Project Management Institute

A GUIDE TO THE PROJECT MANAGEMENT BODY OF KNOWLEDGE

(PMBOK® Guide)—Fourth Edition

An American National Standard
ANSI/PMI 99-001-2008

ISBN: 978-1-933890-51-7

Published by:
Project Management Institute, Inc.
14 Campus Boulevard
Newtown Square, Pennsylvania 19073-3299 USA.
Phone: +1-610-356-4600
Fax: +1-610-356-4647
E-mail: customercare@pmi.org
Internet: www.PMI.org

PMI Publications welcomes corrections and comments on its books. Please feel free to send comments on typographical, formatting, or other errors. Simply make a copy of the relevant page of the book, mark the error, and send it to: Book Editor, PMI Publications, 14 Campus Boulevard, Newtown Square, PA 19073-3299 USA.

To inquire about discounts for resale or educational purposes, please contact the PMI Book Service Center.
PMI Book Service Center
P.O. Box 932683, Atlanta, GA 31193-2683 USA
Phone: 1-866-276-4764 (within the U.S. or Canada) or +1-770-280-4129 (globally)
Fax: +1-770-280-4113
E-mail: book.orders@pmi.org

10 9 8 7 6

NOTICE

The Project Management Institute, Inc. (PMI) standards and guideline publications, of which the document contained herein is one, are developed through a voluntary consensus standards development process. This process brings together volunteers and/or seeks out the views of persons who have an interest in the topic covered by this publication. While PMI administers the process and establishes rules to promote fairness in the development of consensus, it does not write the document and it does not independently test, evaluate, or verify the accuracy or completeness of any information or the soundness of any judgments contained in its standards and guideline publications.

PMI disclaims liability for any personal injury, property or other damages of any nature whatsoever, whether special, indirect, consequential or compensatory, directly or indirectly resulting from the publication, use of application, or reliance on this document. PMI disclaims and makes no guaranty or warranty, expressed or implied, as to the accuracy or completeness of any information published herein, and disclaims and makes no warranty that the information in this document will fulfill any of your particular purposes or needs. PMI does not undertake to guarantee the performance of any individual manufacturer or seller's products or services by virtue of this standard or guide.

In publishing and making this document available, PMI is not undertaking to render professional or other services for or on behalf of any person or entity, nor is PMI undertaking to perform any duty owed by any person or entity to someone else. Anyone using this document should rely on his or her own independent judgment or, as appropriate, seek the advice of a competent professional in determining the exercise of reasonable care in any given circumstances. Information and other standards on the topic covered by this publication may be available from other sources, which the user may wish to consult for additional views or information not covered by this publication.

PMI has no power, nor does it undertake to police or enforce compliance with the contents of this document. PMI does not certify, test, or inspect products, designs, or installations for safety or health purposes. Any certification or other statement of compliance with any health or safety-related information in this document shall not be attributable to PMI and is solely the responsibility of the certifier or maker of the statement.

TABLE OF CONTENTS

LIST OF TABLES AND FIGURES

PREFACE TO THE FOURTH EDITION

This document supersedes *A Guide to the Project Management Body of Knowledge (PMBOK® Guide)* – Third Edition. In the time since its publication, the Project Management Institute (PMI) received thousands of valuable recommendations for improvements to the *PMBOK® Guide* – Third Edition that have been reviewed and, as appropriate, incorporated into the fourth edition.

As a result of those inputs and growth of the Project Management Body of Knowledge, PMI volunteers prepared an updated version of the *PMBOK® Guide.* The project charter to update the *PMBOK® Guide* – Third Edition was to:

1. Revise the standard so that it would not conflict with any other PMI standards.

2. Ensure that the information contained in the standard was cohesive in concept and clear in writing style, and that terminology was well defined and congruous with the other publications' terminology.

3. Research the way life cycles are currently being used in projects and revise or expand them as necessary.

4. Examine the five Project Management Process Groups and the 44 project management description processes to determine whether combining, deleting, or adding new processes would add clarity to the standard.

5. Ensure that Knowledge Area updates are congruent with the work done in defining the processes, inputs, and outputs defined by the standards group.

The major differences between the Third Edition and the Fourth Edition are summarized below:

1. All process names are in a verb–noun format.

2. A standard approach to discussing enterprise environmental factors and organizational process assets was employed.

3. A standard approach for discussing requested changes, preventive actions, corrective actions, and defect repairs was employed.

4. The processes decreased from 44 to 42. Two processes were deleted, two processes were added, and 6 processes were reconfigured into 4 processes in the Project Procurement Management Knowledge Area.

5. To provide clarity, a distinction was made between the project management plan and project documents used to manage the project.

6. The distinction between the information in the Project Charter and the Project Scope Statement was clarified.

7. The process flow diagrams at the beginning of Chapters 4 through 12 have been deleted.

8. A data flow diagram for each process has been created to show the related processes for the inputs and outputs.

9. A new appendix was added that addresses key interpersonal skills that a project manager utilizes when managing a project.

The *PMBOK® Guide* – Fourth Edition maintains the organization from the third edition and is organized into three sections:

Section 1, The Project Management Framework, provides a basis for understanding project management. There are two chapters in this section.

Chapter 1, Introduction, presents a basis and purpose for the standard. It defines what a project is and discusses project management and the relationship between project, program, and portfolio management. The role of the project manager is also discussed.

Chapter 2, Project Life Cycle and Organization, provides an overview of the project life cycle and its relationship to the product life cycle. It describes the project phases and their relationship to each other and to the project, and includes an overview of organizational structure that can influence the project and the way the project is managed.

Section 2, The Standard for Project Management, defines the project management processes and defines the inputs and outputs for each process.

Chapter 3, Project Management Processes for a Project, defines the five Process Groups: Initiating, Planning, Executing, Monitoring and Controlling, and Closing. This chapter maps the Project Management Knowledge Areas to the specific Project Management Process Groups.

Section 3, The Project Management Knowledge Areas, describes the Project Management Knowledge Areas; lists the project management processes; and defines the inputs, tools and techniques, and outputs for each area. Each of the nine chapters focuses on a specific Knowledge Area.

Chapter 4, Project Integration Management, defines the processes and activities that integrate the various elements of project management. This chapter includes:

- Develop Project Charter
- Develop Project Management Plan
- Direct and Manage Project Execution
- Monitor and Control Project Work
- Perform Integrated Change Control
- Close Project or Phase

Chapter 5, Project Scope Management, shows the processes involved in ensuring the project includes all the work required, and only the work required, for completing the project successfully. This chapter includes:

- Collect Requirements
- Define Scope
- Create WBS
- Verify Scope
- Control Scope

Chapter 6, Project Time Management, focuses on the processes that are used to help ensure the timely completion of the project. This chapter includes:

- Define Activities
- Sequence Activities
- Estimate Activity Resources
- Estimate Activity Durations
- Develop Schedule
- Control Schedule

Chapter 7, Project Cost Management, describes the processes involved in planning, estimating, budgeting, and controlling costs so that the project can be completed within the approved budget. This chapter includes:

- Estimate Costs
- Determine Budget
- Control Costs

Chapter 8, Project Quality Management, describes the processes involved in planning for, monitoring, controlling, and assuring the quality requirements of the project are achieved. This chapter includes:

- Plan Quality
- Perform Quality Assurance
- Perform Quality Control

Chapter 9, Project Human Resource Management describes the processes involved in the planning, acquisition, development, and management of the project team. This chapter includes:

- Develop Human Resource Plan
- Acquire Project Team
- Develop Project Team
- Manage Project Team

Chapter 10, Project Communications Management, identifies the processes involved in ensuring timely and appropriate generation, collection, dissemination, storage, and ultimate disposition of project information. This chapter includes:

- Identify Stakeholders
- Plan Communications
- Distribute Information
- Manage Stakeholder Expectations
- Report Performance

Chapter 11, Project Risk Management, describes the processes involved with identifying, analyzing, and controlling risks for the project. This chapter includes:

- Plan Risk Management
- Identify Risks
- Perform Qualitative Risk Analysis
- Perform Quantitative Risk Analysis
- Plan Risk Responses
- Monitor and Control Risks

Chapter 12, Project Procurement Management, describes the processes involved with purchasing or acquiring products, services, or results for the project. This chapter includes:

- Plan Procurements
- Conduct Procurements
- Administer Procurements
- Close Procurements

SECTION I

THE PROJECT MANAGEMENT FRAMEWORK

Chapter 1

- Introduction

Chapter 2

- Project Life Cycle and Organization

CHAPTER 1

INTRODUCTION

A Guide to the Project Management Body of Knowledge (PMBOK® Guide) is a recognized standard for the project management profession. A standard is a formal document that describes established norms, methods, processes, and practices. As with other professions such as law, medicine, and accounting, the knowledge contained in this standard evolved from the recognized good practices of project management practitioners who contributed to the development of this standard.

The first two chapters of the *PMBOK® Guide* provide an introduction to key concepts in the project management field. Chapter 3 is the standard for project management. As such, it summarizes the processes, inputs, and outputs that are considered good practices on most projects most of the time. Chapters 4 through 12 are the guide to the project management body of knowledge. They expand on the information in the standard by describing the inputs and outputs as well as tools and techniques used in managing projects.

The *PMBOK® Guide* provides guidelines for managing individual projects. It defines project management and related concepts and describes the project management life cycle and the related processes.

This chapter defines several key terms and identifies external environmental and internal organizational factors that surround or influence a project's success. An overview of the *PMBOK® Guide* is in the following sections:

1.1 Purpose of the *PMBOK® Guide*

1.2 What is a Project?

1.3 What is Project Management?

1.4 Relationships Among Project Management, Program Management, and Portfolio Management

1.5 Project Management and Operations Management

1.6 Role of a Project Manager

1.7 Project Management Body of Knowledge

1.8 Enterprise Environmental Factors

1.1 Purpose of the *PMBOK® Guide*

The increasing acceptance of project management indicates that the application of appropriate knowledge, processes, skills, tools, and techniques can have a significant impact on project success. The *PMBOK® Guide* identifies that subset of the project management body of knowledge generally recognized as good practice. "Generally recognized" means the knowledge and practices described are applicable to most projects most of the time, and there is consensus about their value and usefulness. "Good practice" means there is general agreement that the application of these skills, tools, and techniques can enhance the chances of success over a wide range of projects. Good practice does not mean the knowledge described should always be applied uniformly to all projects; the organization and/or project management team is responsible for determining what is appropriate for any given project.

The *PMBOK® Guide* also provides and promotes a common vocabulary within the project management profession for discussing, writing, and applying project management concepts. Such a standard vocabulary is an essential element of a professional discipline.

The Project Management Institute (PMI) views this standard as a foundational project management reference for its professional development programs and certifications.

As a foundational reference, this standard is neither complete nor all-inclusive. This standard is a guide rather than a methodology. One can use different methodologies and tools to implement the framework. Appendix D discusses application area extensions, and Appendix E lists sources of further information on project management.

In addition to the standards that establish guidelines for project management processes, tools, and techniques, the *Project Management Institute Code of Ethics and Professional Conduct* guides practitioners of the profession of project management and describes the expectations practitioners have of themselves and others. The *Project Management Institute Code of Ethics and Professional Conduct* is specific about the basic obligation of responsibility, respect, fairness, and honesty. It requires that practitioners demonstrate a commitment to ethical and professional conduct. It carries the obligation to comply with laws, regulations, and organizational and professional policies. Since practitioners come from diverse backgrounds and cultures, the *Code of Ethics and Professional Conduct* applies globally. When dealing with any stakeholder, practitioners should be committed to honest and fair practices and respectful dealings. The *Project Management Institute Code of Ethics and Professional Conduct* is posted on the PMI website (http://www.pmi.org). Acceptance of the code is a requirement for the PMP® certification by PMI.

1.2 What is a Project?

A project is a temporary endeavor undertaken to create a unique product, service, or result. The temporary nature of projects indicates a definite beginning and end. The end is reached when the project's objectives have been achieved or when the project is terminated because its objectives will not or cannot be met, or when the need for the project no longer exists. Temporary does not necessarily mean short in duration. Temporary does not generally apply to the product, service, or result created by the project; most projects are undertaken to create a lasting outcome. For example, a project to build a national monument will create a result expected to last centuries. Projects can also have social, economic, and environmental impacts that far outlast the projects themselves.

Every project creates a unique product, service, or result. Although repetitive elements may be present in some project deliverables, this repetition does not change the fundamental uniqueness of the project work. For example, office buildings are constructed with the same or similar materials or by the same team, but each location is unique—with a different design, different circumstances, different contractors, and so on.

An ongoing work effort is generally a repetitive process because it follows an organization's existing procedures. In contrast, because of the unique nature of projects, there may be uncertainties about the products, services, or results that the project creates. Project tasks can be new to a project team, which necessitates more dedicated planning than other routine work. In addition, projects are undertaken at all organizational levels. A project can involve a single person, a single organizational unit, or multiple organizational units.

A project can create:

- A product that can be either a component of another item or an end item in itself,

- A capability to perform a service (e.g., a business function that supports production or distribution), or

- A result such as an outcome or document (e.g., a research project that develops knowledge that can be used to determine whether a trend is present or a new process will benefit society).

Examples of projects include, but are not limited to:

- Developing a new product or service,

- Effecting a change in the structure, staffing, or style of an organization,

- Developing or acquiring a new or modified information system,

- Constructing a building or infrastructure, or

- Implementing a new business process or procedure.

1.3 What is Project Management?

Project management is the application of knowledge, skills, tools, and techniques to project activities to meet the project requirements. Project management is accomplished through the appropriate application and integration of the 42 logically grouped project management processes comprising the 5 Process Groups. These 5 Process Groups are:

- Initiating,

- Planning,

- Executing,

- Monitoring and Controlling, and

- Closing.

Managing a project typically includes:

- Identifying requirements,

- Addressing the various needs, concerns, and expectations of the stakeholders as the project is planned and carried out,

- Balancing the competing project constraints including, but not limited to:

  o Scope,

  o Quality,

  o Schedule,

  o Budget,

  o Resources, and

  o Risk.

The specific project will influence the constraints on which the project manager needs to focus.

The relationship among these factors is such that if any one factor changes, at least one other factor is likely to be affected. For example, if the schedule is shortened, often the budget needs to be increased to add additional resources to complete the same amount of work in less time. If a budget increase is not possible, the scope or quality may be reduced to deliver a product in less time for the same budget. Project stakeholders may have differing ideas as to which factors are the most important, creating an even greater challenge. Changing the project requirements may create additional risks. The project team must be able to assess the situation and balance the demands in order to deliver a successful project.

Because of the potential for change, the project management plan is iterative and goes through progressive elaboration throughout the project's life cycle. Progressive elaboration involves continuously improving and detailing a plan as more-detailed and specific information and more accurate estimates become available. Progressive elaboration allows a project management team to manage to a greater level of detail as the project evolves.

1.4 Relationships Among Project Management, Program Management, and Portfolio Management

In mature project management organizations, project management exists in a broader context governed by program management and portfolio management. As Figure 1-1 illustrates, organizational strategies and priorities are linked and have relationships between portfolios and programs, and between programs and individual projects. Organizational planning impacts the projects by means of project prioritization based on risk, funding, and the organization's strategic plan. Organizational planning can direct the funding and support for the component projects on the basis of risk categories, specific lines of business, or general types of projects, such as infrastructure and internal process improvement.

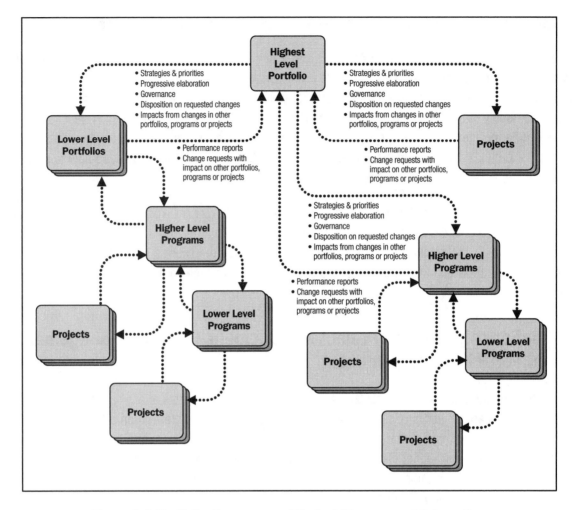

Figure 1-1. Portfolio, Program, and Project Management Interactions

Projects, programs, and portfolios have different approaches. Table 1-1 shows the comparison of project, program, and portfolio views across several domains including change, leadership, management, and others.

1.4.1   Portfolio Management

A portfolio refers to a collection of projects or programs and other work that are grouped together to facilitate effective management of that work to meet strategic business objectives. The projects or programs of the portfolio may not necessarily be interdependent or directly related. For example, an infrastructure firm that has the strategic objective of "maximizing the return on its investments" may put together a portfolio that includes a mix of projects in oil and gas, power, water, roads, rail, and airports. From this mix, the firm may choose to manage related projects as one program. All of the power projects may be grouped together as a power program. Similarly, all of the water projects may be grouped together as a water program.

Portfolio management refers to the centralized management of one or more portfolios, which includes identifying, prioritizing, authorizing, managing, and controlling projects, programs, and other related work, to achieve specific strategic business objectives. Portfolio management focuses on ensuring that projects and programs are reviewed to prioritize resource allocation, and that the management of the portfolio is consistent with and aligned to organizational strategies.

Table 1-1. Comparative Overview of Project, Program, and Portfolio Management

	PROJECTS	PROGRAMS	PORTFOLIOS
Scope	Projects have defined objectives. Scope is progressively elaborated throughout the project life cycle.	Programs have a larger scope and provide more significant benefits.	Portfolios have a business scope that changes with the strategic goals of the organization.
Change	Project managers expect change and implement processes to keep change managed and controlled.	The program manager must expect change from both inside and outside the program and be prepared to manage it.	Portfolio managers continually monitor changes in the broad environment.
Planning	Project managers progressively elaborate high-level information into detailed plans throughout the project life cycle.	Program managers develop the overall program plan and create high-level plans to guide detailed planning at the component level.	Portfolio managers create and maintain necessary processes and communication relative to the aggregate portfolio.
Management	Project managers manage the project team to meet the project objectives.	Program managers manage the program staff and the project managers; they provide vision and overall leadership.	Portfolio managers may manage or coordinate portfolio management staff.
Success	Success is measured by product and project quality, timeliness, budget compliance, and degree of customer satisfaction.	Success is measured by the degree to which the program satisfies the needs and benefits for which it was undertaken.	Success is measured in terms of aggregate performance of portfolio components.
Monitoring	Project managers monitor and control the work of producing the products, services or results that the project was undertaken to produce.	Program managers monitor the progress of program components to ensure the overall goals, schedules, budget, and benefits of the program will be met.	Portfolio managers monitor aggregate performance and value indicators.

1.4.2 Program Management

A program is defined as a group of related projects managed in a coordinated way to obtain benefits and control not available from managing them individually. Programs may include elements of related work outside the scope of the discrete projects in the program. A project may or may not be part of a program but a program will always have projects.

Program management is defined as the centralized coordinated management of a program to achieve the program's strategic objectives and benefits. Projects within a program are related through the common outcome or collective capability. If the relationship between projects is only that of a shared client, seller, technology, or resource, the effort should be managed as a portfolio of projects rather than as a program.

Program management focuses on the project interdependencies and helps to determine the optimal approach for managing them. Actions related to these interdependencies may include:

- Resolving resource constraints and/or conflicts that affect multiple projects within the program;
- Aligning organizational/strategic direction that affects project and program goals and objectives; and
- Resolving issues and change management within a shared governance structure.

An example of a program would be a new communications satellite system with projects for design of the satellite and of the ground stations, construction of each, integration of the system, and launch of the satellite.

1.4.3 Projects and Strategic Planning

Projects are often utilized as a means of achieving an organization's strategic plan. Projects are typically authorized as a result of one or more of the following strategic considerations:

- Market demand (e.g., a car company authorizing a project to build more fuel-efficient cars in response to gasoline shortages),
- Strategic opportunity/business need (e.g., a training company authorizing a project to create a new course to increase its revenues),
- Customer request (e.g., an electric utility authorizing a project to build a new substation to serve a new industrial park),
- Technological advance (e.g., an electronics firm authorizing a new project to develop a faster, cheaper, and smaller laptop after advances in computer memory and electronics technology), and
- Legal requirements (e.g., a chemical manufacturer authorizes a project to establish guidelines for the handling of a new toxic material).

Projects, within programs or portfolios, are a means of achieving organizational goals and objectives, often in the context of a strategic plan. Although a group of projects within a program can have discrete benefits, they can also contribute to the benefits of the program, to the objectives of the portfolio, and to the strategic plan of the organization.

Organizations manage portfolios based on their strategic plan, which may dictate a hierarchy to the portfolio, program, or projects involved. One goal of portfolio management is to maximize the value of the portfolio by the careful examination of its components—the constituent programs, projects, and other related work. Those components contributing the least to the portfolio's strategic objectives may be excluded. In this way, an organization's strategic plan becomes the primary factor guiding investments in projects. At the same time, projects provide feedback to programs and portfolios by means of status reports and change requests that may impact other projects, programs, or portfolios. The needs of the projects, including the resource needs, are rolled up and communicated back to the portfolio level, which in turn sets the direction for organizational planning.

1.4.4 Project Management Office

A project management office (PMO) is an organizational body or entity assigned various responsibilities related to the centralized and coordinated management of those projects under its domain. The responsibilities of a PMO can range from providing project management support functions to actually being responsible for the direct management of a project.

The projects supported or administered by the PMO may not be related, other than by being managed together. The specific form, function, and structure of a PMO is dependent upon the needs of the organization that it supports.

A PMO may be delegated the authority to act as an integral stakeholder and a key decision maker during the beginning of each project, to make recommendations, or to terminate projects or take other actions as required to keep business objectives consistent. In addition, the PMO may be involved in the selection, management, and deployment of shared or dedicated project resources.

A primary function of a PMO is to support project managers in a variety of ways which may include, but are not limited to:

- Managing shared resources across all projects administered by the PMO;
- Identifying and developing project management methodology, best practices, and standards;
- Coaching, mentoring, training, and oversight;
- Monitoring compliance with project management standards, policies, procedures, and templates via project audits;
- Developing and managing project policies, procedures, templates, and other shared documentation (organizational process assets); and
- Coordinating communication across projects.

Project managers and PMOs pursue different objectives and, as such, are driven by different requirements. All of these efforts, however, are aligned with the strategic needs of the organization. Differences between the role of project managers and a PMO may include the following:

- The project manager focuses on the specified project objectives, while the PMO manages major program scope changes which may be seen as potential opportunities to better achieve business objectives.

- The project manager controls the assigned project resources to best meet project objectives while the PMO optimizes the use of shared organizational resources across all projects.

- The project manager manages the constraints (scope, schedule, cost, and quality, etc.) of the individual projects while the PMO manages the methodologies, standards, overall risk/opportunity, and interdependencies among projects at the enterprise level.

1.5 Project Management and Operations Management

Operations are an organizational function performing the ongoing execution of activities that produce the same product or provide a repetitive service. Examples include: production operations, manufacturing operations, and accounting operations. Though temporary in nature, projects can help achieve the organizational goals when they are aligned with the organization's strategy. Organizations sometimes change their operations, products, or systems by creating strategic business initiatives. Projects require project management while operations require business process management or operations management. Projects can intersect with operations at various points during the product life cycle, such as:

- At each closeout phase;

- When developing a new product, upgrading a product, or expanding outputs;

- Improvement of operations or the product development process; or

- Until the divestment of the operations at the end of the product life cycle.

At each point, deliverables and knowledge are transferred between the project and operations for implementation of the delivered work. This occurs through a transfer of project resources to operations toward the end of the project, or through a transfer of operational resources to the project at the start.

Operations are permanent endeavors that produce repetitive outputs, with resources assigned to do basically the same set of tasks according to the standards institutionalized in a product life cycle. Unlike the ongoing nature of operations, projects are temporary endeavors.

1.6 Role of a Project Manager

The project manager is the person assigned by the performing organization to achieve the project objectives. The role of a project manager is distinct from a functional manager or operations manager. Typically the functional manager is focused on providing management oversight for an administrative area, and operations managers are responsible for a facet of the core business.

Depending on the organizational structure, a project manager may report to a functional manager. In other cases, a project manager may be one of several project managers who report to a portfolio or program manager that is ultimately responsible for enterprise-wide projects. In this type of structure, the project manager works closely with the portfolio or program manager to achieve the project objectives and to ensure the project plan aligns with the overarching program plan.

Many of the tools and techniques for managing projects are specific to project management. However, understanding and applying the knowledge, tools, and techniques that are recognized as good practice is not sufficient for effective project management. In addition to any area-specific skills and general management proficiencies required for the project, effective project management requires that the project manager possess the following characteristics:

- **Knowledge.** This refers to what the project manager knows about project management.

- **Performance.** This refers to what the project manager is able to do or accomplish while applying their project management knowledge.

- **Personal.** This refers to how the project manager behaves when performing the project or related activity. Personal effectiveness encompasses attitudes, core personality characteristics and leadership—the ability to guide the project team while achieving project objectives and balancing the project constraints.

1.7 Project Management Body of Knowledge

The *PMBOK® Guide* is the standard for managing most projects most of the time across many types of industries. This standard describes the project management processes, tools, and techniques used to manage a project toward a successful outcome.

This standard is unique to the project management field and has interrelationships to other project management disciplines such as program management and portfolio management.

Project management standards do not address all details of every topic. This standard is limited to single projects and the project management processes that are generally recognized as good practice. Other standards may be consulted for additional information on the broader context in which projects are accomplished. Management of programs is addressed in *The Standard for Program Management,* and management of portfolios is addressed in *The Standard for Portfolio Management.* Examination of an enterprise's project management process capabilities is addressed in *Organizational Project Management Maturity Model (OPM3®).*

1.8 Enterprise Environmental Factors

Enterprise environmental factors refer to both internal and external environmental factors that surround or influence a project's success. These factors may come from any or all of the enterprises involved in the project. Enterprise environmental factors may enhance or constrain project management options and may have a positive or negative influence on the outcome. They are considered as inputs to most planning processes.

Enterprise environmental factors include, but are not limited to:

- Organizational culture, structure, and processes;

- Government or industry standards (e.g., regulatory agency regulations, codes of conduct, product standards, quality standards, and workmanship standards);

- Infrastructure (e.g., existing facilities and capital equipment);

- Existing human resources (e.g., skills, disciplines, and knowledge, such as design, development, law, contracting, and purchasing);

- Personnel administration (e.g., staffing and retention guidelines, employee performance reviews and training records, overtime policy, and time tracking);

- Company work authorization systems;

- Marketplace conditions;

- Stakeholder risk tolerances;

- Political climate;

- Organization's established communications channels;

- Commercial databases (e.g., standardized cost estimating data, industry risk study information, and risk databases); and

- Project management information systems (e.g., an automated tool, such as a scheduling software tool, a configuration management system, an information collection and distribution system, or web interfaces to other online automated systems).

CHAPTER 2

PROJECT LIFE CYCLE AND ORGANIZATION

Projects and project management take place in an environment that is broader than that of the project itself. Understanding this broader context helps ensure that work is carried out in alignment with the goals of the enterprise and managed in accordance with the established practice methodologies of the organization. This chapter describes the basic structure of a project as well as other important high-level considerations including how projects impact ongoing operational work, the influence of stakeholders beyond the immediate project team, and how organizational structure affects the way the project is staffed, managed, and executed. The following major sections are discussed:

2.1 The Project Life Cycle—Overview

2.2 Projects vs. Operational Work

2.3 Stakeholders

2.4 Organizational Influences on Project Management

2.1 The Project Life Cycle—Overview

A project life cycle is a collection of generally sequential and sometimes overlapping project phases whose name and number are determined by the management and control needs of the organization or organizations involved in the project, the nature of the project itself, and its area of application. A life cycle can be documented with a methodology. The project life cycle can be determined or shaped by the unique aspects of the organization, industry or technology employed. While every project has a definite start and a definite end, the specific deliverables and activities that take place in between will vary widely with the project. The life cycle provides the basic framework for managing the project, regardless of the specific work involved.

2.1.1 Characteristics of the Project Life Cycle

Projects vary in size and complexity. No matter how large or small, simple or complex, all projects can be mapped to the following life cycle structure (see Figure 2-1):

- Starting the project,
- Organizing and preparing,
- Carrying out the project work, and
- Closing the project.

This generic life cycle structure is often referred to when communicating with upper management or other entities less familiar with the details of the project. This high-level view can provide a common frame of reference for comparing projects—even if they are dissimilar in nature.

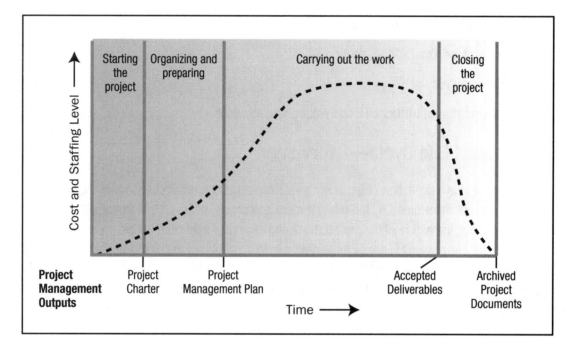

Figure 2-1. Typical Cost and Staffing Levels Across the Project Life Cycle

The generic life cycle structure generally displays the following characteristics:

- Cost and staffing levels are low at the start, peak as the work is carried out, and drop rapidly as the project draws to a close. The dashed line in Figure 2-1 illustrates this typical pattern.

- Stakeholder influences, risk, and uncertainty, (as illustrated in Figure 2-2) are greatest at the start of the project. These factors decrease over the life of the project.

- Ability to influence the final characteristics of the project's product, without significantly impacting cost, is highest at the start of the project and decreases as the project progresses towards completion. Figure 2-2 illustrates the idea that the cost of changes and correcting errors typically increases substantially as the project approaches completion.

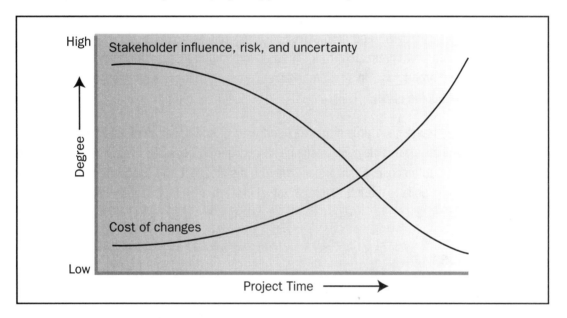

Figure 2-2. Impact of Variable Based on Project Time

Within the context of the generic life cycle structure, a project manager may determine the need for more effective control over certain deliverables. Large and complex projects in particular may require this additional level of control. In such instances, the work carried out to complete the project's objective may benefit from being formally divided into phases.

2.1.2   Product vs. Project Life Cycle Relationships

The product life cycle consists of generally sequential, non-overlapping product phases determined by the manufacturing and control need of the organization. The last product life cycle phase for a product is generally the product's retirement. Project life cycles occur in one or more phases of a product life cycle. Care should be taken to distinguish the project life cycle from the product life cycle. All projects have a purpose or objective, but in those cases where the objective is a service or result, there may be a life cycle for the service or result, not a product life cycle.

When the output of the project is related to a product, there are many possible relationships. For instance, the development of a new product could be a project on its own. Alternatively, an existing product might benefit from a project to add new functions or features, or a project might be created to develop a new model. Many facets of the product life cycle lend themselves to being run as projects, for example, performing a feasibility study, conducting market research, running an advertising campaign, installing a product, holding focus groups, conducting a product trial in a test market, etc. In each of these examples, the project life cycle would differ from the product life cycle.

Since one product may have many projects associated with it, additional efficiencies may be gained by managing all related projects collectively. For instance, a number of separate projects may be related to the development of a new automobile. Each project may be distinct, but still contributes a key deliverable necessary to bring the automobile to market. Oversight of all projects by a higher authority could significantly increase the likelihood of success.

2.1.3   Project Phases

Project phases are divisions within a project where extra control is needed to effectively manage the completion of a major deliverable. Project phases are typically completed sequentially, but can overlap in some project situations. The high level nature of project phases makes them an element of the project life cycle. A project phase is not a Project Management Process Group.

The phase structure allows the project to be segmented into logical subsets for ease of management, planning, and control. The number of phases, the need for phases, and the degree of control applied depend on the size, complexity, and potential impact of the project. Regardless of the number of phases comprising a project, all phases have similar characteristics:

- When phases are sequential, the close of a phase ends with some form of transfer or handoff of the work product produced as the phase deliverable. This phase end represents a natural point to reassess the effort underway and to change or terminate the project if necessary. These points are referred to as phase exits, milestones, phase gates, decision gates, stage gates, or kill points.

- The work has a distinct focus that differs from any other phase. This often involves different organizations and different skill sets.

- The primary deliverable or objective of the phase requires an extra degree of control to be successfully achieved. The repetition of processes across all five Process Groups, as described in Chapter 3, provides that additional degree of control, and defines the boundaries of the phase.

Although many projects may have similar phase names with similar deliverables, few are identical. Some will have only one phase, as shown in Figure 2-3. Other projects may have many phases. Figure 2-4 shows an example of a project with three phases. Different phases typically have a different duration or length.

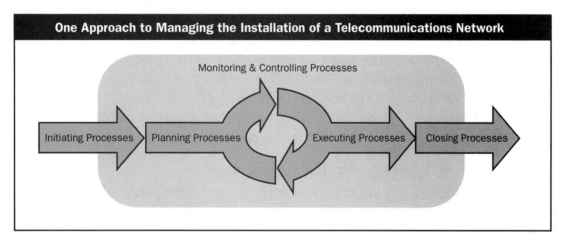

Figure 2-3. Example of a Single-Phase Project

There is no single way to define the ideal structure for a project. Although industry common practices will often lead to the use of a preferred structure, projects in the same industry—or even in the same organization— may have significant variation. Some organizations have established policies that standardize all projects, while others allow the project management team to choose the most appropriate for their individual project. For instance, one organization may treat a feasibility study as routine pre-project work, another may treat it as the first phase of a project, and a third might treat the feasibility study as a separate, stand-alone project. Likewise, one project team might divide a project into two phases where a different project team might choose to manage all the work as a single phase. Much depends on the nature of the specific project and the style of the project team or organization.

.1 Project Governance Across the Life Cycle

Project governance provides a comprehensive, consistent method of controlling the project and ensuring its success. The project governance approach should be described in the project management plan. A project's governance must fit within the larger context of the program or organization sponsoring it.

Within those constraints, as well as the additional limitations of time and budget, it is up to the project manager and the project management team to determine the most appropriate method of carrying out the project. Decisions must be made regarding who will be involved, what resources are necessary, and the general approach to completing the work. Another important consideration is whether more than one phase will be involved and, if so, the specific phased structure for the individual project.

The phase structure provides a formal basis for control. Each phase is formally initiated to specify what is allowed and expected for that phase. A management review is often held to reach a decision to start the activities of a phase. This is especially true when a prior phase has not yet completed. An example would be when an organization chooses a life cycle where more than one phase of the project progresses simultaneously. The beginning of a phase is also a time to revalidate earlier assumptions, review risks and define in more detail the processes necessary to complete the phase deliverable(s). For example, if a particular phase does not require purchasing any new materials or equipment, there would be no need to carry out the activities or processes associated with procurement.

A project phase is generally concluded and formally closed with a review of the deliverables to determine completeness and acceptance. A phase-end review can achieve the combined goal of obtaining authorization to close the current phase and start the subsequent one. The end of a phase represents a natural point to reassess the effort underway and to change or terminate the project if necessary. A review of both key deliverables and project performance to date to a) determine if the project should continue into its next phase and b) detect and correct errors cost effectively should be regarded as good practice. Formal phase completion does not necessarily include authorizing the subsequent phase. For instance, if the risk is deemed to be too great for the project to continue or if the objectives are no longer required, a phase can be closed with the decision to not initiate any other phases.

.2 Phase-to-Phase Relationships

When projects are multi-phased, the phases are part of a generally sequential process designed to ensure proper control of the project and attain the desired product, service, or result. However, there are situations when a project might benefit from overlapping or concurrent phases.

There are three basic types of phase-to-phase relationships:

- *A sequential relationship,* where a phase can only start once the previous phase is complete. Figure 2-4 shows an example of a project with entirely sequential phases. The step-by-step nature of this approach reduces uncertainty, but may eliminate options for reducing the schedule.

- *An overlapping relationship,* where the phase starts prior to completion of the previous one (see Figure 2-5). This can sometimes be applied as an example of the schedule compression technique called fast tracking. Overlapping phases may increase risk and can result in rework if a subsequent phase progresses before accurate information is available from the previous phase.

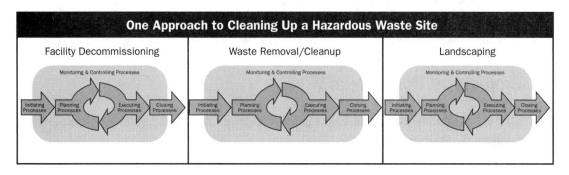

Figure 2-4. Example of a Three-Phase Project Figure

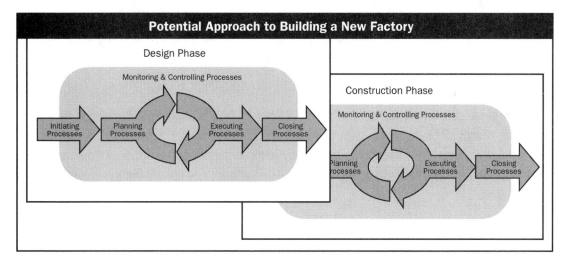

2-5. Example of a Project with Overlapping Phases

- *An iterative relationship,* where only one phase is planned at any given time and the planning for the next is carried out as work progresses on the current phase and deliverables. This approach is useful in largely undefined, uncertain, or rapidly changing environments such as research, but it can reduce the ability to provide long term planning. The scope is then managed by continuously delivering increments of the product and prioritizing requirements to minimize project risks and maximize product business value. It also can entail having all of the project team members (e.g. designers, developers, etc.) available throughout the project or, at a minimum, for two consecutive phases.

For multi-phase projects, more than one phase-to-phase relationship could occur during the project life cycle. Considerations such as level of control required, effectiveness, and degree of uncertainty determine the relationship to be applied between phases. Based on those considerations, all three relationships could occur between different phases of a single project.

2.2 Projects vs. Operational Work

Organizations perform work to achieve a set of objectives. In many organizations the work performed can be categorized as either project or operations work.

These two types of work share a number of characteristics as follows:

- Performed by individuals,
- Limited by constraints, including resource constraints,
- Planned, executed, monitored and controlled, and
- Performed to achieve organizational objectives or strategic plans.

Projects and operations differ primarily in that operations are ongoing and produce repetitive products, services, or results. Projects (along with team members and often the opportunity) are temporary and end. Conversely, operations work is ongoing and sustains the organization over time. Operations work does not terminate when its current objectives are met but instead follow new directions to support the organization's strategic plans.

Operations work supports the business environment where projects are executed. As a result, there is generally a significant amount of interaction between the operations departments and the project team as they work together to achieve project goals. An example of this is when a project is created to redesign a product. The project manager may work with multiple operational managers to research consumer preferences, draw up technical specifications, build a prototype, test it, and begin manufacturing. The team will interface with the operational departments to determine the manufacturing capacity of current equipment, or to determine the most appropriate time to transition production lines to produce the new product.

The amount of resources supplied from operations will vary from project to project. One example of this interaction is when individuals from operations are assigned as dedicated project resources. Their operational expertise is used to carry out and assist in the completion of project deliverables by working with the rest of the project team to complete the project.

Depending on the nature of the project, the deliverables may modify or contribute to the existing operations work. In this case, the operations department will integrate the deliverables into future business practices. Examples of these types of projects can include, but are not limited to:

- Developing a new product or service that is added to an organization's product line to be marketed and sold,

- Installing products or services that will require ongoing support,

- Internal projects that will affect the structure, staffing levels, or culture of an organization, or

- Developing, acquiring, or enhancing an operational department's information system.

2.3 Stakeholders

Stakeholders are persons or organizations (e.g., customers, sponsors, the performing organization, or the public), who are actively involved in the project or whose interests may be positively or negatively affected by the performance or completion of the project. Stakeholders may also exert influence over the project, its deliverables, and the project team members. The project management team must identify both internal and external stakeholders in order to determine the project requirements and expectations of all parties involved. Furthermore, the project manager must manage the influence of the various stakeholders in relation to the project requirements to ensure a successful outcome. Figure 2-6 illustrates the relationship between the project, the project team, and other common stakeholders.

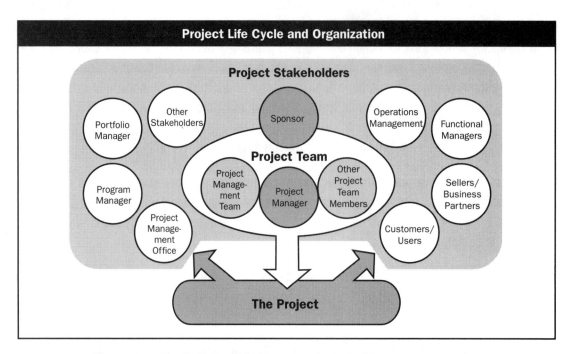

Figure 2-6. The Relationship Between Stakeholders and the Project

Stakeholders have varying levels of responsibility and authority when participating on a project and these can change over the course of the project life cycle. Their responsibility and authority may range from occasional contributions in surveys and focus groups to full project sponsorship, which includes providing financial and political support. Stakeholders can have an adverse impact on the project objectives.

Stakeholder identification is a continuous process and can be difficult. For instance, it could be argued that an assembly-line worker whose future employment depends on the outcome of a new product-design project is a stakeholder. Identifying stakeholders and understanding their relative degree of influence on a project is critical. Failure to do so can extend the timeline and raise costs substantially. An example is late recognition that the legal department is a significant stakeholder which results in delays and increased expenses due to legal requirements.

A project can be perceived as having both positive and negative results by the stakeholders. Some stakeholders benefit from a successful project, while other stakeholders perceive negative outcomes from a project's success, for example, business leaders from a community that will benefit from an industrial expansion project by positive economic benefits to the community. In the case of stakeholders with positive expectations from the project, their interests are best served by helping the project succeed. The interests of negative stakeholders are served by impeding the project's progress. Overlooking negative stakeholders can result in an increased likelihood of failure. An important part of a project manager's responsibility is to manage stakeholder expectations. This can be difficult because stakeholders often have very different or conflicting objectives. Part of the project manager's responsibility is to balance these interests and ensure that the project team interacts with stakeholders in a professional and cooperative manner. The following are some examples of project stakeholders.

- **Customers/users.** The customers/users are the persons or organizations that will use the project's product or service or result. Customers/users may be internal and/or external to the performing organization. There may also be multiple layers of customers. For example, the customers for a new pharmaceutical product can include the doctors who prescribe it, the patients who use it, and the insurers who pay for it. In some application areas, customers and users are synonymous, while in others, customers refer to the entity acquiring the project's product, and users refer to those who will directly utilize the project's product.

- **Sponsor.** A sponsor is the person or group that provides the financial resources, in cash or in kind, for the project. When a project is first conceived, the sponsor champions the project. This includes serving as spokesperson to higher levels of management to gather support throughout the organization and promote the benefits that the project will bring. The sponsor leads the project through the engagement or selection process until formally authorized, and plays a significant role in the development of the initial scope and charter.

  For issues that are beyond the control of the project manager, the sponsor serves as an escalation path. The sponsor may also be involved in other important issues such as authorizing changes in scope, phase-end reviews, and go/no-go decisions when risks are particularly high.

- **Portfolio managers/portfolio review board.** Portfolio managers are responsible for the high-level governance of a collection of projects or programs, which may or may not be interdependent. Portfolio review boards are committees usually made up of the organization's executives who act as a project selection panel. They review each project for its return on investment, the value of the project, risks associated with taking on the project, and other attributes of the project.

- **Program managers.** Program managers are responsible for managing related projects in a coordinated way to obtain benefits and control not available from managing them individually. Program managers interact with each project manager to provide support and guidance on individual projects.

- **Project management office.** A project management office (PMO) is an organizational body or entity assigned various responsibilities related to the centralized and coordinated management of those projects under its domain. The responsibilities of a PMO can range from providing project management support functions to actually being responsible for the direct management of a project. The PMO can be a stakeholder if it has direct or indirect responsibility for the outcome of the project. The PMO can provide but is not limited to:

    o Administrative support services such as policies, methodologies, and templates;

    o Training, mentoring, and coaching of project managers;

    o Project support, guidance, and training on how to manage projects and the use of tools;

    o Resource alignment of project staff; and/or

    o Centralized communication among project managers, project sponsors, managers, and other stakeholders.

- **Project managers.** Project managers are assigned by the performing organization to achieve the project objectives. This is a challenging, high-profile role with significant responsibility and shifting priorities. It requires flexibility, good judgment, strong leadership and negotiating skills, and a solid knowledge of project management practices. A project manager must be able to understand project detail, but manage from the overall project perspective. As the person responsible for the success of the project, a project manager is in charge of all aspects of the project including, but not limited to:

    o Developing the project management plan and all related component plans,

    o Keeping the project on track in terms of schedule and budget,

    o Identifying, monitoring, and responding to risk, and

    o Providing accurate and timely reporting of project metrics.

The project manager is the lead person responsible for communicating with all stakeholders, particularly the project sponsor, project team, and other key stakeholders. The project manager occupies the center of the interactions between stakeholders and the project itself.

- **Project team.** A project team is comprised of the project manager, project management team, and other team members who carry out the work but who are not necessarily involved with management of the project. This team is comprised of individuals from different groups with knowledge of a specific subject matter or with a specific skill set who carry out the work of the project.

- **Functional managers.** Functional managers are key individuals who play a management role within an administrative or functional area of the business, such as human resources, finance, accounting, or procurement. They are assigned their own permanent staff to carry out the ongoing work, and they have a clear directive to manage all tasks within their functional area of responsibility. The functional manager may provide subject matter expertise or their function may provide services to the project.

- **Operations management.** Operations managers are individuals who have a management role in a core business area, such as research and development, design, manufacturing, provisioning, testing, or maintenance. Unlike functional managers, these managers deal directly with producing and maintaining the saleable products or services of the enterprise. Depending on the type of project, a formal handoff occurs upon completion to pass technical project documentation and other permanent records into the hands of the appropriate operations management group. Operations management would then incorporate the handed off project into normal operations and provide the long term support.

- **Sellers/business partners.** Sellers, also called vendors, suppliers, or contractors, are external companies that enter into a contractual agreement to provide components or services necessary for the project. Business partners are also external companies, but they have a special relationship with the enterprise, sometimes attained through a certification process. Business partners provide specialized expertise or fill a specified role such as installation, customization, training, or support.

2.4 Organizational Influences on Project Management

The organizational culture, style, and structure influence how projects are performed. An organization's degree of project management maturity and its project management systems can also influence the project. When a project involves external entities as part of a joint venture or partnering, the project will be influenced by more than one enterprise. The following sections describe organizational characteristics and structures within an enterprise that are likely to influence the project.

2.4.1 Organizational Cultures and Styles

Cultures and styles may have a strong influence on a project's ability to meet its objectives. Cultures and styles are typically known as "cultural norms." The "norms" include a common knowledge regarding how to approach getting the work done, what means are considered acceptable for getting the work done, and who is influential in facilitating the work getting done.

Most organizations have developed unique cultures that manifest in numerous ways including, but not limited to:

- Shared visions, values, norms, beliefs, and expectations,

- Policies, methods, and procedures,

- View of authority relationships, and

- Work ethic and work hours.

The organizational culture is an enterprise environmental factor as described in Section 1.8. Therefore, a project manager should understand the different organizational styles and cultures that may affect a project. For example, in some cases the person shown at the top of an organization chart may be a figurehead who is not truly in charge. The project manager must know which individuals in the organization are the decision makers and work with them to influence project success.

2.4.2 Organizational Structure

Organizational structure is an enterprise environmental factor which can affect the availability of resources and influence how projects are conducted. Organizational structures range from functional to projectized, with a variety of matrix structures between them. Table 2-1 shows key project-related characteristics of the major types of organizational structures.

Table 2-1. Organizational Influences on Projects

Organization Structure / Project Characteristics	Functional	Matrix			Projectized
		Weak Matrix	Balanced Matrix	Strong Matrix	
Project Manager's Authority	Little or None	Limited	Low to Moderate	Moderate to High	High to Almost Total
Resource Availability	Little or None	Limited	Low to Moderate	Moderate to High	High to Almost Total
Who controls the project budget	Functional Manager	Functional Manager	Mixed	Project Manager	Project Manager
Project Manager's Role	Part-time	Part-time	Full-time	Full-time	Full-time
Project Management Administrative Staff	Part-time	Part-time	Part-time	Full-time	Full-time

The classic functional organization, shown in Figure 2-7, is a hierarchy where each employee has one clear superior. Staff members are grouped by specialty, such as production, marketing, engineering, and accounting at the top level. Specialties may be further subdivided into functional organizations, such as mechanical and electrical engineering. Each department in a functional organization will do its project work independent of other departments.

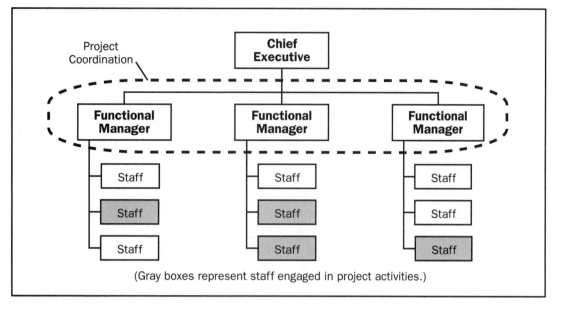

Figure 2-7. Functional Organization

Matrix organizations, as shown in Figures 2-8 through 2-10, are a blend of functional and projectized characteristics. Weak matrices maintain many of the characteristics of a functional organization, and the project manager role is more of a coordinator or expediter than that of a true project manager. Strong matrices have many of the characteristics of the projectized organization, and can have full-time project managers with considerable authority and full-time project administrative staff. While the balanced matrix organization recognizes the need for a project manager, it does not provide the project manager with the full authority over the project and project funding. Table 2-1 provides additional details of the various matrix organizational structures.

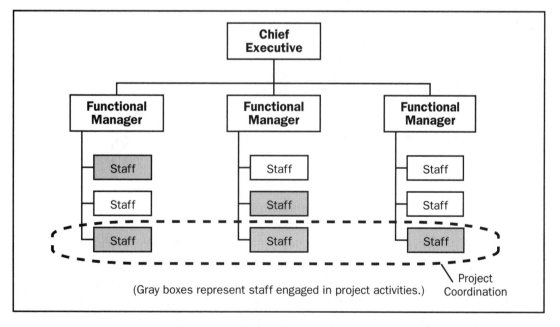

Figure 2-8. Weak Matrix Organization

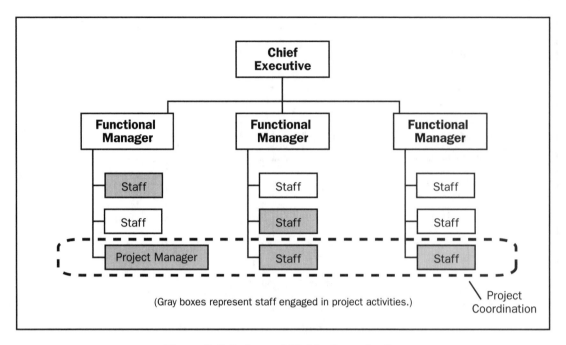

Figure 2-9. Balanced Matrix Organization

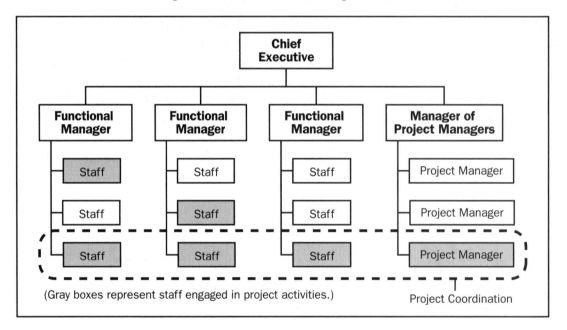

Figure 2-10. Strong Matrix Organization

At the opposite end of the spectrum to the functional organization is the projectized organization, shown in Figure 2-11. In a projectized organization, team members are often co-located, most of the organization's resources are involved in project work, and project managers have a great deal of independence and authority. Projectized organizations often have organizational units called departments, but these groups either report directly to the project manager or provide support services to the various projects.

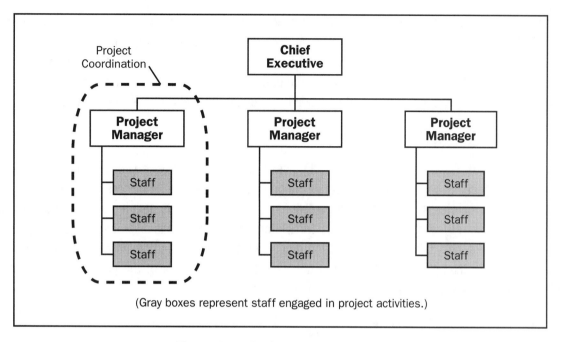

(Gray boxes represent staff engaged in project activities.)

Figure 2-11. Projectized Organization

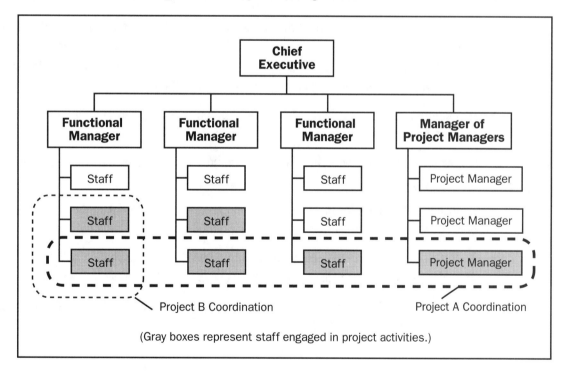

(Gray boxes represent staff engaged in project activities.)

Figure 2-12. Composite Organization

Many organizations involve all these structures at various levels, as shown in Figure 2-12 (composite organization). For example, even a fundamentally functional organization may create a special project team to handle a critical project. Such a team may have many of the characteristics of a project team in a projectized organization. The team may include full-time staff from different functional departments, may develop its own set of operating procedures, and may operate outside the standard, formalized reporting structure.

2.4.3 Organizational Process Assets

Organizational process assets include any or all process related assets, from any or all of the organizations involved in the project that can be used to influence the project's success. These process assets include formal and informal plans, policies, procedures, and guidelines. The process assets also include the organization's knowledge bases such as lessons learned and historical information. Organizational process assets may include completed schedules, risk data, and earned value data. Updating and adding to the organizational process assets as necessary throughout the project are generally the responsibility of the project team members. Organizational process assets may be grouped into two categories:

.1 Processes and Procedures

The organization's processes and procedures for conducting work include but are not limited to:

- Organizational standard processes such as standards, policies (e.g., safety and health policy, ethics policy, and project management policy), standard product and project life cycles, and quality policies and procedures (e.g., process audits, improvement targets, checklists, and standardized process definitions for use in the organization);

- Standardized guidelines, work instructions, proposal evaluation criteria, and performance measurement criteria;

- Templates (e.g., risk, work breakdown structure, project schedule network diagram, and contract templates);

- Guidelines and criteria for tailoring the organization's set of standard processes to satisfy the specific needs of the project;

- Organization communication requirements (e.g., specific communication technology available, allowed communication media, record retention policies, and security requirements);

- Project closure guidelines or requirements (e.g., final project audits, project evaluations, product validations, and acceptance criteria);

- Financial controls procedures (e.g., time reporting, required expenditure and disbursement reviews, accounting codes, and standard contract provisions);

- Issue and defect management procedures defining issue and defect controls, issue and defect identification and resolution, and action item tracking;

- Change control procedures, including the steps by which official company standards, policies, plans, and procedures—or any project documents—will be modified, and how any changes will be approved and validated;

- Risk control procedures, including risk categories, probability definition and impact, and probability and impact matrix; and

- Procedures for prioritizing, approving, and issuing work authorizations.

.2 Corporate Knowledge Base

The organizational corporate knowledge base for storing and retrieving information includes but is not limited to:

- Process measurement databases used to collect and make available measurement data on processes and products,

- Project files (e.g., scope, cost, schedule, and performance measurement baselines, project calendars, project schedule network diagrams, risk registers, planned response actions, and defined risk impact),

- Historical information and lessons learned knowledge bases (e.g., project records and documents, all project closure information and documentation, information about both the results of previous project selection decisions and previous project performance information, and information from the risk management effort),

- Issue and defect management databases containing issue and defect status, control information, issue and defect resolution, and action item results,

- Configuration management knowledge bases containing the versions and baselines of all official company standards, policies, procedures, and any project documents, and

- Financial databases containing information such as labor hours, incurred costs, budgets and any project cost overruns.

SECTION II

THE STANDARD FOR PROJECT MANAGEMENT OF A PROJECT

Chapter 3

- Project Management Processes for a Project

CHAPTER 3

PROJECT MANAGEMENT PROCESSES FOR A PROJECT

Project management is the application of knowledge, skills, tools, and techniques to project activities to meet project requirements. This application of knowledge requires the effective management of appropriate processes.

A process is a set of interrelated actions and activities performed to achieve a pre-specified product, result, or service. Each process is characterized by its inputs, the tools and techniques that can be applied, and the resulting outputs. As explained in Chapters 1 and 2, the project manager must consider organizational process assets and enterprise environmental factors. These must be taken into account for every process, even if they are not explicitly listed as inputs in the process specification. Organizational process assets provide guidelines and criteria for tailoring the organization's processes to the specific needs of the project. Enterprise environmental factors may constrain the project management options.

In order for a project to be successful, the project team must:

- Select appropriate processes required to meet the project objectives,

- Use a defined approach that can be adopted to meet requirements,

- Comply with requirements to meet stakeholder needs and expectations, and

- Balance the competing demands of scope, time, cost, quality, resources, and risk to produce the specified product, service, or result.

The project processes are performed by the project team and generally fall into one of two major categories:

- *Project management processes* ensure the effective flow of the project throughout its existence. These processes encompass the tools and techniques involved in applying the skills and capabilities described in the Knowledge Areas (Chapters 4 through 12).

- *Product-oriented processes* specify and create the project's product. Product-oriented processes are typically defined by the project life cycle (as discussed in Section 2.1.2) and vary by application area. The scope of the project cannot be defined without some basic understanding of how to create the specified product. For example, various construction techniques and tools must be considered when determining the overall complexity of the house to be built.

This standard describes only the project management processes. Although product-oriented processes are outside the scope of this standard, they should not be ignored by the project manager. Project management processes and product-oriented processes overlap and interact throughout the life of a project.

Project management processes apply globally and across industry groups. Good practice means there is general agreement that the application of project management processes has been shown to enhance the chances of success over a wide range of projects.

> **This does not mean that the knowledge, skills, and processes described should always be applied uniformly on all projects. For any given project, the project manager, in collaboration with the project team, is always responsible for determining which processes are appropriate, and the appropriate degree of rigor for each process.**

Project managers and their teams should carefully address each process and its constituent inputs and outputs. This chapter should be used as a guide for those processes they must consider in managing their project. This effort is known as tailoring.

Project management is an integrative undertaking requiring each project and product process to be appropriately aligned and connected with the other processes to facilitate coordination. Actions taken during one process typically affect that process and other related processes. For example, a scope change typically affects project cost, but may not affect the communication plan or product quality. These process interactions often require tradeoffs among project requirements and objectives, and the specific performance tradeoffs will vary from project to project and organization to organization. Successful project management includes actively managing these interactions to meet sponsor, customer, and other stakeholder requirements. In some circumstances, a process or set of processes will need to be iterated several times in order to achieve the required outcome.

Projects exist within an organization and cannot operate as a closed system. They require input data from the organization and beyond, and deliver capabilities back to the organization. The project processes may generate information to improve the management of future projects.

This standard describes the nature of project management processes in terms of the integration between the processes, their interactions, and the purposes they serve. Project management processes are grouped into five categories known as Project Management Process Groups (or Process Groups):

- **Initiating Process Group.** Those processes performed to define a new project or a new phase of an existing project by obtaining authorization to start the project or phase.

- **Planning Process Group.** Those processes required to establish the scope of the project, refine the objectives, and define the course of action required to attain the objectives that the project was undertaken to achieve.

- **Executing Process Group.** Those processes performed to complete the work defined in the project management plan to satisfy the project specifications.

- **Monitoring and Controlling Process Group.** Those processes required to track, review, and regulate the progress and performance of the project; identify any areas in which changes to the plan are required; and initiate the corresponding changes.

- **Closing Process Group.** Those processes performed to finalize all activities across all Process Groups to formally close the project or phase.

The remainder of this chapter provides information for project management of a single project organized as a network of interlinked processes, details the project management processes, and includes the following major sections:

3.1 Common Project Management Process Interactions

3.2 Project Management Process Groups

3.3 Initiating Process Group

3.4 Planning Process Group

3.5 Executing Process Group

3.6 Monitoring and Controlling Process Group

3.7 Closing Process Group

3.1 Common Project Management Process Interactions

The project management processes are presented as discrete elements with well-defined interfaces. However, in practice they overlap and interact in ways that are not completely detailed here. Most experienced project management practitioners recognize there is more than one way to manage a project. The required Process Groups and their constituent processes are guides for applying appropriate project management knowledge and skills during the project. The application of the project management processes is iterative, and many processes are repeated during the project.

The integrative nature of project management requires the Monitoring and Controlling Process Group to interact with the other Process Groups, as shown in Figure 3-1. In addition, since management of a project is a finite effort, the Initiating Process Group begins the project, and the Closing Process Group ends it.

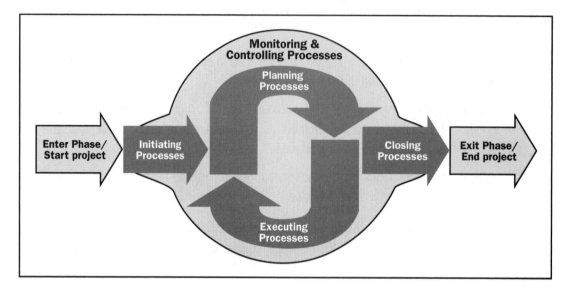

Figure 3-1. Project Management Process Groups

Project Management Process Groups are linked by the outputs they produce. The Process Groups are seldom either discrete or one-time events; they are overlapping activities that occur throughout the project. The output of one process generally becomes an input to another process or is a deliverable of the project. The Planning Process Group provides the Executing Process Group with the project management plan and project documents, and, as the project progresses, it often entails updates to the project management plan and the project documents. Figure 3-2 illustrates how the Process Groups interact and shows the level of overlap at various times. If the project is divided into phases, the Process Groups interact within each phase.

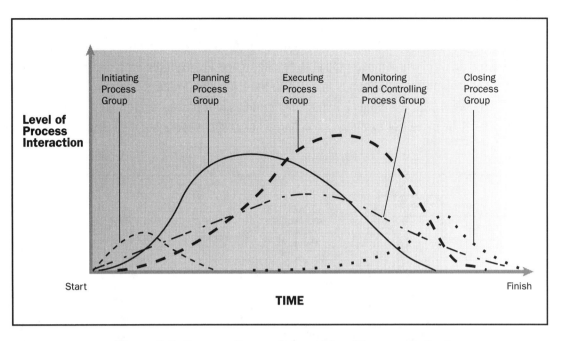

Figure 3-2. Process Groups Interact in a Phase or Project

An example of this would be the exit of a design phase, which requires customer acceptance of the design document. Once it is available, the design document provides the product description for the Planning and Executing Process Groups in one or more subsequent phases. When a project is divided into phases, the Process Groups are invoked as appropriate to effectively drive the project to completion in a controlled manner. In multi-phase projects, processes are repeated within each phase until the criteria for phase completion have been satisfied. Additional information on project life cycles and project phases is provided in Chapter 2.

3.2 Project Management Process Groups

The following sections identify and describe the five Project Management Process Groups required for any project. These five Process Groups have clear dependencies and are typically performed in the same sequence on each project. They are independent of application areas or industry focus. Individual Process Groups and individual constituent processes are often iterated prior to completing the project. The constituent processes can have interactions within a Process Group and among Process Groups. The nature of these interactions varies from project to project and may or may not be performed in a particular order.

The process flow diagram, Figure 3-3, provides an overall summary of the basic flow and interactions among Process Groups and specific stakeholders. A Process Group includes the constituent project management processes that are linked by the respective inputs and outputs where the result or outcome of one process becomes the input to another. **The Process Groups are not project phases.** As projects are separated into distinct phases or subprojects such as feasibility study, concept development, design, prototype, build, test, etc., all of the Process Groups would normally be repeated for each phase or subproject.

Table 3-1 reflects the mapping of the 42 project management processes into the 5 Project Management Process Groups and the nine Project Management Knowledge Areas. The project management processes are shown in the Process Group in which most of the activity takes place. For example, when a process that normally takes place in the Planning Process Group is updated in the Executing Process Group, it is not considered a new process. The iterative nature of project management means that processes from any group may be used throughout the project life cycle. For example, executing a risk response triggers the Identify Risks process to evaluate the impact.

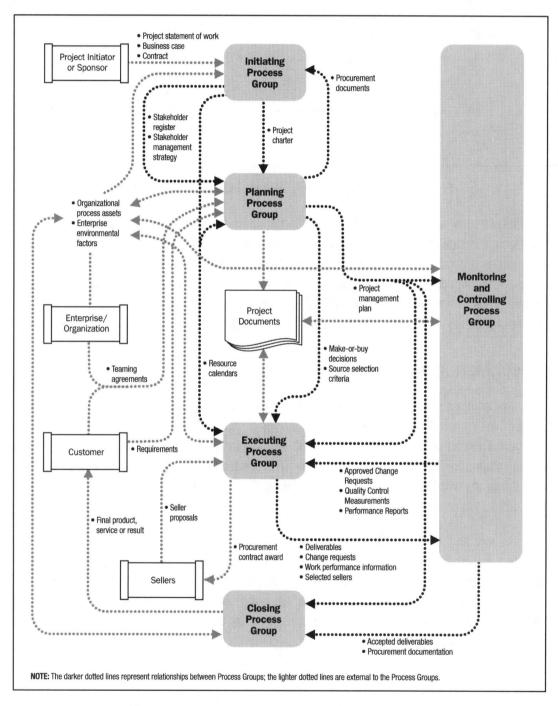

Figure 3-3. Project Management Process Interactions

Table 3-1. Project Management Process Groups and Knowledge Areas Mapping

Knowledge Areas	Project Management Process Groups				
	Initiating Process Group	Planning Process Group	Executing Process Group	Monitoring & Controlling Process Group	Closing Process Group
4. Project Integration Management	4.1 Develop Project Charter	4.2 Develop Project Management Plan	4.3 Direct and Manage Project Execution	4.4 Monitor and Control Project Work 4.5 Perform Integrated Change Control	4.6 Close Project or Phase
5. Project Scope Management		5.1 Collect Requirements 5.2 Define Scope 5.3 Create WBS		5.4 Verify Scope 5.5 Control Scope	
6. Project Time Management		6.1 Define Activities 6.2 Sequence Activities 6.3 Estimate Activity Resources 6.4 Estimate Activity Durations 6.5 Develop Schedule		6.6 Control Schedule	
7. Project Cost Management		7.1 Estimate Costs 7.2 Determine Budget		7.3 Control Costs	
8. Project Quality Management		8.1 Plan Quality	8.2 Perform Quality Assurance	8.3 Perform Quality Control	
9. Project Human Resource Management		9.1 Develop Human Resource Plan	9.2 Acquire Project Team 9.3 Develop Project Team 9.4 Manage Project Team		
10. Project Communications Management	10.1 Identify Stakeholders	10.2 Plan Communications	10.3 Distribute Information 10.4 Manage Stakeholder Expectations	10.5 Report Performance	
11. Project Risk Management		11.1 Plan Risk Management 11.2 Identify Risks 11.3 Perform Qualitative Risk Analysis 11.4 Perform Quantitative Risk Analysis 11.5 Plan Risk Responses		11.6 Monitor and Control Risks	
12. Project Procurement Management		12.1 Plan Procurements	12.2 Conduct Procurements	12.3 Administer Procurements	12.4 Close Procurements

3.3 Initiating Process Group

The Initiating Process Group consists of those processes performed to define a new project or a new phase of an existing project by obtaining authorization to start the project or phase. Within the initiating processes, the initial scope is defined and initial financial resources are committed. Internal and external stakeholders who will interact and influence the overall outcome of the project are identified. If not already assigned, the project manager will be selected. This information is captured in the project charter and stakeholder register. When the project charter is approved, the project becomes officially authorized. Although the project management team may help write the project charter, approval and funding are handled external to the project boundaries (Figure 3-4).

As part of the Initiating Process Group, many large or complex projects may be divided into separate phases. In such projects the Initiating processes are carried out during subsequent phases to validate the decisions made during the original Develop Project Charter and Identify Stakeholders processes. Invoking the Initiating processes at the start of each phase helps keep the project focused on the business need the project was undertaken to address. The success criteria are verified, and the influence and objectives of the project stakeholders are reviewed. A decision is then made as to whether the project should be continued, delayed, or discontinued.

Involving the customers and other stakeholders during initiation generally improves the probability of shared ownership, deliverable acceptance, and customer and other stakeholder satisfaction.

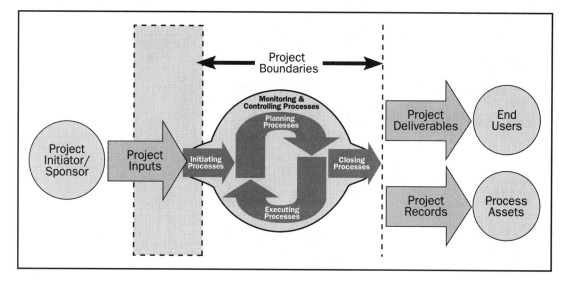

Figure 3-4. Project Boundaries

Initiating processes may be performed by organizational, program, or portfolio processes external to the project's scope of control. For example, prior to commencing a project, the need for high-level requirements may be documented as part of a larger organizational initiative. The feasibility of the new undertaking may be established through a process of evaluating alternatives. Clear descriptions of the project objectives are developed, including the reasons why a specific project is the best alternative to satisfy the requirements. The documentation for this decision may also contain the initial project scope statement, deliverables, project duration, and a forecast of the resources for the organization's investment analysis. As part of the Initiating processes the project manager is given the authority to apply organizational resources to the subsequent project activities.

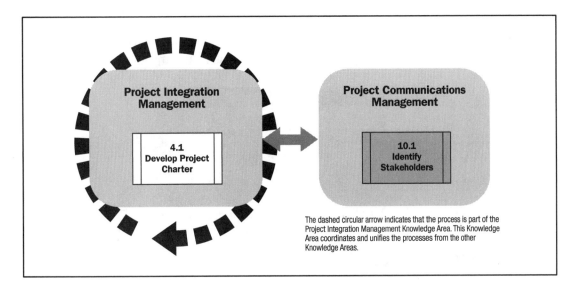

Figure 3-5. Initiating Process Group

The Initiating Process Group (Figure 3-5) includes the following project management processes (Figures 3-6 and 3-7):

3.3.1 Develop Project Charter

Develop Project Charter is the process of developing a document that formally authorizes a project or a phase and documenting initial requirements that satisfy the stakeholder's needs and expectations. In multi-phase projects, this process is used to validate or refine the decisions made during the previous iteration of Develop Project Charter.

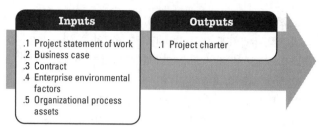

Figure 3-6. Develop Project Charter: Inputs and Outputs

3.3.2   Identify Stakeholders

Identify Stakeholders is the process of identifying all people or organizations impacted by the project, and documenting relevant information regarding their interests, involvement, and impact on project success.

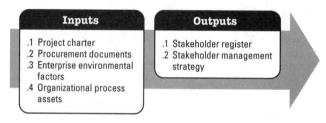

Figure 3-7. Identify Stakeholders: Inputs and Outputs

3.4 Planning Process Group

The Planning Process Group consists of those processes performed to establish the total scope of the effort, define and refine the objectives, and develop the course of action required to attain those objectives. The planning processes develop the project management plan and the project documents that will be used to carry out the project. The multi-dimensional nature of project management creates repeated feedback loops for additional analysis. As more project information or characteristics are gathered and understood, additional planning may be required. Significant changes occurring throughout the project life cycle trigger a need to revisit one or more of the planning processes and, possibly, some of the initiating processes. This progressive detailing of the project management plan is often called "rolling wave planning," indicating that planning and documentation are iterative and ongoing processes.

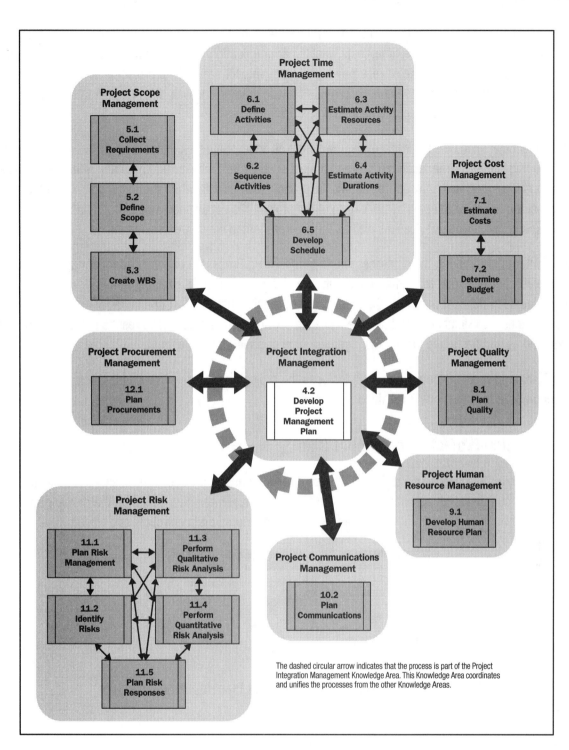

Figure 3-8. Planning Process Group

The project management plan and project documents developed as outputs from the Planning Process Group will explore all aspects of the scope, time, costs, quality, communication, risk, and procurements. Updates arising from approved changes during the project may significantly impact parts of the project management plan and the project documents. Updates to these documents provide greater precision with respect to schedule, costs, and resource requirements to meet the defined project scope.

The project team should encourage involvement from all appropriate stakeholders when planning the project and developing the project management plan and project documents. Since the feedback and refinement process cannot continue indefinitely, procedures set by the organization dictate when the initial planning effort ends. These procedures will be affected by the nature of the project, the established project boundaries, appropriate monitoring and controlling activities, as well as the environment in which the project will be performed.

Other interactions among the processes within the Planning Process Group are dependent upon the nature of the project. For example, for some projects there will be little or no identifiable risk until after significant planning has been done. At that time, the team might recognize that the cost and schedule targets are overly aggressive, thus involving considerably more risk than previously understood. The results of the iterations are documented as updates to the project management plan or project documents.

The Planning Process Group (Figure 3-8) includes the project management processes identified in Figures 3-9 through 3-28 (see Sections 3.4.1 through 3.4.20).

3.4.1 Develop Project Management Plan

Develop Project Management Plan is the process of documenting the actions necessary to define, prepare, integrate, and coordinate all subsidiary plans. The project management plan becomes the primary source of information for how the project will be planned, executed, monitored and controlled, and closed.

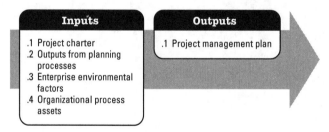

Figure 3-9. Develop Project Management Plan: Inputs and Outputs

3.4.2   Collect Requirements

Collect Requirements is the process of defining and documenting stakeholders' needs to meet the project objectives.

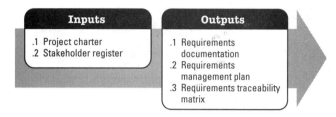

Figure 3-10. Collect Requirements: Inputs and Outputs

3.4.3   Define Scope

Define Scope is the process of developing a detailed description of the project and product.

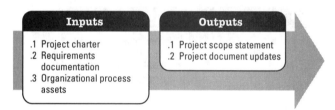

Figure 3-11. Define Scope: Inputs and Outputs

3.4.4   Create WBS

Create Work Breakdown Structure is the process of subdividing project deliverables and project work into smaller, more manageable components.

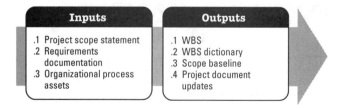

Figure 3-12. Create WBS: Inputs and Outputs

3.4.5 Define Activities

Define Activities is the process of identifying the specific actions to be performed to produce the project deliverables.

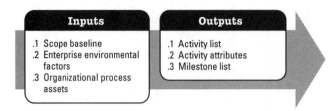

Figure 3-13. Define Activities: Inputs and Outputs

3.4.6 Sequence Activities

Sequence Activities is the process of identifying and documenting relationships among the project activities.

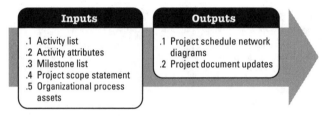

Figure 3-14. Sequence Activities: Inputs and Outputs

3.4.7 Estimate Activity Resources

Estimate Activity Resources is the process of estimating the type and quantities of material, people, equipment, or supplies required to perform each activity.

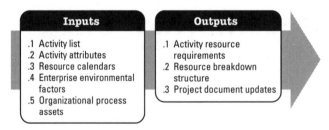

Figure 3-15. Estimate Activity Resources: Inputs and Outputs

3.4.8   Estimate Activity Durations

Estimate Activity Durations is the process of approximating the number of work periods needed to complete individual activities with estimated resources.

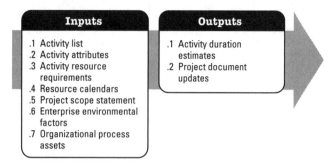

Figure 3-16. Estimate Activity Durations: Inputs and Outputs

3.4.9   Develop Schedule

Develop Schedule is the process of analyzing activity sequences, durations, resource requirements, and schedule constraints to create the project schedule.

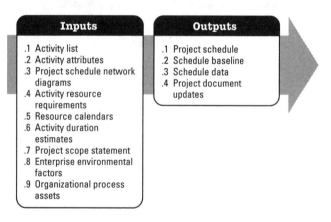

Figure 3-17. Develop Schedule: Inputs and Outputs

3.4.10 Estimate Costs

Estimate Costs is the process of developing an approximation of the monetary resources needed to complete project activities.

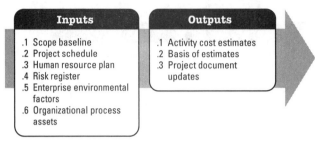

Inputs	Outputs
.1 Scope baseline .2 Project schedule .3 Human resource plan .4 Risk register .5 Enterprise environmental factors .6 Organizational process assets	.1 Activity cost estimates .2 Basis of estimates .3 Project document updates

Figure 3-18. Estimate Costs: Inputs and Outputs

3.4.11 Determine Budget

Determine Budget is the process of aggregating the estimated costs of individual activities or work packages to establish an authorized cost baseline.

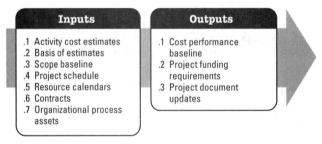

Inputs	Outputs
.1 Activity cost estimates .2 Basis of estimates .3 Scope baseline .4 Project schedule .5 Resource calendars .6 Contracts .7 Organizational process assets	.1 Cost performance baseline .2 Project funding requirements .3 Project document updates

Figure 3-19. Determine Budget: Inputs and Outputs

3.4.12 Plan Quality

Plan Quality is the process of identifying quality requirements and/or standards for the project and product, and documenting how the project will demonstrate compliance.

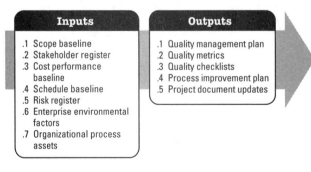

Inputs	Outputs
.1 Scope baseline .2 Stakeholder register .3 Cost performance baseline .4 Schedule baseline .5 Risk register .6 Enterprise environmental factors .7 Organizational process assets	.1 Quality management plan .2 Quality metrics .3 Quality checklists .4 Process improvement plan .5 Project document updates

Figure 3-20. Plan Quality: Inputs and Outputs

3.4.13 Develop Human Resource Plan

Develop Human Resource Plan is the process of identifying and documenting project roles, responsibilities, and required skills, reporting relationships, and creating a staffing management plan.

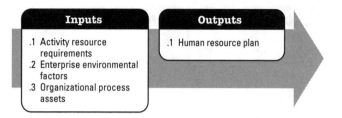

Figure 3-21. Develop Human Resource Plan: Inputs and Outputs

3.4.14 Plan Communications

Plan Communications is the process of determining project stakeholder information needs and defining a communication approach.

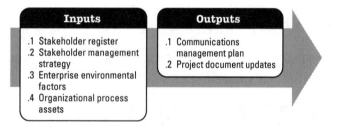

Figure 3-22. Plan Communications: Inputs and Outputs

3.4.15 Plan Risk Management

Plan Risk Management is the process of defining how to conduct risk management activities for a project.

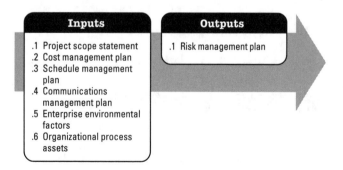

Figure 3-23. Plan Risk Management: Inputs and Outputs

3.4.16 Identify Risks

Identify Risks is the process of determining which risks may affect the project and documenting their characteristics.

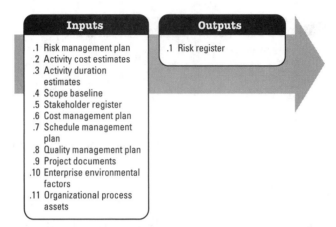

Inputs

.1 Risk management plan
.2 Activity cost estimates
.3 Activity duration estimates
.4 Scope baseline
.5 Stakeholder register
.6 Cost management plan
.7 Schedule management plan
.8 Quality management plan
.9 Project documents
.10 Enterprise environmental factors
.11 Organizational process assets

Outputs

.1 Risk register

Figure 3-24. Identify Risks: Inputs and Outputs

3.4.17 Perform Qualitative Risk Analysis

Perform Qualitative Risk Analysis is the process of prioritizing risks for further analysis or action by assessing and combining their probability of occurrence and impact.

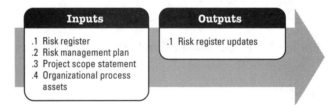

Inputs

.1 Risk register
.2 Risk management plan
.3 Project scope statement
.4 Organizational process assets

Outputs

.1 Risk register updates

Figure 3-25. Perform Qualitative Risk Analysis: Inputs and Outputs

3.4.18 Perform Quantitative Risk Analysis

Perform Quantitative Risk Analysis is the process of numerically analyzing the effect of identified risks on overall project objectives.

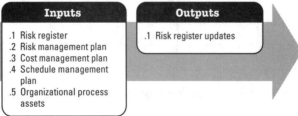

Inputs

.1 Risk register
.2 Risk management plan
.3 Cost management plan
.4 Schedule management plan
.5 Organizational process assets

Outputs

.1 Risk register updates

Figure 3-26. Perform Quantitative Risk Analysis: Inputs and Outputs

3.4.19 Plan Risk Responses

Plan Risk Responses is the process of developing options and actions to enhance opportunities and to reduce threats to project objectives.

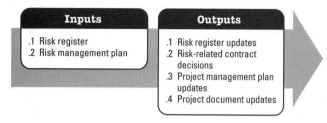

Figure 3-27. Plan Risk Responses: Inputs and Outputs

3.4.20 Plan Procurements

Plan Procurements is the process of documenting project purchasing decisions, specifying the approach, and identifying potential sellers.

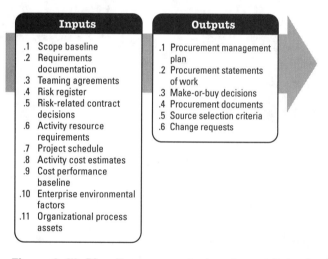

Figure 3-28. Plan Procurements: Inputs and Outputs

3.5 Executing Process Group

The Executing Process Group consist of those processes performed to complete the work defined in the project management plan to satisfy the project specifications. This Process Group involves coordinating people and resources, as well as integrating and performing the activities of the project in accordance with the project management plan (Figure 3-29).

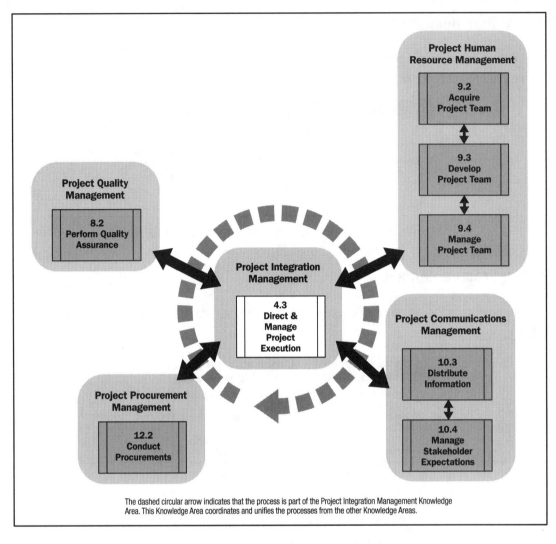

The dashed circular arrow indicates that the process is part of the Project Integration Management Knowledge Area. This Knowledge Area coordinates and unifies the processes from the other Knowledge Areas.

Figure 3-29. Executing Process Group

During project execution, results may require planning updates and re-baselining. This can include changes to expected activity durations, changes in resource productivity and availability, and unanticipated risks. Such variances may affect the project management plan or project documents and may require detailed analysis and development of appropriate project management responses. The results of the analysis can trigger change requests that, if approved, may modify the project management plan or other project documents and possibly require establishing new baselines. A large portion of the project's budget will be expended in performing the Executing Process Group processes. The Executing Process Group includes the following project management processes (Figure 3-30 through 3-37):

3.5.1 Direct and Manage Project Execution

Direct and Manage Project Execution is the process of performing the work defined in the project management plan to achieve the project's objectives.

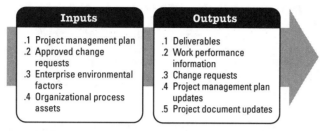

Inputs
- .1 Project management plan
- .2 Approved change requests
- .3 Enterprise environmental factors
- .4 Organizational process assets

Outputs
- .1 Deliverables
- .2 Work performance information
- .3 Change requests
- .4 Project management plan updates
- .5 Project document updates

Figure 3-30. Direct and Manage Project Execution: Inputs and Outputs

3.5.2 Perform Quality Assurance

Perform Quality Assurance is the process of auditing the quality requirements and the results from quality control measurements to ensure appropriate quality standards and operational definitions are used.

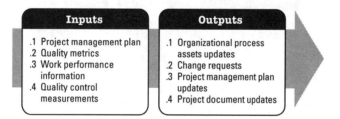

Inputs
- .1 Project management plan
- .2 Quality metrics
- .3 Work performance information
- .4 Quality control measurements

Outputs
- .1 Organizational process assets updates
- .2 Change requests
- .3 Project management plan updates
- .4 Project document updates

Figure 3-31. Perform Quality Assurance: Inputs and Outputs

3.5.3 Acquire Project Team

Acquire Project Team is the process of confirming human resource availability and obtaining the team necessary to complete project assignments.

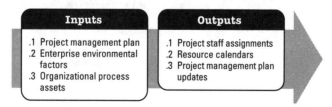

Inputs
- .1 Project management plan
- .2 Enterprise environmental factors
- .3 Organizational process assets

Outputs
- .1 Project staff assignments
- .2 Resource calendars
- .3 Project management plan updates

Figure 3-32. Acquire Project Team: Inputs and Outputs

3.5.4   Develop Project Team

Develop Project Team is the process of improving the competencies, team interaction, and the overall team environment to enhance project performance.

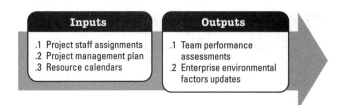

Figure 3-33. Develop Project Team: Inputs and Outputss

3.5.5   Manage Project Team

Manage Project Team is the process of tracking team member performance, providing feedback, resolving issues, and managing changes to optimize project performance.

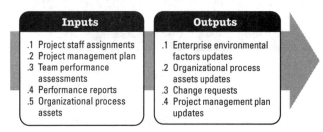

Figure 3-34. Manage Project Team: Inputs and Outputs

3.5.6   Distribute Information

Distribute Information is the process of making relevant information available to project stakeholders as planned.

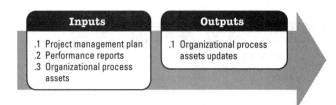

Figure 3-35. Distribute Information: Inputs and Outputs

3.5.7 Manage Stakeholder Expectations

Manage Stakeholder Expectations is the process of communicating and working with stakeholders to meet their needs and addressing issues as they occur.

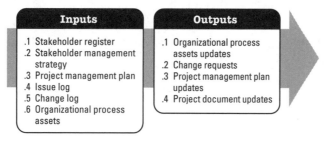

Figure 3-36. Manage Stakeholder Expectations: Inputs and Outputs

3.5.8 Conduct Procurements

Conduct Procurements is the process of obtaining seller responses, selecting a seller, and awarding a contract.

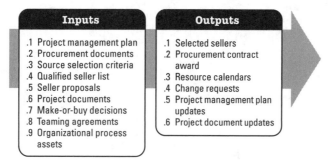

Figure 3-37. Conduct Procurements: Inputs and Outputs

3.6 Monitoring and Controlling Process Group

The Monitoring and Controlling Process Group consists of those processes required to track, review, and regulate the progress and performance of the project; identify any areas in which changes to the plan are required; and initiate the corresponding changes. The key benefit of this Process Group is that project performance is observed and measured regularly and consistently to identify variances from the project management plan. The Monitoring and Controlling Process Group also includes:

- Controlling changes and recommending preventive action in anticipation of possible problems,

- Monitoring the ongoing project activities against the project management plan and the project performance baseline, and

- Influencing the factors that could circumvent integrated change control so only approved changes are implemented.

This continuous monitoring provides the project team insight into the health of the project and identifies any areas requiring additional attention. The Monitoring and Controlling Process Group not only monitors and controls the work being done within a Process Group, but also monitors and controls the entire project effort. In multi-phase projects, the Monitoring and Controlling Process Group coordinates project phases in order to implement corrective or preventive actions to bring the project into compliance with the project management plan. This review can result in recommended and approved updates to the project management plan. For example, a missed activity finish date may require adjustments to the current staffing plan, reliance on overtime, or trade-offs between budget and schedule objectives.

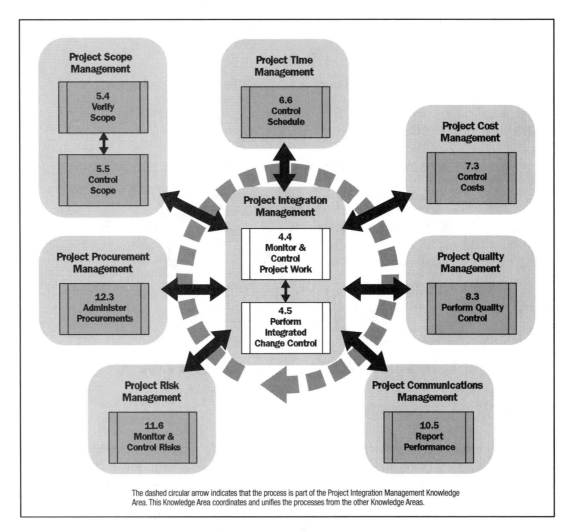

The dashed circular arrow indicates that the process is part of the Project Integration Management Knowledge Area. This Knowledge Area coordinates and unifies the processes from the other Knowledge Areas.

Figure 3-38. Monitoring & Controlling Process Group

The Monitoring and Controlling Process Group (Figure 3-38) includes the following project management processes (Figures 3-39 through 3-48):

3.6.1 Monitor and Control Project Work

Monitor and Control Project Work is the process of tracking, reviewing, and regulating the progress to meet the performance objectives defined in the project management plan. Monitoring includes status reporting, progress measurement, and forecasting. Performance reports provide information on the project's performance with regard to scope, schedule, cost, resources, quality, and risk, which can be used as inputs to other processes.

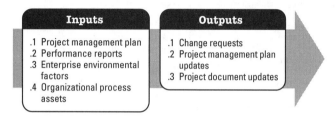

Inputs	Outputs
.1 Project management plan	.1 Change requests
.2 Performance reports	.2 Project management plan
.3 Enterprise environmental	updates
factors	.3 Project document updates
.4 Organizational process	
assets	

Figure 3-39. Monitor and Control Project Work: Inputs and Outputs

3.6.2 Perform Integrated Change Control

Perform Integrated Change Control is the process of reviewing all change requests, approving changes, and managing changes to the deliverables, organizational process assets, project documents, and the project management plan.

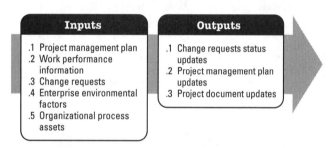

Inputs	Outputs
.1 Project management plan	.1 Change requests status
.2 Work performance	updates
information	.2 Project management plan
.3 Change requests	updates
.4 Enterprise environmental	.3 Project document updates
factors	
.5 Organizational process	
assets	

Figure 3-40. Perform Integrated Change Control: Inputs and Outputs

3.6.3 Verify Scope

Verify Scope is the process of formalizing acceptance of the completed project deliverables.

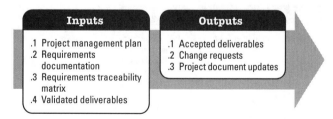

Inputs	Outputs
.1 Project management plan	.1 Accepted deliverables
.2 Requirements	.2 Change requests
documentation	.3 Project document updates
.3 Requirements traceability	
matrix	
.4 Validated deliverables	

Figure 3-41. Verify Scope: Inputs and Outputs

3.6.4   Control Scope

Control Scope is the process of monitoring the status of the project and product scope and managing changes to the scope baseline.

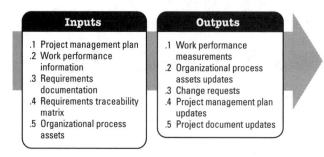

Figure 3-42. Control Scope: Inputs and Outputs

3.6.5   Control Schedule

Control Schedule is the process of monitoring the status of the project to update project progress and managing changes to the schedule baseline.

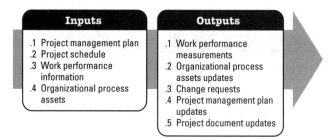

Figure 3-43. Control Schedule: Inputs and Outputs

3.6.6   Control Costs

Control Costs is the process of monitoring the status of the project to update the project budget and managing changes to the cost baseline.

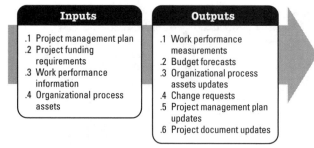

Figure 3-44. Control Costs: Inputs and Outputs

3.6.7   Perform Quality Control

Perform Quality Control is the process of monitoring and recording results of executing the quality activities to assess performance and recommend necessary changes.

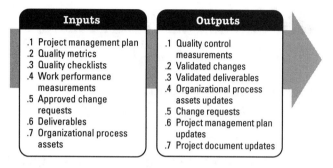

Figure 3-45. Perform Quality Control: Inputs and Outputs

3.6.8   Report Performance

Report Performance is the process of collecting and distributing performance information including status reports, progress measurements, and forecasts.

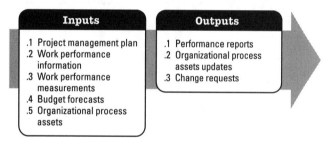

Figure 3-46. Report Performance: Inputs and Outputs

3.6.9   Monitor and Control Risks

Monitor and Control Risks is the process of implementing risk response plans, tracking identified risks, monitoring residual risks, identifying new risks, and evaluating risk process effectiveness throughout the project.

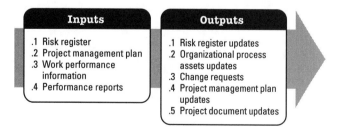

Figure 3-47. Monitor and Control Risks: Inputs and Outputs

3.6.10 Administer Procurements

Administer Procurements is the process of managing procurement relationships, monitoring contract performance, and making changes and corrections as needed.

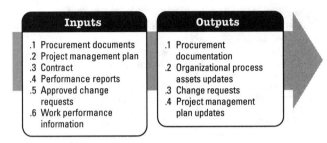

Figure 3-48. Administer Procurements: Inputs and Outputs

3.7 Closing Process Group

The Closing Process Group consists of those processes performed to finalize all activities across all Project Management Process Groups to formally complete the project, phase, or contractual obligations. This Process Group, when completed, verifies that the defined processes are completed within all the Process Groups to close the project or a project phase, as appropriate, and formally establishes that the project or project phase is complete. At project or phase closure, the following may occur:

- Obtain acceptance by the customer or sponsor,

- Conduct post-project or phase-end review,

- Record impacts of tailoring to any process,

- Document lessons learned,

- Apply appropriate updates to organizational process assets,

- Archive all relevant project documents in the Project Management Information System (PMIS) to be used as historical data, and

- Close out procurements.

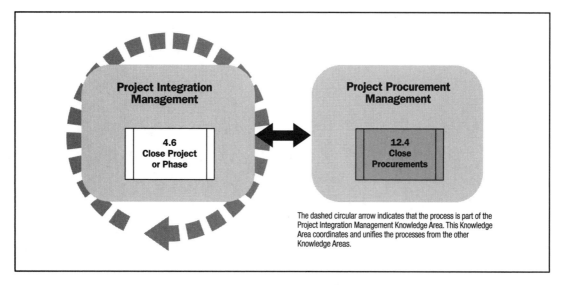

Figure 3-49. Closing Process Group

The closing Process Group (Figure 3-49) includes the following project management processes (Figures 3-50 and 3-51):

3.7.1   Close Project or Phase

Close Project or Phase is the process of finalizing all activities across all of the management Process Groups to formally complete the project or phase.

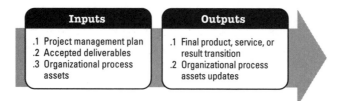

Figure 3-50. Close Project or Phase: Inputs and Outputs

3.7.2   Close Procurements

Close Procurements is the process of completing each project procurement.

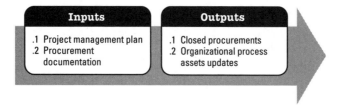

Figure 3-51. Close Procurements: Inputs and Outputs

SECTION III

THE PROJECT MANAGEMENT KNOWLEDGE AREAS

Section III

- Introduction

Chapter 4

- Project Integration Management

Chapter 5

- Project Scope Management

Chapter 6

- Project Time Management

Chapter 7

- Project Cost Management

Chapter 8

- Project Quality Management

Chapter 9

- Project Human Resource Management

Chapter 10

- Project Communications Management

Chapter 11

- Project Risk Management

Chapter 12

- Project Procurement Management

References

SECTION III INTRODUCTION

DATA FLOW DIAGRAMS

A data flow diagram is provided in each Knowledge Area chapter (Chapters 4 through 12). The data flow diagram is a summary level depiction of the process inputs and process outputs that flow down through all the processes within a specific Knowledge Area. Although the processes are presented here as discrete elements with well-defined interfaces, in practice they are iterative and can overlap and interact in ways not detailed here.

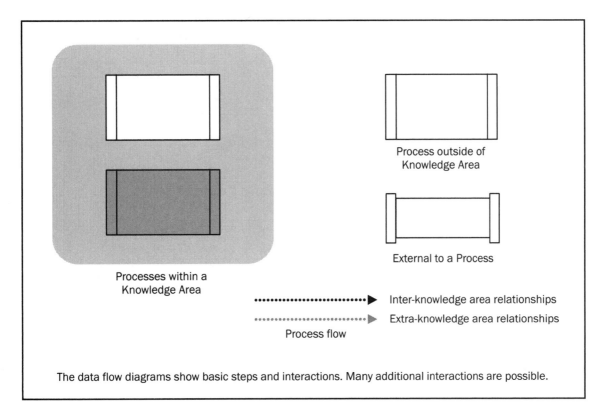

Processes within a
Knowledge Area

Process outside of
Knowledge Area

External to a Process

Process flow

Inter-knowledge area relationships

Extra-knowledge area relationships

The data flow diagrams show basic steps and interactions. Many additional interactions are possible.

Figure III-1. Data Flow Diagram Legend

CHAPTER 4

PROJECT INTEGRATION MANAGEMENT

Project Integration Management includes the processes and activities needed to identify, define, combine, unify, and coordinate the various processes and project management activities within the Project Management Process Groups. In the project management context, integration includes characteristics of unification, consolidation, articulation, and integrative actions that are crucial to project completion, successfully managing stakeholder expectations, and meeting requirements. Project Integration Management entails making choices about resource allocation, making trade-offs among competing objectives and alternatives, and managing the interdependencies among the project management Knowledge Areas. The project management processes are usually presented as discrete processes with defined interfaces while, in practice, they overlap and interact in ways that cannot be completely detailed in the *PMBOK® Guide.*

Figure 4-1 provides an overview of Project Integration Management processes, which are as follows:

4.1 Develop Project Charter—The process of developing a document that formally authorizes a project or a phase and documenting initial requirements that satisfy the stakeholder's needs and expectations.

4.2 Develop Project Management Plan—The process of documenting the actions necessary to define, prepare, integrate, and coordinate all subsidiary plans.

4.3 Direct and Manage Project Execution—The process of performing the work defined in the project management plan to achieve the project's objectives.

4.4 Monitor and Control Project Work—The process of tracking, reviewing, and regulating the progress to meet the performance objectives defined in the project management plan.

4.5 Perform Integrated Change Control—The process of reviewing all change requests, approving changes, and managing changes to the deliverables, organizational process assets, project documents, and the project management plan.

4.6 Close Project or Phase—The process of finalizing all activities across all of the Project Management Process Groups to formally complete the project or phase.

The need for Project Integration Management is evident in situations where individual processes interact. For example, a cost estimate needed for a contingency plan involves integrating the processes in the cost, time, and risk Knowledge Areas. When additional risks associated with various staffing alternatives are identified, then one or more of those processes may be revisited. The project deliverables may also need to be integrated with ongoing operations of either the performing organization or the customer's organization, or with the long-term strategic planning that takes future problems and opportunities into consideration. Project Integration Management also includes the activities needed to manage project documents to ensure consistency with the project management plan and product deliverables.

Most experienced project management practitioners know there is no single way to manage a project. They apply project management knowledge, skills, and required processes in a different order and with varying rigor to achieve the desired project performance. However, the perception that a particular process is not required does not mean that it should not be addressed. The project manager and project team must address every process to determine the level of implementation for each process for each project. If a project has more than one phase, the same level of rigor should be applied to processes within each phase of the project.

The integrative nature of projects and project management can be understood by thinking of other types of activities performed while completing a project. Examples of some activities performed by the project management team are:

- Analyze and understand the scope. This includes the project and product requirements, criteria, assumptions, constraints, and other influences related to a project, and how each will be managed or addressed within the project.

- Understand how to take the identified information and then transform it into a project management plan using a structured approach as described in the PMBOK® Guide.

- Perform activities to produce project deliverables.

- Measure and monitor all aspects of the project's progress and take appropriate action to meet project objectives.

Among the processes in the Project Management Process Groups, the links are often iterated. The Planning Process Group provides the Executing Process Group with a documented project management plan early in the project and then facilitates updates to the project management plan if changes occur as the project progresses.

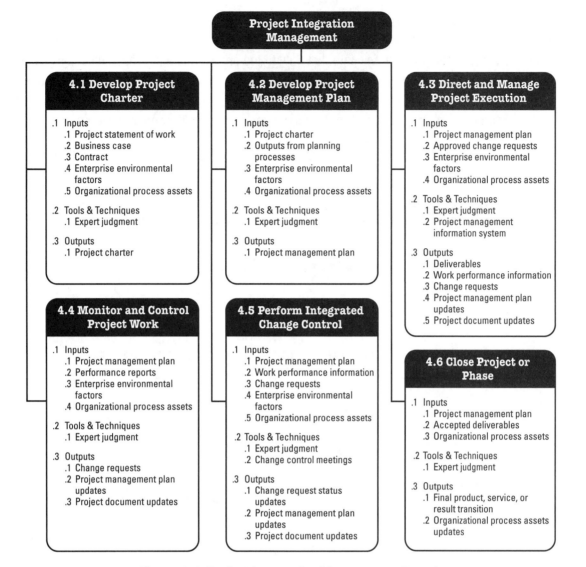

Figure 4-1. Project Integration Management Overview

4.1 Develop Project Charter

Develop Project Charter is the process of developing a document that formally authorizes a project or a phase and documenting initial requirements that satisfy the stakeholders' needs and expectations. It establishes a partnership between the performing organization and the requesting organization (or customer, in the case of external projects). The approved project charter formally initiates the project. A project manager is identified and assigned as early in the project as is feasible, preferably while the project charter is being developed and always prior to the start of planning. It is recommended that the project manager participate in the development of the project charter, as the project charter provides the project manager with the authority to apply resources to project activities.

Projects are authorized by someone external to the project such as a sponsor, PMO, or portfolio steering committee. The project initiator or sponsor should be at a level that is appropriate to funding the project. They will either create the project charter or delegate that duty to the project manager. The initiator's signature on the charter authorizes the project. Projects are authorized due to internal business needs or external influences. This usually triggers the creation of a needs analysis, business case, or description of the situation the project will address. Chartering a project links the project to the strategy and ongoing work of the organization.

Figure 4-2 shows the inputs, tools and techniques, and outputs for this process and the data flow diagram is displayed in Figure 4-3.

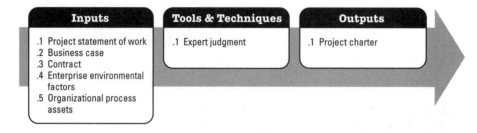

Figure 4-2. Develop Project Charter: Inputs, Tools & Techniques, and Outputs

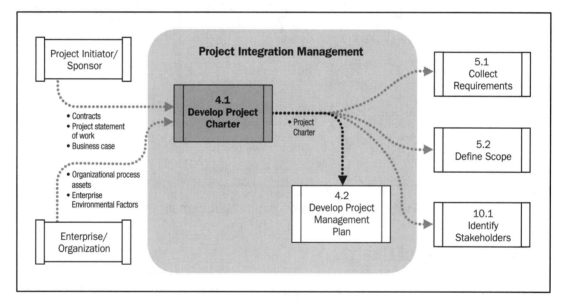

Figure 4-3. Develop Project Charter Data Flow Diagram

4.1.1 Develop Project Charter: Inputs

.1 Project Statement of Work

The statement of work (SOW) is a narrative description of products or services to be delivered by the project. For internal projects, the project initiator or sponsor provides the statement of work based on business needs, product, or service requirements. For external projects, the statement of work can be received from the customer as part of a bid document, for example, request for proposal, request for information, request for bid, or as part of a contract. The SOW references:

- **Business need.** An organization's business need may be based on a market demand, technological advance, legal requirement, or government regulation.

- **Product scope description.** This documents the characteristics of the product that the project will be undertaken to create. The description should also document the relationship between the products or services being created and the business need that the project will address.

- **Strategic plan.** The strategic plan documents the organization's strategic goals. Therefore, all projects should be aligned with the strategic plan.

.2 Business Case

The business case or similar document provides the necessary information from a business standpoint to determine whether or not the project is worth the required investment. Typically the business need and the cost-benefit analysis are contained in the business case to justify the project. The requesting organization or customer, in the case of external projects, may write the business case. The business case is created as a result of one or more of the following:

- Market demand (e.g., a car company authorizing a project to build more fuel-efficient cars in response to gasoline shortages),

- Organizational need (e.g., a training company authorizing a project to create a new course to increase its revenues),

- Customer request (e.g., an electric utility authorizing a project to build a new substation to serve a new industrial park),

- Technological advance (e.g., an electronics firm authorizing a new project to develop a faster, cheaper, and smaller laptop after advances in computer memory and electronics technology),

- Legal requirement (e.g., a paint manufacturer authorizing a project to establish guidelines for handling toxic materials),

- Ecological impacts (e.g., a company undertakes a project to lessen its environmental impact), or

- Social need (e.g., a non-governmental organization in a developing country authorizing a project to provide potable water systems, latrines, and sanitation education to communities suffering from high rates of cholera).

In the case of multi-phase projects, the business case may be periodically reviewed to ensure that the project is on track to deliver the business benefits. In the early stages of the project life cycle, periodic review of the business case by the sponsoring organization also helps to confirm that the project is still required.

.3 Contract

A contract is an input if the project is being done for an external customer.

.4 Enterprise Environmental Factors

The enterprise environmental factors that can influence the Develop Project Charter process include, but are not limited to:

- Governmental or industry standards,

- Organization infrastructure, and

- Marketplace conditions.

.5 Organizational Process Assets

The organizational process assets that can influence the Develop Project Charter process include, but are not limited to:

- Organizational standard processes, policies, and standardized process definitions for use in the organization;

- Templates (e.g., project charter template); and

- Historical information and lessons learned knowledge base.

4.1.2 Develop Project Charter: Tools and Techniques

.1 Expert Judgment

Expert judgment is often used to assess the inputs used to develop the project charter. Such judgment and expertise is applied to any technical and management details during this process. Such expertise is provided by any group or individual with specialized knowledge or training, and is available from many sources, including:

- Other units within the organization,

- Consultants,

- Stakeholders, including customers or sponsors,

- Professional and technical associations,

- Industry groups,

- Subject matter experts, and

- Project management office (PMO).

4.1.3 Develop Project Charter: Outputs

.1 Project Charter

The project charter documents the business needs, current understanding of the customer's needs, and the new product, service, or result that it is intended to satisfy, such as:

- Project purpose or justification,

- Measurable project objectives and related success criteria,

- High-level requirements,

- High-level project description,

- High-level risks,

- Summary milestone schedule,

- Summary budget,

- Project approval requirements (what constitutes project success, who decides the project is successful, and who signs off on the project),

- Assigned project manager, responsibility, and authority level, and

- Name and authority of the sponsor or other person(s) authorizing the project charter.

4.2 Develop Project Management Plan

Develop Project Management Plan is the process of documenting the actions necessary to define, prepare, integrate, and coordinate all subsidiary plans. The project management plan defines how the project is executed, monitored and controlled, and closed. The project management plan content will vary depending upon the application area and complexity of the project. The project management plan is developed through a series of integrated processes until project closure. This process results in a project management plan that is progressively elaborated by updates and controlled and approved through the Perform Integrated Change Control (Section 4.5) process.

Figure 4-4 shows the inputs, tools and techniques, and outputs for this process and the data flow diagram is displayed in Figure 4-5.

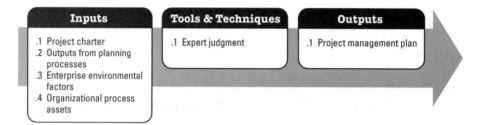

Inputs	Tools & Techniques	Outputs
.1 Project charter .2 Outputs from planning processes .3 Enterprise environmental factors .4 Organizational process assets	.1 Expert judgment	.1 Project management plan

Figure 4-4. Develop Project Management Plan: Inputs, Tools & Techniques, and Outputs

4.2.1 Develop Project Management Plan: Inputs

.1 Project Charter

Described in Section 4.1.3.1.

.2 Outputs from Planning Processes

Outputs from many of the planning processes described in Chapters 5 through 12 are integrated to create the project management plan. Any baselines and subsidiary management plans that are an output from other planning processes are inputs to this process. In addition, updates to these documents can necessitate updates to the project management plan.

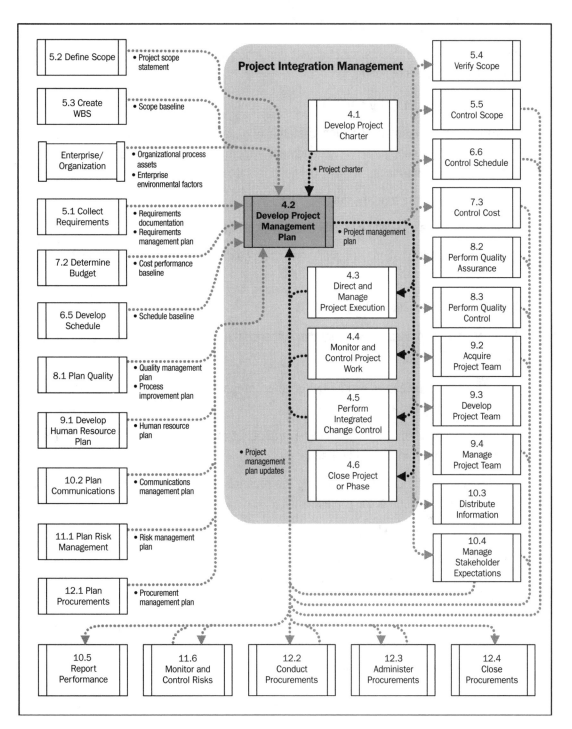

Figure 4-5. Develop Project Management Plan Data Flow Diagram

.3 Enterprise Environmental Factors

The enterprise environmental factors that can influence the Develop Project Management Plan process include, but are not limited to:

- Governmental or industry standards,

- Project management information systems (e.g., an automated tool, such as a scheduling software tool, a configuration management system, an information collection and distribution system, or web interfaces to other online automated systems),

- Organizational structure and culture,

- Infrastructure (e.g., existing facilities and capital equipment), and

- Personnel administration (e.g., hiring and firing guidelines, employee performance reviews, and training records).

.4 Organizational Process Assets

The organizational process assets that can influence the Develop Project Management Plan process include, but are not limited to:

- Standardized guidelines, work instructions, proposal evaluation criteria, and performance measurement criteria,

- Project management plan template—Elements of the project management plan that may be updated include, but are not limited to:

  o Guidelines and criteria for tailoring the organization's set of standard processes to satisfy the specific needs of the project, and

  o Project closure guidelines or requirements like the product validation and acceptance criteria,

- Change control procedures including the steps by which official company standards, policies, plans, and procedures, or any project documents will be modified and how any changes will be approved and validated,

- Project files from past projects (e.g., scope, cost, schedule and performance measurement baselines, project calendars, project schedule network diagrams, risk registers, planned response actions, and defined risk impact),

- Historical information and lessons learned knowledge base, and

- Configuration management knowledge base containing the versions and baselines of all official company standards, policies, procedures, and any project documents.

4.2.2 Develop Project Management Plan: Tools and Techniques

.1 Expert Judgment

When developing the project management plan, expert judgment is utilized to:

- Tailor the process to meet the project needs,

- Develop technical and management details to be included in the project management plan,

- Determine resources and skill levels needed to perform project work,

- Define the level of configuration management to apply on the project, and

- Determine which project documents will be subject to the formal change control process.

4.2.3 Develop Project Management Plan: Outputs

.1 Project Management Plan

The project management plan integrates and consolidates all of the subsidiary management plans and baselines from the planning processes and includes but is not limited to:

- The life cycle selected for the project and the processes that will be applied to each phase,

- Results of the tailoring by the project management team as follows:

  o Project management processes selected by the project management team,

  o Level of implementation of each selected process,

  o Descriptions of the tools and techniques to be used for accomplishing those processes, and

  o How the selected processes will be used to manage the specific project, including the dependencies and interactions among those processes, and the essential inputs and outputs.

- How work will be executed to accomplish the project objectives,

- A change management plan that documents how changes will be monitored and controlled,

- A configuration management plan that documents how configuration management will be performed,

- How integrity of the performance measurement baselines will be maintained,

- Need and techniques for communication among stakeholders, and

- Key management reviews for content, extent, and timing to facilitate addressing open issues and pending decisions.

The project management plan can be either summary level or detailed, and can be composed of one or more subsidiary plans. Each of the subsidiary plans is detailed to the extent required by the specific project. Once the project management plan is baselined, it may only be changed when a change request is generated and approved through the Perform Integrated Change Control process.

Project baselines include, but are not limited to:

- Schedule baseline,

- Cost performance baseline, and

- Scope baseline.

Subsidiary plans include, but are not limited to:

- Scope management plan (introduction to Chapter 5),

- Requirements management plan (Section 5.1.3.2),

- Schedule management plan (introduction to Chapter 6),

- Cost management plan (introduction to Chapter 7),

- Quality management plan (Section 8.1.3.1),

- Process improvement plan (Section 8.1.3.4),

- Human resource plan (Section 9.1.3.1),

- Communications management plan (Section 10.2.3.1),

- Risk management plan (Section 11.1.3.1), and

- Procurement management plan (Section 12.1.3.1).

Often the scope, schedule, and cost baseline will be combined into a performance measurement baseline that is used as an overall project baseline against which integrated performance can be measured. The performance measurement baseline is used for earned value measurements.

4.3 Direct and Manage Project Execution

Direct and Manage Project Execution is the process of performing the work defined in the project management plan to achieve the project's objectives. These activities include, but are not limited to:

- Perform activities to accomplish project requirements;
- Create project deliverables;
- Staff, train, and manage the team members assigned to the project;
- Obtain, manage, and use resources including materials, tools, equipment, and facilities;
- Implement the planned methods and standards;
- Establish and manage project communication channels, both external and internal to the project team;
- Generate project data, such as cost, schedule, technical and quality progress, and status to facilitate forecasting;
- Issue change requests and adapt approved changes into the project's scope, plans, and environment;
- Manage risks and implement risk response activities;
- Manage sellers and suppliers; and
- Collect and document lessons learned, and implement approved process improvement activities.

The project manager, along with the project management team, directs the performance of the planned project activities, and manages the various technical and organizational interfaces that exist within the project. The Direct and Manage Project Execution process is directly affected by the project application area. Deliverables are produced as outputs from processes performed to accomplish the project work planned and scheduled in the project management plan. Work performance information, about the completion status of the deliverables and what has been accomplished, is collected as part of project execution and is fed into the performance reporting process. The work performance information will also be used as an input to the Monitoring and Controlling Process Group.

Direct and Manage Project Execution also requires implementation of approved changes covering:

- **Corrective action.** Documented direction for executing the project work to bring expected future performance of the project work in line with the project management plan.
- **Preventive action.** A documented direction to perform an activity that can reduce the probability of negative consequences associated with project risks.
- **Defect repair.** The formally documented identification of a defect in a project component with a recommendation to either repair the defect or completely replace the component.

Figure 4-6 shows the inputs, tools and techniques, and outputs for this process and the data flow diagram is displayed in Figure 4-7.

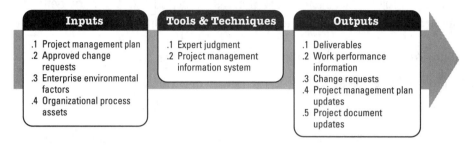

Figure 4-6. Direct and Manage Project Execution: Inputs, Tools & Techniques, and Outputs

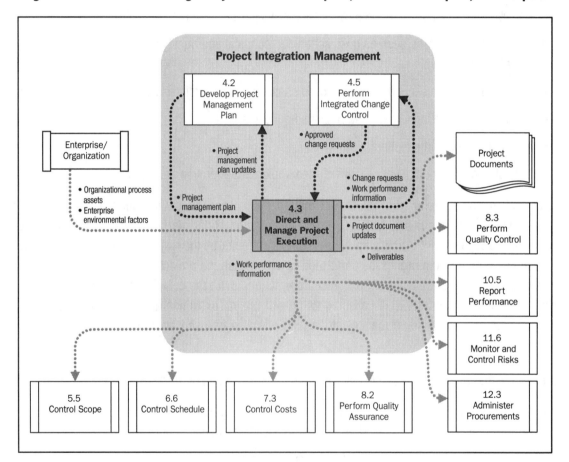

Figure 4-7. Direct and Manage Project Execution Data Flow Diagram

4.3.1 Direct and Manage Project Execution: Inputs

.1 Project Management Plan

Described in Section 4.2.3.1.

.2 Approved Change Requests

As part of the Perform Integrated Change Control process, a change control status update will indicate that some changes are approved and some are not. Approved change requests are scheduled for implementation by the project team. Approved change requests are the documented, authorized changes to expand or reduce project scope. The approved change requests can also modify policies, the project management plan, procedures, costs, or budgets; or revise schedules. Approved change requests may require implementation of preventive or corrective actions.

.3 Enterprise Environmental Factors

The enterprise environmental factors which can influence the Direct and Manage Project Execution process include, but are not limited to:

- Organizational, company or customer culture and structure,

- Infrastructure (e.g., existing facilities and capital equipment),

- Personnel administration (e.g., hiring and firing guidelines, employee performance reviews, and training records),

- Stakeholder risk tolerances, and.

- Project management information systems (e.g., an automated tool suite, such as a scheduling software tool, a configuration management system, an information collection and distribution system or web interfaces to other online automated systems).

.4 Organizational Process Assets

The organizational process assets that can influence the Direct and Manage Project Execution process include, but are not limited to:

- Standardized guidelines and work instructions;

- Communication requirements defining allowed communication media, record retention, and security requirements;

- Issue and defect management procedures defining issue and defect controls, issue and defect identification and resolution, and action item tracking;

- Process measurement database used to collect and make available measurement data on processes and products;

- Project files from prior projects (e.g., scope, cost, schedule, performance measurement baselines, project calendars, project schedule, network diagrams, risk registers, planned response actions, and defined risk impact); and

- Issue and defect management database containing historical issue and defect status, control information, issue and defect resolution, and action item results.

4.3.2 Direct and Manage Project Execution: Tools and Techniques

.1 Expert Judgment

Expert judgment is used to assess the inputs needed to direct and manage execution of the project management plan. Such judgment and expertise is applied to all technical and management details during this process. This expertise is provided by the project manager and the project management team using specialized knowledge or training. Additional expertise is available from many sources, including:

- Other units within the organization,

- Consultants,

- Stakeholders, including customers or sponsors, and

- Professional and technical associations.

.2 Project Management Information System

The project management information system, part of the enterprise environmental factors, provides access to an automated tool, such as a scheduling software tool, a configuration management system, an information collection and distribution system, or web interfaces to other online automated systems used during the Direct and Manage Project Execution effort.

4.3.3 Direct and Manage Project Execution: Outputs

.1 Deliverables

An approved deliverable is any unique and verifiable product, result, or capability to perform a service that must be produced to complete a process, phase, or project.

.2 Work Performance Information

Information from project activities is routinely collected as the project progresses. This information can be related to various performance results including, but not limited to:

- Deliverable status,

- Schedule progress, and

- Costs incurred.

.3 Change Requests

When issues are found while project work is being performed, change requests are issued which may modify project policies or procedures, project scope, project cost or budget, project schedule, or project quality. Other change requests cover needed preventive or corrective actions to forestall negative impact later in the project. Requests for a change can be direct or indirect, externally or internally initiated, and can be optional or legally/contractually mandated and can include:

- **Corrective action.** Documented direction for executing the project work to bring expected future performance of the project work in line with the project management plan.

- **Preventive action.** A documented direction to perform an activity that can reduce the probability of negative consequences associated with project risks.

- **Defect repair.** The formally documented identification of a defect in a project component with a recommendation to either repair the defect or completely replace the component.

- **Updates.** Changes to formally controlled documentation, plans, etc., to reflect modified or additional ideas or content.

.4 Project Management Plan Updates

Elements of the project management plan that may be updated include, but are not limited to:

- Requirements management plan,

- Schedule management plan,

- Cost management plan,

- Quality management plan,

- Human resource plan,

- Communications management plan,

- Risk management plan,

- Procurement management plan, and

- Project baselines.

.5 Project Document Updates

Project documents that may be updated include, but are not limited to:

- Requirements documents,

- Project logs (issue, assumptions, etc.),

- Risk register, and

- Stakeholder register.

4.4 Monitor and Control Project Work

Monitor and Control Project Work is the process of tracking, reviewing, and regulating the progress to meet the performance objectives defined in the project management plan. Monitoring is an aspect of project management performed throughout the project. Monitoring includes collecting, measuring, and distributing performance information, and assessing measurements and trends to effect process improvements. Continuous monitoring gives the project management team insight into the health of the project, and identifies any areas that may require special attention. Control includes determining corrective or preventive actions or replanning and following up on action plans to determine if the actions taken resolved the performance issue. The Monitor and Control Project Work process is concerned with:

- Comparing actual project performance against the project management plan;

- Assessing performance to determine whether any corrective or preventive actions are indicated, and then recommending those actions as necessary;

- Identifying new risks and analyzing, tracking, and monitoring existing project risks to make sure the risks are identified, their status is reported, and that appropriate risk response plans are being executed;

- Maintaining an accurate, timely information base concerning the project's product(s) and their associated documentation through project completion;

- Providing information to support status reporting, progress measurement, and forecasting;

- Providing forecasts to update current cost and current schedule information; and

- Monitoring implementation of approved changes as they occur.

Figure 4-8 shows the inputs, tools and techniques, and outputs for this process and the data flow diagram is displayed in Figure 4-9.

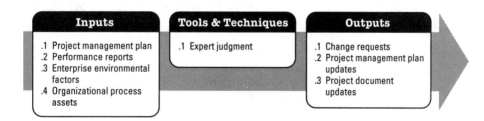

Figure 4-8. Monitor and Control Project Work: Inputs, Tools & Techniques, and Outputs

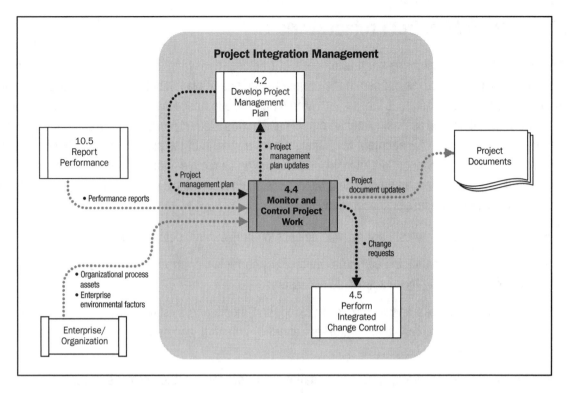

Figure 4-9. Monitor and Control Project Work Data Flow Diagram

4.4.1 Monitor and Control Project Work: Inputs

.1 Project Management Plan

Described in Section 4.2.3.1.

.2 Performance Reports

Reports should be prepared by the project team detailing activities, accomplishments, milestones, identified issues, and problems. Performance reports can be used to report the key information including, but not limited to:

- Current status,
- Significant accomplishments for the period,
- Scheduled activities,
- Forecasts, and
- Issues.

.3 Enterprise Environmental Factors

The enterprise environmental factors that can influence the Monitor and Control Project Work process include, but are not limited to:

- Governmental or industry standards (e.g., regulatory agency regulations, product standards, quality standards, and workmanship standards),

- Company work authorization system,

- Stakeholder risk tolerances, and

- Project management information systems (e.g., an automated tool suite, such as a scheduling software tool, a configuration management system, an information collection and distribution system or web interfaces to other online automated systems).

.4 Organizational Process Assets

The organizational process assets that can influence the Monitor and Control Project Work process include but are not limited to:

- Organization communication requirements,

- Financial controls procedures (e.g., time reporting, accounting codes, expenditure and disbursement reviews, and standard contract provisions),

- Issue and defect management procedures,

- Risk control procedures including risk categories, probability definition and impact, and probability and impact matrix,

- Process measurement database used to make available measurement data on processes and products, and

- Lessons learned database.

4.4.2 Monitor and Control Project Work: Tools and Techniques

.1 Expert Judgment

Expert judgment is used by the project management team to interpret the information provided by the monitor and control processes. The project manager, in collaboration with the team, determines the actions required to ensure project performance matches expectations.

4.4.3 Monitor and Control Project Work: Outputs

.1 Change Requests

As a result of comparing planned results to actual results, change requests may be issued which may expand, adjust, or reduce project or product scope. Changes can impact the project management plan, project documents, or product deliverables. Changes may include, but are not limited to the following:

- **Corrective action.** A documented direction for executing the project work to bring expected future performance of the project work in line with the project management plan.

- **Preventive action.** A documented direction to perform an activity that can reduce the probability of negative consequences associated with project risks.

- **Defect repair.** The formally documented identification of a defect in a project component with a recommendation to either repair the defect or completely replace the component.

.2 Project Management Plan Updates

Project management plan elements that may be updated include, but are not limited to:

- Schedule management plan,

- Cost management plan,

- Quality management plan,

- Scope baseline,

- Schedule baseline, and

- Cost performance baseline.

.3 Project Document Updates

Project documents that may be updated include, but are not limited to:

- Forecasts,

- Performance reports, and

- Issue log.

4.5 Perform Integrated Change Control

Perform Integrated Change Control is the process of reviewing all change requests, approving changes and managing changes to the deliverables, organizational process assets, project documents and the project management plan. The Perform Integrated Change Control process is conducted from project inception through completion. The project management plan, the project scope statement, and other deliverables are maintained by carefully and continuously managing changes, either by rejecting changes or by approving changes thereby assuring that only approved changes are incorporated into a revised baseline.

The Perform Integrated Change Control process includes the following change management activities in differing levels of detail, based upon the progress of project execution:

- Influencing the factors that circumvent integrated change control so that only approved changes are implemented;

- Reviewing, analyzing, and approving change requests promptly, which is essential, as a slow decision may negatively affect time, cost, or the feasibility of a change;

- Managing the approved changes;

- Maintaining the integrity of baselines by releasing only approved changes for incorporation into the project management plan and project documents;

- Reviewing, approving, or denying all recommended corrective and preventive actions;

- Coordinating changes across the entire project (e.g., a proposed schedule change will often affect cost, risk, quality, and staffing); and

- Documenting the complete impact of change requests.

Changes may be requested by any stakeholder involved with the project. Although they may be initiated verbally, they should always be recorded in written form and entered into the change management and/or configuration management system. Change requests are subject to the process specified in the change control and configuration control systems. Those change request processes may require information on estimated time impacts and estimated cost impacts.

Every documented change request must be either approved or rejected by some authority within the project management team or an external organization. On many projects, the project manager is given authority to approve certain types of change requests as defined in the project's roles and responsibilities documentation. Whenever required, the Perform Integrated Change Control process includes a change control board (CCB) responsible for approving or rejecting change requests. The roles and responsibilities of these boards are clearly defined within the configuration control and change control procedures, and are agreed upon by appropriate stakeholders. Many large organizations provide for a multi-tiered board structure, separating responsibilities among the boards. If the project is being provided under a contract, then some proposed changes may need to be approved by the customer as per the contract.

Approved change requests can require new or revised cost estimates, activity sequences, schedule dates, resource requirements, and analysis of risk response alternatives. These changes can require adjustments to the project management plan or other project management plans/documents. The applied level of change control is dependent upon the application area, complexity of the specific project, contract requirements, and the context and environment in which the project is performed.

A configuration management system with integrated change control provides a standardized, effective, and efficient way to centrally manage approved changes and baselines within a project. Configuration control is focused on the specification of both the deliverables and the processes while change control is focused on identifying, documenting and controlling changes to the project and the product baselines. Project-wide application of the configuration management system, including change control processes, accomplishes three main objectives:

- Establishes an evolutionary method to consistently identify and request changes to established baselines, and to assess the value and effectiveness of those changes,

- Provides opportunities to continuously validate and improve the project by considering the impact of each change, and

- Provides the mechanism for the project management team to consistently communicate all approved and rejected changes to the stakeholders.

Some of the configuration management activities included in the integrated change control process are as follows:

- **Configuration identification.** Selection and identification of a configuration item provides the basis for which product configuration is defined and verified, products and documents are labeled, changes are managed, and accountability is maintained.

- **Configuration status accounting.** Information is recorded and reported as to when appropriate data about the configuration item should be provided. This information includes a listing of approved configuration identification, status of proposed changes to the configuration, and the implementation status of approved changes.

- **Configuration verification and audit.** Configuration verification and configuration audits ensure the composition of a project's configuration items is correct and that corresponding changes are registered, assessed, approved, tracked, and correctly implemented. This ensures the functional requirements defined in the configuration documentation have been met.

Figure 4-10 shows the inputs, tools and techniques, and outputs for this process and the data flow diagram is displayed in Figure 4-11.

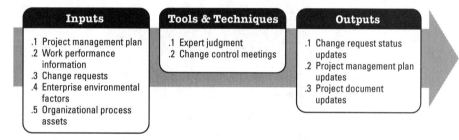

Figure 4-10. Perform Integrated Change Control: Inputs, Tools & Techniques, and Outputs

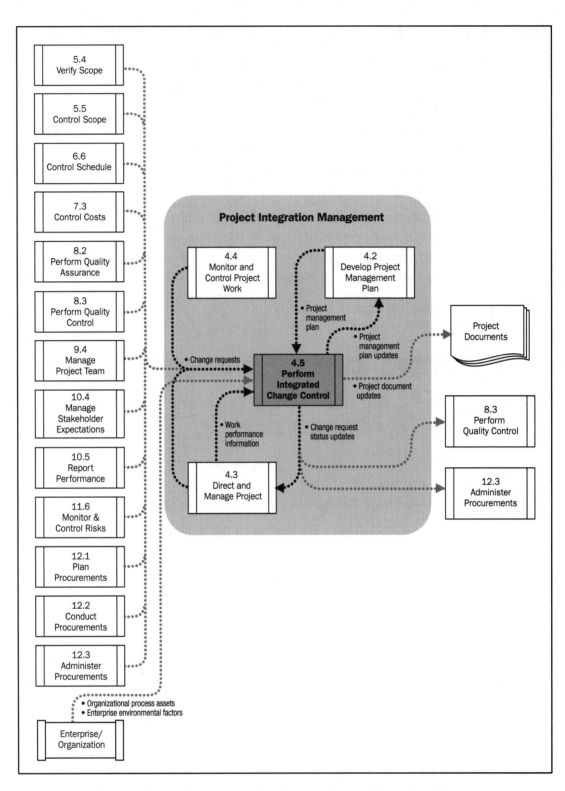

Figure 4-11. Perform Integrated Change Control Data Flow Diagram

4.5.1 Perform Integrated Change Control: Inputs

.1 Project Management Plan

Described in Section 4.2.3.1.

.2 Work Performance Information

Described in Section 4.3.3.2.

.3 Change Requests

All of the monitoring and control processes and many of the executing processes produce change requests as an output. Change requests can include corrective action, preventive action, and defect repairs. However, corrective and preventive actions do not normally affect the project baselines, only the performance against the baselines.

.4 Enterprise Environmental Factors

The following enterprise environmental factor can influence the Integrated Change Control process: project management information system (e.g., an automated tool, such as a scheduling software tool, a configuration management system, an information collection and distribution system or web interfaces to other online automated systems). This is not a complete list, but it should be considered on most projects.

.5 Organizational Process Assets

The organizational process assets that can influence the Perform Integrated Change Control process include, but are not limited to:

- Change control procedures, including the steps by which official company standards, policies, plans, and other project documents will be modified, and how any changes will be approved, validated, and implemented;

- Procedures for approving and issuing change authorizations;

- Process measurement database used to collect and make available measurement data on processes and products;

- Project files (e.g., scope, cost, schedule and, performance measurement baselines, project calendars, project schedule network diagrams, risk registers, planned response actions, and defined risk impact); and

- Configuration management knowledge base containing the versions and baselines of all official company standards, policies, procedures, and any project documents.

4.5.2 Perform Integrated Change Control: Tools and Techniques

.1 Expert Judgment

In addition to the project management team's expert judgment, stakeholders may be asked to provide their expertise and may be asked to sit on the change control board. Such judgment and expertise is applied to any technical and management details during this process and may be provided by various sources, for example:

- Consultants,

- Stakeholders, including customers or sponsors,

- Professional and technical associations,

- Industry groups,

- Subject matter experts, and

- Project management office (PMO).

.2 Change Control Meetings

A change control board is responsible for meeting and reviewing the change requests and approving or rejecting those change requests. The roles and responsibilities of these boards are clearly defined and are agreed upon by appropriate stakeholders. All change control board decisions are documented and communicated to the stakeholders for information and follow-up actions.

4.5.3 Perform Integrated Change Control: Outputs

If a change request is deemed feasible but outside the project scope, its approval requires a baseline change. If the change request is not deemed feasible, the change request will be rejected and possibly sent back to the requester for additional information.

.1 Change Request Status Updates

Change requests are processed according to the change control system by the project manager or by an assigned team member. Approved change requests will be implemented by the Direct and Manage Project Execution process. The status of all changes, approved or not, will be updated in the change request log as part of the project document updates.

.2 Project Management Plan Updates

Elements of the project management plan that may be updated include but are not limited to:

- Any subsidiary management plans, and

- Baselines that are subject to the formal change control process.

Changes to baselines should only show the changes from the current time forward. Past performance may not be changed. This protects the integrity of the baselines and the historical data of past performance.

.3 Project Document Updates

Project documents that may be updated as a result of the Perform Integrated Change Control process include the change request log and any documents that are subject to the formal change control process.

4.6 Close Project or Phase

Close Project or Phase is the process of finalizing all activities across all of the Project Management Process Groups to formally complete the project or phase. When closing the project, the project manager will review all prior information from the previous phase closures to ensure that all project work is complete and that the project has met its objectives. Since project scope is measured against the project management plan, the project manager will review that document to ensure completion before considering the project closed. The Close Project or Phase process also establishes the procedures to investigate and document the reasons for actions taken if a project is terminated before completion.

This includes all of the activities necessary for administrative closure of the project or phase, including step-by-step methodologies that address:

- Actions and activities necessary to satisfy completion or exit criteria for the phase or project;

- Actions and activities necessary to transfer the project's products, services, or results to the next phase or to production and/or operations; and

- Activities needed to collect project or phase records, audit project success or failure, gather lessons learned and archive project information for future use by the organization.

Figure 4-12 shows the inputs, tools and techniques, and outputs for this process and the data flow diagram is displayed in Figure 4-13.

Inputs	Tools & Techniques	Outputs
.1 Project management plan .2 Accepted deliverables .3 Organizational process assets	.1 Expert judgment	.1 Final product, service, or result transition .2 Organizational process assets updates

Figure 4-12. Close Project or Phase: Inputs, Tools & Techniques, and Outputs

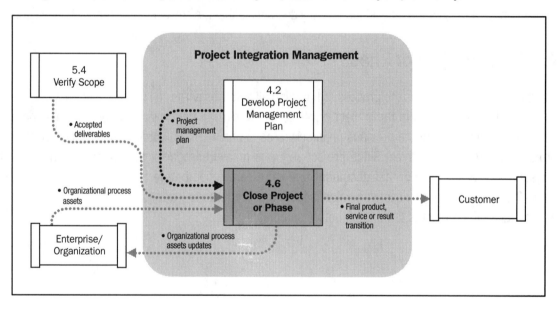

Figure 4-13. Close Project or Phase Data Flow Diagram

4.6.1 Close Project or Phase: Inputs

.1 Project Management Plan

Described in Section 4.2.3.1.

.2 Accepted Deliverables

Those deliverables that have been accepted through the Verify Scope process in Section 5.4.

.3 Organizational Process Assets

The organizational process assets that can influence the Close Project or Phase process include, but are not limited to:

- Project or phase closure guidelines or requirements (e.g., project audits, project evaluations, and transition criteria), and

- Historical information and lessons learned knowledge base (e.g., project records and documents, all project closure information and documentation, information about both the results of previous project selection decisions and previous project performance information, and information from the risk management effort).

4.6.2 Close Project or Phase: Tools and Techniques

.1 Expert Judgment

Expert judgment is applied when performing administrative closure activities. These experts ensure the project or phase closure is performed to the appropriate standards.

4.6.3 Close Project or Phase: Outputs

.1 Final Product, Service, or Result Transition

This output refers to the transition of the final product, service, or result that the project was authorized to produce (or in the case of phase closure, the intermediate product, service, or result of that phase).

.2 Organizational Process Assets Updates

The organizational process assets that are updated as a result of the Close Project or Phase process include, but are not limited to:

- **Project files.** Documentation resulting from the project's activities, for example, project management plan, scope, cost, schedule and project calendars, risk registers, change management documentation, planned risk response actions, and risk impact.

- **Project or phase closure documents.** Project or phase closure documents, consisting of formal documentation that indicates completion of the project or phase and the transfer of the completed project or phase deliverables to others, such as an operations group or to the next phase. During project closure the project manager reviews prior phase documentation, customer acceptance documentation from the Verify Scope process (Section 5.4) and the contract (if applicable), to ensure that all project requirements are complete prior to finalizing the closure of the project. If the project was terminated prior to completion, the formal documentation indicates why the project was terminated and formalizes the procedures for the transfer of the finished and unfinished deliverables of the cancelled project to others.

- **Historical information.** Historical information and lessons learned information are transferred to the lessons learned knowledge base for use by future projects or phases. This can include information on issues and risks as well as techniques that worked well that can be applied to future projects.

CHAPTER 5

PROJECT SCOPE MANAGEMENT

Project Scope Management includes the processes required to ensure that the project includes all the work required, and only the work required, to complete the project successfully. Managing the project scope is primarily concerned with defining and controlling what is and is not included in the project. Figure 5-1 provides an overview of the Project Scope Management processes, which include the following:

5.1 Collect Requirements—The process of defining and documenting stakeholders' needs to meet the project objectives.

5.2 Define Scope—The process of developing a detailed description of the project and product.

5.3 Create WBS—The process of subdividing project deliverables and project work into smaller, more manageable components.

5.4 Verify Scope—The process of formalizing acceptance of the completed project deliverables.

5.5 Control Scope—The process of monitoring the status of the project and product scope and managing changes to the scope baseline.

These processes interact with each other and with the processes in the other Knowledge Areas. Each process can involve effort from one or more persons, based on the needs of the project. Each process occurs at least once in every project and occurs in one or more of the project phases, if the project is divided into phases. Although the processes are presented here as discrete components with well-defined interfaces, in practice they will overlap and interact in ways not detailed here. Process interactions are discussed in detail in Chapter 3, Project Management Processes. In the project context, the term scope can refer to:

- **Product scope.** The features and functions that characterize a product, service, or result; and/or

- **Project scope.** The work that needs to be accomplished to deliver a product, service, or result with the specified features and functions.

The processes used to manage project scope, as well as the supporting tools and techniques, vary by application area and are usually defined as part of the project life cycle. The approved detailed project scope statement and its associated WBS and WBS dictionary are the scope baseline for the project. This baselined scope is then monitored, verified, and controlled throughout the lifecycle of the project.

Although not shown here as a discrete process, the work involved in performing the five processes of Project Scope Management is preceded by a planning effort by the project management team. This planning effort is part of the Develop Project Management Plan process (Section 4.2), which produces a scope management plan that provides guidance on how project scope will be defined, documented, verified, managed, and controlled. The scope management plan may be formal or informal, highly detailed, or broadly framed, based upon the needs of the project.

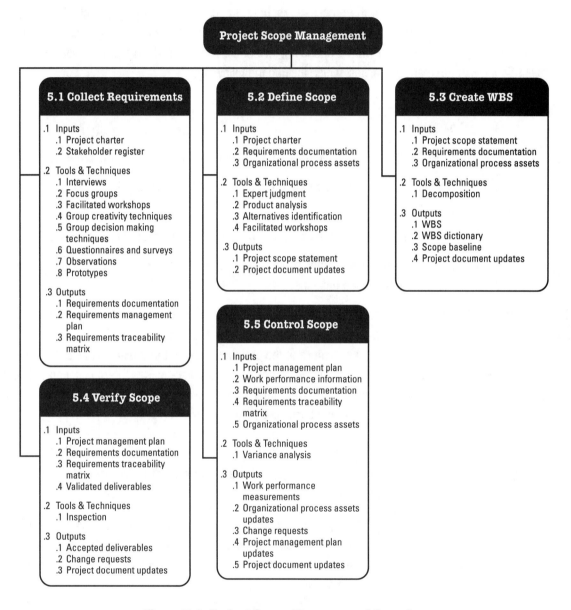

Figure 5-1. Project Scope Management Overview

Completion of the project scope is measured against the project management plan (Section 4.2.3.1). Completion of the product scope is measured against the product requirements (Section 5.1). The Project Scope Management processes need to be well integrated with the other Knowledge Area processes, so that the work of the project will result in delivery of the specified product scope.

5.1 Collect Requirements

Collect Requirements is the process of defining and documenting stakeholders' needs to meet the project objectives. The project's success is directly influenced by the care taken in capturing and managing project and product requirements. Requirements include the quantified and documented needs and expectations of the sponsor, customer, and other stakeholders. These requirements need to be elicited, analyzed, and recorded in enough detail to be measured once project execution begins. Collecting requirements is defining and managing customer expectations. Requirements become the foundation of the WBS. Cost, schedule, and quality planning are all built upon these requirements. The development of requirements begins with an analysis of the information contained in the project charter (Section 4.1.3.1) and the stakeholder register (Section 10.1.3.1).

Many organizations categorize requirements into project requirements and product requirements. Project requirements can include business requirements, project management requirements, delivery requirements, etc. Product requirements can include information on technical requirements, security requirements, performance requirements etc.

Figure 5-2 shows the inputs, tools and techniques, and outputs for the Collect Requirements process, and Figure 5-3 provides a summary of the basic flow and interactions within this process.

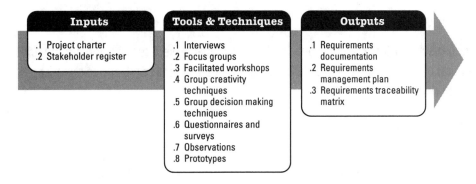

Figure 5-2. Collect Requirements: Inputs, Tools & Techniques, and Outputs

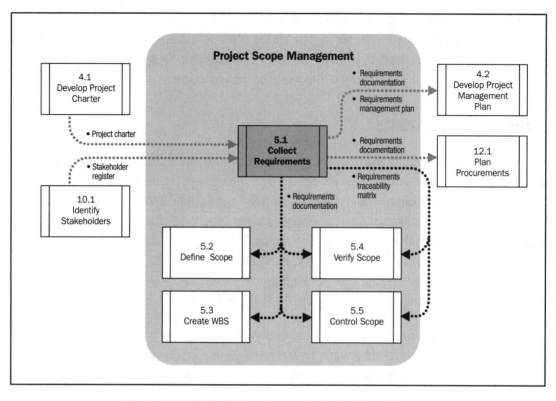

Figure 5-3. Collect Requirements Data Flow Diagram

5.1.1   Collect Requirements: Inputs

.1 Project Charter

The project charter is used to provide the high-level project requirements and high-level product description of the project so that detailed product requirements can be developed. The project charter is described in Section 4.1.

.2 Stakeholder Register

The stakeholder register is used to identify stakeholders that can provide information on detailed project and product requirements. The stakeholder register is described in Section 10.1.

5.1.2 Collect Requirements: Tools and Techniques

.1 Interviews

An interview is a formal or informal approach to discover information from stakeholders by talking to them directly. It is typically performed by asking prepared and spontaneous questions and recording the responses. Interviews are often conducted "one-on-one," but may involve multiple interviewers and/or multiple interviewees. Interviewing experienced project participants, stakeholders, and subject matter experts can aid in identifying and defining the features and functions of the desired project deliverables.

.2 Focus groups

Focus groups bring together prequalified stakeholders and subject matter experts to learn about their expectations and attitudes about a proposed product, service, or result. A trained moderator guides the group through an interactive discussion, designed to be more conversational than a one-on-one interview.

.3 Facilitated Workshops

Requirements workshops are focused sessions that bring key cross-functional stakeholders together to define product requirements. Workshops are considered a primary technique for quickly defining cross-functional requirements and reconciling stakeholder differences. Because of their interactive group nature, well-facilitated sessions can build trust, foster relationships, and improve communication among the participants which can lead to increased stakeholder consensus. Another benefit of this technique is that issues can be discovered and resolved more quickly than in individual sessions.

For example, facilitated workshops called Joint Application Development (or Design) (JAD) sessions are used in the software development industry. These facilitated sessions focus on bringing users and the development team together to improve the software development process. In the manufacturing industry, Quality Function Deployment (QFD) is an example of another facilitated workshop technique that helps determine critical characteristics for new product development. QFD starts by collecting customer needs, also known as Voice of the Customer (VOC). These needs are then objectively sorted and prioritized, and goals are set for achieving them.

.4 Group Creativity Techniques

Several group activities can be organized to identify project and product requirements. Some of the group creativity techniques that can be used are:

- **Brainstorming.** A technique used to generate and collect multiple ideas related to project and product requirements.

- **Nominal group technique.** This technique enhances brainstorming with a voting process used to rank the most useful ideas for further brainstorming or for prioritization.

- **The Delphi Technique.** A selected group of experts answers questionnaires and provides feedback regarding the responses from each round of requirements gathering. The responses are only available to the facilitator to maintain anonymity.

- **Idea/mind mapping.** Ideas created through individual brainstorming are consolidated into a single map to reflect commonality and differences in understanding, and generate new ideas.

- **Affinity diagram.** This technique allows large numbers of ideas to be sorted into groups for review and analysis.

.5 Group Decision Making Techniques

Group decision making is an assessment process of multiple alternatives with an expected outcome in the form of future actions resolution. These techniques can be used to generate, classify, and prioritize product requirements.

There are multiple methods of reaching a group decision, for example:

- **Unanimity.** Everyone agrees on a single course of action.

- **Majority.** Support from more than 50% of the members of the group.

- **Plurality.** The largest block in a group decides even if a majority is not achieved.

- **Dictatorship.** One individual makes the decision for the group.

Almost any of the decision methods described previously can be applied to the group techniques used in the requirements gathering process.

.6 Questionnaires and Surveys

Questionnaires and surveys are written sets of questions designed to quickly accumulate information from a wide number of respondents. Questionnaires and/or surveys are most appropriate with broad audiences, when quick turnaround is needed, and where statistical analysis is appropriate.

.7 Observations

Observations provide a direct way of viewing individuals in their environment and how they perform their jobs or tasks and carry out processes. It is particularly helpful for detailed processes when the people that use the product have difficulty or are reluctant to articulate their requirements. Observation, also called "job shadowing," is usually done externally by the observer viewing the user performing his or her job. It can also be done by a "participant observer" who actually performs a process or procedure to experience how it is done to uncover hidden requirements.

.8 Prototypes

Prototyping is a method of obtaining early feedback on requirements by providing a working model of the expected product before actually building it. Since prototypes are tangible, it allows stakeholders to experiment with a model of their final product rather than only discussing abstract representations of their requirements. Prototypes support the concept of progressive elaboration because they are used in iterative cycles of mock-up creation, user experimentation, feedback generation, and prototype revision. When enough feedback cycles have been performed, the requirements obtained from the prototype are sufficiently complete to move to a design or build phase.

5.1.3 Collect Requirements: Outputs

.1 Requirements Documentation

Requirements documentation describes how individual requirements meet the business need for the project. Requirements may start out at a high level and become progressively more detailed as more is known. Before being baselined, requirements must be unambiguous (measurable and testable), traceable, complete, consistent, and acceptable to key stakeholders. The format of a requirements document may range from a simple document listing all the requirements categorized by stakeholder and priority, to more elaborate forms containing executive summary, detailed descriptions, and attachments.

Components of requirements documentation can include, but, are not limited to:

- Business need or opportunity to be seized, describing the limitations of the current situation and why the project has been undertaken;

- Business and project objectives for traceability;

- Functional requirements, describing business processes, information, and interaction with the product, as appropriate which can be documented textually in a requirements list, in models, or both;

- Non-functional requirements, such as level of service, performance, safety, security, compliance, supportability, retention/purge, etc.;

- Quality requirements;

- Acceptance criteria;

- Business rules stating the guiding principles of the organization;

- Impacts to other organizational areas, such as the call center, sales force, technology groups;

- Impacts to other entities inside or outside the performing organization;

- Support and training requirements; and

- Requirements assumptions and constraints.

.2 Requirements Management Plan

The requirements management plan documents how requirements will be analyzed, documented, and managed throughout the project. The phase-to-phase relationship, described in Section 2.1.3.2, strongly influences how requirements are managed. The project manager must choose the most effective relationship for the project and document this approach in the requirements management plan. Many of the requirements management plan components are based on that relationship.

Components of the requirements management plan can include, but are not limited to:

- How requirements activities will be planned, tracked, and reported;

- Configuration management activities such as how changes to the product, service, or result requirements will be initiated, how impacts will be analyzed, how they will be traced, tracked, and reported, as well as the authorization levels required to approve these changes;

- Requirements prioritization process;

- Product metrics that will be used and the rationale for using them; and

- Traceability structure, that is, which requirements attributes will be captured on the traceability matrix and to which other project documents requirements will be traced.

.3 Requirements Traceability Matrix

The requirements traceability matrix is a table that links requirements to their origin and traces them throughout the project life cycle. The implementation of a requirements traceability matrix helps ensure that each requirement adds business value by linking it to the business and project objectives. It provides a means to track requirements throughout the project life cycle, helping to ensure that requirements approved in the requirements documentation are delivered at the end of the project. Finally, it provides a structure for managing changes to the product scope.

This process includes, but is not limited to tracing:

- Requirements to business needs, opportunities, goals, and objectives;

- Requirements to project objectives;

- Requirements to project scope/WBS deliverables;

- Requirements to product design;

- Requirements to product development;

- Requirements to test strategy and test scenarios; and

- High-level requirements to more detailed requirements.

Attributes associated with each requirement can be recorded in the requirements traceability matrix. These attributes help to define key information about the requirement. Typical attributes used in the requirements traceability matrix may include: a unique identifier, a textual description of the requirement, the rationale for inclusion, owner, source, priority, version, current status (such as active, cancelled, deferred, added, approved) and date completed. Additional attributes to ensure that the requirement has met stakeholders' satisfaction may include stability, complexity, and acceptance criteria.

5.2 Define Scope

Define Scope is the process of developing a detailed description of the project and product. The preparation of a detailed project scope statement is critical to project success and builds upon the major deliverables, assumptions, and constraints that are documented during project initiation. During planning, the project scope is defined and described with greater specificity as more information about the project is known. Existing risks, assumptions, and constraints are analyzed for completeness; additional risks, assumptions, and constraints are added as necessary. Figure 5-4 shows the inputs, tools and techniques, and outputs for the Define Scope process, and Figure 5-5 provides a summary of the basic flow and interactions within this process.

Inputs	Tools & Techniques	Outputs
.1 Project charter	.1 Expert judgment	.1 Project scope statement
.2 Requirements documentation	.2 Product analysis	.2 Project document updates
.3 Organizational process assets	.3 Alternatives identification	
	.4 Facilitated workshops	

Figure 5-4. Define Scope: Inputs, Tools & Techniques, and Outputs

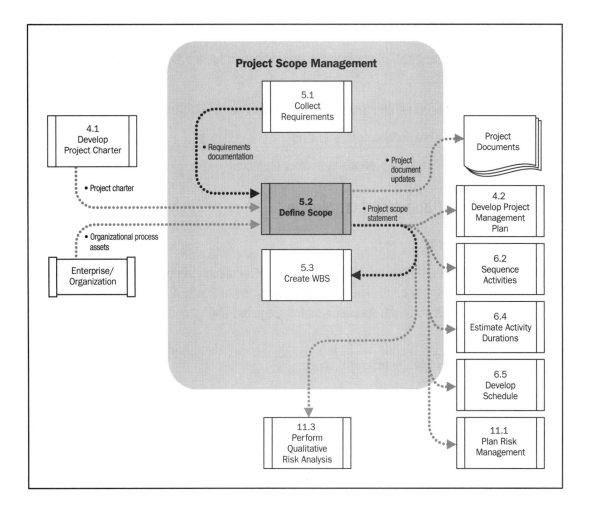

Figure 5-5. Define Scope Data Flow Diagram

5.2.1 Define Scope: Inputs

.1 Project Charter

The project charter provides the high-level project description and product characteristics. It also contains project approval requirements. The project charter is described in Section 4.1.3.1. If a project charter is not used in the performing organization, then comparable information needs to be acquired or developed, and used as a basis for the detailed project scope statement.

.2 Requirements Documentation

Described in Section 5.1.3.1.

.3 Organizational Process Assets

Examples of organizational process assets that can influence the Define Scope process include, but are not limited to:

- Policies, procedures, and templates for a project scope statement,

- Project files from previous projects, and

- Lessons learned from previous phases or projects.

5.2.2 Define Scope: Tools and Techniques

.1 Expert Judgment

Expert judgment is often used to analyze the information needed to develop the project scope statement. Such judgment and expertise is applied to any technical details. Such expertise is provided by any group or individual with specialized knowledge or training, and is available from many sources, including:

- Other units within the organization,

- Consultants,

- Stakeholders, including customers or sponsors,

- Professional and technical associations,

- Industry groups, and

- Subject matter experts.

.2 Product Analysis

For projects that have a product as a deliverable, as opposed to a service or result, product analysis can be an effective tool. Each application area has one or more generally accepted methods for translating high-level product descriptions into tangible deliverables. Product analysis includes techniques such as product breakdown, systems analysis, requirements analysis, systems engineering, value engineering, and value analysis.

.3 Alternatives Identification

Identifying alternatives is a technique used to generate different approaches to execute and perform the work of the project. A variety of general management techniques can be used such as brainstorming, lateral thinking, pair wise comparisons, etc.

.4 Facilitated Workshops

Described in Section 5.1.2.3.

5.2.3 Define Scope: Outputs

.1 Project Scope Statement

The project scope statement describes, in detail, the project's deliverables and the work required to create those deliverables. The project scope statement also provides a common understanding of the project scope among project stakeholders. It may contain explicit scope exclusions that can assist in managing stakeholder expectations. It enables the project team to perform more detailed planning, guides the project team's work during execution, and provides the baseline for evaluating whether requests for changes or additional work are contained within or outside the project's boundaries.

The degree and level of detail to which the project scope statement defines the work that will be performed and the work that is excluded can determine how well the project management team can control the overall project scope. The detailed project scope statement includes, either directly, or by reference to other documents, the following:

- **Product scope description.** Progressively elaborates the characteristics of the product, service, or result described in the project charter and requirements documentation.

- **Product acceptance criteria.** Defines the process and criteria for accepting completed products, services, or results.

- **Project deliverables.** Deliverables include both the outputs that comprise the product or service of the project, as well as ancillary results, such as project management reports and documentation. The deliverables may be described at a summary level or in great detail.

- **Project exclusions.** Generally identifies what is excluded as from the project. Explicitly stating what is out of scope for the project helps to manage stakeholders' expectations.

- **Project constraints.** Lists and describes the specific project constraints associated with the project scope that limits the team's options, for example, a predefined budget or any imposed dates or schedule milestones that are issued by the customer or performing organization. When a project is performed under contract, contractual provisions will generally be constraints. Information on constraints may be listed in the project scope statement or in a separate log.

- **Project assumptions.** Lists and describes the specific project assumptions associated with the project scope and the potential impact of those assumptions if they prove to be false. Project teams frequently identify, document, and validate assumptions as part of their planning process. Information on assumptions may be listed in the project scope statement or in a separate log.

.2 Project Document Updates

Project documents that may be updated include, but are not limited to:

- Stakeholder register,
- Requirements documentation, and
- Requirements traceability matrix.

5.3 Create WBS

Create WBS is the process of subdividing project deliverables and project work into smaller, more manageable components. The work breakdown structure (WBS) is a deliverable-oriented hierarchical decomposition of the work to be executed by the project team to accomplish the project objectives and create the required deliverables, with each descending level of the WBS representing an increasingly detailed definition of the project work. The WBS organizes and defines the total scope of the project, and represents the work specified in the current approved project scope statement. See Figures 5-6 and 5-7.

The planned work is contained within the lowest level WBS components, which are called work packages. A work package can be scheduled, cost estimated, monitored, and controlled. In the context of the WBS, work refers to work products or deliverables that are the result of effort and not to the effort itself. Figure 5-6 shows the inputs, tools and techniques, and outputs for the Create WBS process, and Figure 5-7 provides a summary of the basic flow and interactions within this process.

For specific information regarding work breakdown structures, refer to the *Practice Standard for Work Breakdown Structures* – Second Edition [1][1].

Inputs	Tools & Techniques	Outputs
.1 Project scope statement .2 Requirements documentation .3 Organizational process assets	.1 Decomposition	.1 WBS .2 WBS dictionary .3 Scope baseline .4 Project document updates

Figure 5-6. Create WBS: Inputs, Tools & Techniques, and Outputs

[1] The boldface numbers in brackets refer to the list of references at the end of this standard.

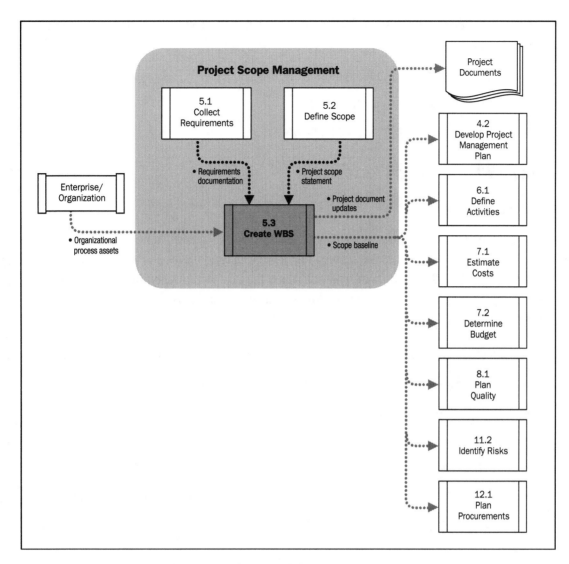

Figure 5-7. Create WBS Data Flow Diagram

5.3.1 Create WBS: Inputs

.1 Project Scope Statement

Described in Section 5.2.3.1.

.2 Requirements Documentation

Described in Section 5.1.3.1.

.3 Organizational Process Assets

The organizational process assets that can influence the Create WBS process include, but are not limited to:

- Policies, procedures, and templates for the WBS,

- Project files from previous projects, and

- Lessons learned from previous projects.

5.3.2 Create WBS: Tools and Techniques

.1 Decomposition

Decomposition is the subdivision of project deliverables into smaller, more manageable components until the work and deliverables are defined to the work package level. The work package level is the lowest level in the WBS, and is the point at which the cost and activity durations for the work can be reliably estimated and managed. The level of detail for work packages will vary with the size and complexity of the project.

Decomposition of the total project work into work packages generally involves the following activities:

- Identifying and analyzing the deliverables and related work,

- Structuring and organizing the WBS,

- Decomposing the upper WBS levels into lower level detailed components,

- Developing and assigning identification codes to the WBS components, and

- Verifying that the degree of decomposition of the work is necessary and sufficient.

A portion of a WBS with some branches of the WBS decomposed down through the work package level is shown in Figure 5-8.

The WBS structure can be created in a number of forms, such as:

- Using phases of the project life cycle as the first level of decomposition, with the product and project deliverables inserted at the second level, as shown in Figure 5-9;

- Using major deliverables as the first level of decomposition, as shown in Figure 5-10; and

- Using subprojects which may be developed by organizations outside the project team, such as contracted work. The seller then develops the supporting contract work breakdown structure as part of the contracted work.

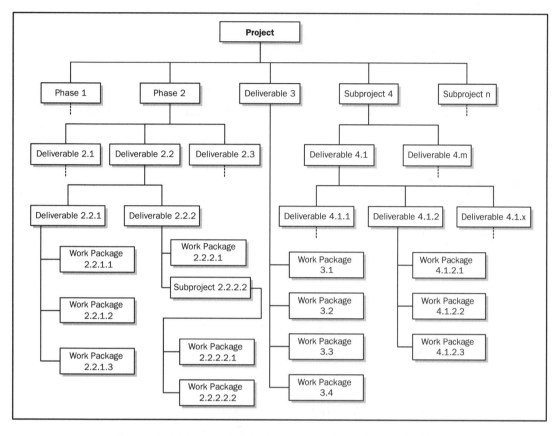

Figure 5-8. Sample Work Breakdown Structure with Some Branches Decomposed Down Through Work Packages

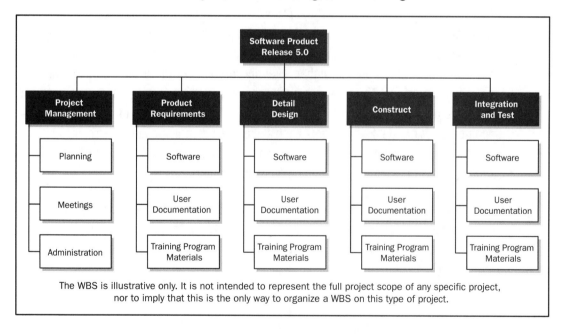

The WBS is illustrative only. It is not intended to represent the full project scope of any specific project, nor to imply that this is the only way to organize a WBS on this type of project.

Figure 5-9. Sample Work Breakdown Structure Organized by Phase

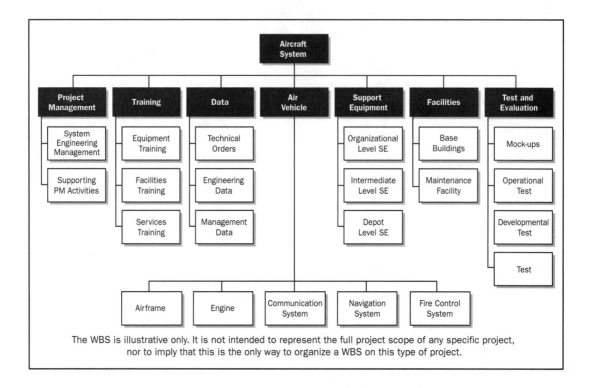

Figure 5-10. Sample Work Breakdown with Major Deliverables

Decomposition of the upper level WBS components requires subdividing the work for each of the deliverables or subprojects into its fundamental components, where the WBS components represent verifiable products, services, or results. The WBS can be structured as an outline, an organizational chart, a fishbone diagram, or other method. Verifying the correctness of the decomposition requires determining that the lower-level WBS components are those that are necessary and sufficient for completion of the corresponding higher level deliverables. Different deliverables can have different levels of decomposition. To arrive at a work package, the work for some deliverables needs to be decomposed only to the next level, while others need additional levels of decomposition. As the work is decomposed to greater levels of detail, the ability to plan, manage, and control the work is enhanced. However, excessive decomposition can lead to non-productive management effort, inefficient use of resources, and decreased efficiency in performing the work.

Decomposition may not be possible for a deliverable or subproject that will be accomplished far into the future. The project management team usually waits until the deliverable or subproject is clarified so the details of the WBS can be developed. This technique is sometimes referred to as rolling wave planning.

The WBS represents all product and project work, including the project management work. The total of the work at the lowest levels must roll up to the higher levels so that nothing is left out and no extra work is completed. This is sometimes called the 100% rule.

The PMI *Practice Standard for Work Breakdown Structures* - Second Edition provides guidance for the generation, development, and application of work breakdown structures. This standard contains industry-specific examples of WBS templates that can be tailored to specific projects in a particular application area.

5.3.3 Create WBS: Outputs

.1 WBS

The WBS is a deliverable-oriented hierarchical decomposition of the work to be executed by the project team, to accomplish the project objectives and create the required deliverables, with each descending level of the WBS representing an increasingly detailed definition of the project work. The WBS is finalized by establishing control accounts for the work packages and a unique identifier from a code of accounts. These identifiers provide a structure for hierarchical summation of costs, schedule, and resource information. A control account is a management control point where scope, cost, and schedule are integrated and compared to the earned value for performance measurement. Control accounts are placed at selected management points in the WBS. Each control account may include one or more work packages, but each of the work packages must be associated with only one control account.

.2 WBS Dictionary

The WBS dictionary is a document generated by the Create WBS process that supports the WBS. The WBS dictionary provides more detailed descriptions of the components in the WBS, including work packages and control accounts. Information in the WBS dictionary includes, but is not limited to:

- Code of account identifier,
- Description of work,
- Responsible organization,

- List of schedule milestones,

- Associated schedule activities,

- Resources required,

- Cost estimates,

- Quality requirements,

- Acceptance criteria,

- Technical references, and

- Contract information.

.3 Scope Baseline

The scope baseline is a component of the project management plan. Components of the scope baseline include:

- **Project scope statement.** The project scope statement includes the product scope description, and the project deliverables, and defines the product user acceptance criteria.

- **WBS.** The WBS defines each deliverable and the decomposition of the deliverables into work packages.

- **WBS dictionary.** The WBS dictionary has a detailed description of work and technical documentation for each WBS element.

.4 Project Document Updates

Project documents that may be updated include, but are not limited to requirements documentation. If approved change requests result from the Create WBS process, then the requirements documentation may need to be updated to include approved changes.

5.4 Verify Scope

Verify Scope is the process of formalizing acceptance of the completed project deliverables. Verifying scope includes reviewing deliverables with the customer or sponsor to ensure that they are completed satisfactorily and obtaining formal acceptance of deliverables by the customer or sponsor. Scope verification differs from quality control in that scope verification is primarily concerned with acceptance of the deliverables, while quality control is primarily concerned with correctness of the deliverables and meeting the quality requirements specified for the deliverables. Control Quality is generally performed before Verify Scope, but these two processes can be performed in parallel. Figure 5-11 provides the associated inputs, tools and techniques, and outputs. The process flow diagram, Figure 5-12, provides an overall summary of the basic flow and interactions within this process.

Inputs	Tools & Techniques	Outputs
.1 Project management plan .2 Requirements documentation .3 Requirements traceability matrix .4 Validated deliverables	.1 Inspection	.1 Accepted deliverables .2 Change requests .3 Project document updates

Figure 5-11. Verify Scope: Inputs, Tools & Techniques, and Outputs

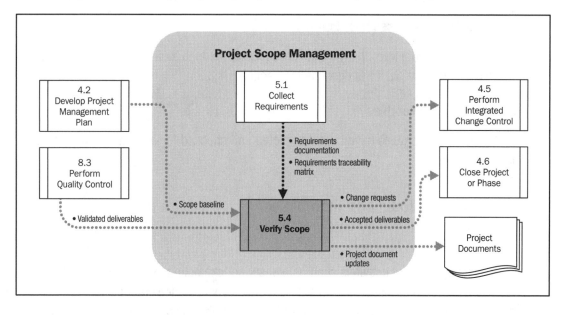

Figure 5-12. Verify Scope Data Flow Diagram

5.4.1 Verify Scope: Inputs

.1 Project Management Plan

The project management plan described in Section 4.2.3.1 contains the scope baseline. Components of the scope baseline include:

- **Project scope statement.** The project scope statement includes the product scope description, includes the project deliverables, and defines the product user acceptance criteria.

- **WBS.** The WBS defines each deliverable and the decomposition of the deliverables into work packages.

- **WBS dictionary.** The WBS dictionary has a detailed description of work and technical documentation for each WBS element.

.2 Requirements Documentation

The requirements documentation lists all the project, product, technical, and other types of requirements that must be present for the project and product, along with their acceptance criteria. Requirements documentation is described in Section 5.1.3.1.

.3 Requirements Traceability Matrix

The requirements traceability matrix links requirements to their origin and tracks them throughout the project life cycle, which is described in Section 5.1.3.3.

.4 Validated Deliverables

Validated deliverables have been completed and checked for correctness by the Perform Quality Control process.

5.4.2 Verify Scope: Tools and Techniques

.1 Inspection

Inspection includes activities such as measuring, examining, and verifying to determine whether work and deliverables meet requirements and product acceptance criteria. Inspections are sometimes called reviews, product reviews, audits, and walkthroughs. In some application areas, these different terms have narrow and specific meanings.

5.4.3　Verify Scope: Outputs

.1 Accepted Deliverables

Deliverables that meet the acceptance criteria are formally signed off and approved by the customer or sponsor. Formal documentation received from the customer or sponsor acknowledging formal stakeholder acceptance of the project's deliverables is forwarded to the Close Project or Phase process (4.6).

.2　Change Requests

Those completed deliverables that have not been formally accepted are documented, along with the reasons for non-acceptance. Those deliverables may require a change request for defect repair. The change requests are processed for review and disposition through the Perform Integrated Change Control process (see Section 4.5).

.3　Project Document Updates

Project documents that may be updated as a result of the Verify Scope process include any documents that define the product or report status on product completion.

5.5 Control Scope

Control Scope is the process of monitoring the status of the project and product scope and managing changes to the scope baseline. Controlling the project scope ensures all requested changes and recommended corrective or preventive actions are processed through the Perform Integrated Change Control process (see Section 4.5). Project scope control is also used to manage the actual changes when they occur and is integrated with the other control processes. Uncontrolled changes are often referred to as project scope creep. Change is inevitable, thereby mandating some type of change control process. Figure 5-13 provides the associated inputs, tools and techniques, and outputs; and the process flow diagram, Figure 5-14, provides an overall summary of the basic flow and interactions within this process.

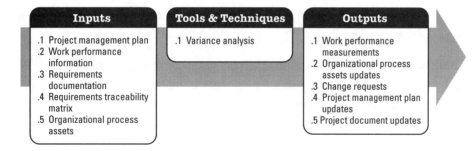

Inputs	Tools & Techniques	Outputs
.1 Project management plan .2 Work performance information .3 Requirements documentation .4 Requirements traceability matrix .5 Organizational process assets	.1 Variance analysis	.1 Work performance measurements .2 Organizational process assets updates .3 Change requests .4 Project management plan updates .5 Project document updates

Figure 5-13. Control Scope: Inputs, Tools & Techniques, and Outputs

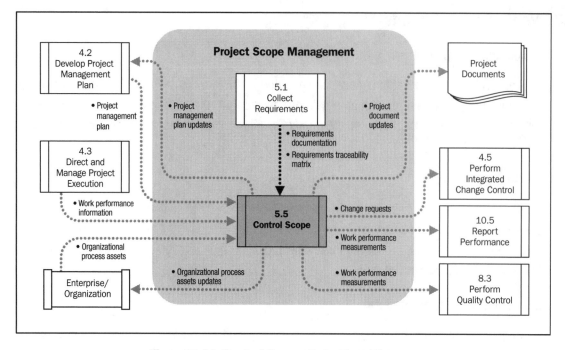

Figure 5-14. Control Scope Data Flow Diagram

5.5.1 Control Scope: Inputs

.1 Project Management Plan

The project management plan described in Section 4.2.3.1 contains the following information that is used to control scope:

- **Scope baseline.** The scope baseline is compared to actual results to determine if a change, corrective action, or preventive action is necessary.

- **Scope management plan.** The scope management plan describes how the project scope will be managed and controlled.

- **Change management plan.** The change management plan defines the process for managing change on the project.

- **Configuration management plan.** The configuration management plan defines those items that are configurable, those items that require formal change control, and the process for controlling changes to such items.

- **Requirements management plan.** The requirements management plan can include how requirements activities will be planned, tracked, and reported and how changes to the product, service, or result requirements will be initiated. It also describes how impacts will be analyzed and the authorization levels required to approve these changes;

.2 Work Performance Information

Information about project progress, such as which deliverables have started, their progress and which deliverables have finished.

.3 Requirements Documentation

Described in Section 5.1.3.1.

.4 Requirements Traceability Matrix

Described in Section 5.1.3.3.

.5 Organizational Process Assets

The organizational process assets that can influence the Control Scope process include but are not limited to:

- Existing formal and informal scope control-related policies, procedures, and guidelines,

- Monitoring and reporting methods to be used.

5.5.2　Control Scope: Tools and Techniques

.1 Variance Analysis

Project performance measurements are used to assess the magnitude of variation from the original scope baseline. Important aspects of project scope control include determining the cause and degree of variance relative to the scope baseline (Section 5.3.3.3) and deciding whether corrective or preventive action is required.

5.5.3 Control Scope: Outputs

.1 Work Performance Measurements

Measurements can include planned vs. actual technical performance or other scope performance measurements. This information is documented and communicated to stakeholders.

.2 Organizational Process Assets Updates

Organizational process assets that may be updated include, but are not limited to:

- Causes of variances,
- Corrective action chosen and the reasons, and
- Other types of lessons learned from project scope control.

.3 Change Requests

Analysis of scope performance can result in a change request to the scope baseline or other components of the project management plan. Change requests can include preventive or corrective actions or defect repairs. Change requests are processed for review and disposition according to the Perform Integrated Change Control process (Section 4.5).

.4 Project Management Plan Updates

- **Scope Baseline Updates.** If the approved change requests have an effect upon the project scope, then the scope statement, the WBS, and the WBS dictionary are revised and reissued to reflect the approved changes.

- **Other Baseline Updates.** If the approved change requests have an effect on the project scope, then the corresponding cost baseline and schedule baselines are revised and reissued to reflect the approved changes.

.5 Project Document Updates

Project documents that may be updated include, but are not limited to:

- Requirements documentation, and
- Requirements traceability matrix.

CHAPTER 6

PROJECT TIME MANAGEMENT

Project Time Management includes the processes required to manage timely completion of the project. Figure 6-1 provides an overview of the Project Time Management processes, which are as follows:

6.1 Define Activities—The process of identifying the specific actions to be performed to produce the project deliverables.

6.2 Sequence Activities—The process of identifying and documenting relationships among the project activities.

6.3 Estimate Activity Resources—The process of estimating the type and quantities of material, people, equipment, or supplies required to perform each activity.

6.4 Estimate Activity Durations—The process of approximating the number of work periods needed to complete individual activities with estimated resources.

6.5 Develop Schedule—The process of analyzing activity sequences, durations, resource requirements, and schedule constraints to create the project schedule.

6.6 Control Schedule—The process of monitoring the status of the project to update project progress and managing changes to the schedule baseline.

These processes interact with each other and with processes in the other Knowledge Areas. Each process can involve effort from one group or person, based on the needs of the project. Each process occurs at least once in every project and occurs in one or more of the project phases, if the project is divided into phases. Although the processes are presented here as discrete components with well-defined interfaces, in practice they can overlap and interact in ways not detailed here. Process interactions are discussed in detail in Chapter 3.

Some advanced practitioners distinguish the printed project schedule information (schedule) from the schedule data and calculations that produce the schedule, by referring to the scheduling engine populated with project data as the *schedule model*. However, in general practice the schedule and the schedule model are referred to as the schedule. Therefore, the *PMBOK® Guide* uses the term *schedule*. On some projects, especially those of smaller scope, defining activities, sequencing activities, estimating activity resources, estimating activity durations, and developing the schedule are so tightly linked that they are viewed as a single process that can be performed by a person over a relatively short period of time. These processes are presented here as distinct processes because the tools and techniques for each are different.

Although not shown here as a discrete process, the work involved in performing the six processes of Project Time Management is preceded by a planning effort by the project management team. This planning effort is part of the Develop Project Management Plan process (Section 4.2), which produces a schedule management plan that selects a scheduling methodology, a scheduling tool, and sets the format and establishes criteria for developing and controlling the project schedule. A scheduling methodology defines the rules and approaches for the scheduling process. Some of the better known methodologies include critical path method (CPM) and critical chain.

The project time management processes and their associated tools and techniques are documented in the schedule management plan. The schedule management plan is contained in, or is a subsidiary plan of, the project management plan, and may be formal or informal, highly detailed or broadly framed, based upon the needs of the project, and includes appropriate control thresholds.

Developing the project schedule uses the outputs from the processes to define activities, sequence activities, estimate activity resources, and estimate activity durations in combination with the scheduling tool to produce the schedule. The finalized and approved schedule is the baseline that will be used in the Control Schedule process (6.6). As the project activities are being performed, the majority of effort in the Project Time Management Knowledge Area will occur in the Control Schedule process (Section 6.6) to ensure completion of project work in a timely manner. Figure 6-2 provides a scheduling overview that shows how the scheduling methodology, scheduling tool, and outputs from the Project Time Management processes interact to create a project schedule.

Figure 6-1. Project Time Management Overview

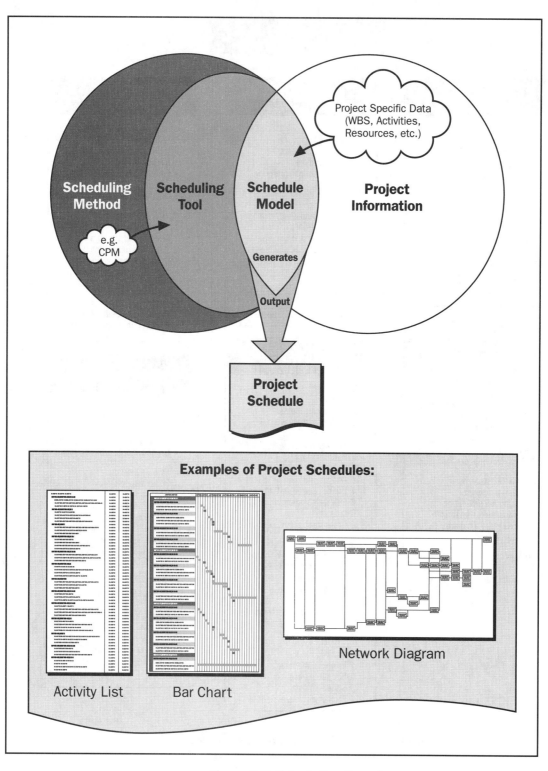

Figure 6-2. Scheduling Overview

6.1 Define Activities

Define Activities is the process of identifying the specific actions to be performed to produce the project deliverables. The Create WBS process identifies the deliverables at the lowest level in the Work Breakdown Structure (WBS), the work package. Project work packages are typically decomposed into smaller components called activities that represent the work necessary to complete the work package. Activities provide a basis for estimating, scheduling, executing, and monitoring and controlling the project work. Implicit in this process is defining and planning the schedule activities such that the project objectives will be met. See Figures 6-3 and 6-4.

Inputs	Tools & Techniques	Outputs
.1 Scope baseline .2 Enterprise environmental factors .3 Organizational process assets	.1 Decomposition .2 Rolling wave planning .3 Templates .4 Expert judgment	.1 Activity list .2 Activity attributes .3 Milestone list

Figure 6-3. Define Activities: Inputs, Tools & Techniques, and Outputs

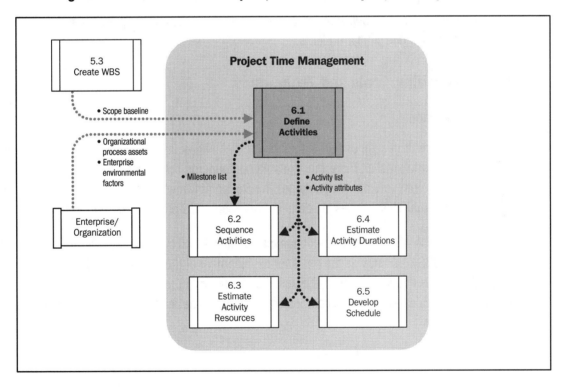

Figure 6-4. Define Activities Data Flow Diagram

6.1.1　Define Activities: Inputs

.1　Scope Baseline

The project deliverables, constraints, and assumptions documented in the project scope baseline (Section 5.3.3.3) are considered explicitly while defining activities.

.2　Enterprise Environmental Factors

The enterprise environmental factors that can influence the Define Activities process include, but are not limited to, the project management information system (PMIS).

.3　Organizational Process Assets

The organizational process assets that can influence the Define Activities process include, but are not limited to:

- Existing formal and informal activity planning-related policies, procedures, and guidelines, such as the scheduling methodology, that are considered in developing the activity definitions, and

- Lessons-learned knowledge base containing historical information regarding activities lists used by previous similar projects.

6.1.2　Define Activities: Tools and Techniques

.1　Decomposition

The technique of decomposition, as applied to defining activities, involves subdividing the project work packages into smaller, more manageable components called activities. Activities represent the effort needed to complete a work package. The Define Activities process defines the final outputs as activities rather than deliverables, as done in the Create WBS process (Section 5.3).

The activity list, WBS, and WBS dictionary can be developed either sequentially or concurrently, with the WBS and WBS dictionary as the basis for development of the final activity list. Each work package within the WBS is decomposed into the activities required to produce the work package deliverables. Involving team members in the decomposition can lead to better and more accurate results.

.2 Rolling Wave Planning

Rolling wave planning is a form of progressive elaboration planning where the work to be accomplished in the near term is planned in detail and future work is planned at a higher level of the WBS. Therefore, work can exist at various levels of detail depending on where it is in the project life cycle. For example, during early strategic planning, when information is less defined, work packages may be decomposed to the milestone level. As more is known about the upcoming events in the near term it can be decomposed into activities.

.3 Templates

A standard activity list or a portion of an activity list from a previous project is often usable as a template for a new project. The related activity attributes information in the templates can also contain other descriptive information useful in defining activities. Templates can also be used to identify typical schedule milestones.

.4 Expert Judgment

Project team members or other experts, who are experienced and skilled in developing detailed project scope statements, the WBS, and project schedules, can provide expertise in defining activities.

6.1.3 Define Activities: Outputs

.1 Activity List

The activity list is a comprehensive list including all schedule activities required on the project. The activity list includes the activity identifier and a scope of work description for each activity in sufficient detail to ensure that project team members understand what work is required to be completed.

.2 Activity Attributes

Activity attributes extend the description of the activity by identifying the multiple components associated with each activity. The components for each activity evolve over time. During the initial stages of the project they include the Activity ID, WBS ID, and Activity Name, and when completed may include activity codes, activity description, predecessor activities, successor activities, logical relationships, leads and lags (Section 6.2.2.3), resource requirements, imposed dates, constraints, and assumptions. Activity attributes can be used to identify the person responsible for executing the work, geographic area, or place where the work has to be performed, and activity type such as level of effort (LOE), discrete effort, and apportioned effort (AE). Activity attributes are used for schedule development and for selecting, ordering, and sorting the planned schedule activities in various ways within reports. The number of attributes varies by application area.

.3 Milestone List

A milestone is a significant point or event in the project. A milestone list identifies all milestones and indicates whether the milestone is mandatory, such as those required by contract, or optional, such as those based upon historical information.

6.2 Sequence Activities

Sequence Activities is the process of identifying and documenting relationships among the project activities. Activities are sequenced using logical relationships. Every activity and milestone except the first and last are connected to at least one predecessor and one successor. It may be necessary to use lead or lag time between activities to support a realistic and achievable project schedule. Sequencing can be performed by using project management software or by using manual or automated techniques. See Figure 6-5 and Figure 6-6.

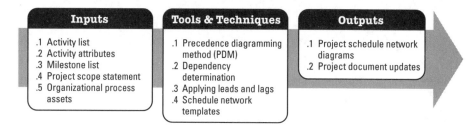

Figure 6-5. Sequence Activities: Inputs, Tools & Techniques, and Outputs

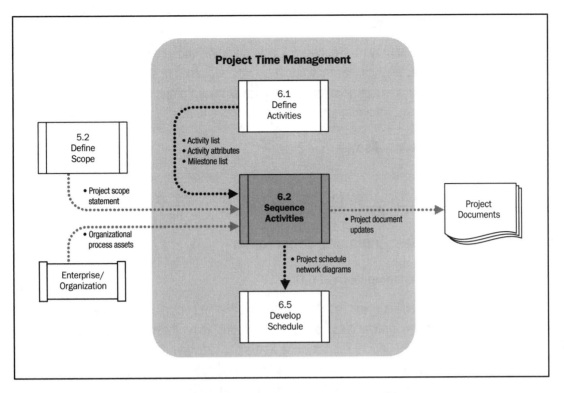

Figure 6-6. Sequence Activities Data Flow Diagram

6.2.1 Sequence Activities: Inputs

.1 Activity List

Described in Section 6.1.3.1.

.2 Activity Attributes

Described in Section 6.1.3.2. Activity attributes may describe a necessary sequence of events or defined predecessor or successor relationships.

.3 Milestone List

Described in Section 6.1.3.3. The milestone list may have scheduled dates for specific milestones.

.4 Project Scope Statement

The project scope statement (Section 5.2.3.1) contains the product scope description, which includes product characteristics that may affect activity sequencing, such as the physical layout of a plant to be constructed or subsystem interfaces on a software project. While these effects are often apparent in the activity list, the product scope description is generally reviewed to ensure accuracy.

.5 Organizational Process Assets

The organizational process assets that can influence the Sequence Activities process include, but are not limited to, project files from the corporate knowledge base used for scheduling methodology.

6.2.2 Sequence Activities: Tools and Techniques

.1 Precedence Diagramming Method (PDM)

PDM is a method used in Critical Path Methodology (CPM) for constructing a project schedule network diagram that uses boxes or rectangles, referred to as nodes, to represent activities, and connects them with arrows that show the logical relationships that exist between them. Figure 6-7 shows a simple project schedule network diagram drawn using PDM. This technique is also called Activity-On-Node (AON), and is the method used by most project management software packages.

PDM includes four types of dependencies or logical relationships:

- **Finish-to-start (FS).** The initiation of the successor activity depends upon the completion of the predecessor activity.

- **Finish-to-finish (FF).** The completion of the successor activity depends upon the completion of the predecessor activity.

- **Start-to-start (SS).** The initiation of the successor activity depends upon the initiation of the predecessor activity.

- **Start-to-finish (SF).** The completion of the successor activity depends upon the initiation of the predecessor activity.

In PDM, finish-to-start is the most commonly used type of precedence relationship. The start-to-finish relationship is rarely used but is included here for a complete list of the PDM relationship types.

.2 Dependency Determination

Three types of dependencies are used to define the sequence among the activities:

- **Mandatory dependencies.** Mandatory dependencies are those that are contractually required or inherent in the nature of the work. The project team determines which dependencies are mandatory during the process of sequencing the activities. Mandatory dependencies often involve physical limitations, such as on a construction project where it is impossible to erect the superstructure until after the foundation has been built, or on an electronics project, where a prototype must be built before it can be tested. Mandatory dependencies are also sometimes referred to as hard logic.

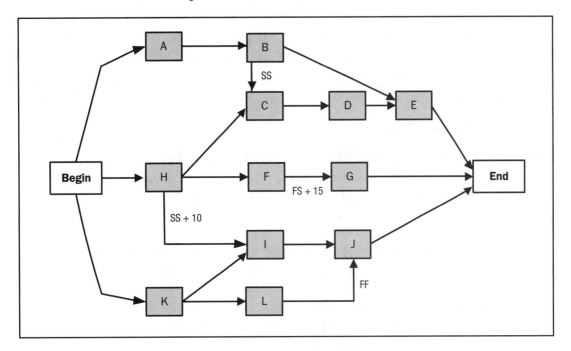

Figure 6-7. Precedence Diagramming Method

- **Discretionary dependencies.** The project team determines which dependencies are discretionary during the process of sequencing the activities. Discretionary dependencies are sometimes referred to as preferred logic, preferential logic, or soft logic. Discretionary dependencies are established based on knowledge of best practices within a particular application area or some unusual aspect of the project where a specific sequence is desired, even though there may be other acceptable sequences. Discretionary dependencies should be fully documented since they can create arbitrary total float values and can limit later scheduling options. When fast tracking techniques are employed, these discretionary dependencies should be reviewed and considered for modification or removal.

- **External dependencies.** The project management team determines which dependencies are external during the process of sequencing the activities. External dependencies involve a relationship between project activities and non-project activities. These dependencies are usually outside the project team's control. For example, the testing activity in a software project can be dependent on the delivery of hardware from an external source, or governmental environmental hearings may need to be held before site preparation can begin on a construction project.

.3 Applying Leads and Lags

The project management team determines the dependencies that may require a lead or a lag to accurately define the logical relationship. The use of leads and lags should not replace schedule logic. Activities and their related assumptions should be documented.

A lead allows an acceleration of the successor activity. For example, on a project to construct a new office building, the landscaping could be scheduled to start 2 weeks prior to the scheduled punch list completion. This would be shown as a finish-to-start with a 2-week lead.

A lag directs a delay in the successor activity. For example, a technical writing team can begin editing the draft of a large document 15 days after they begin writing it. This could be shown as a start-to-start relationship with a 15-day lag.

.4 Schedule Network Templates

Standardized schedule network diagram templates can be used to expedite the preparation of networks of project activities. They can include an entire project or only a portion of it. Portions of a project schedule network diagram are often referred to as a subnetwork or a fragment network. Subnetwork templates are especially useful when a project includes several identical or nearly identical deliverables, such as floors on a high-rise office building, clinical trials on a pharmaceutical research project, coding program modules on a software project, or the start-up phase of a development project.

6.2.3 Sequence Activities: Outputs

.1 Project Schedule Network Diagrams

Project schedule network diagrams are schematic displays of the project's schedule activities and the logical relationships among them, also referred to as dependencies. Figure 6-7 illustrates a project schedule network diagram. A project schedule network diagram can be produced manually or by using project management software. It can include full project details, or have one or more summary activities. A summary narrative can accompany the diagram and describe the basic approach used to sequence the activities. Any unusual activity sequences within the network should be fully described within the narrative.

.2 Project Document Updates

Project documents that may be updated include, but are not limited to:

- Activity lists,
- Activity attributes, and
- Risk register.

6.3 Estimate Activity Resources

Estimate Activity Resources is the process of estimating the type and quantities of material, people, equipment, or supplies required to perform each activity. See Figures 6-8 and 6-9. The Estimate Activity Resource process is closely coordinated with the Estimate Costs process (Section 7.1). For example:

- A construction project team will need to be familiar with local building codes. Such knowledge is often readily available from local sellers. However, if the local labor pool lacks experience with unusual or specialized construction techniques, the additional cost for a consultant might be the most effective way to secure knowledge of the local building codes.

- An automotive design team will need to be familiar with the latest in automated assembly techniques. The requisite knowledge might be obtained by hiring a consultant, by sending a designer to a seminar on robotics, or by including someone from manufacturing as a member of the project team.

Figure 6-8. Estimate Activity Resources: Inputs, Tools & Techniques, and Outputs

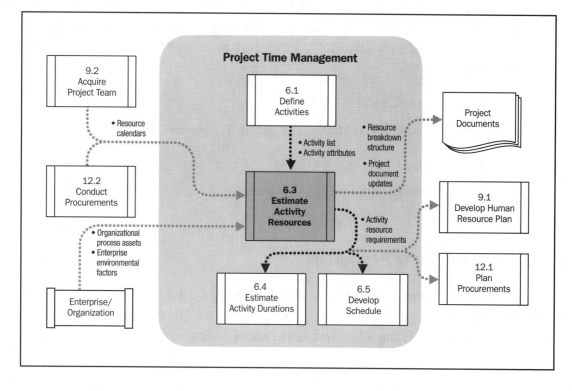

Figure 6-9. Estimate Activity Resources Data Flow Diagram

6.3.1　Estimate Activity Resources: Inputs

.1　Activity List

The activity list (Section 6.1.3.1) identifies the activities which will need resources.

.2　Activity Attributes

The activity attributes (Section 6.1.3.2) developed during the Define Activities and Sequence Activities processes provide the primary data input for use in estimating those resources required for each activity in the activity list.

.3　Resource Calendars

Information on which resources (such as people, equipment, and material) are potentially available during planned activity period, described in Sections 9.2.3.2 and 12.2.3.3, is used for estimating resource utilization. Resource calendars specify when and how long identified project resources will be available during the project. This information may be at the activity or project level. This knowledge includes consideration of attributes such as resource experience and/or skill level, as well as various geographical locations from which the resources originate and when they may be available.

The composite resource calendar includes the availability, capabilities, and skills of human resources (Section 9.2). For example, during the early phases of an engineering design project, the pool of resources might include junior and senior engineers in large numbers. During later phases of the same project, however, the pool can be limited to those individuals who are knowledgeable about the project as a result of having worked on the earlier phases of the project.

.4　Enterprise Environmental Factors

The enterprise environmental factors that can influence the Estimate Activity Resources process include but are not limited to resource availability and skills.

.5 Organizational Process Assets

The organizational process assets that can influence the Estimate Activity Resources process include but are not limited to:

- Policies and procedures regarding staffing,

- Policies and procedures relating to rental and purchase of supplies and equipment, and

- Historical information regarding types of resources used for similar work on previous projects.

6.3.2 Estimate Activity Resources: Tools and Techniques

.1 Expert Judgment

Expert judgment is often required to assess the resource-related inputs to this process. Any group or person with specialized knowledge in resource planning and estimating can provide such expertise.

.2 Alternatives Analysis

Many schedule activities have alternative methods of accomplishment. They include using various levels of resource capability or skills, different size or type of machines, different tools (hand versus automated), and make-or-buy decisions regarding the resource (Section 12.1.3.3).

.3 Published Estimating Data

Several companies routinely publish updated production rates and unit costs of resources for an extensive array of labor trades, material, and equipment for different countries and geographical locations within countries.

.4 Bottom-Up Estimating

When an activity cannot be estimated with a reasonable degree of confidence, the work within the activity is decomposed into more detail. The resource needs are estimated. These estimates are then aggregated into a total quantity for each of the activity's resources. Activities may or may not have dependencies between them that can affect the application and use of resources. If there are dependencies, this pattern of resource usage is reflected and documented in the estimated requirements of the activity.

.5 Project Management Software

Project management software has the capability to help plan, organize, and manage resource pools and develop resource estimates. Depending on the sophistication of the software, resource breakdown structures, resource availability, resource rates and various resource calendars can be defined to assist in optimizing resource utilization.

6.3.3 Estimate Activity Resources: Outputs

.1 Activity Resource Requirements

The output of the Estimate Activity Resources process identifies the types and quantities of resources required for each activity in a work package. These requirements can then be aggregated to determine the estimated resources for each work package. The amount of detail and the level of specificity of the resource requirement descriptions can vary by application area. The resource requirements documentation for each activity can include the basis of estimate for each resource, as well as the assumptions that were made in determining which types of resources are applied, their availability, and what quantities are used.

.2 Resource Breakdown Structure

The resource breakdown structure is a hierarchical structure of the identified resources by resource category and resource type. Examples of resource categories include labor, material, equipment, and supplies. Resource types can include the skill level, grade level or other information as appropriate to the project. The resource breakdown structure is useful for organizing and reporting project schedule data with resource utilization information.

.3 Project Document Updates

Project documents that may be updated include, but are not limited to:

- Activity list,
- Activity attributes, and
- Resource calendars.

6.4 Estimate Activity Durations

Estimate Activity Durations is the process of approximating the number of work periods needed to complete individual activities with estimated resources. Estimating activity durations uses information on activity scope of work, required resource types, estimated resource quantities, and resource calendars. The inputs for the estimates of activity duration originate from the person or group on the project team who is most familiar with the nature of the work in the specific activity. The duration estimate is progressively elaborated, and the process considers the quality and availability of the input data. For example, as the project engineering and design work evolves, more detailed and precise data is available, and the accuracy of the duration estimates improves. Thus, the duration estimate can be assumed to be progressively more accurate and of better quality. See Figure 6-10 and Figure 6-11.

The Estimate Activity Durations process requires that the amount of work effort required to complete the activity is estimated and the amount of resources to be applied to complete the activity is estimated; these are used to approximate the number of work periods (activity duration) needed to complete the activity. All data and assumptions that support duration estimating are documented for each estimate of activity duration.

Most project management software for scheduling will handle this situation by using a project calendar and alternative work-period resource calendars that are usually identified by the resources that require specific work periods. In addition to the sequencing logic, the activities will be performed according to the project calendar and the appropriate resource calendars.

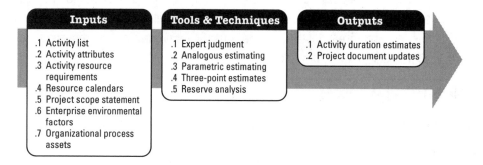

Inputs	Tools & Techniques	Outputs
.1 Activity list .2 Activity attributes .3 Activity resource requirements .4 Resource calendars .5 Project scope statement .6 Enterprise environmental factors .7 Organizational process assets	.1 Expert judgment .2 Analogous estimating .3 Parametric estimating .4 Three-point estimates .5 Reserve analysis	.1 Activity duration estimates .2 Project document updates

Figure 6-10. Estimate Activity Durations: Inputs, Tools & Techniques, and Outputs

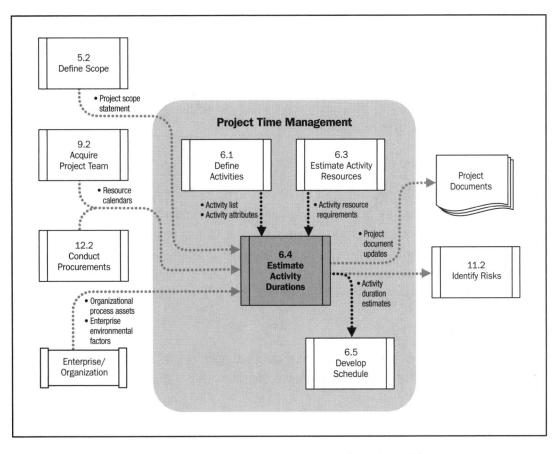

Figure 6-11. Estimate Activity Durations Data Flow Diagram

6.4.1 Estimate Activity Durations: Inputs

.1 Activity List

Described in Section 6.1.3.1.

.2 Activity Attributes

Described in Section 6.1.3.2.

.3 Activity Resource Requirements

The estimated activity resource requirements (Section 6.3.3.1) will have an effect on the duration of the activity, since the resources assigned to the activity and the availability of those resources will significantly influence the duration of most activities. For example, if additional or lower-skilled resources are assigned to an activity, there may be reduced efficiency or productivity due to increased communication, training, and coordination needs.

.4 Resource Calendars

The resource calendar (Section 6.3.1.3), developed as part of the Estimating Activity Resources process, can include the type, availability, and capabilities of human resources (Section 9.2.3.2). The type, quantity, availability, and capability, when applicable, of both equipment and material resources, which could significantly influence the duration of schedule activities, are also considered. For example, when a senior and a junior staff member are assigned full time, a senior staff member can generally be expected to complete a given activity in less time than a junior staff member.

.5 Project Scope Statement

The constraints and assumptions from the project scope statement (Section 5.2.3.1) are considered when estimating the activity durations. Examples of assumptions include, but are not limited to:

- Existing conditions,
- Availability of information, and
- Length of the reporting periods.

Examples of constraints include, but are not limited to:

- Available skilled resources, and
- Contract terms and requirements.

.6 Enterprise Environmental Factors

The enterprise environmental factors that can influence the Estimate Activity Durations process include, but are not limited to:

- Duration estimating databases and other reference data,
- Productivity metrics, and
- Published commercial information.

.7 Organizational Process Assets

The organizational process assets that can influence the Estimate Activity Durations process include but are not limited to:

- Historical duration information,

- Project calendars,

- Scheduling methodology, and

- Lessons learned.

6.4.2 Estimate Activity Durations: Tools and Techniques

.1 Expert Judgment

Expert judgment, guided by historical information, can provide duration estimate information or recommended maximum activity durations from prior similar projects. Expert judgment can also be used to determine whether to combine methods of estimating and how to reconcile differences between them.

.2 Analogous Estimating

Analogous estimating uses parameters such as duration, budget, size, weight, and complexity, from a previous, similar project, as the basis for estimating the same parameter or measure for a future project. When estimating durations, this technique relies on the actual duration of previous, similar projects as the basis for estimating the duration of the current project. It is a gross value estimating approach, sometimes adjusted for known differences in project complexity.

Analogous duration estimating is frequently used to estimate project duration when there is a limited amount of detailed information about the project for example, in the early phases of a project. Analogous estimating uses historical information and expert judgment.

Analogous estimating is generally less costly and time consuming than other techniques, but it is also generally less accurate. Analogous duration estimates can be applied to a total project or to segments of a project and may be used in conjunction with other estimating methods. Analogous estimating is most reliable when the previous activities are similar in fact and not just in appearance, and the project team members preparing the estimates have the needed expertise.

.3 Parametric Estimating

Parametric estimating uses a statistical relationship between historical data and other variables (e.g., square footage in construction) to calculate an estimate for activity parameters, such as cost, budget, and duration.

Activity durations can be quantitatively determined by multiplying the quantity of work to be performed by labor hours per unit of work. For example, activity duration can be estimated on a design project by the number of drawings multiplied by the number of labor hours per drawing, or a cable installation in meters of cable multiplied by the number of labor hours per meter. For example, if the assigned resource is capable of installing 25 meters of cable per hour, the duration required to install 1,000 meters would be 40 hours. (1,000 meters divided by 25 meters per hour).

This technique can produce higher levels of accuracy depending upon the sophistication and underlying data built into the model. Parametric time estimates can be applied to a total project or to segments of a project, in conjunction with other estimating methods.

.4 Three-Point Estimates

The accuracy of activity duration estimates can be improved by considering estimation uncertainty and risk. This concept originated with the Program Evaluation and Review Technique (PERT). PERT uses three estimates to define an approximate range for an activity's duration:

- **Most likely (t_M).** The duration of the activity, given the resources likely to be assigned, their productivity, realistic expectations of availability for the activity, dependencies on other participants, and interruptions.

- **Optimistic (t_O).** The activity duration is based on analysis of the best-case scenario for the activity.

- **Pessimistic (t_P).** The activity duration is based on analysis of the worst-case scenario for the activity.

PERT analysis calculates an **Expected** (t_E) activity duration using a weighted average of these three estimates:

$$t_E = (t_O + 4t_M + t_P) /6$$

Duration estimates based on this equation (or even on a simple average of the three points) may provide more accuracy, and the three points clarify the range of uncertainty of the duration estimates.

.5 Reserve Analysis

Duration estimates may include contingency reserves, (sometimes referred to as time reserves or buffers) into the overall project schedule to account for schedule uncertainty. The contingency reserve may be a percentage of the estimated activity duration, a fixed number of work periods, or may be developed by using quantitative analysis methods.

As more precise information about the project becomes available, the contingency reserve may be used, reduced, or eliminated. Contingency should be clearly identified in schedule documentation.

6.4.3 Estimate Activity Durations: Outputs

.1 Activity Duration Estimates

Activity duration estimates are quantitative assessments of the likely number of work periods that will be required to complete an activity. Duration estimates do not include any lags as described in 6.2.2.3. Activity duration estimates may include some indication of the range of possible results. For example:

- 2 weeks ± 2 days to indicate that the activity will take at least eight days and no more than twelve (assuming a five-day workweek).

- 15% probability of exceeding three weeks to indicate a high probability—85% percent—that the activity will take three weeks or less.

.2 Project Document Updates

Project documents that may be updated include, but are not limited to:

- Activity attributes, and

- Assumptions made in developing the activity duration estimate such as skill levels and availability.

6.5 Develop Schedule

Develop Schedule is the process of analyzing activity sequences, durations, resource requirements, and schedule constraints to create the project schedule. Entering the activities, durations, and resources into the scheduling tool generates a schedule with planned dates for completing project activities. Developing an acceptable project schedule is often an iterative process. It determines the planned start and finish dates for project activities and milestones. Schedule development can require the review and revision of duration estimates and resource estimates to create an approved project schedule that can serve as a baseline to track progress. Revising and maintaining a realistic schedule continues throughout the project as work progresses, the project management plan changes, and the nature of risk events evolves. See Figures 6-12 and 6-13.

For more specific information regarding scheduling, refer to the *Practice Standard for Scheduling* [**2**].

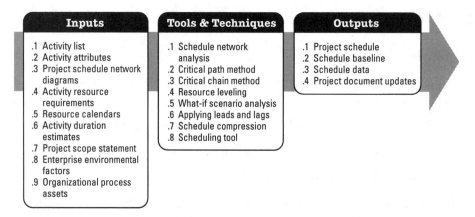

Inputs	Tools & Techniques	Outputs
.1 Activity list	.1 Schedule network analysis	.1 Project schedule
.2 Activity attributes	.2 Critical path method	.2 Schedule baseline
.3 Project schedule network diagrams	.3 Critical chain method	.3 Schedule data
.4 Activity resource requirements	.4 Resource leveling	.4 Project document updates
.5 Resource calendars	.5 What-if scenario analysis	
.6 Activity duration estimates	.6 Applying leads and lags	
.7 Project scope statement	.7 Schedule compression	
.8 Enterprise environmental factors	.8 Scheduling tool	
.9 Organizational process assets		

Figure 6-12. Develop Schedule: Inputs, Tools & Techniques, and Outputs

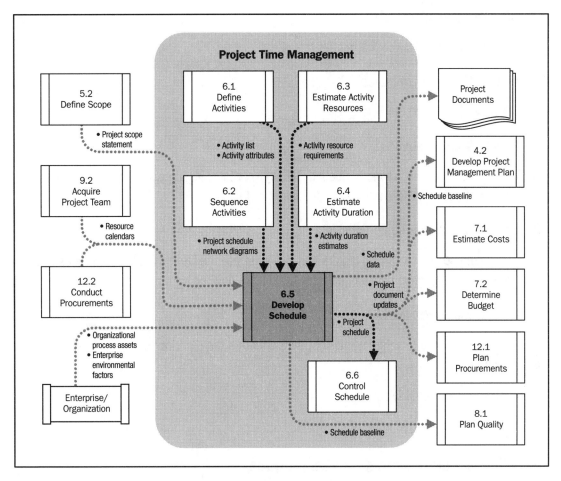

Figure 6-13. Develop Schedule Data Flow Diagram

6.5.1   Develop Schedule: Inputs

.1 Activity List

Described in Section 6.1.3.1.

.2 Activity Attributes

Described in Section 6.1.3.2.

.3 Project Schedule Network Diagrams

Described in Section 6.2.3.1.

.4 Activity Resource Requirements

Described in Section 6.3.3.1.

.5 Resource Calendars

Described in Sections 6.3.1.3.

.6 Activity Duration Estimates

Described in Section 6.4.3.1.

.7 Project Scope Statement

The project scope statement (Section 5.2.3.1) contains assumptions and constraints that can impact the development of the project schedule.

.8 Enterprise Environmental Factors

The enterprise environmental factors that can influence the Develop Schedule process include, but are not limited to, a scheduling tool that can be used in developing the schedule.

.9 Organizational Process Assets

The organizational process assets that can influence the Develop Schedule process include, but are not limited to:

- Scheduling methodology, and
- Project calendar.

6.5.2 Develop Schedule: Tools and Techniques

.1 Schedule Network Analysis

Schedule network analysis is a technique that generates the project schedule. It employs various analytical techniques, such as critical path method, critical chain method, what-if analysis, and resource leveling to calculate the early and late start and finish dates for the uncompleted portions of project activities. Some network paths may have points of path convergence or path divergence that can be identified and used in schedule compression analysis or other analyses.

.2 Critical Path Method

The critical path method calculates the theoretical early start and finish dates, and late start and finish dates, for all activities without regard for any resource limitations, by performing a forward and backward pass analysis through the schedule network. The resulting early and late start and finish dates are not necessarily the project schedule; rather, they indicate the time periods within which the activity could be scheduled, given activity durations, logical relationships, leads, lags, and other known constraints.

Calculated early start and finish dates, and late start and finish dates, may be affected by activity total float, which provides schedule flexibility and, may be positive, negative, or zero. On any network path, the schedule flexibility is measured by the positive difference between early and late dates, and is termed "total float." Critical paths have either a zero or negative total float, and schedule activities on a critical path are called "critical activities." A critical path is normally characterized by zero total float on the critical path. Networks can have multiple near critical paths. Adjustments to activity durations, logical relationships, leads and lags, or other schedule constraints may be necessary to produce network paths with a zero or positive total float. Once the total float for a network path has been calculated then the free float, the amount of time that an activity can be delayed without delaying the early start date of any immediate successor activity within the network path, can also be determined.

.3 Critical Chain Method

Critical chain is a schedule network analysis technique that modifies the project schedule to account for limited resources. Initially, the project schedule network diagram is built using duration estimates with required dependencies and defined constraints as inputs. The critical path is then calculated. After the critical path is identified, resource availability is entered and the resource-limited schedule result is determined. The resulting schedule often has an altered critical path.

The resource-constrained critical path is known as the critical chain. The critical chain method adds duration buffers that are non-work schedule activities to manage uncertainty. One buffer, placed at the end of the critical chain, is known as the project buffer and protects the target finish date from slippage along the critical chain. Additional buffers, known as feeding buffers, are placed at each point that a chain of dependent tasks not on the critical chain feeds into the critical chain. Feeding buffers thus protect the critical chain from slippage along the feeding chains. The size of each buffer should account for the uncertainty in the duration of the chain of dependent tasks leading up to that buffer. Once the buffer schedule activities are determined, the planned activities are scheduled to their latest possible planned start and finish dates. Consequently, in lieu of managing the total float of network paths, the critical chain method focuses on managing remaining buffer durations against the remaining durations of task chains.

.4 Resource Leveling

Resource leveling is a schedule network analysis technique applied to a schedule that has already been analyzed by the critical path method. Resource leveling can be used when shared or critical required resources are only available at certain times, are only available in limited quantities, or to keep resource usage at a constant level. Resource leveling is necessary when resources have been over-allocated, such as when a resource has been assigned to two or more activities during the same time period, when shared or critical required resources are only available at certain times or are only available in limited quantities. Resource leveling can often cause the original critical path to change.

.5 What-If Scenario Analysis

This is an analysis of the question "What if the situation represented by scenario 'X' happens?" A schedule network analysis is performed using the schedule to compute the different scenarios, such as delaying a major component delivery, extending specific engineering durations, or introducing external factors, such as a strike or a change in the permitting process. The outcome of the what-if scenario analysis can be used to assess the feasibility of the project schedule under adverse conditions, and in preparing contingency and response plans to overcome or mitigate the impact of unexpected situations. Simulation involves calculating multiple project durations with different sets of activity assumptions. The most common technique is Monte Carlo Analysis (Section 11.4.2.2), in which a distribution of possible activity durations is defined for each activity and used to calculate a distribution of possible outcomes for the total project.

.6 Applying Leads and Lags

Leads and lags (Section 6.2.2.3) are refinements applied during network analysis to develop a viable schedule.

.7 Schedule Compression

Schedule compression shortens the project schedule without changing the project scope, to meet schedule constraints, imposed dates, or other schedule objectives. Schedule compression techniques include:

- **Crashing.** A schedule compression technique in which cost and schedule tradeoffs are analyzed to determine how to obtain the greatest amount of compression for the least incremental cost. Examples of crashing could include approving overtime, bringing in additional resources, or paying to expedite delivery to activities on the critical path. Crashing only works for activities where additional resources will shorten the duration. Crashing does not always produce a viable alternative and may result in increased risk and/or cost.

- **Fast tracking.** A schedule compression technique in which phases or activities normally performed in sequence are performed in parallel. An example is constructing the foundation for a building before completing all of the architectural drawings. Fast tracking may result in rework and increased risk. Fast tracking only works if activities can be overlapped to shorten the duration.

.8 Scheduling Tool

Automated scheduling tools expedite the scheduling process by generating start and finish dates based on the inputs of activities, network diagrams, resources and activity durations. A scheduling tool can be used in conjunction with other project management software applications as well as manual methods.

6.5.3   Develop Schedule: Outputs

.1 Project Schedule

As a minimum, the project schedule includes a planned start date and planned finish date for each activity. If resource planning is done at an early stage, then the project schedule would remain preliminary until resource assignments have been confirmed and scheduled start and finish dates are established. This process usually happens no later than completion of the project management plan (Section 4.2.3.1). A project target schedule may also be developed with a defined target start and target finish for each activity. The project schedule may be presented in summary form, sometimes referred to as the master schedule or milestone schedule, or presented in detail. Although a project schedule can be presented in tabular form, it is more often presented graphically, using one or more of the following formats:

- **Milestone charts.** These charts are similar to bar charts, but only identify the scheduled start or completion of major deliverables and key external interfaces. An example is the milestone schedule portion of Figure 6-14.

- **Bar charts.** These charts, with bars representing activities, show activity start and end dates, as well as expected durations. Bar charts are relatively easy to read, and are frequently used in management presentations. For control and management communication, the broader, more comprehensive summary activity, sometimes referred to as a hammock activity, is used between milestones or across multiple interdependent work packages, and is displayed in bar chart reports. An example is the summary schedule portion of Figure 6-14 that is presented in a WBS structured format.

- **Project schedule network diagrams.** These diagrams, with activity date information, usually show both the project network logic and the project's critical path schedule activities. These diagrams can be presented in the activity-on-node diagram format, as shown in Figure 6-7, or presented in a time-scaled schedule network diagram format that is sometimes called a logic bar chart, as shown for the detailed schedule in Figure 6-14. This example also shows how each work package is planned as a series of related activities.

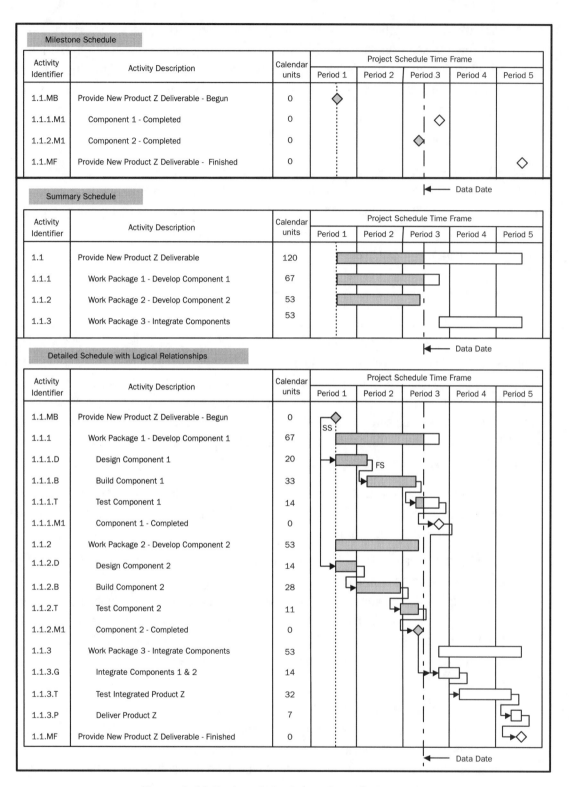

Figure 6-14. Project Schedule—Graphic Examples

Figure 6-14 shows the schedule for a sample project being executed, with the work in progress reported through the data date, which is sometimes also called the as-of date or status date. For a simple project schedule, Figure 6-14 gives a graphic display of a milestone schedule, a summary schedule, and a detailed schedule. Figure 6-14 also visually shows the relationships among the three different levels of schedule presentation.

.2 Schedule Baseline

A schedule baseline is a specific version of the project schedule developed from the schedule network analysis. It is accepted and approved by the project management team as the schedule baseline with baseline start dates and baseline finish dates. The schedule baseline is a component of the project management plan.

.3 Schedule Data

The schedule data for the project schedule includes at least the schedule milestones, schedule activities, activity attributes, and documentation of all identified assumptions and constraints. The amount of additional data varies by application area. Information frequently supplied as supporting detail includes, but is not limited to:

- Resource requirements by time period, often in the form of a resource histogram,

- Alternative schedules, such as best-case or worst-case, not resource-leveled, or resource-leveled, with or without imposed dates, and

- Scheduling of contingency reserves.

Schedule data could include such items as resource histograms, cash-flow projections, and order and delivery schedules.

.4 Project Document Updates

Project documents that may be updated include, but are not limited to:

- **Activity resource requirements.** Resource leveling can have a significant effect on preliminary estimates of the types and quantities of resources required. If the resource-leveling analysis changes the project resource requirements, then the project resource requirements are updated.

- **Activity attributes.** Activity attributes (Section 6.1.3.2) are updated to include any revised resource requirements and any other revisions generated by the Develop Schedule process.

- **Calendar.** The calendar for each project may use different calendar units as the basis for scheduling the project.

- **Risk register.** The risk register may need to be updated to reflect opportunities or threats perceived through scheduling assumptions.

6.6 Control Schedule

Control Schedule is the process of monitoring the status of the project to update project progress and manage changes to the schedule baseline. See Figure 6-15 and Figure 6-16. Schedule control is concerned with:

- Determining the current status of the project schedule,

- Influencing the factors that create schedule changes,

- Determining that the project schedule has changed, and

- Managing the actual changes as they occur.

Control Schedule is a component of the Perform Integrated Change Control process (Section 4.5).

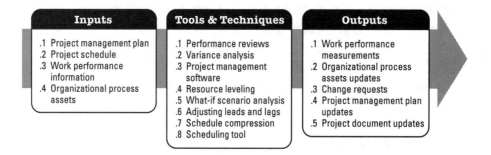

Figure 6-15. Control Schedule Overview: Inputs, Tools & Techniques, and Outputs

---

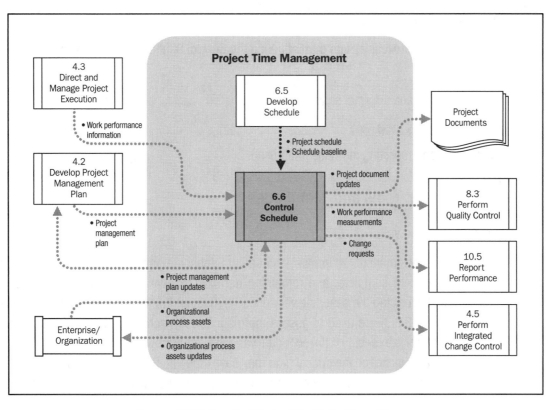

Figure 6-16. Control Schedule Data Flow Diagram

6.6.1 Control Schedule: Inputs

.1 Project Management Plan

The project management plan described in Section 4.2.3.1 contains the schedule management plan and the schedule baseline. The schedule management plan describes how the schedule will be managed and controlled. The schedule baseline is used to compare with actual results to determine if a change, corrective action, or preventive action is necessary.

.2 Project Schedule

The most recent version of the project schedule with notations to indicate updates, completed activities, and started activities as of the indicated data date.

.3 Work Performance Information

Information about project progress, such as which activities have started, their progress, and which activities have finished.

.4 Organizational Process Assets

The organizational process assets that influence the Control Schedule process include but are not limited to:

- Existing formal and informal schedule control-related policies, procedures, and guidelines;

- Schedule control tools; and

- Monitoring and reporting methods to be used.

6.6.2 Control Schedule: Tools and Techniques

.1 Performance Reviews

Performance reviews measure, compare, and analyze schedule performance such as actual start and finish dates, percent complete, and remaining duration for work in progress. If earned value management (EVM) is utilized the schedule variance (SV) (Section 7.3.2.1) and schedule performance index (SPI) (Section 7.3.2.3) are used to assess the magnitude of schedule variations. An important part of schedule control is to decide if the schedule variation requires corrective action. For example, a major delay on any activity not on the critical path may have little effect on the overall project schedule, while a much shorter delay on a critical or near-critical activity may require immediate action.

If using the critical chain scheduling method (6.5.2.3), comparing the amount of buffer remaining to the amount of buffer needed to protect the delivery date can help determine schedule status. The difference between the buffer needed and the buffer remaining can determine whether corrective action is appropriate.

.2 Variance Analysis

Schedule performance measurements (SV, SPI) are used to assess the magnitude of variation to the original schedule baseline. The total float variance is also an essential planning component to evaluate project time performance. Important aspects of project schedule control include determining the cause and degree of variance relative to the schedule baseline (Section 6.5.3.2) and deciding whether corrective or preventive action is required.

.3 Project Management Software

Project management software for scheduling provides the ability to track planned dates versus actual dates, and to forecast the effects of changes to the project schedule.

.4 Resource Leveling

Resource leveling as described in Section 6.5.2.4, is used to optimize the distribution of work among resources.

.5 What-If Scenario Analysis

What-if scenario analysis is used to review various scenarios to bring the schedule into alignment with the plan. Described in Section 6.5.2.5.

.6 Adjusting Leads and Lags

Adjusting leads and lags is used to find ways to bring project activities that are behind into alignment with plan.

.7 Schedule Compression

Schedule compression techniques are used to find ways to bring project activities that are behind into alignment with the plan. Described in Section 6.5.2.7.

.8 Scheduling Tool

Schedule data is updated and compiled into the schedule to reflect actual progress of the project and remaining work to be completed. The scheduling tool and the supporting schedule data are used in conjunction with manual methods or other project management software to perform schedule network analysis to generate an updated project schedule.

6.6.3　Control Schedule: Outputs

.1 Work Performance Measurements

The calculated SV and SPI values for WBS components, in particular the work packages and control accounts, are documented and communicated to stakeholders.

.2 Organizational Process Assets Updates

Organizational process assets that may be updated include but are not limited to:

- Causes of variances,
- Corrective action chosen and the reasons, and
- Other types of lessons learned from project schedule control.

.3 Change Requests

Schedule variance analysis, along with review of progress reports, results of performance measures, and modifications to the project schedule can result in change requests to the schedule baseline and/or to other components of the project management plan. Change requests are processed for review and disposition through the Perform Integrated Change Control process (4.5). Preventive actions may include recommended changes to reduce the probability of negative schedule variances.

.4 Project Management Plan Updates

Elements of the project management plan that may be updated include but are not limited to:

- **Schedule baseline.** Changes to the schedule baseline are incorporated in response to approved change requests (Section 4.4.3.1) related to project scope changes, activity resources, or activity duration estimates.

- **Schedule management plan.** The schedule management plan may be updated to reflect a change in the way the schedule is managed.

- **Cost baseline.** The cost baseline may be updated to reflect changes caused by compression or crashing techniques.

.5 Project Document Updates

Project documents that may be updated include but are not limited to:

- **Schedule Data.** New project schedule network diagrams may be developed to display approved remaining durations and modifications to the work plan. In some cases, project schedule delays can be so severe that development of a new target schedule with forecasted start and finish dates is needed to provide realistic data for directing the work, and for measuring performance and progress.

- **Project Schedule.** An updated project schedule will be generated from the updated schedule data to reflect the schedule changes and manage the project.

CHAPTER 7

PROJECT COST MANAGEMENT

Project Cost Management includes the processes involved in estimating, budgeting, and controlling costs so that the project can be completed within the approved budget. Figure 7-1 provides an overview of the Project Cost Management processes which include the following:

7.1 Estimate Costs—The process of developing an approximation of the monetary resources needed to complete project activities.

7.2 Determine Budget—The process of aggregating the estimated costs of individual activities or work packages to establish an authorized cost baseline.

7.3 Control Costs—The process of monitoring the status of the project to update the project budget and managing changes to the cost baseline.

These processes interact with each other and with processes in the other Knowledge Areas as well. Each process can involve effort from one group or person, based upon the needs of the project. Each process occurs at least once in every project and occurs in one or more project phases, if the project is divided into phases. Although the processes are presented here as discrete elements with well-defined interfaces, in practice they may overlap and interact in ways not detailed here. Process interactions are discussed in detail in Chapter 3.

On some projects, especially ones of smaller scope, cost estimating and cost budgeting are so tightly linked that they are viewed as a single process that can be performed by a single person over a relatively short period of time. These processes are presented here as distinct processes because the tools and techniques for each are different. The ability to influence cost is greatest at the early stages of the project, making early scope definition critical (Section 5.2).

The work involved in performing the three processes of Project Cost Management is preceded by a planning effort of the project management team. This planning effort is part of the Develop Project Management Plan process (Section 4.2), which produces a cost management plan that sets out the format and establishes the criteria for planning, structuring, estimating, budgeting, and controlling project costs. The cost management processes and their associated tools and techniques are usually selected during the project life cycle definition (Section 2.1), and are documented in the cost management plan. For example, the cost management plan can establish the following:

- **Level of accuracy.** Activity cost estimates will adhere to a rounding of the data to a prescribed precision (e.g., $100, $1,000), based on the scope of the activities and magnitude of the project, and may include an amount for contingencies.

- **Units of measure.** Each unit used in measurements (such as staff hours, staff days, weeks, or lump sum) is defined for each of the resources.

- **Organizational procedures links.** The work breakdown structure (WBS) (Section 5.3.3.1) provides the framework for the cost management plan, allowing for consistency with the estimates, budgets, and control of costs. The WBS component used for the project cost accounting is called the control account (CA). Each control account is assigned a unique code or account number(s) that links directly to the performing organization's accounting system.

- **Control thresholds.** Variance thresholds for monitoring cost performance may be specified to indicate an agreed-upon amount of variation to be allowed before some action needs to be taken. Thresholds are typically expressed as percentage deviations from the baseline plan.

- **Rules of performance measurement.** Earned value management (EVM) rules of performance measurement are set. For example, the cost management plan could:

  o Define the WBS and points at which measurement of control accounts will be performed,

  o Establish the earned value measurement techniques (e.g., weighted milestones, fixed-formula, percent complete, etc.) to be employed, and

  o Specify the earned value management computation equations for determining the projected estimate at completion (EAC) forecasts and other tracking methodologies.

For more specific information regarding earned value management, refer to the *Practice Standard for Earned Value Management* [3].

- **Reporting formats.** The formats and frequency for the various cost reports are defined.

- **Process descriptions.** Descriptions of each of the three cost management processes are documented.

All of this information is included in the cost management plan, a component of the project management plan, either as text within the body of the plan or as appendices. The cost management plan may be formal or informal, highly detailed or broadly framed, based upon the needs of the project.

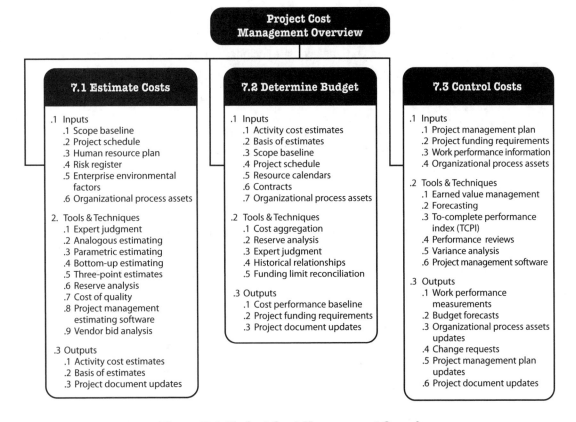

Figure 7-1. Project Cost Management Overview

Project Cost Management should consider the stakeholder requirements for capturing costs. Different stakeholders will measure project costs in different ways and at different times. For example, the cost of an acquired item can be measured when the acquisition decision is made or committed, the order is placed, the item is delivered, or the actual cost is incurred or recorded for project accounting purposes.

Project Cost Management is primarily concerned with the cost of the resources needed to complete project activities. Project Cost Management should also consider the effect of project decisions on the subsequent recurring cost of using, maintaining, and supporting the product, service, or result of the project. For example, limiting the number of design reviews can reduce the cost of the project but could do so by increasing the customer's operating costs.

In many organizations, predicting and analyzing the prospective financial performance of the project's product is done outside the project. In others, such as a capital facilities project, Project Cost Management can include this work. When such predictions and analyses are included, Project Cost Management may address additional processes and numerous general management techniques such as return on investment, discounted cash flow, and investment payback analysis.

The cost management planning effort occurs early in project planning and sets the framework for each of the cost management processes so that performance of the processes will be efficient and coordinated.

7.1 Estimate Costs

Estimate Costs is the process of developing an approximation of the monetary resources needed to complete project activities. See Figures 7-2 and 7-3. Cost estimates are a prediction that is based on the information known at a given point in time. It includes the identification and consideration of costing alternatives to initiate and complete the project. Cost trade-offs and risks must be considered, such as make versus buy, buy versus lease, and the sharing of resources in order to achieve optimal costs for the project.

Cost estimates are generally expressed in units of some currency (i.e., dollars, euro, yen, etc.), although in some instances other units of measure, such as staff hours or staff days, are used to facilitate comparisons by eliminating the effects of currency fluctuations.

Cost estimates should be refined during the course of the project to reflect additional detail as it becomes available. The accuracy of a project estimate will increase as the project progresses through the project life cycle. Hence cost estimating is an iterative process from phase to phase. For example, a project in the initiation phase could have a rough order of magnitude (ROM) estimate in the range of ±50%. Later in the project, as more information is known, estimates could narrow to a range of ±10%. In some organizations, there are guidelines for when such refinements can be made and the degree of accuracy that is expected.

Sources of input information are derived from the outputs of project processes in other Knowledge Areas. Once received, all of this information will remain available as inputs to all three of the cost management processes.

Costs are estimated for all resources that will be charged to the project. This includes, but is not limited to, labor, materials, equipment, services, and facilities, as well as special categories such as an inflation allowance or contingency costs. A cost estimate is a quantitative assessment of the likely costs for resources required to complete the activity.

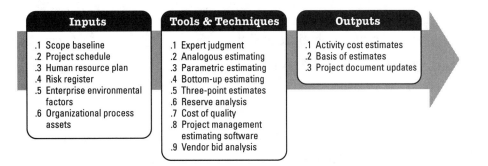

Inputs	Tools & Techniques	Outputs
.1 Scope baseline .2 Project schedule .3 Human resource plan .4 Risk register .5 Enterprise environmental factors .6 Organizational process assets	.1 Expert judgment .2 Analogous estimating .3 Parametric estimating .4 Bottom-up estimating .5 Three-point estimates .6 Reserve analysis .7 Cost of quality .8 Project management estimating software .9 Vendor bid analysis	.1 Activity cost estimates .2 Basis of estimates .3 Project document updates

Figure 7-2. Estimate Costs: Inputs, Tools & Techniques, and Outputs

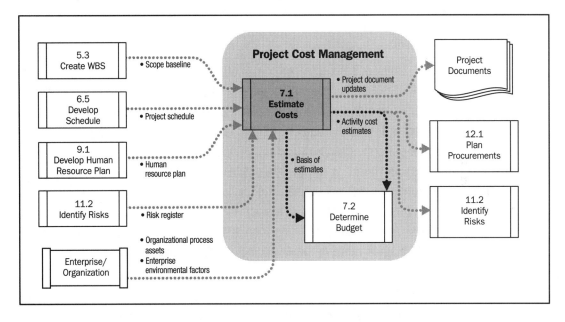

Figure 7-3. Estimate Costs Data Flow Diagram

7.1.1 Estimate Costs: Inputs

.1 Scope Baseline

- **Scope statement.** The scope statement (Section 5.2.3.1) provides the product description, acceptance criteria, key deliverables, project boundaries, assumptions, and constraints about the project. One basic assumption that needs to be made when estimating project costs is whether the estimates will be limited to direct project costs only or whether the estimates will also include indirect costs. Indirect costs are those costs that cannot be directly traced to a specific project and therefore will be accumulated and allocated equitably over multiple projects by some approved and documented accounting procedure. One of the most common constraints for many projects is a limited project budget. Examples of other constraints are required delivery dates, available skilled resources, and organizational policies.

- **Work breakdown structure.** The project WBS (Section 5.3.3.1) provides the relationships among all the components of the project and the project deliverables (Section 4.3.3.1).

- **WBS dictionary.** The WBS dictionary (Section 5.3.3.2) and related detailed statements of work provide an identification of the deliverables and a description of the work in each WBS component required to produce each deliverable.

Additional information that may be found in the scope baseline that includes requirements with contractual and legal implications are health, safety, security, performance, environmental, insurance, intellectual property rights, licenses, and permits. All of this information should be considered when developing the cost estimates.

.2 Project Schedule

The type and quantity of resources and the amount of time which those resources are applied to complete the work of the project are major factors in determining the project cost. Schedule activity resources and their respective durations are used as key inputs to this process. Estimate Activity Resources (Section 6.3) involves determining the availability and quantities required of staff and material needed to perform schedule activities. It is closely coordinated with cost estimating. Activity duration estimates (Section 6.4.3.1) will affect cost estimates on any project where the project budget includes an allowance for the cost of financing (including interest charges) and where resources are applied per unit of time for the duration of the activity. Activity duration estimates can also affect cost estimates that have time-sensitive costs included in them, such as union labor with regularly expiring collective bargaining agreements or materials with seasonal cost variations.

.3 Human Resource Plan

Project staffing attributes, personnel rates, and related rewards/recognition (Section 9.1.3.1) are necessary components for developing the project cost estimates.

.4 Risk Register

The risk register (Section 11.2.3.1) should be reviewed to consider risk mitigation costs. Risks, which can be either threats or opportunities, typically have an impact on both activity and overall project costs. As a general rule, when the project experiences a negative risk event, the near-term cost of the project will usually increase, and there will sometimes be a delay in the project schedule.

.5 Enterprise Environmental Factors

The enterprise environmental factors that influence the Estimate Costs process include, but are not limited to:

- Market conditions. Market conditions describe what products, services, and results are available in the market, from whom, and under what terms and conditions. Regional and/or global supply and demand conditions greatly influence resource costs.

- Published commercial information. Resource cost rate information is often available from commercial databases that track skills and human resource costs, and provide standard costs for material and equipment. Published seller price lists are another source of information.

.6 Organizational Process Assets

The organizational process assets that influence the Estimate Costs process include but are not limited to:

- Cost estimating policies,
- Cost estimating templates,
- Historical information, and
- Lessons learned.

7.1.2 Estimate Costs: Tools and Techniques

.1 Expert Judgment

Cost estimates are influenced by numerous variables such as labor rates, material costs, inflation, risk factors, and other variables. Expert judgment, guided by historical information, provides valuable insight about the environment and information from prior similar projects. Expert judgment can also be used to determine whether to combine methods of estimating and how to reconcile differences between them.

.2 Analogous Estimating

Analogous cost estimating uses the values of parameters, such as scope, cost, budget, and duration or measures of scale such as size, weight, and complexity, from a previous, similar project as the basis for estimating the same parameter or measure for a current project. When estimating costs, this technique relies on the actual cost of previous, similar projects as the basis for estimating the cost of the current project. It is a gross value estimating approach, sometimes adjusted for known differences in project complexity.

Analogous cost estimating is frequently used to estimate a parameter when there is a limited amount of detailed information about the project, for example, in the early phases of a project. Analogous cost estimating uses historical information and expert judgment.

Analogous cost estimating is generally less costly and time consuming than other techniques, but it is also generally less accurate. Analogous cost estimates can be applied to a total project or to segments of a project, used in conjunction with other estimating methods. Analogous estimating is most reliable when the previous projects are similar in fact and not just in appearance, and the project team members preparing the estimates have the needed expertise.

.3 Parametric Estimating

Parametric estimating uses a statistical relationship between historical data and other variables (e.g., square footage in construction) to calculate an estimate for activity parameters, such as cost, budget, and duration. This technique can produce higher levels of accuracy depending upon the sophistication and underlying data built into the model. Parametric cost estimates can be applied to a total project or to segments of a project, in conjunction with other estimating methods.

.4 Bottom-Up Estimating

Bottom-up estimating is a method of estimating a component of work. The cost of individual work packages or activities is estimated with the greatest level of specified detail. The detailed cost is then summarized or "rolled up" to higher levels for subsequent reporting and tracking purposes. The cost and accuracy of bottom-up cost estimating is typically influenced by the size and complexity of the individual activity or work package.

.5 Three-Point Estimates

The accuracy of single-point activity cost estimates can be improved by considering estimation uncertainty and risk. This concept originated with the program evaluation and review technique (PERT). PERT uses three estimates to define an approximate range for an activity's cost:

- **Most likely (c_M).** The cost of the activity, based on realistic effort assessment for the required work and any predicted expenses.

- **Optimistic (c_O).** The activity cost based on analysis of the best-case scenario for the activity.

- **Pessimistic (c_P).** The activity cost based on analysis of the worst-case scenario for the activity.

PERT analysis calculated an expected (c_E) activity cost using a weighted average of these three estimates:

$$c_E = \frac{c_O + 4c_M + c_P}{6}$$

Cost estimates based on this equation (or even on a simple average of the three points) may provide more accuracy, and the three points clarify the range of uncertainty of the cost estimates.

.6 Reserve Analysis

Cost estimates may include contingency reserves (sometimes called contingency allowances) to account for cost uncertainty. The contingency reserve may be a percentage of the estimated cost, a fixed number, or may be developed by using quantitative analysis methods.

As more precise information about the project becomes available, the contingency reserve may be used, reduced or eliminated. Contingency should be clearly identified in cost documentation. Contingency reserves are part of the funding requirements.

.7 Cost of Quality (COQ)

Assumptions about costs of quality (Section 8.1.2.2) may be used to prepare the activity cost estimate.

.8 Project Management Estimating Software

Project management cost estimating software applications, computerized spreadsheets, simulation, and statistical tools are becoming more widely accepted to assist with cost estimating. Such tools can simplify the use of some cost estimating techniques and thereby facilitate rapid consideration of cost estimate alternatives.

.9 Vendor Bid Analysis

Cost estimating methods may include analysis of what the project should cost, based on the responsive bids from qualified vendors. Where projects are awarded to a vendor under competitive processes, additional cost estimating work can be required of the project team to examine the price of individual deliverables and to derive a cost that supports the final total project cost.

7.1.3 Estimate Costs: Outputs

.1 Activity Cost Estimates

Activity cost estimates are quantitative assessments of the probable costs required to complete project work. Cost estimates can be presented in summary form or in detail. Costs are estimated for all resources that are applied to the activity cost estimate. This includes, but is not limited to, direct labor, materials, equipment, services, facilities, information technology, and special categories such as an inflation allowance or a cost contingency reserve. Indirect costs, if they are included in the project estimate, can be included at the activity level or at higher levels.

.2 Basis of Estimates

The amount and type of additional details supporting the cost estimate vary by application area. Regardless of the level of detail, the supporting documentation should provide a clear and complete understanding of how the cost estimate was derived.

Supporting detail for activity cost estimates may include:

- Documentation of the basis of the estimate (i.e., how it was developed),
- Documentation of all assumptions made,
- Documentation of any known constraints,
- Indication of the range of possible estimates (e.g., $10,000 (±10%) to indicate that the item is expected to cost between a range of values), and
- Indication of the confidence level of the final estimate.

.3 Project Document Updates

Project documents that may be updated include, but are not limited to, the risk register.

7.2 Determine Budget

Determine Budget is the process of aggregating the estimated costs of individual activities or work packages to establish an authorized cost baseline. This baseline includes all authorized budgets, but excludes management reserves. See Figures 7-4 and 7-5.

Project budgets constitute the funds authorized to execute the project. Project cost performance will be measured against the authorized budget.

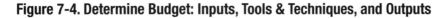

Figure 7-4. Determine Budget: Inputs, Tools & Techniques, and Outputs

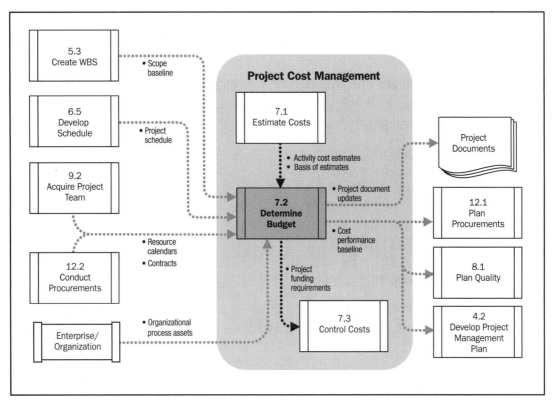

Figure 7-5. Determine Budget Data Flow Diagram

Figure 7-5. Determine Budget Data Flow Diagram

7.2.1 Determine Budget: Inputs

.1 Activity Cost Estimates

Cost estimates (Section 7.1.3.1) for each activity within a work package are aggregated to obtain a cost estimate for each work package.

.2 Basis of Estimates

Supporting detail for cost estimates should be specified as described in Section 7.1.3.2. Any basic assumptions dealing with the inclusion or exclusion of indirect costs in the project budget are specified in the basis of estimates.

.3 Scope Baseline

- **Scope Statement.** Formal limitations by period for the expenditure of project funds can be mandated by the organization, by contract (Section 12.2.3.2) or by other entities such as government agencies. These funding constraints are reflected in the project scope statement.

- **Work breakdown structure.** The project WBS (Section 5.3.3.1) provides the relationships among all the project deliverables and their various components.

- **WBS dictionary.** The WBS dictionary (Section 5.3.3.2) and related detailed statements of work provide an identification of the deliverables and a description of the work in each WBS component required to produce each deliverable.

.4 Project Schedule

The project schedule (Section 6.5.3.1), as part of the project management plan, includes planned start and finish dates for the project's activities, milestones, work packages, planning packages, and control accounts. This information can be used to aggregate costs to the calendar periods in which the costs are planned to be incurred.

.5 Resource Calendars

Resource calendars provide information on which resources are assigned to the project and when they are assigned. This information can be used to indicate resource costs over the duration of the project.

.6 Contracts

Applicable contract information and costs relating to products, services, or results that have been purchased are included when determining the budget.

.7 Organizational Process Assets

The organizational process assets that influence the Determine Budget process include, but are not limited to:

- Existing formal and informal cost budgeting-related policies, procedures, and guidelines,

- Cost budgeting tools, and

- Reporting methods.

7.2.2 Determine Budget: Tools and Techniques

.1 Cost Aggregation

Cost estimates are aggregated by work packages in accordance with the WBS. The work package cost estimates are then aggregated for the higher component levels of the WBS (such as control accounts) and ultimately for the entire project.

.2 Reserve Analysis

Budget reserve analysis can establish both the contingency reserves and the management reserves for the project. Contingency reserves are allowances for unplanned but potentially required changes that can result from realized risks identified in the risk register. Management reserves are budgets reserved for unplanned changes to project scope and cost. The project manager may be required to obtain approval before obligating or spending management reserve. Management reserves are not a part of the project cost baseline, but may be included in the total budget for the project. They are not included as a part of the earned value measurement calculations.

.3 Expert Judgment

Judgment provided based upon expertise in an application area, Knowledge Area, discipline, industry, etc., as appropriate for the activity being performed should be used in determining the budget. Such expertise may be provided by any group or person with specialized education, knowledge, skill, experience, or training. Expert judgment is available from many sources, including, but not limited to:

- Other units within the performing organization,

- Consultants,

- Stakeholders, including customers,

- Professional and technical associations, and

- Industry groups.

.4 Historical Relationships

Any historical relationships that result in parametric estimates or analogous estimates involve the use of project characteristics (parameters) to develop mathematical models to predict total project costs. Such models can be simple (e.g., residential home construction is based on a certain cost per square foot of space) or complex (e.g., one model of software development costing uses multiple separate adjustment factors, each of which has numerous points within it).

Both the cost and accuracy of analogous and parametric models can vary widely. They are most likely to be reliable when:

- Historical information used to develop the model is accurate,

- Parameters used in the model are readily quantifiable, and

- Models are scalable, such that they work for a large project, a small project, and phases of a project.

.5 Funding Limit Reconciliation

The expenditure of funds should be reconciled with any funding limits on the commitment of funds for the project. A variance between the funding limits and the planned expenditures will sometimes necessitate the rescheduling of work to level out the rate of expenditures. This can be accomplished by placing imposed date constraints for work into the project schedule.

7.2.3   Determine Budget: Outputs

.1   Cost Performance Baseline

The cost performance baseline is an authorized time-phased budget at completion (BAC) used to measure, monitor, and control overall cost performance on the project. It is developed as a summation of the approved budgets by time period and is typically displayed in the form of an S-curve, as is illustrated in Figure 7-6. In the earned value management technique the cost performance baseline is referred to as the performance measurement baseline (PMB).

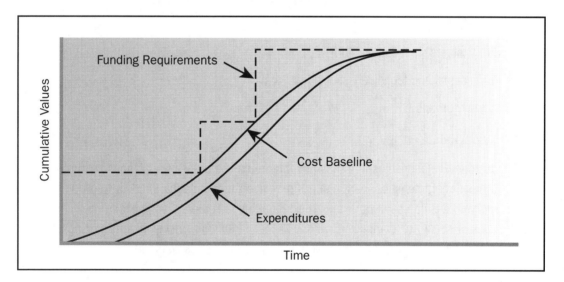

Figure 7-6. Cost Baseline, Expenditures, and Funding Requirements

.2 Project Funding Requirements

Total funding requirements and periodic funding requirements (e.g., quarterly, annually) are derived from the cost baseline. The cost baseline will include projected expenditures plus anticipated liabilities. Funding often occurs in incremental amounts that are not continuous, which appear as steps as shown in Figure 7-6. The total funds required are those included in the cost baseline, plus management reserves, if any.

.3 Project Document Updates

Project documents that may be updated include but are not limited to:

- Risk register,
- Cost estimates, and
- Project schedule.

7.3 Control Costs

Control Costs is the process of monitoring the status of the project to update the project budget and managing changes to the cost baseline. See Figures 7-7 and 7-8. Updating the budget involves recording actual costs spent to date. Any increase to the authorized budget can only be approved through the Perform Integrated Change Control process (Section 4.5). Monitoring the expenditure of funds without regard to the value of work being accomplished for such expenditures has little value to the project other than to allow the project team to stay within the authorized funding. Thus much of the effort of cost control involves analyzing the relationship between the consumption of project funds to the physical work being accomplished for such expenditures. The key to effective cost control is the management of the approved cost performance baseline and the changes to that baseline.

Project cost control includes:

- Influencing the factors that create changes to the authorized cost baseline,
- Ensuring that all change requests are acted on in a timely manner,
- Managing the actual changes when and as they occur,
- Ensuring that cost expenditures do not exceed the authorized funding, by period and in total for the project,
- Monitoring cost performance to isolate and understand variances from the approved cost baseline,
- Monitoring work performance against funds expended,

- Preventing unapproved changes from being included in the reported cost or resource usage,

- Informing appropriate stakeholders of all approved changes and associated cost, and

- Acting to bring expected cost overruns within acceptable limits.

Project cost control seeks out the causes of positive and negative variances and is part of the Perform Integrated Change Control process (Section 4.5).

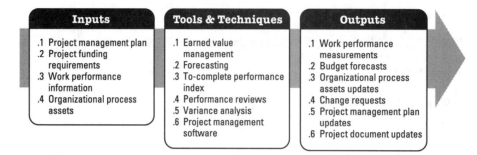

Inputs	Tools & Techniques	Outputs
.1 Project management plan .2 Project funding requirements .3 Work performance information .4 Organizational process assets	.1 Earned value management .2 Forecasting .3 To-complete performance index .4 Performance reviews .5 Variance analysis .6 Project management software	.1 Work performance measurements .2 Budget forecasts .3 Organizational process assets updates .4 Change requests .5 Project management plan updates .6 Project document updates

Figure 7-7. Control Costs: Inputs, Tools & Techniques, and Outputs

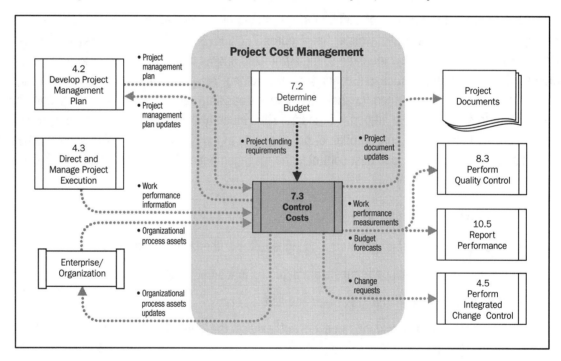

Figure 7-8. Control Costs Data Flow Diagram

7.3.1 Control Costs: Inputs

.1 Project Management Plan

The project management plan described in Section 4.2.3.1 contains the following information that is used to control cost:

- **Cost Performance baseline.** The cost performance baseline is compared with actual results to determine if a change, corrective action or preventive action is necessary.

- **Cost management plan.** The cost management plan describes how the project costs will be managed and controlled (Introduction to Chapter 7).

.2 Project Funding Requirements

Project funding requirements are described in Section 7.2.3.2.

.3 Work Performance Information

Work performance information includes information about project progress, such as which deliverables have started, their progress and which deliverables have finished. Information also includes costs that have been authorized and incurred, and estimates for completing project work.

4 Organizational Process Assets

The organizational process assets that can influence the Control Costs process include, but are not limited to:

- Existing formal and informal cost control-related policies, procedures, and guidelines;

- Cost control tools; and

- Monitoring and reporting methods to be used.

7.3.2 Control Costs: Tools and Techniques

.1 Earned Value Management

Earned value management (EVM) in its various forms is a commonly used method of performance measurement. It integrates project scope, cost, and schedule measures to help the project management team assess and measure project performance and progress. It is a project management technique that requires the formation of an integrated baseline against which performance can be measured for the duration of the project. The principles of EVM can be applied to all projects, in any industry. EVM develops and monitors three key dimensions for each work package and control account:

- **Planned value.** Planned value (PV) is the authorized budget assigned to the work to be accomplished for an activity or work breakdown structure component. It includes the detailed authorized work, plus the budget for such authorized work, allocated by phase over the life of the project. The total of the PV is sometimes referred to as the performance measurement baseline (PMB). The total planned value for the project is also known as Budget At Completion (BAC).

- **Earned value.** Earned value (EV) is the value of work performed expressed in terms of the approved budget assigned to that work for an activity or work breakdown structure component. It is the authorized work that has been completed, plus the authorized budget for such completed work. The EV being measured must be related to the PV baseline (PMB), and the EV measured cannot be greater than the authorized PV budget for a component. The term EV is often used to describe the percentage completion of a project. A progress measurement criteria should be established for each WBS component to measure work in progress. Project managers monitor EV, both incrementally to determine current status and cumulatively to determine the long-term performance trends.

- **Actual cost.** Actual cost (AC) is the total cost actually incurred and recorded in accomplishing work performed for an activity or work breakdown structure component. It is the total cost incurred in accomplishing the work that the EV measured. The AC has to correspond in definition to whatever was budgeted for in the PV and measured in the EV (e.g., direct hours only, direct costs only, or all costs including indirect costs). The AC will have no upper limit; whatever is spent to achieve the EV will be measured.

Variances from the approved baseline will also be monitored:

- **Schedule variance.** Schedule variance (SV) is a measure of schedule performance on a project. It is equal to the earned value (EV) minus the planned value (PV). The EVM schedule variance is a useful metric in that it can indicate a project falling behind its baseline schedule. The EVM schedule variance will ultimately equal zero when the project is completed because all of the planned values will have been earned. EVM SVs are best used in conjunction with critical path methodology (CPM) scheduling and risk management. Equation: $SV = EV - PV$.

- **Cost variance.** Cost variance (CV) is a measure of cost performance on a project. It is equal to the earned value (EV) minus the actual costs (AC). The cost variance at the end of the project will be the difference between the budget at completion (BAC) and the actual amount spent. The EVM CV is particularly critical because it indicates the relationship of physical performance to the costs spent. Any negative EVM CV is often non-recoverable to the project. Equation: $CV = EV - AC$.

The SV and CV values can be converted to efficiency indicators to reflect the cost and schedule performance of any project for comparison against all other projects or within a portfolio of projects. The variances and indices are useful for determining project status and providing a basis for estimating project cost and schedule outcome.

- **Schedule performance index.** The schedule performance index (SPI) is a measure of progress achieved compared to progress planned on a project. It is sometimes used in conjunction with the cost performance index (CPI) to forecast the final project completion estimates. An SPI value less than 1.0 indicates less work was completed than was planned. An SPI greater than 1.0 indicates that more work was completed than was planned. Since the SPI measures all project work, the performance on the critical path must also be analyzed to determine whether the project will finish ahead of or behind its planned finish date. The SPI is equal to the ratio of the EV to the PV. Equation: SPI = EV/PV.

- **Cost performance index.** The cost performance index (CPI) is a measure of the value of work completed compared to the actual cost or progress made on the project. It is considered the most critical EVM metric and measures the cost efficiency for the work completed. A CPI value less than 1.0 indicates a cost overrun for work completed. A CPI value greater than 1.0 indicates a cost underrun of performance to date. The CPI is equal to the ratio of the EV to the AC. Equation: CPI = EV/AC.

The three parameters of planned value, earned value, and actual cost can be monitored and reported on both a period-by-period basis (typically weekly or monthly) and on a cumulative basis. Figure 7-9 uses S-curves to display EV data for a project that is performing over budget and behind the work plan.

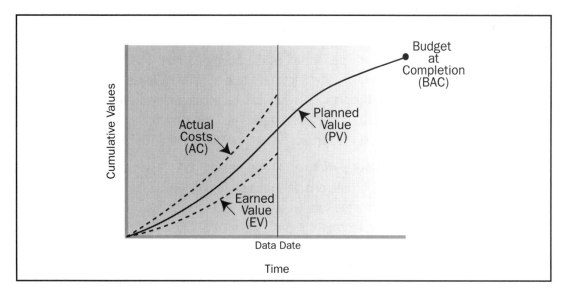

Figure 7-9. Earned Value, Planned Value, and Actual Costs

.2 Forecasting

As the project progresses, the project team can develop a forecast for the estimate at completion (EAC) that may differ from the budget at completion (BAC) based on the project performance. If it becomes obvious that the BAC is no longer viable, the project manager should develop a forecasted EAC. Forecasting the EAC involves making estimates or predictions of conditions and events in the project's future based on information and knowledge available at the time of the forecast. Forecasts are generated, updated, and reissued based on work performance information (Section 4.3.3.2) provided as the project is executed. The work performance information covers the project's past performance and any information that could impact the project in the future.

EACs are typically based on the actual costs incurred for work completed, plus an estimate to complete (ETC) the remaining work. It is incumbent on the project team to predict what it may encounter to perform the ETC, based on its experience to date. The EVM method works well in conjunction with manual forecasts of the required EAC costs. The most common EAC forecasting approach is a manual, bottom-up summation by the project manager and project team.

The project manager's bottom-up EAC method builds upon the actual costs and experience incurred for the work completed, and requires a new estimate to complete the remaining project work. This method may be problematic in that it interferes with the conduct of project work. The personnel who are performing the project work have to stop working to provide a detailed bottom-up ETC of the remaining work. Typically there is no separate budget to perform the ETC, so additional costs are incurred for the project to conduct the ETC. Equation: EAC = AC + bottom-up ETC.

The project manager's manual EAC can be quickly compared with a range of calculated EACs representing various risk scenarios. While EVM data can quickly provide many statistical EACs, only three of the more common methods are described as follows:

- **EAC forecast for ETC work performed at the budgeted rate.** This EAC method accepts the actual project performance to date (whether favorable or unfavorable) as represented by the actual costs, and predicts that all future ETC work will be accomplished at the budgeted rate. When actual performance is unfavorable, the assumption that future performance will improve should be accepted only when supported by project risk analysis. Equation: EAC = AC + BAC – EV.

- **EAC forecast for ETC work performed at the present CPI.** This method assumes what the project has experienced to date can be expected to continue in the future. The ETC work is assumed to be performed at the same cumulative cost performance index (CPI) as that incurred by the project to date. Equation: EAC = BAC / cumulative CPI.

- **EAC forecast for ETC work considering both SPI and CPI factors.** In this forecast, the ETC work will be performed at an efficiency rate that considers both the cost and schedule performance indices. It assumes both a negative cost performance to date, and a requirement to meet a firm schedule commitment by the project. This method is most useful when the project schedule is a factor impacting the ETC effort. Variations of this method weigh the CPI and SPI at different values (e.g., 80/20, 50/50, or some other ratio) according to the project manager's judgment. Equation: AC + [(BAC – EV) / (cumulative CPI x cumulative SPI)].

Each of these approaches can be correct for any given project and will provide the project management team with an "early warning" signal if the EAC forecasts are not within acceptable tolerances.

.3 To-Complete Performance Index (TCPI)

The to-complete performance index (TCPI) is the calculated projection of cost performance that must be achieved on the remaining work to meet a specified management goal, such as the BAC or the EAC. If it becomes obvious that the BAC is no longer viable, the project manager develops a forecasted estimate at completion (EAC). Once approved, the EAC effectively supersedes the BAC as the cost performance goal. Equation for the TCPI based on the BAC: (BAC – EV) / (BAC – AC).

The TCPI is conceptually displayed in Figure 7-10. The equation for the TCPI is shown in the lower left as the work remaining (defined as the BAC minus the EV) divided by the funds remaining (which can be either the BAC minus the AC, or the EAC minus the AC).

If the cumulative CPI falls below the baseline plan (as shown in Figure 7-10), all future work of the project will need to immediately be performed in the range of the TCPI (BAC) (as reflected in the top line of Figure 7-10) to stay within the authorized BAC. Whether this level of performance is achievable is a judgment call based on a number of considerations, including risks, schedule, and technical performance. Once management acknowledges that the BAC is no longer attainable, the project manager will prepare a new estimate at completion (EAC) for the work, and once approved, the project will work to the new EAC value. This level of performance is displayed as the TCPI (EAC) line. The equation for the TCPI based on the EAC: (BAC – EV) / (EAC – AC).

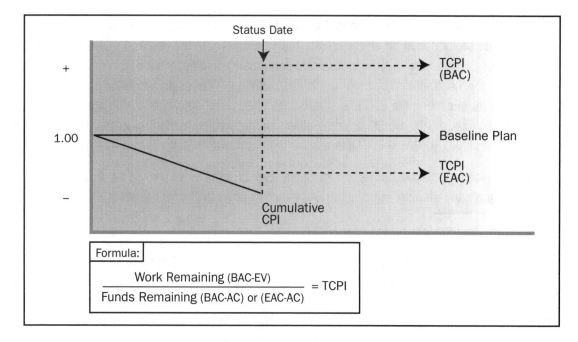

Figure 7-10. To-Complete Performance Index (TCPI)

.4 Performance Reviews

Performance reviews compare cost performance over time, schedule activities or work packages overrunning and under running the budget, and estimated funds needed to complete work in progress. If EVM is being used, the following information is determined:

- **Variance analysis.** Variance analysis as used in EVM compares actual project performance to planned or expected performance. Cost and schedule variances are the most frequently analyzed.

- **Trend analysis.** Trend analysis examines project performance over time to determine if performance is improving or deteriorating. Graphical analysis techniques are valuable for understanding performance to date and for comparison to future performance goals in the form of BAC versus EAC and completion dates.

- **Earned value performance.** Earned value management compares the baseline plan to actual schedule and cost performance.

.5 Variance Analysis

Cost performance measurements (CV, CPI) are used to assess the magnitude of variation to the original cost baseline. Important aspects of project cost control include determining the cause and degree of variance relative to the cost performance baseline (Section 7.2.3.1) and deciding whether corrective or preventive action is required. The percentage range of acceptable variances will tend to decrease as more work is accomplished. The larger percentage variances allowed at the start of the project can decrease as the project nears completion.

.6 Project Management Software

Project management software is often used to monitor the three EVM dimensions (PV, EV, and AC), to display graphical trends, and to forecast a range of possible final project results.

7.3.3 Control Costs: Outputs

.1 Work Performance Measurements

The calculated CV, SV, CPI, and SPI values for WBS components, in particular the work packages and control accounts, are documented and communicated to stakeholders.

.2 Budget Forecasts

Either a calculated EAC value or a bottom-up EAC value is documented and communicated to stakeholders.

.3 Organizational Process Assets Updates

Organizational process assets that may be updated include, but are not limited to:

- Causes of variances,
- Corrective action chosen and the reasons, and
- Other types of lessons learned from project cost control.

.4 Change Requests

Analysis of project performance can result in a change request to the cost performance baseline or other components of the project management plan. Change requests can include preventive or corrective actions and are processed for review and disposition through the Perform Integrated Change Control process (Section 4.5).

.5 Project Management Plan Updates

Elements of the project management plan that may be updated include, but are not limited to:

- **Cost performance baseline.** Changes to the cost performance baseline are incorporated in response to approved changes in scope, activity resources, or cost estimates. In some cases, cost variances can be so severe that a revised cost baseline is needed to provide a realistic basis for performance measurement.

- **Cost management plan.**

.6 Project Document Updates

Project documents that may be updated include, but are not limited to:

- Cost estimates, and
- Basis of estimates.

CHAPTER 8

PROJECT QUALITY MANAGEMENT

Project Quality Management includes the processes and activities of the performing organization that determine quality policies, objectives, and responsibilities so that the project will satisfy the needs for which it was undertaken. It implements the quality management system through policy and procedures with continuous process improvement activities conducted throughout, as appropriate.

Figure 8-1 provides an overview of the Project Quality Management processes which include the following:

8.1 Plan Quality—The process of identifying quality requirements and/or standards for the project and product, and documenting how the project will demonstrate compliance.

8.2 Perform Quality Assurance—The process of auditing the quality requirements and the results from quality control measurements to ensure appropriate quality standards and operational definitions are used.

8.3 Perform Quality Control—The process of monitoring and recording results of executing the quality activities to assess performance and recommend necessary changes.

These processes interact with each other and with the processes in the other Knowledge Areas. Each process can involve effort from one or more persons or groups based on the project requirements. Each process occurs at least once in every project and occurs in one or more of the project phases, if the project is divided into phases. Although the processes are presented here as discrete elements with well-defined interfaces, in practice they may overlap and interact in ways not detailed here. Process interactions are discussed in detail in Chapter 3.

Project Quality Management addresses the management of the project and the product of the project. It applies to all projects, regardless of the nature of their product. Product quality measures and techniques are specific to the type of product produced by the project. While quality management of software products uses different approaches and measures than building a nuclear power plant, Project Quality Management approaches apply to both. In either case, failure to meet product or project quality requirements can have serious negative consequences for any or all of the project stakeholders. For example:

- Meeting customer requirements by overworking the project team may result in increased employee attrition, errors, or rework.

- Meeting project schedule objectives by rushing planned quality inspections may result in undetected errors.

Quality and grade are not the same. Quality is "the degree to which a set of inherent characteristics fulfill requirements [4]." Grade is a category assigned to products or services having the same functional use but different technical characteristics [5]. While a quality level that fails to meet quality requirements is always a problem, low grade may not be. For example, a software product can be of high quality (no obvious defects, readable manual) and low grade (a limited number of features), or of low quality (many defects, poorly organized user documentation) and high grade (numerous features). The project manager and the project management team are responsible for managing the tradeoffs involved to deliver the required levels of both quality and grade.

Precision and accuracy are not equivalent. Precision means the values of repeated measurements are clustered and have little scatter. Accuracy means that the measured value is very close to the true value. Precise measurements are not necessarily accurate. A very accurate measurement is not necessarily precise. The project management team must determine appropriate levels of accuracy and precision.

The basic approach to quality management described in this section is intended to be compatible with that of the International Organization for Standardization (ISO). This is compatible with proprietary approaches to quality management such as those recommended by Deming, Juran, Crosby, and others, and non-proprietary approaches such as Total Quality Management (TQM), Six Sigma, failure mode and effect analysis (FMEA), design reviews, voice of the customer, cost of quality (COQ), and continuous improvement.

Modern quality management complements project management. Both disciplines recognize the importance of:

- **Customer satisfaction.** Understanding, evaluating, defining, and managing expectations so that customer requirements are met. This requires a combination of conformance to requirements (to ensure the project produces what it was created to produce) and fitness for use (the product or service must satisfy real needs).

- **Prevention over inspection.** One of the fundamental tenets of modern quality management states that quality is planned, designed, and built in—not inspected in. The cost of preventing mistakes is generally much less than the cost of correcting them when they are found by inspection.

- **Continuous improvement.** The plan-do-check-act cycle is the basis for quality improvement as defined by Shewhart and modified by Deming. In addition, quality improvement initiatives undertaken by the performing organization, such as TQM and Six Sigma, should improve the quality of the project's management as well as the quality of the project's product. Process improvement models include Malcolm Baldrige, Organizational Project Management Maturity Model (OPM3®), and Capability Maturity Model Integrated (CMMI®).

- **Management Responsibility.** Success requires the participation of all members of the project team, but remains the responsibility of management to provide the resources needed to succeed.

Cost of quality (COQ) refers to the total cost of all efforts related to quality throughout the product life cycle. Project decisions can impact operational costs of quality as a result of product returns, warranty claims, and recall campaigns. Therefore, due to the temporary nature of a project, the sponsoring organization may choose to invest in product quality improvement, especially defect prevention and appraisal, to reduce the external cost of quality.

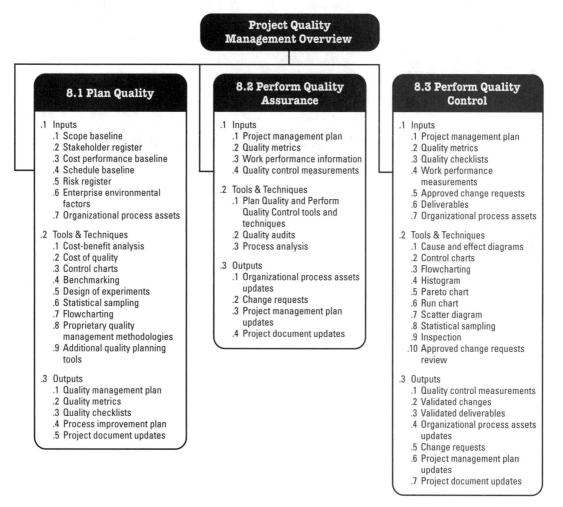

Figure 8-1. Project Quality Management Overview

8.1 Plan Quality

Plan Quality is the process of identifying quality requirements and/or standards for the project and product, and documenting how the project will demonstrate compliance. See Figures 8-2 and 8-3.

Quality planning should be performed in parallel with the other project planning processes. For example, proposed changes in the product to meet identified quality standards may require cost or schedule adjustments and a detailed risk analysis of the impact to plans.

The quality planning techniques discussed here are those most frequently used on projects. There are many others that may be useful on certain projects or in some application areas.

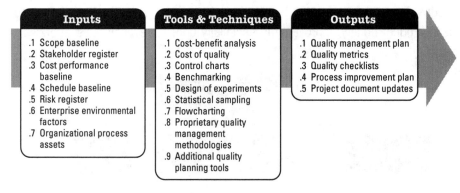

Inputs	Tools & Techniques	Outputs
.1 Scope baseline	.1 Cost-benefit analysis	.1 Quality management plan
.2 Stakeholder register	.2 Cost of quality	.2 Quality metrics
.3 Cost performance baseline	.3 Control charts	.3 Quality checklists
.4 Schedule baseline	.4 Benchmarking	.4 Process improvement plan
.5 Risk register	.5 Design of experiments	.5 Project document updates
.6 Enterprise environmental factors	.6 Statistical sampling	
.7 Organizational process assets	.7 Flowcharting	
	.8 Proprietary quality management methodologies	
	.9 Additional quality planning tools	

Figure 8-2. Plan Quality Inputs, Tools & Techniques, and Outputs

8.1.1 Plan Quality: Inputs

.1 Scope Baseline

- **Scope statement.** The scope statement contains the project description, major project deliverables, and acceptance criteria. The product scope description will often contain details of technical issues and other concerns that can affect quality planning. The definition of acceptance criteria can significantly increase or decrease project costs and quality costs. Satisfying all acceptance criteria implies the needs of the customer have been met.

- **WBS.** The WBS identifies the deliverables, the work packages and the control accounts used to measure project performance.

- **WBS Dictionary.** The WBS dictionary defines technical information for WBS elements.

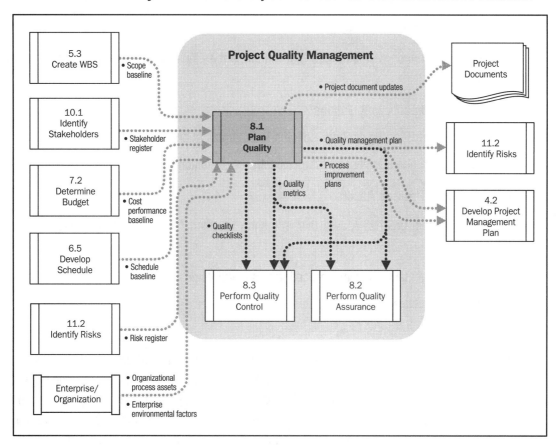

Figure 8-3. Plan Quality Data Flow Diagram

.2 Stakeholder Register

The stakeholder register identifies stakeholders with a particular interest in, or impact on, quality.

.3 Cost Performance Baseline

The cost performance baseline documents the accepted time phase used to measure cost performance (Section 7.2.3.1).

.4 Schedule Baseline

The schedule baseline documents the accepted schedule performance measures including start and finish dates (Section 6.5.3.2).

.5 Risk Register

The risk register contains information on threats and opportunities that may impact quality requirements (Section 11.2.3.1).

.6 Enterprise Environmental Factors

The enterprise environmental factors that influence the Plan Quality process include, but are not limited to:

- Governmental agency regulations,

- Rules, standards, and guidelines specific to the application area, and

- Working/operating conditions of the project/product which may affect project quality.

.7 Organizational Process Assets

The organizational process assets that influence the Plan Quality process include, but are not limited to:

- Organizational quality policies, procedures, and guidelines,

- Historical databases,

- Lessons learned from previous projects, and

- Quality policy, as endorsed by senior management, which sets the intended direction of a performing organization with regard to quality. The quality policy of the performing organization for their products often can be adopted "as is" for use by the project. If the performing organization lacks a formal quality policy, or if the project involves multiple performing organizations (as with a joint venture), the project management team will need to develop a quality policy for the project. Regardless of the origin of the quality policy, the project management team must ensure that the project stakeholders are fully aware of the policy used for the project through the appropriate distribution of information.

8.1.2 Plan Quality: Tools and Techniques

.1 Cost-Benefit Analysis

The primary benefits of meeting quality requirements can include less rework, higher productivity, lower costs, and increased stakeholder satisfaction. A business case for each quality activity compares the cost of the quality step to the expected benefit.

.2 Cost of Quality (COQ)

Cost of quality includes all costs incurred over the life of the product by investment in preventing nonconformance to requirements, appraising the product or service for conformance to requirements, and failing to meet requirements (rework). Failure costs are often categorized into internal (found by the project) and external (found by the customer). Failure costs are also called cost of poor quality. Figure 8-4 provides some examples to consider in each area.

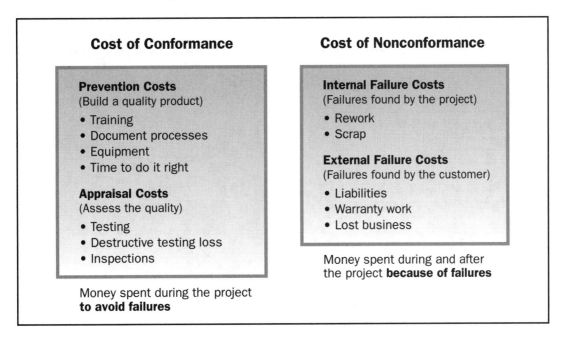

Figure 8-4. Cost of Quality

.3 Control Charts

Control charts are used to determine whether or not a process is stable or has predictable performance. Upper and lower specification limits are based on requirements of the contract. They reflect the maximum and minimum values allowed. There may be penalties associated with exceeding the specification limits. Upper and lower control limits are set by the project manager and appropriate stakeholders to reflect the points at which corrective action will be taken to prevent exceeding specification limits. For repetitive processes, the control limits are generally $\pm 3\sigma$. A process is considered out of control when a data point exceeds a control limit or if seven consecutive points are above or below the mean.

Control charts can be used to monitor various types of output variables. Although used most frequently to track repetitive activities required for producing manufactured lots, control charts may also be used to monitor cost and schedule variances, volume, and frequency of scope changes, or other management results to help determine if the project management processes are in control. Figure 8-5 shows a control chart that tracks recorded project hours. Figure 8-6 shows measured product defects compared to fixed limits.

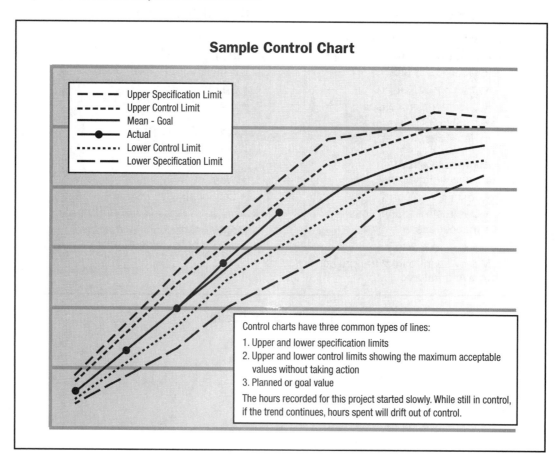

Figure 8-5. Sample Control Chart

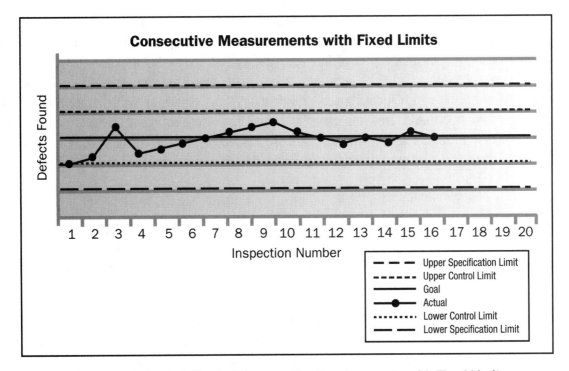

Figure 8-6. Control Chart of Consecutive Measurements with Fixed Limits

.4 Benchmarking

Benchmarking involves comparing actual or planned project practices to those of comparable projects to identify best practices, generate ideas for improvement, and provide a basis for measuring performance. These other projects can be within the performing organization or outside of it and can be within the same or in another application area.

.5 Design of Experiments

Design of experiments (DOE) is a statistical method for identifying which factors may influence specific variables of a product or process under development or in production. DOE should be used during the Plan Quality process to determine the number and type of tests and their impact on cost of quality.

DOE also plays a role in the optimization of products or processes. DOE can be used to reduce the sensitivity of product performance to sources of variations caused by environmental or manufacturing differences. One important aspect of this technique is that it provides a statistical framework for systematically changing all of the important factors, rather than changing the factors one at a time. Analysis of the experimental data should provide the optimal conditions for the product or process, highlight the factors that influence the results, and reveal the presence of interactions and synergy among the factors. For example, automotive designers use this technique to determine which combination of suspension and tires will produce the most desirable ride characteristics at a reasonable cost.

.6 Statistical Sampling

Statistical sampling involves choosing part of a population of interest for inspection (for example, selecting ten engineering drawings at random from a list of seventy-five). Sample frequency and sizes should be determined during the Plan Quality process so the cost of quality will include the number of tests, expected scrap, etc.

There is a substantial body of knowledge on statistical sampling. In some application areas it may be necessary for the project management team to be familiar with a variety of sampling techniques to assure the sample selected actually represents the population of interest.

.7 Flowcharting

A flowchart is a graphical representation of a process showing the relationships among process steps. There are many styles, but all process flowcharts show activities, decision points, and the order of processing. During quality planning, flowcharting can help the project team anticipate quality problems that might occur. An awareness of potential problems can result in the development of test procedures or approaches for dealing with them. Figure 8-7 is an example of a process flowchart for design reviews.

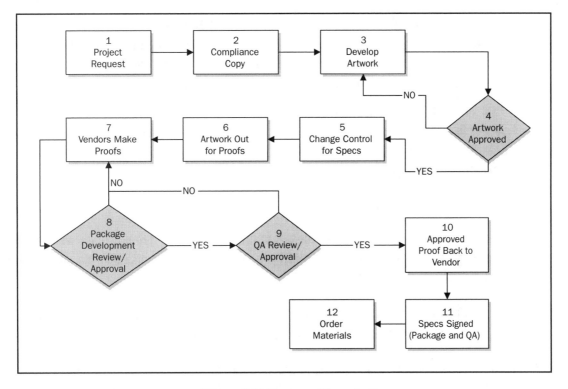

Figure 8-7. Process Flowchart

.8 Quality Management Methodologies

These include Six Sigma, Lean Six Sigma, Quality Function Deployment, CMMI®, etc. Many other methodologies exist—this is not intended to be a recommended or complete list of examples.

.9 Additional Quality Planning Tools

Other quality planning tools are often used to better define the quality requirements and plan effective quality management activities. These include, but are not limited to:

- **Brainstorming** (defined in Section 11.2.2.2).

- **Affinity diagrams,** used to visually identify logical groupings based on natural relationships.

- **Force field analysis,** which are diagrams of the forces for and against change.

- **Nominal group techniques,** to allow ideas to be brainstormed in small groups and then reviewed by a larger group.

- **Matrix diagrams,** which include two, three, or four groups of information and show relationships between factors, causes, and objectives. Data in a matrix is organized in rows and columns with intersecting cells that can be filled with information that describes the demonstrated relationship between the items located in the row and column.

- **Prioritization matrices,** which provide a way of ranking a diverse set of problems and/or issues (usually generated through brainstorming) by their importance.

8.1.3   Plan Quality: Outputs

.1   Quality Management Plan

The quality management plan describes how the project management team will implement the performing organization's quality policy. It is a component or a subsidiary plan of the project management plan (Section 4.2.3.1).

The quality management plan provides input to the overall project management plan and includes quality control, quality assurance, and continuous process improvement approaches for the project.

The quality management plan may be formal or informal, highly detailed, or broadly framed. The style and detail is determined by the requirements of the project. The quality management plan should be reviewed early in the project to ensure that decisions are based on accurate information. The benefits of this review can include reduction of cost and schedule overruns caused by rework.

.2   Quality Metrics

A quality metric is an operational definition that describes, in very specific terms, a project or product attribute and how the quality control process will measure it. A measurement is an actual value. The tolerance defines the allowable variations on the metrics. For example, a metric related to the quality objective of staying within the approved budget by ± 10% could be to measure the cost of every deliverable and determine the percent variance from the approved budget for that deliverable. Quality metrics are used in the quality assurance and quality control processes. Some examples of quality metrics include on-time performance, budget control, defect frequency, failure rate, availability, reliability, and test coverage.

.3 Quality Checklists

A checklist is a structured tool, usually component-specific, used to verify that a set of required steps has been performed. Checklists range from simple to complex based on project requirements and practices. Many organizations have standardized checklists available to ensure consistency in frequently performed tasks. In some application areas, checklists are also available from professional associations or commercial service providers. Quality checklists are used in the quality control process.

.4 Process Improvement Plan

The process improvement plan is a subsidiary of the project management plan (Section 4.2.3.1). The process improvement plan details the steps for analyzing processes to identify activities which enhance their value. Areas to consider include:

- **Process boundaries.** Describes the purpose of processes, their start and end, their inputs/ outputs, the data required, the owner, and the stakeholders.

- **Process configuration.** A graphic depiction of processes, with interfaces identified, used to facilitate analysis.

- **Process metrics.** Along with control limits, allows analysis of process efficiency.

- **Targets for improved performance.** Guides the process improvement activities.

.5 Project Document Updates

Project documents that may be updated include, but are not limited to:

- Stakeholder register, and

- Responsibility Assignment Matrix (Section 9.1.2.1).

8.2 Perform Quality Assurance

Perform Quality Assurance is the process of auditing the quality requirements and the results from quality control measurements to ensure appropriate quality standards and operational definitions are used. See Figures 8-8 and 8-9. Perform Quality Assurance is an execution process that uses data created during Perform Quality Control (Section 8.3).

A quality assurance department, or similar organization, often oversees quality assurance activities. Quality assurance support, regardless of the unit's title, may be provided to the project team, the management of the performing organization, the customer or sponsor, as well as other stakeholders not actively involved in the work of the project.

Perform Quality Assurance also provides an umbrella for continuous process improvement, which is an iterative means for improving the quality of all processes. Continuous process improvement reduces waste and eliminates activities that do not add value. This allows processes to operate at increased levels of efficiency and effectiveness.

Inputs	Tools & Techniques	Outputs
.1 Project management plan .2 Quality metrics .3 Work performance information .4 Quality control measurements	.1 Plan Quality and Perform Quality Control tools and techniques .2 Quality audits .3 Process analysis	.1 Organizational process assets updates .2 Change requests .3 Project management plan updates .4 Project document updates

Figure 8-8. Perform Quality Assurance: Inputs, Tools & Techniques, and Outputs

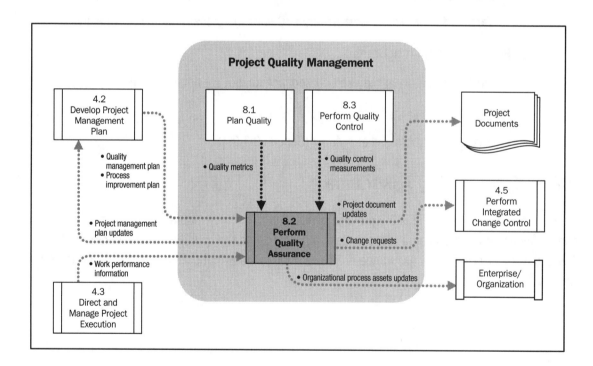

Figure 8-9. Perform Quality Assurance Data Flow Diagram

8.2.1 Perform Quality Assurance: Inputs

.1 Project Management Plan

The project management plan described in Section 4.2.3.1 contains the following information that is used to assure quality:

- **Quality management plan.** The quality management plan describes how quality assurance will be performed within the project.

- **Process improvement plan.** The process improvement plan details the steps for analyzing processes to identify activities which enhance their value.

.2 Quality Metrics

Described in Section 8.1.3.2.

.3 Work Performance Information

Performance information from project activities is routinely collected as the project progresses. Performance results which may support the audit process include, but are not limited to:

- Technical performance measures,

- Project deliverables status,

- Schedule progress, and

- Costs incurred.

.4 Quality Control Measurements

Quality control measurements are the results of quality control activities. They are used to analyze and evaluate the quality standards and processes of the performing organization (Section 8.3.3.1).

8.2.2 Perform Quality Assurance: Tools and Techniques

.1 Plan Quality and Perform Quality Control Tools and Techniques

Tools and techniques from Plan Quality and Perform Quality Control, are discussed in Section 8.1.2. Section 8.3.2 can also be used for quality assurance activities.

.2 Quality Audits

A quality audit is a structured, independent review to determine whether project activities comply with organizational and project policies, processes, and procedures. The objectives of a quality audit are:

- Identify all the good/best practices being implemented,

- Identify all the gaps/shortcomings,

- Share the good practices introduced or implemented in similar projects in the organization and/ or industry,

- Proactively offer assistance in a positive manner to improve implementation of processes to help the team raise productivity, and

- Highlight contributions of each audit in the lessons learned repository of the organization.

The subsequent effort to correct any deficiencies should result in a reduced cost of quality and an increase in sponsor or customer acceptance of the project's product. Quality audits may be scheduled or random and may be conducted by internal or external auditors.

Quality audits can confirm the implementation of approved change requests including corrective actions, defect repairs, and preventive actions.

.3 Process Analysis

Process analysis follows the steps outlined in the process improvement plan to identify needed improvements. This analysis also examines problems experienced, constraints experienced, and non-value-added activities identified during process operation. Process analysis includes root cause analysis—a specific technique to identify a problem, discover the underlying causes that lead to it, and develop preventive actions.

8.2.3 Perform Quality Assurance: Outputs

.1 Organizational Process Assets Updates

Elements of the organizational process assets that may be updated include, but are not limited to, the quality standards.

.2 Change Requests

Quality improvement includes taking action to increase the effectiveness and/or efficiency of the policies, processes, and procedures of the performing organization. Change requests are created and used as input into the Perform Integrated Change Control (Section 4.5) process to allow full consideration of the recommended improvements. Change requests can be used to take corrective action or preventive action or to perform defect repair.

.3 Project Management Plan Updates

Elements of the project management plan that may be updated include, but are not limited to:

- Quality management plan,
- Schedule management plan, and
- Cost management plan.

.4 Project Document Updates

Project documents that may be updated include, but are not limited to:

- Quality audits reports,
- Training plans, and
- Process documentation.

8.3 Perform Quality Control

Perform Quality Control is the process of monitoring and recording results of executing the quality activities to assess performance and recommend necessary changes. Quality control is performed throughout the project. Quality standards include project processes and product goals. Project results include deliverables and project management results, such as cost and schedule performance. Quality control is often performed by a quality control department or similarly titled organizational unit. Quality control activities identify causes of poor process or product quality and recommend and/or take action to eliminate them. See Figures 8-10 and 8-11.

The project management team should have a working knowledge of statistical quality control, especially sampling and probability, to help evaluate quality control outputs. Among other subjects, the team may find it useful to know the differences between the following pairs of terms:

- Prevention (keeping errors out of the process) and inspection (keeping errors out of the hands of the customer).

- Attribute sampling (the result either conforms or does not conform) and variables sampling (the result is rated on a continuous scale that measures the degree of conformity).

- Tolerances (specified range of acceptable results) and control limits (thresholds, which can indicate whether the process is out of control).

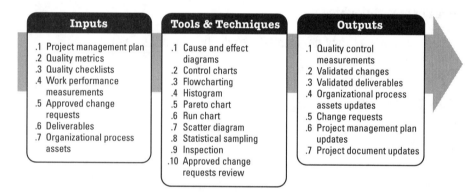

Figure 8-10. Perform Quality Control: Inputs, Tools & Techniques, and Outputs

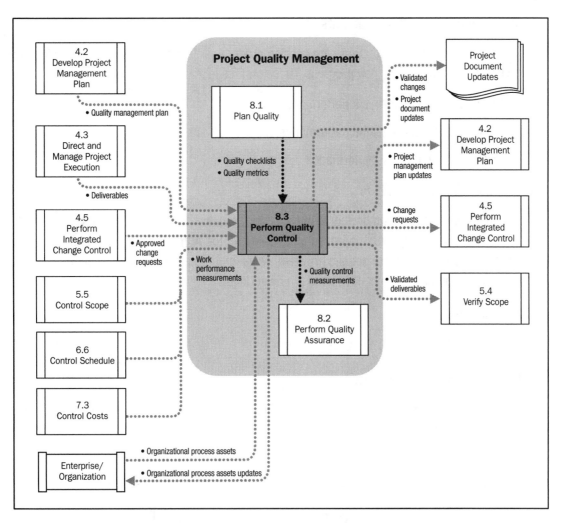

Figure 8-11. Perform Quality Control Data Flow Diagram

8.3.1 Perform Quality Control: Inputs

.1 Project Management Plan

The project management plan described in Section 4.2.3.1 contains the quality management plan, which is used to control quality. The quality management plan describes how quality control will be performed within the project.

.2 Quality Metrics

Described in Section 8.1.3.2.

.3 Quality Checklists

Described in Section 8.1.3.3.

.4 Work Performance Measurements

Work performance measurements are used to produce project activity metrics to evaluate actual progress as compared to planned progress. These metrics include, but are not limited to:

- Planned vs. actual technical performance,

- Planned vs. actual schedule performance, and

- Planned vs. actual cost performance.

.5 Approved Change Requests

As part of the Perform Integrated Change Control process a change control status update will indicate that some changes are approved and some are not. Approved change requests can include modifications such as defect repairs, revised work methods and revised schedule. The timely implementation of approved changes needs to be verified.

.6 Deliverables

Described in Section 4.3.3.1.

.7 Organizational Process Assets

The organizational process assets that can influence the Perform Quality Control process include, but are not limited to:

- Quality standards and policies,

- Standard work guidelines, and

- Issue and defect reporting procedures and communication policies.

8.3.2 Perform Quality Control: Tools and Techniques

The first seven of these tools and techniques are known as Ishikawa's seven basic tools of quality.

.1 Cause and Effect Diagrams

Cause and effect diagrams, also called Ishikawa diagrams or fishbone diagrams, illustrate how various factors might be linked to potential problems or effects. Figures 8-12 and 8-13 are examples of cause and effect diagrams. A possible root cause can be uncovered by continuing to ask "why" or "how" along one of the lines. "Why-Why" and "How-How" diagrams may be used in root cause analysis. Cause and effect diagrams are also used in risk analysis (Section 11.2.2.5).

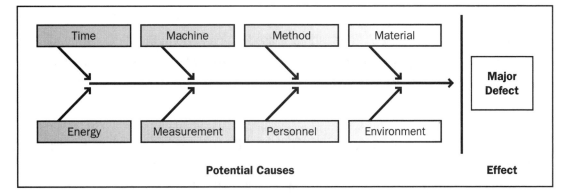

Figure 8-12. Classic Sources of Problems to Consider

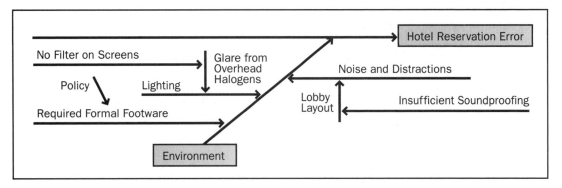

Figure 8-13. Environment Bone Expanded by Brainstorming

.2 Control Charts

Control charts are described in Section 8.1.2.3. In this tool, the appropriate data is collected and analyzed to indicate the quality status of project processes and products. Control charts illustrate how a process behaves over time and when a process is subject to special cause variation, resulting in an out-of-control condition. They graphically answer the question: "Is this process variance within acceptable limits?" The pattern of data points on a control chart may reveal random fluctuating values, sudden process jumps, or a gradual trend in increased variation. By monitoring the output of a process over time, a control chart can help assess whether the application of process changes resulted in the desired improvements.

When a process is within acceptable limits it is in control and does not need to be adjusted. Conversely, when a process is outside acceptable limits, the process should be adjusted. Seven consecutive points above or below the central line indicate a process that is out of control. The upper control limit and lower control limit are usually set at ±3σ, where 1σ is one standard deviation.

.3 Flowcharting

Described in Section 8.1.2.7, flowcharting is used during Perform Quality Control to determine a failing process step(s) and identify potential process improvement opportunities. Flowcharting is also used in risk analysis (Section 11.2.2.5).

.4 Histogram

A histogram is a vertical bar chart showing how often a particular variable state occurred. Each column represents an attribute or characteristic of a problem/situation. The height of each column represents the relative frequency of the characteristic. This tool helps illustrates the most common cause of problems in a process by the number and relative heights of the bars. Figure 8-14 is an example of an unordered histogram showing causes of late time entry by a project team.

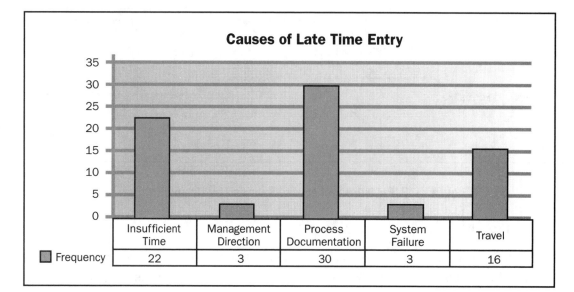

	Insufficient Time	Management Direction	Process Documentation	System Failure	Travel
Frequency	22	3	30	3	16

Figure 8-14. Histogram

.5 Pareto Chart

A Pareto chart, also referred to as a Pareto diagram, is a specific type of histogram, ordered by frequency of occurrence. It shows how many defects were generated by type or category of identified cause (Figure 8-15). Rank ordering is used to focus corrective action. The project team should address the causes creating the greatest number of defects first.

Pareto diagrams are conceptually related to Pareto's Law, which holds that a relatively small number of causes will typically produce a majority of the problems or defects. This is commonly referred to as the 80/20 principle, where 80% of the problems are due to 20% of the causes. Pareto diagrams can also be used to summarize various types of data for 80/20 analyses.

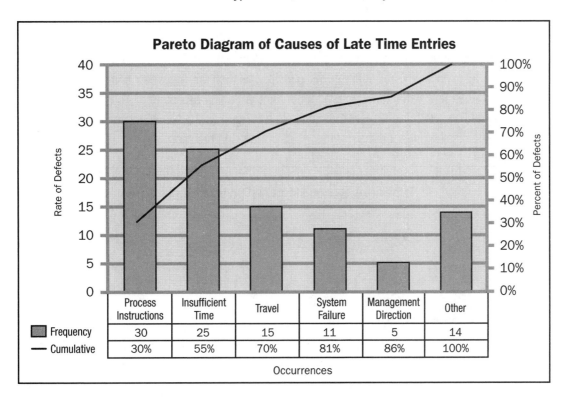

Pareto Diagram of Causes of Late Time Entries

	Process Instructions	Insufficient Time	Travel	System Failure	Management Direction	Other
Frequency	30	25	15	11	5	14
Cumulative	30%	55%	70%	81%	86%	100%

Occurrences

Figure 8-15. Pareto Diagram

.6 Run Chart

Similar to a control chart without displayed limits, a run chart shows the history and pattern of variation. A run chart is a line graph that shows data points plotted in the order in which they occur. Run charts show trends in a process over time, variation over time, or declines or improvements in a process over time. Trend analysis is performed using run charts and involves mathematical techniques to forecast future outcomes based on historical results. Trend analysis is often used to monitor:

- **Technical performance.** How many errors or defects have been identified, and how many remain uncorrected?

- **Cost and schedule performance.** How many activities per period were completed with significant variances?

.7 Scatter Diagram

A scatter diagram (Figure 8-16) shows the relationship between two variables. This tool allows the quality team to study and identify the possible relationship between changes observed in two variables. Dependent variables versus independent variables are plotted. The closer the points are to a diagonal line, the more closely they are related. Figure 8-16 shows the correlation between the timecard submission date and the number of days traveling per month.

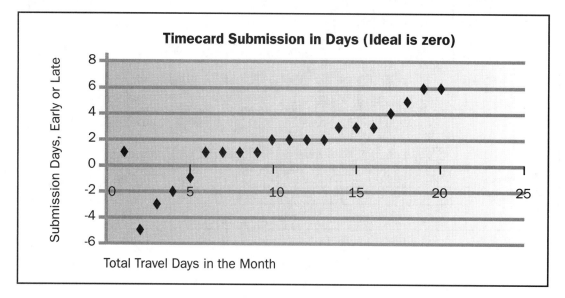

Figure 8-16. Scatter Diagram

.8 Statistical Sampling

Described in Section 8.1.2.6. Samples are selected and tested as defined in the quality plan.

.9 Inspection

An inspection is the examination of a work product to determine whether it conforms to documented standards. The results of an inspection generally include measurements and may be conducted at any level. For example, the results of a single activity can be inspected, or the final product of the project can be inspected. Inspections may be called reviews, peer reviews, audits, or walkthroughs. In some application areas, these terms have narrow and specific meanings. Inspections are also used to validate defect repairs.

.10 Approved Change Requests Review

All approved change requests should be reviewed to verify that they were implemented as approved.

8.3.3 Perform Quality Control: Outputs

.1 Quality Control Measurements

Quality control measurements are the documented results of quality control activities in the format specified during quality planning.

.2 Validated Changes

Any changed or repaired items are inspected and will be either accepted or rejected before notification of the decision is provided. Rejected items may require rework.

.3 Validated Deliverables

A goal of quality control is to determine the correctness of deliverables. The results of the execution quality control processes are validated deliverables. Validated deliverables are an input to Verify Scope (5.4.1.4) for formalized acceptance.

.4 Organizational Process Assets Updates

Elements of the organizational process assets that may be updated include, but are not limited to:

- **Completed checklists.** When checklists are used, the completed checklists become part of the project's records (Section 4.1.1.5).

- **Lessons learned documentation.** The causes of variances, the reasoning behind the corrective action chosen, and other types of lessons learned from quality control are documented so they become part of the historical database for both the project and the performing organization. Lessons learned are documented throughout the project life cycle, but at a minimum, during project closure.

.5 Change Requests

If the recommended corrective or preventive actions or a defect repair requires a change to the project management plan, a change request (Section 4.4.3.1) should be initiated in accordance with the defined Perform Integrated Change Control (4.5) process.

.6 Project Management Plan Updates

Elements of the project management plan that may be updated include, but are not limited to:

- Quality management plan, and
- Process improvement plan.

.7 Project Document Updates

Project documents that may be updated include, but are not limited to, quality standards.

CHAPTER 9

PROJECT HUMAN RESOURCE MANAGEMENT

Project Human Resource Management includes the processes that organize, manage, and lead the project team. The project team is comprised of the people with assigned roles and responsibilities for completing the project. The type and number of project team members can change frequently as the project progresses. Project team members may also be referred to as the project's staff. While the specific roles and responsibilities for the project team members are assigned, the involvement of all team members in project planning and decision making can be beneficial. Early involvement and participation of team members adds their expertise during the planning process and strengthens their commitment to the project.

Figure 9-1 provides an overview of the Project Human Resource Management processes, which are as follows:

9.1 Develop Human Resource Plan—The process of identifying and documenting project roles, responsibilities, and required skills, reporting relationships, and creating a staffing management plan.

9.2 Acquire Project Team—The process of confirming human resource availability and obtaining the team necessary to complete project assignments.

9.3 Develop Project Team—The process of improving the competencies, team interaction, and the overall team environment to enhance project performance.

9.4 Manage Project Team—The process of tracking team member performance, providing feedback, resolving issues, and managing changes to optimize project performance.

The project management team is a subset of the project team and is responsible for the project management and leadership activities such as initiating, planning, executing, monitoring, controlling, and closing the various project phases. This group can also be referred to as the core, executive, or leadership team. For smaller projects, the project management responsibilities can be shared by the entire team or administered solely by the project manager. The project sponsor works with the project management team, typically assisting with matters such as project funding, clarifying scope, monitoring progress, and influencing others in order to benefit the project.

Managing and leading the project team also includes, but is not limited to:

- **Influencing the project team.** Being aware of, and influencing when possible, those human resource factors that may impact the project. This includes team environment, geographical locations of team members, communications among stakeholders, internal and external politics, cultural issues, organizational uniqueness, and other such people factors that may alter the project performance.

- **Professional and ethical behavior.** The project management team should be aware of, subscribe to, and ensure that all team members follow ethical behavior.

The project management processes are usually presented as discrete processes with defined interfaces while, in practice, they overlap and interact in ways that cannot be completely detailed in the *PMBOK® Guide*. Examples of interactions that require additional planning include the following situations:

- After initial team members create a work breakdown structure, additional team members may need to be acquired.

- As additional team members are acquired, their experience levels, or lack thereof, could increase or decrease project risk, creating the need for additional risk planning updates.

- When activity durations are estimated, budgeted, scoped, or planned prior to identifying all project team members and their competency levels, the activity durations may be subject to change.

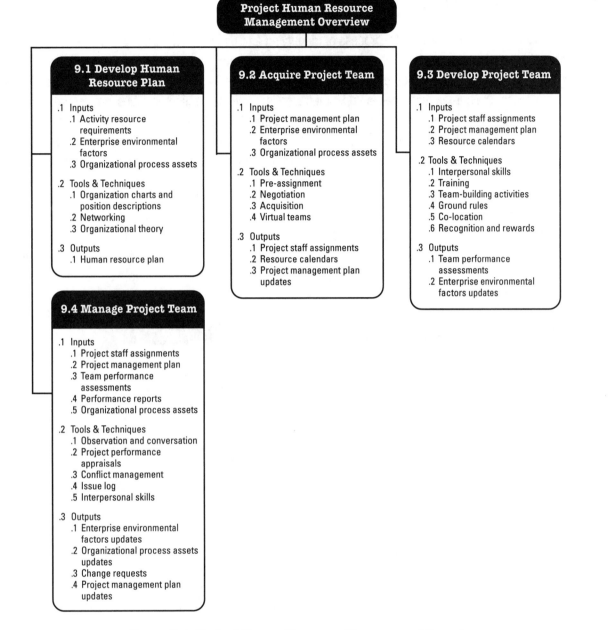

Figure 9-1. Project Human Resource Management Overview

9.1 Develop Human Resource Plan

Develop Human Resource Plan is the process of identifying and documenting project roles, responsibilities, and required skills, reporting relationships, and creating a staffing management plan. (See Figures 9-2 and 9-3). Human resource planning is used to determine and identify human resources with the necessary skills required for project success. The human resource plan documents project roles and responsibilities, project organization charts, and the staffing management plan including the timetable for staff acquisition and release. It may also include identification of training needs, team-building strategies, plans for recognition and rewards programs, compliance considerations, safety issues, and the impact of the staffing management plan on the organization.

Important consideration should be given to the availability of, or competition for, scarce or limited human resources. Project roles can be designated for persons or groups. Those persons or groups can be from inside or outside the organization performing the project. Other projects may be competing for resources with the same competencies or skill sets. Given these factors, project costs, schedules, risks, quality, and other areas may be significantly affected. Effective human resource planning should consider and plan for these factors and develop human resource options.

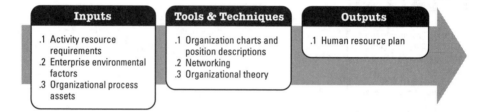

Figure 9-2. Develop Human Resource Plan: Inputs, Tools & Techniques, and Outputs

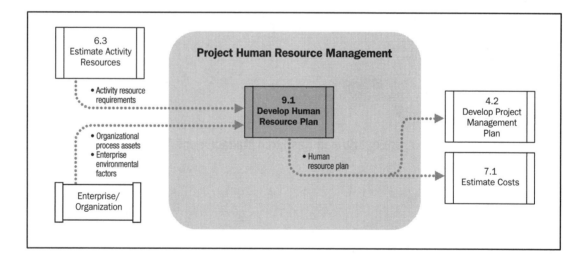

Figure 9-3. Develop Human Resource Plan Data Flow Diagram

9.1.1 Develop Human Resource Plan: Inputs

.1 Activity Resource Requirements

Human resource planning uses activity resource requirements (Section 6.3.3.1) to determine the human resource needs for the project. The preliminary requirements regarding the required people and competencies for the project team members are progressively elaborated as part of the human resource planning process.

.2 Enterprise Environmental Factors

The enterprise environmental factors (Section 1.8) that can influence the Develop Human Resource Plan process include, but are not limited to:

- Organizational culture and structure,
- Existing human resources,
- Personnel administration policies, and
- Marketplace conditions.

.3 Organizational Process Assets

The organizational process assets (Section 2.4.3) that can influence the project team with the Develop Human Resource Plan process include, but are not limited to:

- Organizational standard processes and policies and standardized role descriptions,
- Templates for organizational charts and position descriptions, and
- Historical information on organizational structures that have worked in previous projects.

9.1.2 Develop Human Resource Plan: Tools and Techniques

.1 Organization Charts and Position Descriptions

Various formats exist to document team member roles and responsibilities. Most of the formats fall into one of three types (Figure 9-4): hierarchical, matrix, and text-oriented. Additionally, some project assignments are listed in subsidiary project management plans such as the risk, quality, or communication plans. Regardless of the method utilized, the objective is to ensure that each work package has an unambiguous owner and that all team members have a clear understanding of their roles and responsibilities.

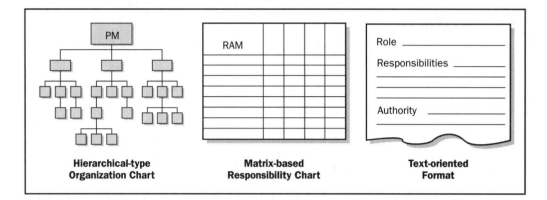

Figure 9-4. Roles and Responsibility Definition Formats

- **Hierarchical-type charts.** The traditional organization chart structure can be used to show positions and relationships in a graphic, top-down format. Work breakdown structures (WBS) designed to show how project deliverables are broken down into work packages provide a way of showing high-level areas of responsibility. While the WBS shows a breakdown of project deliverables, the organizational breakdown structure (OBS) is arranged according to an organization's existing departments, units, or teams with the project activities or work packages listed under each department. An operational department such as information technology or purchasing can see all of its project responsibilities by looking at its portion of the OBS. The resource breakdown structure is another hierarchical chart used to break down the project by types of resources. For example, a resource breakdown structure can depict all of the welders and welding equipment being used in different areas of a ship even though they can be scattered among different branches of the OBS and WBS. The resource breakdown structure is helpful in tracking project costs and can be aligned with the organization's accounting system. It can contain resource categories other than human resources.

- **Matrix-based charts.** A responsibility assignment matrix (RAM) is used to illustrate the connections between work packages or activities and project team members. On larger projects, RAMs can be developed at various levels. For example, a high-level RAM can define what a project team group or unit is responsible for within each component of the WBS, while lower-level RAMs are used within the group to designate roles, responsibilities, and levels of authority for specific activities. The matrix format shows all activities associated with one person and all people associated with one activity. This also ensures that there is only one person accountable for any one task to avoid confusion. One example of a RAM is a RACI (responsible, accountable, consult, and inform) chart, shown in Figure 9-5. The sample chart shows the work to be done in the left column as activities. The assigned resources can be shown as individuals or groups. The RACI is just one type of RAM; the project manager can select other options such as "lead" and "resource" designations or others as appropriate for the project. The RACI is particularly important when the team consists of internal and external resources to ensure clear divisions of roles and expectations.

RACI Chart	Person				
Activity	Ann	Ben	Carlos	Dina	Ed
Define	A	R	I	I	I
Design	I	A	R	C	C
Develop	I	A	R	C	C
Test	A	I	I	R	I

R = Responsible A = Accountable C = Consult I = Inform

Figure 9-5. Responsibility Assignment Matrix (RAM) Using a RACI Format

- **Text-oriented formats.** Team member responsibilities that require detailed descriptions can be specified in text-oriented formats. Usually in outline form, the documents provide information such as responsibilities, authority, competencies, and qualifications. The documents are known by various names including position descriptions and role-responsibility-authority forms. These documents can be used as templates for future projects, especially when the information is updated throughout the current project by applying lessons learned.

- **Other sections of the project management plan.** Some responsibilities related to managing the project are listed and explained in other sections of the project management plan. For example, the risk register lists risk owners, the communication plan lists team members responsible for communication activities, and the quality plan designates those responsible for carrying out quality assurance and quality control activities.

.2 Networking

Networking is the formal and informal interaction with others in an organization, industry, or professional environment. It is a constructive way to understand political and interpersonal factors that will impact the effectiveness of various staffing management options. Human resources networking activities include proactive correspondence, luncheon meetings, informal conversations including meetings and events, trade conferences, and symposia. Networking can be a useful technique at the beginning of a project. It can also be an effective way to enhance project management professional development during the project and after the project ends.

.3 Organizational Theory

Organizational theory provides information regarding the way in which people, teams, and organizational units behave. Effective use of this information can shorten the amount of time, cost, and effort needed to create the human resource planning outputs and improve the likelihood that the planning will be effective. It is important to recognize that different organizational structures have different individual response, individual performance, and personal relationship characteristics.

9.1.3 Develop Human Resource Plan: Outputs

.1 Human Resource Plan

The human resource plan, a part of the project management plan, provides guidance on how project human resources should be defined, staffed, managed, controlled, and eventually released. The human resource plan should include, but not be limited to, the following:

- **Roles and responsibilities.** The following should be addressed when listing the roles and responsibilities needed to complete a project:

  - *Role.* The label describing the portion of a project for which a person is accountable. Examples of project roles are civil engineer, court liaison, business analyst, and testing coordinator. Role clarity concerning authority, responsibilities, and boundaries should be documented.

- ○ *Authority.* The right to apply project resources, make decisions, and sign approvals. Examples of decisions that need clear authority include the selection of a method for completing an activity, quality acceptance, and how to respond to project variances. Team members operate best when their individual levels of authority match their individual responsibilities.

- ○ *Responsibility.* The work that a project team member is expected to perform in order to complete the project's activities.

- ○ *Competency.* The skill and capacity required to complete project activities. If project team members do not possess required competencies, performance can be jeopardized. When such mismatches are identified, proactive responses such as training, hiring, schedule changes, or scope changes are initiated.

- **Project organization charts.** A project organization chart is a graphic display of project team members and their reporting relationships. It can be formal or informal, highly detailed or broadly framed, based on the needs of the project. For example, the project organization chart for a 3,000-person disaster response team will have greater detail than a project organization chart for an internal, twenty-person project.

- **Staffing management plan.** The staffing management plan, a part of the human resources plan within the project management plan, describes when and how human resource requirements will be met. The staffing management plan can be formal or informal, highly detailed or broadly framed, depending upon the needs of the project. The plan is updated continually during the project to direct ongoing team member acquisition and development actions. Information in the staffing management plan varies by application area and project size, but items to consider include:

  - ○ *Staff acquisition.* A number of questions arise when planning the acquisition of project team members. For example, will the human resources come from within the organization or from external, contracted sources? Will team members need to work in a central location or can they work from distant locations? What are the costs associated with each level of expertise needed for the project? How much assistance can the organization's human resource department and functional managers provide to the project management team?

○ *Resource calendars.* The staffing management plan describes necessary time frames for project team members, either individually or collectively, as well as when acquisition activities such as recruiting should start. One tool for charting human resources is a resource histogram. This bar chart illustrates the number of hours a person, department, or entire project team will be needed each week or month over the course of the project. The chart can include a horizontal line that represents the maximum number of hours available from a particular resource. Bars that extend beyond the maximum available hours identify the need for a resource leveling strategy, such as adding more resources or modifying the schedule. An example of a resource histogram is illustrated in Figure 9-6.

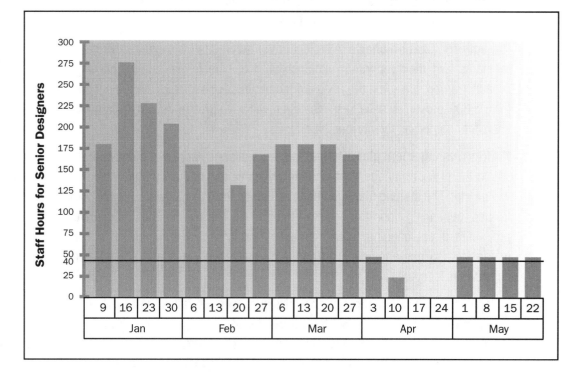

Figure 9-6. Illustrative Resource Histogram

○ *Staff release plan.* Determining the method and timing of releasing team members benefits both the project and team members. When team members are released from a project, the costs associated with those resources are no longer charged to the project, thus reducing project costs. Morale is improved when smooth transitions to upcoming projects are already planned. A staff release plan also helps mitigate human resource risks that may occur during or at the end of a project.

o *Training needs.* If the team members to be assigned are not expected to have the required competencies, a training plan can be developed as part of the project. The plan can also include ways to help team members obtain certifications that would support their ability to benefit the project.

o *Recognition and rewards.* Clear criteria for rewards and a planned system for their use helps promote and reinforce desired behaviors. To be effective, recognition and rewards should be based on activities and performance under a person's control. For example, a team member who is to be rewarded for meeting cost objectives should have an appropriate level of control over decisions that affect expenses. Creating a plan with established times for distribution of rewards ensures that recognition takes place and is not forgotten. Recognition and rewards are part of the Develop Project Team process (Section 9.3).

o *Compliance.* The staffing management plan can include strategies for complying with applicable government regulations, union contracts, and other established human resource policies.

o *Safety.* Policies and procedures that protect team members from safety hazards can be included in the staffing management plan as well as the risk register.

9.2 Acquire Project Team

Acquire Project Team is the process of confirming human resource availability and obtaining the team necessary to complete project assignments. See Figures 9-7 and 9-8. The project management team may or may not have direct control over team member selection because of collective bargaining agreements, use of subcontractor personnel, matrix project environment, internal or external reporting relationships, or other various reasons. It is important that the following factors are considered during the process of acquiring the project team:

- The project manager or project management team should effectively negotiate and influence others who are in a position to provide the required human resources for the project.

- Failure to acquire the necessary human resources for the project may affect project schedules, budgets, customer satisfaction, quality, and risks. It could decrease the probability of success and ultimately result in project cancellation.

- If the human resources are not available due to constraints, economic factors, or previous assignments to other projects, the project manager or project team may be required to assign alternative resources, perhaps with lower competencies, provided there is no violation of legal, regulatory, mandatory, or other specific criteria.

These factors should be considered and planned for in the planning stages of the project. The project manager or project management team will be required to reflect the impact of any unavailability of required human resources in the project schedule, project budget, project risks, project quality, training plans, and the other project management plans as required.

Figure 9-7. Acquire Project Team: Inputs, Tools & Techniques, and Outputs

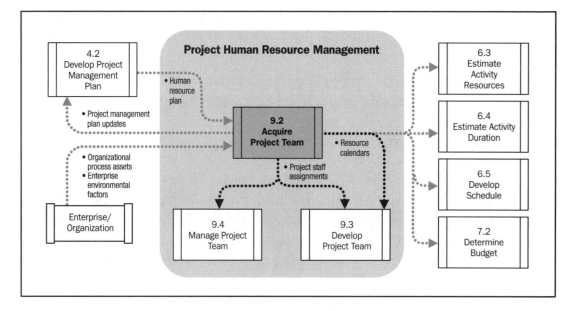

Figure 9-8. Acquire Project Team Data Flow Diagram

9.2.1 Acquire Project Team: Inputs

.1 Project Management Plan

The project management plan described in Section 4.2.3.1 contains the human resource plan which has the following information that is used to provide guidance on how project human resources should be identified, staffed, managed, controlled, and eventually released. It includes:

- Roles and responsibilities defining the positions, skills, and competencies that the project demands,

- Project organization charts indicating the number of people needed for the project, and

- Staffing management plan delineating the time periods each project team member will be needed and other information important to acquiring the project team.

.2 Enterprise Environmental Factors

The enterprise environmental factors that can influence the Acquire Project Team process include, but are not limited to:

- Existing information for human resources including who is available, their competency levels, their prior experience, their interest in working on the project and their cost rate;

- Personnel administration policies such as those that affect outsourcing;

- Organizational structure as described in Section 2.4.2; and

- Location or multiple locations.

.3 Organizational Process Assets

The organizational process assets that can influence the Acquire Project Team process include, but are not limited to, organization standard policies, processes, and procedures.

9.2.2 Acquire Project Team: Tools and Techniques

.1 Pre-Assignment

When project team members are selected in advance they are considered pre-assigned. This situation can occur if the project is the result of specific people being promised as part of a competitive proposal, if the project is dependent upon the expertise of particular persons, or if some staff assignments are defined within the project charter.

.2 Negotiation

Staff assignments are negotiated on many projects. For example, the project management team may need to negotiate with:

- Functional managers to ensure that the project receives appropriately competent staff in the required time frame, and that the project team members will be able, willing, and authorized to work on the project until their responsibilities are completed,

- Other project management teams within the performing organization to appropriately assign scarce or specialized human resources, and

- External organizations, vendors, suppliers, contractors, etc., for appropriate, scarce, specialized, qualified, certified, or other such specified human resources. Special consideration should be given to external negotiating policies, practices, processes, guidelines, legal, and other such criteria.

The project management team's ability to influence others plays an important role in negotiating staff assignments, as do the politics of the organizations involved. For example, a functional manager will weigh the benefits and visibility of competing projects when determining where to assign exceptional performers requested by various project teams.

.3 Acquisition

When the performing organization lacks the in-house staff needed to complete a project, the required services may be acquired from outside sources. This can involve hiring individual consultants or subcontracting work to another organization.

.4 Virtual Teams

The use of virtual teams creates new possibilities when acquiring project team members. Virtual teams can be defined as groups of people with a shared goal who fulfill their roles with little or no time spent meeting face to face. The availability of electronic communication such as e-mail, audio conferencing, web-based meetings and video conferencing has made such teams feasible. The virtual team format makes it possible to:

- Form teams of people from the same company who live in widespread geographic areas,

- Add special expertise to a project team even though the expert is not in the same geographic area,

- Incorporate employees who work from home offices,

- Form teams of people who work different shifts or hours,

- Include people with mobility limitations or disabilities, and

- Move forward with projects that would have been ignored due to travel expenses.

Communication planning becomes increasingly important in a virtual team environment. Additional time may be needed to set clear expectations, facilitate communications, develop protocols for resolving conflict, include people in decision-making, and share credit in successes.

9.2.3 Acquire Project Team: Outputs

.1 Project Staff Assignments

The project is staffed when appropriate people have been assigned through the previously described methods. The documentation of these assignments can include a project team directory, memos to team members, and names inserted into other parts of the project management plan, such as project organization charts and schedules.

.2 Resource Calendars

Resource calendars document the time periods that each project team member can work on the project. Creating a reliable schedule (Section 6.5.3.1) depends on having a good understanding of each person's schedule conflicts, including vacation time and commitments to other projects, to accurately document team member availability.

.3 Project Management Plan Updates

Elements of the project management plan that may be updated include, but are not limited to the human resources plan. For example, when specific people are assigned to project roles and responsibilities, there may not be an exact fit between the staffing requirements indicated in the human resource plan and the individual.

9.3 Develop Project Team

Develop Project Team is the process of improving the competencies, team interaction, and the overall team environment to enhance project performance. Project managers should acquire skills to identify, build, maintain, motivate, lead, and inspire project teams to achieve high team performance and to meet the project's objectives. See Figures 9-9 and 9-10.

Teamwork is a critical factor for project success, and developing effective project teams is one of the primary responsibilities of the project manager. Project managers should create an environment that facilitates teamwork. Project managers should continually motivate their team by providing challenges and opportunities, by providing timely feedback and support as needed, and by recognizing and rewarding good performance. High team performance can be achieved by using open and effective communication, developing trust among team members, managing conflicts in a constructive manner, and encouraging collaborative problem-solving and decision-making. The project manager should request management support and/or influence the appropriate stakeholders to acquire the resources needed to develop effective project teams.

Today project managers operate in a global environment and work on projects characterized by cultural diversity. Team members often have diverse industry experience, multiple languages, and sometimes operate in the "team language" that is a different language or norm than their native one. The project management team should capitalize on cultural differences, focus on developing and sustaining the project team throughout the project life cycle, and promote working together interdependently in a climate of mutual trust. Developing the project team improves the people skills, technical competencies, and overall team environment and project performance. It requires clear, timely, effective, and efficient communication between team members throughout the life of the project. Objectives of developing a project team include, but are not limited to:

- Improve knowledge and skills of team members in order to increase their ability to complete project deliverables, while lowering costs, reducing schedules, and improving quality;

- Improve feelings of trust and agreement among team members in order to raise morale, lower conflict, and increase team work; and

- Create a dynamic and cohesive team culture to improve both individual and team productivity, team spirit, and cooperation, and to allow cross-training and mentoring between team members to share knowledge and expertise.

Figure 9-9. Develop Project Team: Inputs, Tools & Techniques, and Outputs

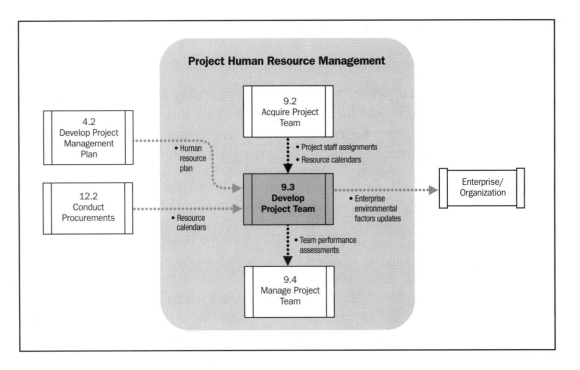

Figure 9-10. Develop Project Team Data Flow Diagram

9.3.1 Develop Project Team: Inputs

.1 Project Staff Assignments

Team development starts with a list of the project team members. Project staff assignment documents (Section 9.2.3.1) identify the people who are on the team.

.2 Project Management Plan

The project management plan described in Section 4.2.3.1 contains the human resource plan (Section 9.1.3.1), which identifies training strategies and plans for developing the project team. Items such as rewards, feedback, additional training, and disciplinary actions can be added to the plan as a result of ongoing team performance assessments and other forms of project team management.

.3 Resource Calendars

Resource calendars identify times when the project team members can participate in team development activities.

9.3.2 Develop Project Team: Tools and Techniques

.1 Interpersonal Skills

These are sometimes known as "soft skills," and are particularly important to team development. The project management team can greatly reduce problems and increase cooperation by understanding the sentiments of project team members, anticipating their actions, acknowledging their concerns, and following up on their issues. Skills such as empathy, influence, creativity, and group facilitation are valuable assets when managing the project team.

.2 Training

Training includes all activities designed to enhance the competencies of the project team members. Training can be formal or informal. Examples of training methods include classroom, online, computer-based, on-the-job training from another project team member, mentoring, and coaching. If project team members lack necessary management or technical skills, such skills can be developed as part of the project work. Scheduled training takes place as stated in the human resource plan. Unplanned training takes place as a result of observation, conversation, and project performance appraisals conducted during the controlling process of managing the project team.

.3 Team-Building Activities

Team-building activities can vary from a five-minute agenda item in a status review meeting to an off-site, professionally facilitated experience designed to improve interpersonal relationships. The objective of team-building activities is to help individual team members work together effectively. Team-building strategies are particularly valuable when team members operate from remote locations without the benefit of face-to-face contact. Informal communication and activities can help in building trust and establishing good working relationships.

One of the most important skills in developing a team environment involves handling project team problems and discussing these as team issues. The entire team should be encouraged to work collaboratively to resolve these issues. To build effective project teams, project managers should obtain top management support, obtain commitment of team members, introduce appropriate rewards and recognition, create a team identity, manage conflicts effectively, promote trust and open communication among team members, and, above all, provide good team leadership.

As an ongoing process, team building is crucial to project success. While team building is essential during the front end of a project, it is a never-ending process. Changes in a project environment are inevitable, and to manage them effectively, a continued or a renewed team-building effort should be applied. The project manager should continually monitor team functioning and performance to determine if any actions are needed to prevent or correct various team problems.

One theory states that there are five stages of development that teams may go through. Usually these stages occur in order. However, it's not uncommon for a team to get stuck in a particular stage or slip to an earlier stage. Also, projects with team members who have worked together in the past could skip a stage.

- **Forming.** This phase is where the team meets and learns about the project and what their formal roles and responsibilities are. Team members tend to be independent and not as open in this phase. For more information, refer to the Tuckman ladder of team development [**6**].

- **Storming.** During this phase, the team begins to address the project work, technical decisions, and the project management approach. If team members are not collaborative and open to differing ideas and perspectives the environment can become destructive.

- **Norming.** In the norming phase, team members begin to work together and adjust work habits and behaviors that support the team. The team begins to trust each other.

- **Performing.** Teams that reach the performing stage function as a well-organized unit. They are interdependent and work through issues smoothly and effectively.

- **Adjourning.** In the adjourning phase, the team completes the work and moves on from the project.

The duration of a particular stage depends upon team dynamics, team size, and team leadership. Project managers should have a good understanding of team dynamics in order to move their team members through all stages in an effective manner.

.4 Ground Rules

Ground rules establish clear expectations regarding acceptable behavior by project team members. Early commitment to clear guidelines decreases misunderstandings and increases productivity. Discussing ground rules allows team members to discover values that are important to one another. All project team members share responsibility for enforcing the rules once they are established.

.5 Co-location

Co-location involves placing many or all of the most active project team members in the same physical location to enhance their ability to perform as a team. Co-location can be temporary, such as at strategically important times during the project, or for the entire project. Co-location strategies can include a team meeting room, places to post schedules, and other conveniences that enhance communication and a sense of community. While co-location is considered a good strategy, the use of virtual teams is sometimes unavoidable.

.6 Recognition and Rewards

Part of the team development process involves recognizing and rewarding desirable behavior. The original plans concerning ways in which to reward people are developed during the Develop Human Resource Plan process. It is important to recognize that a particular reward given to any individual will only be effective if it satisfies a need which is valued by that individual. Award decisions are made, formally or informally, during the process of managing the project team through project performance appraisals (Section 9.4.2.2). Cultural differences should be considered when determining recognition and rewards. For example, developing appropriate team rewards in a culture that encourages individualism can be difficult.

Only desirable behavior should be rewarded. For example, the willingness to work overtime to meet an aggressive schedule objective should be rewarded or recognized; needing to work overtime as the result of poor planning by the team member should not be rewarded. However, the team members should not be punished for poor planning and consistently unrealistic expectations imposed by senior management. Win-lose (zero sum) rewards that only a limited number of project team members can achieve, such as team member of the month, can hurt team cohesiveness. Rewarding behavior that everyone can achieve, such as turning in progress reports on time, tends to increase support among team members.

People are motivated if they feel they are valued in the organization and this value is demonstrated by the rewards given to them. Generally, money is viewed by most as a very tangible aspect of any reward system, but other intangible rewards are also effective. Most project team members are motivated by an opportunity to grow, accomplish, and apply their professional skills to meet new challenges. Public recognition of good performance creates positive reinforcement. A good strategy for project managers is to give the team all possible recognition during the life cycle of the project rather than after the project is completed.

9.3.3 Develop Project Team: Outputs

.1 Team Performance Assessments

As project team development efforts such as training, team building, and co-location are implemented, the project management team makes formal or informal assessments of the project team's effectiveness. Effective team development strategies and activities are expected to increase the team's performance, which increases the likelihood of meeting project objectives. Team performance assessment criteria should be determined by all appropriate parties and incorporated in the Develop Project Team inputs. This is especially important in contract-related or collective bargaining projects.

The performance of a successful team is measured in terms of technical success according to agreed-upon project objectives, performance on project schedule (finished on time), and performance on budget (finished within financial constraints). High-performance teams are characterized by these task-oriented and results-oriented outcomes. They also exhibit specific job-related and people-related qualities that represent indirect measures of project performance.

The evaluation of a team's effectiveness may include indicators such as:

- Improvements in skills that allow individuals to perform assignments more effectively,
- Improvements in competencies that help the team perform better as a team,
- Reduced staff turnover rate, and
- Increased team cohesiveness where team members share information and experiences openly and help each other to improve the overall project performance.

As a result of conducting an evaluation of the team's overall performance, the project management team can identify the specific training, coaching, mentoring, assistance, or changes required to improve the team's performance. This should also include identification of the proper or required resources necessary to achieve and implement the improvements identified in the assessment. These resources and recommendations for team improvement should be well documented and forwarded to the appropriate parties. This is especially important when team members are part of a union, involved in collective bargaining, bound by contract performance clauses, or other related situations.

.2 Enterprise Environmental Factors Updates

The enterprise environmental factors that may be updated as a result of the Develop Project Team process include, but are not limited to, personnel administration, including updates for employee training records and skill assessments.

9.4 Manage Project Team

Manage Project Team is the process of tracking team member performance, providing feedback, resolving issues, and managing changes to optimize project performance. See Figures 9-11 and 9-12. The project management team observes team behavior, manages conflict, resolves issues, and appraises team member performance. As a result of managing the project team, change requests are submitted, the human resource plan is updated, issues are resolved, input is provided for performance appraisals, and lessons learned are added to the organization's database.

Managing the project team requires a variety of management skills for fostering teamwork and integrating the efforts of team members to create high-performance teams. Team management involves a combination of skills with special emphasis on communication, conflict management, negotiation, and leadership. Project managers should provide challenging assignments to team members and provide recognition for high performance.

Figure 9-11. Manage Project Team: Inputs, Tools & Techniques, and Outputs

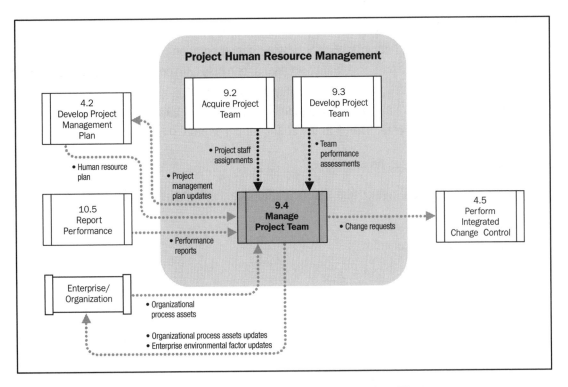

Figure 9-12. Manage Project Team Data Flow Diagram

9.4.1　Manage Project Team: Inputs

.1　Project Staff Assignments

Project staff assignments (Section 9.2.3.1) provides documentation which includes the list of project team members.

.2　Project Management Plan

The project management plan described in Section 4.2.3.1 contains the human resource plan (Section 9.1.3.1). The human resource plan includes, but is not limited to:

- Roles and responsibilities,

- Project organization, and

- The staffing management plan.

.3　Team Performance Assessments

The project management team makes ongoing formal or informal assessments of the project team's performance. By continually assessing the project team's performance, actions can be taken to resolve issues, modify communication, address conflict, and improve team interaction.

.4 Performance Reports

Performance reports (Section 10.5.3.1) provide documentation about the current project status compared to project forecasts. Performance areas that can help with project team management include results from schedule control, cost control, quality control, and scope verification. The information from performance reports and related forecasts assists in determining future human resource requirements, recognition and rewards, and updates to the staffing management plan.

.5 Organizational Process Assets

The organizational process assets that can influence the Manage Project Team process include, but are not limited to:

- Certificates of appreciation,
- Newsletters,
- Websites,
- Bonus structures,
- Corporate apparel, and
- Other organizational perquisites.

9.4.2 Manage Project Team: Tools and Techniques

.1 Observation and Conversation

Observation and conversation are used to stay in touch with the work and attitudes of project team members. The project management team monitors progress toward project deliverables, accomplishments that are a source of pride for team members, and interpersonal issues.

.2 Project Performance Appraisals

Objectives for conducting performance appraisals during the course of a project can include clarification of roles and responsibilities, constructive feedback to team members, discovery of unknown or unresolved issues, development of individual training plans, and the establishment of specific goals for future time periods.

The need for formal or informal project performance appraisals depends on the length of the project, complexity of the project, organizational policy, labor contract requirements, and the amount and quality of regular communication.

.3 Conflict Management

Conflict is inevitable in a project environment. Sources of conflict include scarce resources, scheduling priorities, and personal work styles. Team ground rules, group norms, and solid project management practices like communication planning and role definition, reduce the amount of conflict.

Successful conflict management results in greater productivity and positive working relationships. When managed properly, differences of opinion can lead to increased creativity and better decision making. If the differences become a negative factor, project team members are initially responsible for their resolution. If conflict escalates, the project manager should help facilitate a satisfactory resolution. Conflict should be addressed early and usually in private, using a direct, collaborative approach. If disruptive conflict continues, formal procedures may be used, including disciplinary actions.

When handling conflict in a team environment, project managers should recognize the following characteristics of conflict and the conflict management process:

- Conflict is natural and forces a search for alternatives,
- Conflict is a team issue,
- Openness resolves conflict,
- Conflict resolution should focus on issues, not personalities, and
- Conflict resolution should focus on the present, not the past.

The success of project managers in managing their project teams often depends a great deal on their ability to resolve conflict. Different project managers may have different conflict resolution styles. Factors that influence conflict resolution methods include:

- Relative importance and intensity of the conflict,
- Time pressure for resolving the conflict,
- Position taken by players involved, and
- Motivation to resolve conflict on a long-term or a short-term basis.

There are six general techniques for resolving conflict. As each one has its place and use, these are not given in any particular order:

- **Withdrawing/Avoiding.** Retreating from an actual or potential conflict situation.

- **Smoothing/Accommodating.** Emphasizing areas of agreement rather than areas of difference.

- **Compromising.** Searching for solutions that bring some degree of satisfaction to all parties.

- **Forcing.** Pushing one's viewpoint at the expense of others; offers only win-lose solutions.

- **Collaborating.** Incorporating multiple viewpoints and insights from differing perspectives; leads to consensus and commitment.

- **Confronting/Problem Solving.** Treating conflict as a problem to be solved by examining alternatives; requires a give-and-take attitude and open dialogue.

.4 Issue Log

Issues arise in the course of managing the project team. A written log documents and helps monitor who is responsible for resolving specific issues by a target date. Issue resolution addresses obstacles that can block the team from achieving its goals.

.5 Interpersonal Skills

Project managers use a combination of technical, human, and conceptual skills to analyze situations and interact appropriately with team members. Using appropriate interpersonal skills aids project managers in capitalizing on the strengths of all team members.

There is a wide body of knowledge about interpersonal skills that is appropriate to project work and non-project work. That body of knowledge is too in-depth to cover in this publication. There is expanded coverage of some of the most relevant interpersonal skills used in project management in Appendix G. Some of the interpersonal skills the project managers use most often are briefly covered below.

- **Leadership.** Successful projects require strong leadership skills. Leadership is important through all phases of the project life cycle. It is especially important to communicate the vision and inspire the project team to achieve high performance.

- **Influencing.** Since project managers often have little or no direct authority over their team members in a matrix environment, their ability to influence stakeholders on a timely basis is critical to project success. Key influencing skills include:

- o Ability to be persuasive and clearly articulate points and positions,

- o High levels of active and effective listening skills,

- o Consideration of the various perspectives in any situation, and

- o Gathering relevant and critical information to address important issues and reach agreements while maintaining mutual trust.

- **Effective decision making.** This involves the ability to negotiate and influence the organization and the project management team. Some guidelines for decision making include:

- o Focus on goals to be served,

- o Follow a decision-making process,

- o Study the environmental factors,

- o Develop personal qualities of the team members,

- o Stimulate team creativity, and

- o Manage opportunity and risk.

9.4.3 Manage Project Team: Outputs

.1 Enterprise Environmental Factors Updates

Enterprise environmental factors that may require updates as a result of the Manage Project Team process include, but are not limited to:

- Input to organizational performance appraisals, and

- Personnel skill updates.

.2 Organizational Process Assets Updates

Organizational process assets that may require updates as a result of the Manage Project Team process include, but are not limited to:

- Historical information and lessons learned documentation,

- Templates, and

- Organizational standard processes.

.3 Change Requests

Staffing changes, whether by choice or by uncontrollable events, can affect the rest of the project management plan. When staffing issues disrupt the project management plan, such as causing the schedule to be extended or the budget to be exceeded, a change request can be processed through the Perform Integrated Change Control process. Staffing changes can include moving people to different assignments, outsourcing some of the work, and replacing team members who leave.

Preventive actions are those that can be developed to reduce the probability and/or impact of problems before they occur. These actions may include cross-training to reduce problems during project team member absences and additional role clarification to ensure all responsibilities are fulfilled.

.4 Project Management Plan Updates

Elements of the project management plan that may be updated include, but are not limited to, the staffing management plan.

CHAPTER 10

PROJECT COMMUNICATIONS MANAGEMENT

Project Communications Management includes the processes required to ensure timely and appropriate generation, collection, distribution, storage, retrieval, and ultimate disposition of project information. Project managers spend the majority of their time communicating with team members and other project stakeholders, whether they are internal (at all organizational levels) or external to the organization. Effective communication creates a bridge between diverse stakeholders involved in a project, connecting various cultural and organizational backgrounds, different levels of expertise, and various perspectives and interests in the project execution or outcome.

Figure 10-1 provides an overview of the Project Communications Management processes which include the following:

10.1 Identify Stakeholders—The process of identifying all people or organizations impacted by the project, and documenting relevant information regarding their interests, involvement, and impact on project success.

10.2 Plan Communications—The process of determining the project stakeholder information needs and defining a communication approach.

10.3 Distribute Information—The process of making relevant information available to project stakeholders as planned.

10.4 Manage Stakeholder Expectations—The process of communicating and working with stakeholders to meet their needs and addressing issues as they occur.

10.5 Report Performance—The process of collecting and distributing performance information, including status reports, progress measurements, and forecasts.

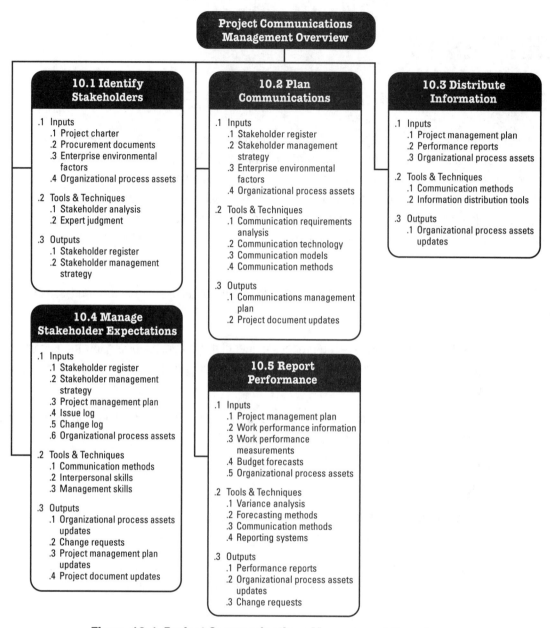

Figure 10-1. Project Communications Management Overview

These processes interact with each other and with processes in the other Knowledge Areas. Each process occurs at least once in every project and, if the project is divided into phases, it could occur in one or more project phases. Although the processes are presented here as discrete elements with well-defined interfaces, in practice they may overlap and interact in ways not detailed here.

Communication activity has many potential dimensions, including:

- Internal (within the project) and external (customer, other projects, the media, the public),
- Formal (reports, memos, briefings) and informal (emails, ad-hoc discussions),
- Vertical (up and down the organization) and horizontal (with peers),
- Official (newsletters, annual report) and unofficial (off the record communications),
- Written and oral, and
- Verbal and non-verbal (voice inflections, body language).

Most communication skills are common for general management and project management, such as, but not limited to:

- Listening actively and effectively,
- Questioning, probing ideas and situations to ensure better understanding,
- Educating to increase team's knowledge so that they can be more effective,
- Fact-finding to identify or confirm information,
- Setting and managing expectations,
- Persuading a person or organization to perform an action,
- Negotiating to achieve mutually acceptable agreements between parties,
- Resolving conflict to prevent disruptive impacts, and
- Summarizing, recapping, and identifying the next steps.

10.1 Identify Stakeholders

Identify Stakeholders is the process of identifying all people or organizations impacted by the project, and documenting relevant information regarding their interests, involvement, and impact on project success. See Figures 10-2 and 10-3. Project stakeholders are persons and organizations such as customers, sponsors, the performing organization, and the public that are actively involved in the project, or whose interests may be positively or negatively affected by the execution or completion of the project. They may also exert influence over the project and its deliverables. Stakeholders may be at different levels within the organization and may possess different authority levels, or may be external to the performing organization for the project. Section 2.3 identifies various types of project stakeholders.

It is critical for project success to identify the stakeholders early in the project, and to analyze their levels of interest, expectations, importance and influence. A strategy can then be developed for approaching each stakeholder and determining the level and timing of stakeholders' involvement to maximize positive influences and mitigate potential negative impacts. The assessment and corresponding strategy should be periodically reviewed during project execution to adjust for potential changes.

Most projects will have a large number of stakeholders. As the project manager's time is limited and must be used as efficiently as possible, these stakeholders should be classified according to their interest, influence, and involvement in the project. This enables the project manager to focus on the relationships necessary to ensure the success of the project.

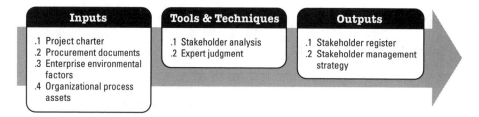

Figure 10-2. Identify Stakeholders: Inputs, Tools & Techniques, and Outputs

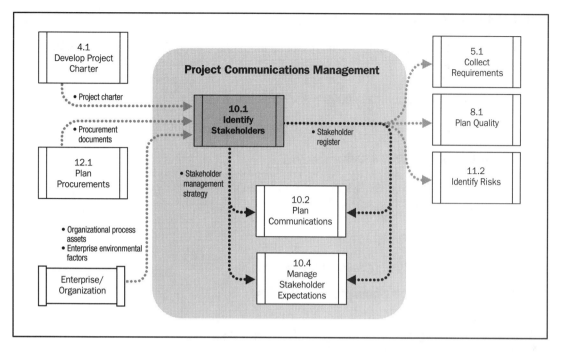

Figure 10-3. Identify Stakeholders Data Flow Diagram

10.1.1 Identify Stakeholders: Inputs

.1 Project Charter

The project charter can provide information about internal and external parties involved in and affected by the project, such as project sponsor(s), customers, team members, groups and departments participating in the project, and other people or organizations affected by the project.

.2 Procurement Documents

If a project is the result of a procurement activity or is based on an established contract, the parties in that contract are key project stakeholders. Other relevant parties, such as suppliers, should also be considered as part of the project stakeholders list.

.3 Enterprise Environmental Factors

The enterprise environmental factors that can influence the Identify Stakeholders process include, but are not limited to:

- Organizational or company culture and structure, and

- Governmental or industry standards (e.g. regulations, product standards).

.4 Organizational Process Assets

The organizational process assets that can influence the Identify Stakeholders process include, but are not limited to:

- Stakeholder register templates,

- Lessons learned from previous projects, and

- Stakeholder registers from previous projects.

10.1.2 Identify Stakeholders: Tools and Techniques

.1 Stakeholder Analysis

Stakeholder analysis is a technique of systematically gathering and analyzing quantitative and qualitative information to determine whose interests should be taken into account throughout the project. It identifies the interests, expectations, and influence of the stakeholders and relates them to the purpose of the project. It also helps identify stakeholder relationships that can be leveraged to build coalitions and potential partnerships to enhance the project's chance of success.

Stakeholder analysis generally follows the steps described below:

- **Step 1:** Identify all potential project stakeholders and relevant information, such as their roles, departments, interests, knowledge levels, expectations, and influence levels. Key stakeholders are usually easy to identify. They include anyone in a decision-making or management role who is impacted by the project outcome, such as the sponsor, the project manager, and the primary customer.

  o Identifying other stakeholders is usually done by interviewing identified stakeholders and expanding the list until all potential stakeholders are included.

- **Step 2:** Identify the potential impact or support each stakeholder could generate, and classify them so as to define an approach strategy. In large stakeholder communities, it is important to prioritize the key stakeholders to ensure the efficient use of effort to communicate and manage their expectations. There are multiple classification models available including, but not limited to:

  o Power/interest grid, grouping the stakeholders based on their level of authority ("power") and their level or concern ("interest") regarding the project outcomes;

  o Power/influence grid, grouping the stakeholders based on their level of authority ("power") and their active involvement ("influence") in the project;

  o Influence/impact grid, grouping the stakeholders based on their active involvement ("influence") in the project and their ability to effect changes to the project's planning or execution ("impact"); and

  o Salience model, describing classes of stakeholders based on their power (ability to impose their will), urgency (need for immediate attention), and legitimacy (their involvement is appropriate).

Figure 10-4 presents an example of a power/interest grid with A-H representing the placement of generic stakeholders.

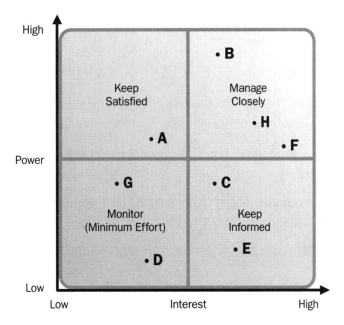

Figure 10-4. Example Power/Interest Grid with Stakeholders

- **Step 3:** Assess how key stakeholders are likely to react or respond in various situations, in order to plan how to influence them to enhance their support and mitigate potential negative impacts.

.2 Expert Judgment

To ensure comprehensive identification and listing of stakeholders, judgment and expertise should be sought from groups or individuals with specialized training or knowledge on the subject area such as:

- Senior management,

- Other units within the organization,

- Identified key stakeholders,

- Project managers who have worked on projects in the same area (directly or through lessons learned),

- Subject matter experts (SMEs) in business or project area,

- Industry groups and consultants, and

- Professional and technical associations.

Expert judgment can be obtained through individual consultations (one-on-one meetings, interviews, etc.) or through a panel format (focus groups, surveys etc).

10.1.3 Identify Stakeholders: Outputs

.1 Stakeholder Register

The main output of the Identify Stakeholders process is the stakeholder register. This contains all details related to the identified stakeholders including, but not limited to:

- **Identification information:** Name, organizational position, location, role in the project, contact information;

- **Assessment information:** Major requirements, main expectations, potential influence in the project, phase in the life cycle with the most interest; and

- **Stakeholder classification:** Internal/external, supporter/neutral/resistor, etc.

.2 Stakeholder Management Strategy

The stakeholder management strategy defines an approach to increase the support and minimize negative impacts of stakeholders throughout the entire project life cycle. It includes elements such as:

- Key stakeholders who can significantly impact the project,

- Level of participation in the project desired for each identified stakeholder, and

- Stakeholder groups and their management (as groups).

A common way of representing the stakeholder management strategy is a stakeholder analysis matrix. An example of a blank matrix with column headers is provided in Figure 10-5.

Stakeholder	Stakeholder Interest(s) in the Project	Assessment of Impact	Potential Strategies for Gaining Support or Reducing Obstacles

Figure 10-5. Sample Stakeholder Analysis Matrix

Some of the information related to certain stakeholder management strategies could be too sensitive to be included in a shared document. The project manager must exercise judgment with regard to the type of information and the level of detail to be included in the stakeholder management strategy.

10.2 Plan Communications

Plan Communications is the process of determining the project stakeholder information needs and defining a communication approach. See Figures 10-6 and 10-7. The Plan Communications process responds to the information and communications needs of the stakeholders; for example, who needs what information, when they will need it, how it will be given to them, and by whom. While all projects share the need to communicate project information, the informational needs and methods of distribution vary widely. Identifying the information needs of the stakeholders and determining a suitable means of meeting those needs are important factors for project success.

Improper communication planning will lead to problems such as delay in message delivery, communication of sensitive information to the wrong audience, or lack of communication to some of the required stakeholders. A communication plan allows the project manager to document the approach to communicate most efficiently and effectively with stakeholders. Effective communication means that the information is provided in the right format, at the right time, and with the right impact. Efficient communication means providing only the information that is needed. On most projects, the communications planning is done very early, such as during project management plan development. This allows appropriate resources, such as time and budget, to be allocated to communication activities. The results of this planning process should be reviewed regularly throughout the project and revised as needed to ensure continued applicability.

The Plan Communications process is tightly linked with enterprise environmental factors, since the organization's structure will have a major effect on the project's communications requirements.

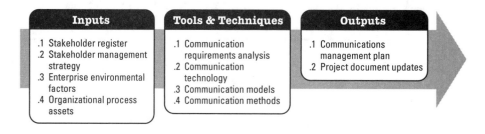

Figure 10-6. Plan Communications: Inputs, Tools & Techniques, and Outputs

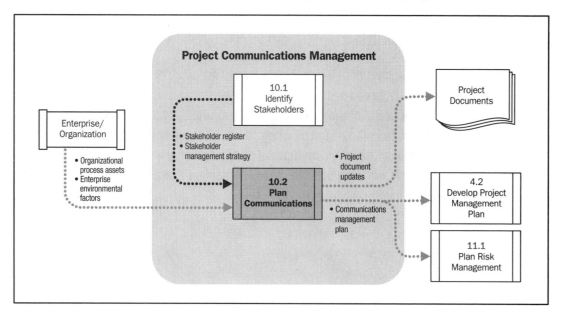

Figure 10-7. Plan Communications Data Flow Diagram

10.2.1 Plan Communications: Inputs

.1 Stakeholder Register

The stakeholder register is described in Section 10.1.3.1.

.2 Stakeholder Management Strategy

Stakeholder management strategy is described in Section 10.1.3.2.

.3 Enterprise Environmental Factors

All enterprise environmental factors are used as inputs for this process since communication must be adapted to the project environment.

.4 Organizational Process Assets

All organizational process assets are used as inputs for the Plan Communications process. Of these, lessons learned and historical information are of particular importance because they can provide insights on both the decisions taken regarding communications issues and the results of those decisions in previous similar projects. These can be used as guiding information to plan the communication activities for the current project.

10.2.2 Plan Communications: Tools and Techniques

.1 Communication Requirements Analysis

The analysis of the communication requirements determines the information needs of the project stakeholders. These requirements are defined by combining the type and format of information needed with an analysis of the value of that information. Project resources are expended only on communicating information that contributes to success, or where a lack of communication can lead to failure.

The project manager should also consider the number of potential communication channels or paths as an indicator of the complexity of a project's communications. The total number of potential communication channels is $n(n-1)/2$, where n represents the number of stakeholders. Thus, a project with 10 stakeholders has $10(10-1)/2 = 45$ potential communication channels. A key component of planning the project's actual communications, therefore, is to determine and limit who will communicate with whom and who will receive what information.

Information typically used to determine project communication requirements includes:

- Organization charts,

- Project organization and stakeholder responsibility relationships,

- Disciplines, departments, and specialties involved in the project,

- Logistics of how many persons will be involved with the project and at which locations,

- Internal information needs (e.g., communicating across organizations),

- External information needs (e.g., communicating with the media, public, or contractors), and

- Stakeholder information from the stakeholder register and the stakeholder management strategy.

.2 Communication Technology

The methods used to transfer information among project stakeholders can vary significantly. For example, a project team may use techniques from brief conversations all the way through to extended meetings, or from simple written documents to material (e.g., schedules and databases) that is accessible online as methods of communication.

Factors that can affect the project include:

- **Urgency of the need for information.** Is project success dependent upon having frequently updated information available on a moment's notice, or would regularly issued written reports suffice?

- **Availability of technology.** Are appropriate systems already in place or do project needs warrant change? For example, do the intended stakeholder(s) have access to a selected communications technology?

- **Expected project staffing.** Are the proposed communication systems compatible with the experience and expertise of the project participants, or is extensive training and learning required?

- **Duration of the project.** Is the available technology likely to change before the project is over?

- **Project environment.** Does the team meet and operate on a face-to-face basis or in a virtual environment?

.3 Communication Models

A basic model of communication, shown in Figure 10-8, demonstrates how information is sent and received between two parties, defined as the sender and the receiver. The key components of the model include:

- **Encode.** To translate thoughts or ideas into a language that is understood by others.

- **Message and feedback-message.** The output of encoding.

- **Medium.** The method used to convey the message.

- **Noise.** Anything that interferes with the transmission and understanding of the message (e.g., distance, unfamiliar technology, lack of background information).

- **Decode.** To translate the message back into meaningful thoughts or ideas.

Figure 10-8 is a basic communication model. Inherent in the model is an action to acknowledge a message. Acknowledgement means that the receiver signals receipt of the message, but not necessarily agreement with the message. Another action is the response to a message, which means that the receiver has decoded, understands, and is replying to the message.

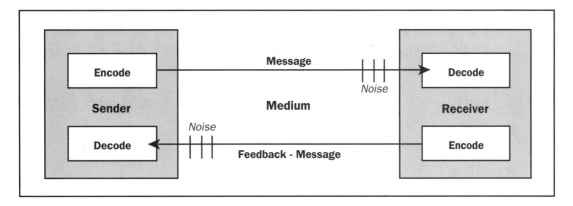

Figure 10-8. Basic Communication Model

The components in the communications model need to be taken into account when discussing project communications. As part of the communications process, the sender is responsible for making the information clear and complete so that the receiver can receive it correctly, and for confirming that it is properly understood. The receiver is responsible for making sure that the information is received in its entirety, understood correctly, and acknowledged. A failure in communication can negatively impact the project.

There are many challenges in using these components to effectively communicate with project stakeholders. Consider a highly technical, multinational project team. For one team member to successfully communicate a technical concept to another team member in a different country can involve encoding the message in the appropriate language, sending the message using a variety of technologies, and having the receiver decode the message and reply or provide feedback. Any noise introduced along the way compromises the original meaning of the message.

.4 Communication Methods

There are several communication methods used to share information among project stakeholders. These methods can be broadly classified into:

- **Interactive communication.** Between two or more parties performing a multidirectional exchange of information. It is the most efficient way to ensure a common understanding by all participants on specified topics, and includes meetings, phone calls, video conferencing, etc.

- **Push communication.** Sent to specific recipients who need to know the information. This ensures that the information is distributed but does not certify that it actually reached or was understood by the intended audience. Push communication includes letters, memos, reports, emails, faxes, voice mails, press releases etc.

- **Pull communication.** Used for very large volumes of information, or for very large audiences, that requires the recipients to access the communication content at their own discretion. These methods include intranet sites, e-learning, and knowledge repositories, etc.

The project manager decides, based on communication requirements, what, how, and when communication methods are to be used in the project.

10.2.3 Plan Communications: Outputs

.1 Communications Management Plan

The communications management plan is contained in or is a subsidiary of the project management plan (Section 4.2.3.1). The communications management plan can be formal or informal, highly detailed or broadly framed, and based on the needs of the project.

The communications management plan usually provides:

- Stakeholder communication requirements;

- Information to be communicated, including language, format, content, and level of detail;

- Reason for the distribution of that information;

- Time frame and frequency for the distribution of required information;

- Person responsible for communicating the information;

- Person responsible for authorizing release of confidential information;

- Person or groups who will receive the information;

- Methods or technologies used to convey the information, such as memos, e-mail, and/or press releases;

- Resources allocated for communication activities, including time and budget;

- Escalation process identifying time frames and the management chain (names) for escalation of issues that cannot be resolved at a lower staff level;

- Method for updating and refining the communications management plan as the project progresses and develops;

- Glossary of common terminology;

- Flow charts of the information flow in the project, workflows with possible sequence of authorization, list of reports, and meeting plans, etc.; and

- Communication constraints, usually derived from specific legislation or regulation, technology, and organizational policies, etc.

The communications management plan can also include guidelines and templates for project status meetings, project team meetings, e-meetings, and e-mail. The use of a project website and project management software can also be included if they are used in the project.

.2 Project Document Updates

Project documents that may be updated include but are not limited to:

- Project schedule,
- Stakeholder register, and
- Stakeholder management strategy.

10.3 Distribute Information

Distribute information is the process of making relevant information available to project stakeholders as planned. See Figures 10-9 and 10-10. It is performed throughout the entire project life cycle and in all management processes. The focus here is mainly in the execution process, which includes implementing the communications management plan, as well as responding to unexpected requests for information. Effective information distribution includes a number of techniques including:

- **Sender-receiver models.** Feedback loops and barriers to communication.

- **Choice of media.** Situation specifics of when to communicate in writing versus orally, when to write an informal memo versus a formal report, and when to communicate face-to-face versus by e-mail.

- **Writing style.** Active versus passive voice, sentence structure, and word choice.

- **Meeting management techniques.** Preparing an agenda and dealing with conflicts.

- **Presentation techniques.** Body language and design of visual aids.

- **Facilitation techniques.** Building consensus and overcoming obstacles.

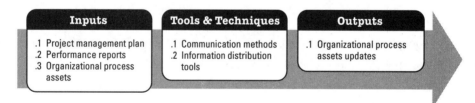

Inputs	Tools & Techniques	Outputs
.1 Project management plan .2 Performance reports .3 Organizational process assets	.1 Communication methods .2 Information distribution tools	.1 Organizational process assets updates

Figure 10-9. Distribute Information: Inputs, Tools & Techniques, and Outputs

---

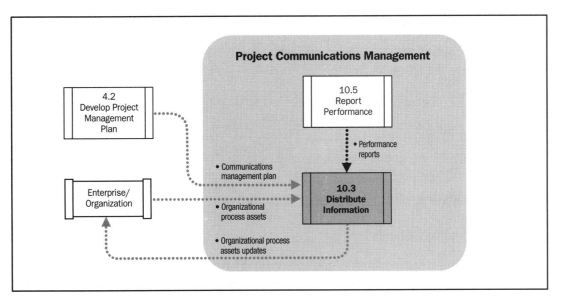

Figure 10-10. Distribute Information Data Flow Diagram

10.3.1 Distribute Information: Inputs

.1 Project Management Plan

The project management plan (Section 4.2.3.1) contains the communications management plan described in Section 10.2.3.1.

.2 Performance Reports

Performance reports are used to distribute project performance and status information, should be made available prior to project meetings, and should be as precise and current as possible.

Forecasts are updated and reissued based on work performance measurements provided as the project is executed. This information is about the project's past performance that could impact the project in the future, for example, estimates at completion and estimates to complete. Forecast information is often generated using earned value methods (see Section 7.3.2.2), but may use other methods such as analogy with past projects, re-estimating remaining work, inclusion of impact of external events in the schedule, and others. This information should be available along with performance information and other important information that must be distributed for decision-making purposes. Forecasting methods are described in Section 10.5.2.2. Additional information on performance reports is provided in Section 10.5.3.1.

.3 Organizational Process Assets

The organizational process assets (see Section 2.4.3) that can influence the Distribute Information process include, but are not limited to:

- Policies, procedures, and guidelines regarding information distribution,
- Templates, and
- Historical information and lessons learned.

10.3.2 Distribute Information: Tools and Techniques

.1 Communication Methods

Individual and group meetings, video and audio conferences, computer chats, and other remote communications methods are used to distribute information.

.2 Information Distribution Tools

Project information can be distributed using a variety of tools, including:

- Hard-copy document distribution, manual filing systems, press releases, and shared-access electronic databases;
- Electronic communication and conferencing tools, such as e-mail, fax, voice mail, telephone, video and web conferencing, websites and web publishing; and
- Electronic tools for project management, such as web interfaces to scheduling and project management software, meeting and virtual office support software, portals, and collaborative work management tools.

10.3.3 Distribute Information: Outputs

.1 Organizational Process Assets Updates

The organizational process assets which may be updated include, but are not limited to:

- **Stakeholder notifications.** Information may be provided to stakeholders about resolved issues, approved changes, and general project status.

- **Project reports.** Formal and informal project reports describe project status and include lessons learned, issues logs, project closure reports, and outputs from other Knowledge Areas (Chapters 4–12).

- **Project presentations.** The project team provides information formally or informally to any or all of the project stakeholders. The information and presentation method should be relevant to the needs of the audience.

- **Project records.** Project records can include correspondence, memos, meeting minutes, and other documents describing the project. This information should, to the extent possible and appropriate, be maintained in an organized manner. Project team members can also maintain records in a project notebook or register, which could be physical or electronic.

- **Feedback from stakeholders.** Information received from stakeholders concerning project operations can be distributed and used to modify or improve future performance of the project.

- **Lessons learned documentation.** Documentation includes the causes of issues, reasoning behind the corrective action chosen, and other types of lessons learned about information distribution. Lessons learned are documented and distributed so that they become part of the historical database for both the project and the performing organization.

10.4 Manage Stakeholder Expectations

Manage Stakeholder Expectations is the process of communicating and working with stakeholders to meet their needs and addressing issues as they occur. See Figures 10-11 and 10-12. Manage Stakeholder Expectations involves communication activities directed toward project stakeholders to influence their expectations, address concerns, and resolve issues, such as:

- Actively managing the expectations of stakeholders to increase the likelihood of project acceptance by negotiating and influencing their desires to achieve and maintain the project goals,

- Addressing concerns that have not become issues yet, usually related to the anticipation of future problems. These concerns need to be uncovered and discussed, and the risks need to be assessed, and

- Clarifying and resolving issues that have been identified. The resolution may result in a change request or may be addressed outside of the project, for example, postponed for another project or phase or deferred to another organizational entity.

Managing expectations helps to increase the probability of project success by ensuring that the stakeholders understand the project benefits and risks. This enables them to be active supporters of the project and to help with risk assessment of project choices. By anticipating people's reaction to the project, preventive actions can be taken to win their support or minimize potential negative impacts.

The project manager is responsible for stakeholder expectations management. Actively managing stakeholder expectations decreases the risk that the project will fail to meet its goals and objectives due to unresolved stakeholder issues, and limits disruptions during the project.

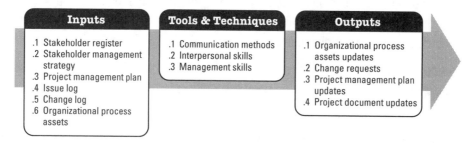

Inputs	Tools & Techniques	Outputs
.1 Stakeholder register .2 Stakeholder management strategy .3 Project management plan .4 Issue log .5 Change log .6 Organizational process assets	.1 Communication methods .2 Interpersonal skills .3 Management skills	.1 Organizational process assets updates .2 Change requests .3 Project management plan updates .4 Project document updates

Figure 10-11. Manage Stakeholder Expectations: Inputs, Tools & Techniques, and Outputs

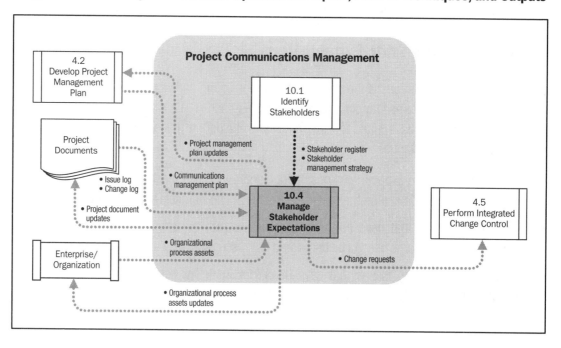

Figure 10-12. Manage Stakeholder Expectations Data Flow Diagram

10.4.1 Manage Stakeholder Expectations: Inputs

.1 Stakeholder Register

The stakeholder register (see Section 10.1.3.1) is a list of the relevant stakeholders for the project. It is used to ensure that all stakeholders are included in the project communications.

.2 Stakeholder Management Strategy

An understanding of stakeholder goals and objectives is used to determine a strategy to manage stakeholder expectations. The strategy is documented in the stakeholder management strategy document (see Section 10.1.3.2).

.3 Project Management Plan

The project management plan (Section 4.2.3.1) contains the communications management plan described in Section 10.2.3.1. Stakeholder requirements and expectations provide an understanding of stakeholder goals, objectives, and level of communication required during the project. The needs and expectations are identified, analyzed, and documented in the communications management plan, which is a subsidiary of the project management plan.

.4 Issue Log

An issue log or action item log can be used to document and monitor the resolution of issues. It can be used to facilitate communication and ensure a common understanding of issues. Issues do not usually rise to the importance of becoming a project or activity but are usually addressed in order to maintain good, constructive working relationships among various stakeholders, including team members.

The issues are clearly stated and categorized based on urgency and potential impact. An owner is assigned an action item for resolution, and a target date is usually established for closure. Unresolved issues can be a major source of conflict and project delays.

.5 Change Log

A change log is used to document changes that occur during a project. These changes and their impact to the project in terms of time, cost, and risk, must be communicated to the appropriate stakeholders.

.6 Organizational Process Assets

The organizational process assets that can influence the Manage Stakeholder Expectations process include, but are not limited to:

- Organizational communication requirements,
- Issue management procedures,
- Change control procedures, and
- Historical information about previous projects.

10.4.2 Manage Stakeholder Expectations: Tools and Techniques

.1 Communication Methods

The methods of communication identified for each stakeholder in the communications management plan are utilized during stakeholder management.

.2 Interpersonal Skills

The project manager applies appropriate interpersonal skills to manage stakeholder expectations. For example:

- Building trust,
- Resolving conflict,
- Active listening, and
- Overcoming resistance to change.

More information on interpersonal skills is found in Appendix G.

.3 Management Skills

Management is the act of directing and controlling a group of people for the purpose of coordinating and harmonizing the group towards accomplishing a goal beyond the scope of individual effort. Management skills used by the project manager include but are not limited to:

- Presentation skills,
- Negotiating,
- Writing skills, and
- Public speaking.

10.4.3 Manage Stakeholder Expectations: Outputs

.1 Organizational Process Assets Updates

Organizational process assets that may be updated include, but are not limited to:

- Causes of issues,
- Reasoning behind corrective actions chosen, and
- Lessons learned from managing stakeholder expectations.

.2 Change Requests

Managing stakeholder expectations may result in a change request to the product or the project. It may also include corrective or preventive actions as appropriate.

.3 Project Management Plan Updates

Elements of the project management plan that may be updated include, but are not limited to, a communications management plan. This is updated when new or changed communication requirements are identified. For example, some communications may no longer be necessary, an ineffective communication method may be replaced by another method, or a new communication requirement may be identified.

.4 Project Document Updates

Project documents that may be updated include, but are not limited to:

- **Stakeholder management strategy.** This is updated as a result of addressing concerns and resolving issues. For example, it may be determined that a stakeholder has additional informational needs.
- **Stakeholder register.** This is updated as information on stakeholders change, when new stakeholders are identified or if registered stakeholders are no longer involved in or impacted by the project, or other updates for specific stakeholders are required.
- **Issue log.** This is updated as new issues are identified and current issues are resolved.

10.5 Report Performance

Report Performance is the process of collecting and distributing performance information, including status reports, progress measurements, and forecasts. See Figures 10-13 and 10-14. The performance reporting process involves the periodic collection and analysis of baseline versus actual data to understand and communicate the project progress and performance as well as to forecast the project results.

Performance reports need to provide information at an appropriate level for each audience. The format may range from a simple status report to more elaborate reports. A simple status report might show performance information, such as percent complete, or status dashboards for each area (i.e., scope, schedule, cost, and quality). More elaborate reports may include:

- Analysis of past performance,
- Current status of risks and issues,
- Work completed during the period,
- Work to be completed next,
- Summary of changes approved in the period, and
- Other relevant information which must be reviewed and discussed.

A complete report should also include forecasted project completion (including time and cost). These reports may be prepared regularly or on an exception basis.

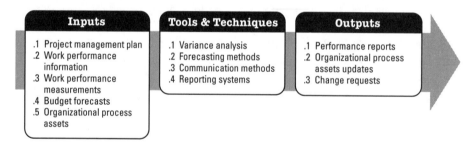

Figure 10-13. Report Performance: Inputs, Tools & Techniques, and Outputs

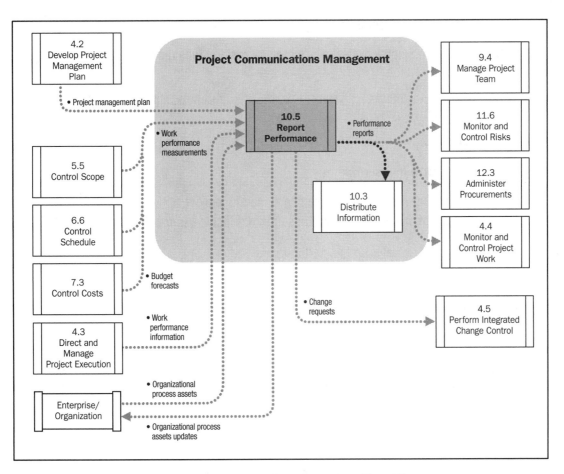

Figure 10-14. Report Performance Data Flow Diagram

10.5.1 Report Performance: Inputs

.1 Project Management Plan

The project management plan provides information on project baselines. The performance measurement baseline is an approved plan for the project work to which the project execution is compared, and deviations are measured for management control. The performance measurement baseline typically integrates scope, schedule, and cost parameters of a project, but may also include technical and quality parameters.

.2 Work Performance Information

Information from project activities is collected on performance results such as:

- Deliverables status,
- Schedule progress, and
- Costs incurred.

.3 Work Performance Measurements

Work performance information is used to generate project activity metrics to evaluate actual progress compared to planned progress. These metrics include, but are not limited to:

- Planned versus actual schedule performance,
- Planned versus actual cost performance, and
- Planned versus actual technical performance.

.4 Budget Forecasts

Budget forecast information from the Control Cost process (7.3.3.2) provide information on the additional funds that are expected to be required for the remaining work, as well as estimates for the completion of the total project work.

.5 Organizational Process Assets

The organizational process assets that can influence the Report Performance process include, but are not limited to:

- Report templates,
- Policies and procedures that define the measures and indicators to be used, and
- Organizationally defined variance limits.

10.5.2 Report Performance: Tools and Techniques

.1 Variance Analysis

Variance analysis is an after-the-fact look at what caused a difference between the baseline and the actual performance. The process for performing variance analysis may vary depending on the application area, the standard used, and the industry. Common steps are:

- Verify the quality of the information collected to ensure that it is complete, consistent with past data, and credible when comparing with other project or status information,

- Determine variances, comparing the actual information with the project baseline and noting all differences both favorable and unfavorable to the project outcome. Earned value management uses specific equations to quantify variances. The technique is explained in detail in Section 7.3.2.1.

- Determine the impact of the variances in the project cost and schedule as well as in other areas of the project (i.e., quality performance adjustments and scope changes, etc.).

If applicable, analyze the trends of the variances and document any findings about the sources of variation and the impact area.

.2 Forecasting Methods

Forecasting is the process of predicting future project performance based on the actual performance to date. Forecasting methods may be classified in different categories:

- **Time series methods.** Time series methods use historical data as the basis for estimating future outcomes. Examples of methods in this category may include earned value, moving average, extrapolation, linear prediction, trend estimation, and growth curve.

- **Causal/econometric methods.** Some forecasting methods use the assumption that it is possible to identify the underlying factors that might influence the variable that is being forecasted. For example, sales of umbrellas might be associated with weather conditions. If the causes are understood, projections of the influencing variables can be made and used in the forecast. Examples of methods in this category include regression analysis using linear regression or non-linear regression, autoregressive moving average (ARMA), and econometrics.

- **Judgmental methods.** Judgmental forecasting methods incorporate intuitive judgments, opinions, and probability estimates. Examples of methods in this category are composite forecasts, surveys, Delphi method, scenario building, technology forecasting, and forecast by analogy.

- **Other methods.** Other methods may include simulation, probabilistic forecasting, and ensemble forecasting.

.3 Communication Methods

Status review meetings can be used to exchange and analyze information about the project progress and performance. The project manager generally uses a push communication technique as defined in 10.2.2.4 to distribute performance reports.

.4 Reporting Systems

A reporting system provides a standard tool for the project manager to capture, store, and distribute information to stakeholders about the project cost, schedule progress, and performance. Software packages allow the project manager to consolidate reports from several systems and facilitate report distribution to the project stakeholders. Examples of distribution formats may include table reporting, spreadsheet analysis, and presentations. Graphic capabilities can be used to create visual representations of project performance information.

10.5.3 Report Performance: Outputs

.1 Performance Reports

Performance reports organize and summarize the information gathered, and present the results of any analysis as compared to the performance measurement baseline. Reports should provide the status and progress information, at the level of detail required by various stakeholders, as documented in the communications management plan. Common formats for performance reports include bar charts, S-curves, histograms, and tables. Variance analysis, earned value analysis, and forecast data is often included as part of performance reporting. Figure 10-15 gives a tabular view of earned value data (Section 7.3.2.1).

Performance reports are issued periodically and their format may range from a simple status report to more elaborate reports. A simple status report might show only performance information such as percent complete, or status dashboards for each area (e.g., scope, schedule, cost, and quality). More elaborate reports may include:

- Analysis of past performance,
- Current status of risks and issues,
- Work completed during the reporting period,
- Work to be completed during the next reporting period,
- Summary of changes approved in the period,
- Results of variance analysis,
- Forecasted project completion (including time and cost), and
- Other relevant information to be reviewed and discussed.

WBS Element	Values			Variance		Performance Index	
	Planned Value (PV)	Earned Value (EV)	Actual Cost (AC)	Schedule EV - PV	Cost EV - AC	Schedule EV ÷ PV	Cost EV ÷ AC
1.0 Pre-Pilot Plan	63,000	58,000	62,500	(5,000)	(4,500)	0.92	0.93
2.0 Checklists	64,000	48,000	46,800	(16,000)	1,200	0.75	1.03
3.0 Curriculum	23,000	20,000	23,500	(3,000)	(3,500)	0.87	0.85
4.0 Mid-Term Evaluation	68,000	68,000	72,500	–	(4,500)	1.00	0.94
5.0 Implementation Support	12,000	10,000	10,000	(2,000)	–	0.83	1.00
6.0 Practice Manual	7,000	6,200	6,000	(800)	200	0.89	1.03
7.0 Roll-Out Plan	20,000	13,500	18,100	(6,500)	(4,600)	0.68	0.75
Totals	257,000	223,700	239,400	(33,300)	(15,700)	0.87	0.93

Figure 10-15. Tabular Performance Report Sample

.2 Organizational Process Assets Updates

The organizational process assets that can be updated include, but are not limited to, report formats and lessons learned documentation, including the causes of issues, reasoning behind the corrective action chosen, and other types of lessons learned about performance reporting. Lessons learned are documented so that they become part of the historical database for both this project and the performing organization.

.3 Change Requests

Analysis of project performance often generates change requests. These change requests are processed through the Perform Integrated Change Control process (Section 4.5) as follows:

- Recommended corrective actions include changes that bring the expected future performance of the project in line with the project management plan, and

- Recommended preventive actions can reduce the probability of incurring future negative project performance.

CHAPTER 11

PROJECT RISK MANAGEMENT

Project Risk Management includes the processes of conducting risk management planning, identification, analysis, response planning, and monitoring and control on a project. The objectives of Project Risk Management are to increase the probability and impact of positive events, and decrease the probability and impact of negative events in the project.

Figure 11-1 provides an overview of Project Risk Management processes, which are as follows:

11.1 Plan Risk Management—The process of defining how to conduct risk management activities for a project.

11.2 Identify Risks—The process of determining which risks may affect the project and documenting their characteristics.

11.3 Perform Qualitative Risk Analysis—The process of prioritizing risks for further analysis or action by assessing and combining their probability of occurrence and impact.

11.4 Perform Quantitative Risk Analysis—The process of numerically analyzing the effect of identified risks on overall project objectives.

11.5 Plan Risk Responses—The process of developing options and actions to enhance opportunities and to reduce threats to project objectives.

11.6 Monitor and Control Risks—The process of implementing risk response plans, tracking identified risks, monitoring residual risks, identifying new risks, and evaluating risk process effectiveness throughout the project.

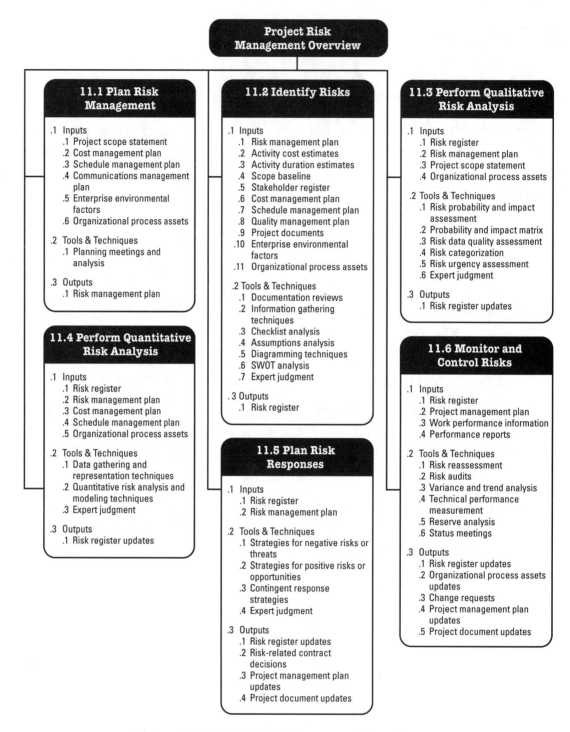

Project Risk Management Overview

11.1 Plan Risk Management

.1 Inputs
.1 Project scope statement
.2 Cost management plan
.3 Schedule management plan
.4 Communications management plan
.5 Enterprise environmental factors
.6 Organizational process assets

.2 Tools & Techniques
.1 Planning meetings and analysis

.3 Outputs
.1 Risk management plan

11.2 Identify Risks

.1 Inputs
.1 Risk management plan
.2 Activity cost estimates
.3 Activity duration estimates
.4 Scope baseline
.5 Stakeholder register
.6 Cost management plan
.7 Schedule management plan
.8 Quality management plan
.9 Project documents
.10 Enterprise environmental factors
.11 Organizational process assets

.2 Tools & Techniques
.1 Documentation reviews
.2 Information gathering techniques
.3 Checklist analysis
.4 Assumptions analysis
.5 Diagramming techniques
.6 SWOT analysis
.7 Expert judgment

.3 Outputs
.1 Risk register

11.3 Perform Qualitative Risk Analysis

.1 Inputs
.1 Risk register
.2 Risk management plan
.3 Project scope statement
.4 Organizational process assets

.2 Tools & Techniques
.1 Risk probability and impact assessment
.2 Probability and impact matrix
.3 Risk data quality assessment
.4 Risk categorization
.5 Risk urgency assessment
.6 Expert judgment

.3 Outputs
.1 Risk register updates

11.4 Perform Quantitative Risk Analysis

.1 Inputs
.1 Risk register
.2 Risk management plan
.3 Cost management plan
.4 Schedule management plan
.5 Organizational process assets

.2 Tools & Techniques
.1 Data gathering and representation techniques
.2 Quantitative risk analysis and modeling techniques
.3 Expert judgment

.3 Outputs
.1 Risk register updates

11.5 Plan Risk Responses

.1 Inputs
.1 Risk register
.2 Risk management plan

.2 Tools & Techniques
.1 Strategies for negative risks or threats
.2 Strategies for positive risks or opportunities
.3 Contingent response strategies
.4 Expert judgment

.3 Outputs
.1 Risk register updates
.2 Risk-related contract decisions
.3 Project management plan updates
.4 Project document updates

11.6 Monitor and Control Risks

.1 Inputs
.1 Risk register
.2 Project management plan
.3 Work performance information
.4 Performance reports

.2 Tools & Techniques
.1 Risk reassessment
.2 Risk audits
.3 Variance and trend analysis
.4 Technical performance measurement
.5 Reserve analysis
.6 Status meetings

.3 Outputs
.1 Risk register updates
.2 Organizational process assets updates
.3 Change requests
.4 Project management plan updates
.5 Project document updates

Figure 11-1. Project Risk Management Overview

These processes interact with each other and with the processes in the other Knowledge Areas. Each process can involve effort from one or more persons based on the needs of the project. Each process occurs at least once in every project and occurs in one or more of the project phases, if the project is divided into phases. Although the processes are presented here as discrete elements with well-defined interfaces, in practice they will overlap and interact in ways not detailed here. Process interactions are discussed in detail in Chapter 3 on Project Management Processes for a Project.

Project risk is always in the future. Risk is an uncertain event or condition that, if it occurs, has an effect on at least one project objective. Objectives can include scope, schedule, cost, and quality. A risk may have one or more causes and, if it occurs, it may have one or more impacts. A cause may be a requirement, assumption, constraint, or condition that creates the possibility of negative or positive outcomes. For example, causes could include the requirement of an environmental permit to do work, or having limited personnel assigned to design the project. The risk event is that the permitting agency may take longer than planned to issue a permit, or, in the case of an opportunity, limited design personnel available and assigned may still be able to get the job done on time, thereby accomplishing work with less resource utilization. If either of these uncertain events occurs, there may be an impact on the project cost, schedule, or performance. Risk conditions could include aspects of the project's or organization's environment that may contribute to project risk, such as immature project management practices, lack of integrated management systems, concurrent multiple projects, or dependency on external participants who cannot be controlled.

Project risk has its origins in the uncertainty present in all projects. Known risks are those that have been identified and analyzed, making it possible to plan responses for those risks. Specific unknown risks cannot be managed proactively, which suggests that the project team should create a contingency plan. A project risk that has occurred can also be considered an issue.

Organizations perceive risk as the effect of uncertainty on their project and organizational objectives. Organizations and stakeholders are willing to accept varying degrees of risk. This is called risk tolerance. Risks that are threats to the project may be accepted if the risks are within tolerances and are in balance with the rewards that may be gained by taking the risks. For example, adopting a fast track schedule (Section 6.5.2.7) is a risk taken to achieve the reward created by an earlier completion date.

Individuals and groups adopt attitudes toward risk that influence the way they respond. These risk attitudes are driven by perception, tolerances, and other biases, which should be made explicit wherever possible. A consistent approach to risk should be developed for each project, and communication about risk and its handling should be open and honest. Risk responses reflect an organization's perceived balance between risk-taking and risk avoidance.

To be successful, the organization should be committed to address risk management proactively and consistently throughout the project. A conscious choice must be made at all levels of the organization to actively identify and pursue effective risk management during the life of the project. Risk exists the moment a project is conceived. Moving forward on a project without a proactive focus on risk management increases the impact that a realized risk can have on the project and can potentially lead to project failure.

11.1 Plan Risk Management

Plan Risk Management is the process of defining how to conduct risk management activities for a project (see Figures 11-2 and 11-3). Careful and explicit planning enhances the probability of success for the five other risk management processes. Planning risk management processes is important to ensure that the degree, type, and visibility of risk management are commensurate with both the risks and the importance of the project to the organization. Planning is also important to provide sufficient resources and time for risk management activities, and to establish an agreed-upon basis for evaluating risks. The Plan Risk Management process should begin as a project is conceived and should be completed early during project planning.

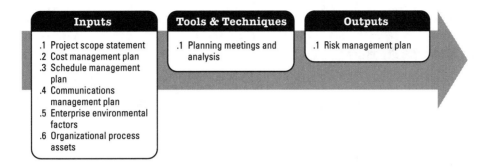

Inputs	Tools & Techniques	Outputs
.1 Project scope statement .2 Cost management plan .3 Schedule management plan .4 Communications management plan .5 Enterprise environmental factors .6 Organizational process assets	.1 Planning meetings and analysis	.1 Risk management plan

Figure 11-2. Plan Risk Management: Inputs, Tools & Techniques, and Outputs

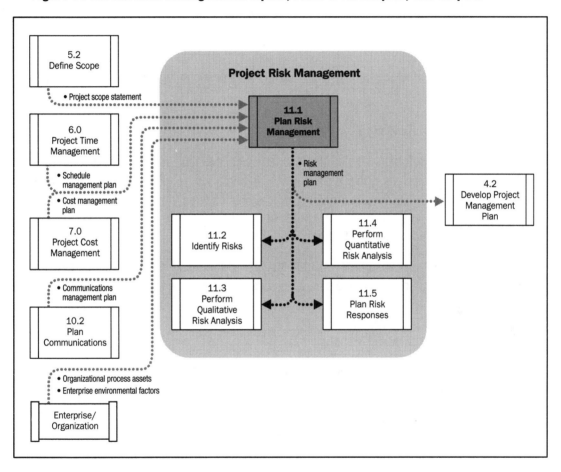

Figure 11-3. Plan Risk Management Data Flow Diagram

11.1.1 Plan Risk Management: Inputs

.1 Project Scope Statement

The project scope statement provides a clear sense of the range of possibilities associated with the project and its deliverables and establishes the framework for how significant the risk management effort may ultimately become. Described in Section 5.2.3.1.

.2 Cost Management Plan

The project cost management plan defines how risk budgets, contingencies, and management reserves will be reported and accessed. Described in Section 7.0.

.3 Schedule Management Plan

The schedule management plan defines how schedule contingencies will be reported and assessed. Described in Section 6.0.

.4 Communications Management Plan

The project communications management plan defines the interactions that will occur on the project, and determines who will be available to share information on various risks and responses at different times (and locations). Described in Section 10.2.3.1.

.5 Enterprise Environmental Factors

The enterprise environmental factors that can influence the Plan Risk Management process include, but are not limited to, risk attitudes and tolerances that describe the degree of risk that an organization will withstand.

.6 Organizational Process Assets

The organizational process assets that can influence the Plan Risk Management process include, but are not limited to:

- Risk categories,
- Common definitions of concepts and terms,
- Risk statement formats,
- Standard templates,
- Roles and responsibilities,

- Authority levels for decision-making,

- Lessons learned, and

- Stakeholder registers, which are also critical assets to be reviewed as components of establishing effective risk management plans.

11.1.2 Plan Risk Management: Tools and Techniques

.1 Planning Meetings and Analysis

Project teams hold planning meetings to develop the risk management plan. Attendees at these meetings may include the project manager, selected project team members and stakeholders, anyone in the organization with responsibility to manage the risk planning and execution activities, and others, as needed.

High-level plans for conducting the risk management activities are defined in these meetings. Risk management cost elements and schedule activities will be developed for inclusion in the project budget and schedule, respectively. Risk contingency reserve application approaches may be established or reviewed. Risk management responsibilities will be assigned. General organizational templates for risk categories and definitions of terms such as levels of risk, probability by type of risk, impact by type of objectives, and the probability and impact matrix will be tailored to the specific project. If templates for other steps in the process do not exist they may be generated in these meetings. The outputs of these activities will be summarized in the risk management plan.

11.1.3 Plan Risk Management: Outputs

.1 Risk Management Plan

The risk management plan describes how risk management will be structured and performed on the project. It becomes a subset of the project management plan (Section 4.2.3.1). The risk management plan includes the following:

- **Methodology.** Defines the approaches, tools, and data sources that may be used to perform risk management on the project.

- **Roles and responsibilities.** Defines the lead, support, and risk management team members for each type of activity in the risk management plan, and clarifies their responsibilities.

- **Budgeting.** Assigns resources, estimates funds needed for risk management for inclusion in the cost performance baseline, and establishes protocols for application of contingency reserve (Section 7.2.3.1).

- **Timing.** Defines when and how often the risk management process will be performed throughout the project life cycle, establishes protocols for application of schedule contingency reserves, and establishes risk management activities to be included in the project schedule (Section 6.5.3.1).

- **Risk categories.** Provides a structure that ensures a comprehensive process of systematically identifying risks to a consistent level of detail and contributes to the effectiveness and quality of the Identify Risks process. An organization can use a previously prepared categorization framework which might take the form of a simple list of categories or might be structured into a Risk Breakdown Structure (RBS). The RBS is a hierarchically organized depiction of the identified project risks arranged by risk category and subcategory that identifies the various areas and causes of potential risks. An example is shown in Figure 11-4.

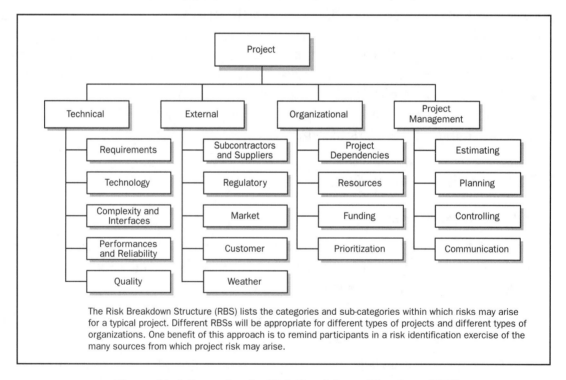

The Risk Breakdown Structure (RBS) lists the categories and sub-categories within which risks may arise for a typical project. Different RBSs will be appropriate for different types of projects and different types of organizations. One benefit of this approach is to remind participants in a risk identification exercise of the many sources from which project risk may arise.

Figure 11-4. Example of a Risk Breakdown Structure (RBS)

- **Definitions of risk probability and impact.** The quality and credibility of the Perform Qualitative Risk Analysis process requires that different levels of the risks' probabilities and impacts be defined. General definitions of probability levels and impact levels are tailored to the individual project during the Plan Risk Management process for use in the Perform Qualitative Risk Analysis process (Section 11.3). Figure 11-5 is an example of definitions of negative impacts that could be used in evaluating risk impacts related to four project objectives. (Similar tables could be established with a positive impact perspective). The figure illustrates both relative and numeric (in this case, nonlinear) approaches.

Defined Conditions for Impact Scales of a Risk on Major Project Objectives (Examples are shown for negative impacts only)					
	Relative or numerical scales are shown				
Project Objective	Very low /.05	Low /.10	Moderate /.20	High /.40	Very high /.80
Cost	Insignificant cost increase	<10% cost increase	10-20% cost increase	20-40% cost increase	>40% cost increase
Time	Insignificant time increase	<5% time increase	5-10% time increase	10-20% time increase	>20% time increase
Scope	Scope decrease barely noticeable	Minor areas of scope affected	Major areas of scope affected	Scope reduction unacceptable to sponsor	Project end item is effectively useless
Quality	Quality degradation barely noticeable	Only very demanding applications are affected	Quality reduction requires sponsor approval	Quality reduction unacceptable to sponsor	Project end item is effectively useless

This table presents examples of risk impact definitions for four different project objectives. They should be tailored in the Risk Management Planning process to the individual project and to the organization's risk thresholds. Impact definitions can be developed for opportunities in a similar way.

Figure 11-5. Definition of Impact Scales for Four Project Objectives

- **Probability and impact matrix.** Risks are prioritized according to their potential implications for having an effect on the project's objectives. A typical approach to prioritizing risks is to use a look-up table or a Probability and Impact Matrix (Section 11.3.2.2). The specific combinations of probability and impact that lead to a risk being rated as "high," "moderate," or "low" importance, with the corresponding importance for planning responses to the risk (Section 11.5), are usually set by the organization.

- **Revised stakeholders' tolerances.** Stakeholders' tolerances, as they apply to the specific project, may be revised in the Plan Risk Management process.

- **Reporting formats.** Defines how the outcomes of the risk management processes will be documented, analyzed, and communicated. It describes the content and format of the risk register as well as any other risk reports required.

- **Tracking.** Documents how risk activities will be recorded for the benefit of the current project, as well as for future needs and lessons learned, as well as whether and how risk management processes will be audited.

11.2 Identify Risks

Identify Risks is the process of determining which risks may affect the project and documenting their characteristics (see Figures 11-6 and 11-7). Participants in risk identification activities can include the following: project manager, project team members, risk management team (if assigned), customers, subject matter experts from outside the project team, end users, other project managers, stakeholders, and risk management experts. While these personnel are often key participants for risk identification, all project personnel should be encouraged to identify risks.

Identify Risks is an iterative process because new risks may evolve or become known as the project progresses through its life cycle. The frequency of iteration and who participates in each cycle will vary by situation. The format of the risk statements should be consistent to ensure the ability to compare the relative effect of one risk event against others on the project. The process should involve the project team so they can develop and maintain a sense of ownership and responsibility for the risks and associated risk response actions. Stakeholders outside the project team may provide additional objective information.

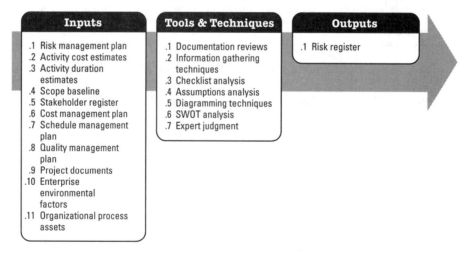

Inputs	Tools & Techniques	Outputs
.1 Risk management plan .2 Activity cost estimates .3 Activity duration estimates .4 Scope baseline .5 Stakeholder register .6 Cost management plan .7 Schedule management plan .8 Quality management plan .9 Project documents .10 Enterprise environmental factors .11 Organizational process assets	.1 Documentation reviews .2 Information gathering techniques .3 Checklist analysis .4 Assumptions analysis .5 Diagramming techniques .6 SWOT analysis .7 Expert judgment	.1 Risk register

Figure 11-6. Identify Risks: Inputs, Tools & Techniques, and Outputs

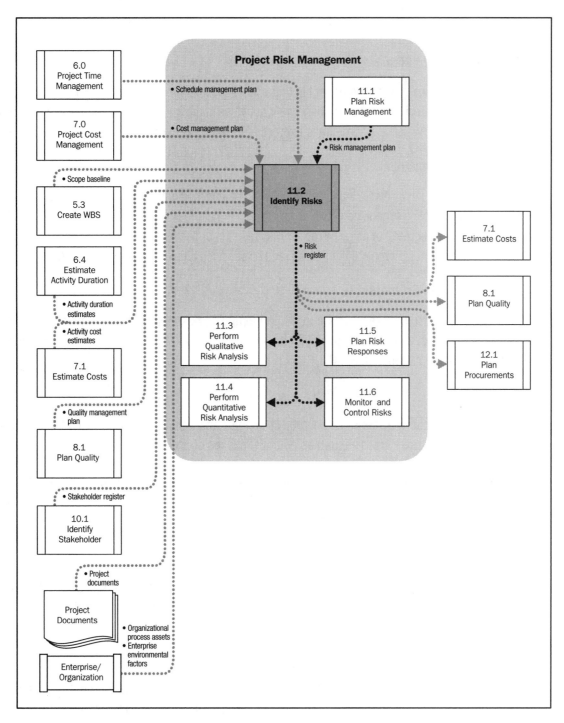

Figure 11-7. Identify Risks Data Flow Diagram

11.2.1 Identify Risks: Inputs

.1 Risk Management Plan

Key inputs from the risk management plan to the Identify Risks process are the assignments of roles and responsibilities, provision for risk management activities in the budget and schedule, and categories of risk (Section 11.1), which are sometimes expressed in a risk breakdown structure (Figure 11-4).

.2 Activity Cost Estimates

Activity cost estimate reviews are useful in identifying risk as they provide a quantitative assessment of the likely cost to complete scheduled activities and ideally are expressed as a range, with the width of the range indicating the degree(s) of risk. The review may result in projections indicating the estimate is either sufficient or insufficient to complete the activity (and hence pose a risk to the project) (Section 7.1.3.1).

.3 Activity Duration Estimates

Activity duration estimate reviews are useful in identifying risks related to the time allowances for the activities or project as a whole, again with the width of the range of such estimates indicating the relative degree(s) of risk (Section 6.4.3.1).

.4 Scope Baseline

Project assumptions are found in the project scope statement (Section 5.2.3.1). Uncertainty in project assumptions should be evaluated as potential causes of project risk.

The WBS is a critical input to identifying risks as it facilitates an understanding of the potential risks at both the micro and macro levels. Risks can be identified and subsequently tracked at summary, control account, and/or work package levels.

.5 Stakeholder Register

Information about the stakeholders will be useful in soliciting inputs for identifying risks as this will ensure that key stakeholders, especially the customer, are interviewed or otherwise participate during the "Identify Risks" process (Section 10.1.3.1).

.6 Cost Management Plan

The risk identification process requires an understanding of the cost management plans found in the project management plan (Section 7.0). The project-specific approach to cost management may generate or alleviate risk by its nature or structure.

.7 Schedule Management Plan

The risk identification process also requires an understanding of the schedule management plan found in the project management plan (Section 6.0). The project-specific approach to schedule management may generate or alleviate risk by its nature or structure.

.8 Quality Management Plan

The risk identification process also requires an understanding of the quality management plan found in the project management plan (Section 8.1.3.1). The project-specific approach to quality management may generate or alleviate risk by its nature or structure.

.9 Project Documents

Project documents include, but are not limited to:

- Assumptions log,
- Work performance reports,
- Earned value reports,
- Network diagrams,
- Baselines, and
- Other project information proven to be valuable in identifying risks.

.10 Enterprise Environmental Factors

The enterprise environmental factors that can influence the Identify Risks process include, but are not limited to:

- Published information, including commercial databases,
- Academic studies,
- Published checklists,
- Benchmarking,
- Industry studies, and
- Risk attitudes.

.11 Organizational Process Assets

The organizational process assets that can influence the Identify Risks process include, but are not limited to:

- Project files, including actual data,

- Organizational and project process controls,

- Risk statement templates, and

- Lessons learned.

11.2.2 Identify Risks: Tools and Techniques

.1 Documentation Reviews

A structured review may be performed of project documentation, including plans, assumptions, previous project files, contracts, and other information. The quality of the plans, as well as consistency between those plans and the project requirements and assumptions, can be indicators of risk in the project.

.2 Information Gathering Techniques

Examples of information gathering techniques used in identifying risk can include:

- **Brainstorming.** The goal of brainstorming is to obtain a comprehensive list of project risks. The project team usually performs brainstorming, often with a multidisciplinary set of experts who are not part of the team. Ideas about project risk are generated under the leadership of a facilitator, either in a traditional free-form brainstorm session with ideas contributed by participants, or structured using mass interviewing techniques such as the nominal group technique. Categories of risk, such as a risk breakdown structure, can be used as a framework. Risks are then identified and categorized by type of risk and their definitions are sharpened.

- **Delphi technique.** The Delphi technique is a way to reach a consensus of experts. Project risk experts participate in this technique anonymously. A facilitator uses a questionnaire to solicit ideas about the important project risks. The responses are summarized and are then recirculated to the experts for further comment. Consensus may be reached in a few rounds of this process. The Delphi technique helps reduce bias in the data and keeps any one person from having undue influence on the outcome.

- **Interviewing.** Interviewing experienced project participants, stakeholders, and subject matter experts can identify risks.

- **Root cause analysis.** Root cause analysis is a specific technique to identify a problem, discover the underlying causes that lead to it, and develop preventive action.

.3 Checklist Analysis

Risk identification checklists can be developed based on historical information and knowledge that has been accumulated from previous similar projects and from other sources of information. The lowest level of the RBS can also be used as a risk checklist. While a checklist can be quick and simple, it is impossible to build an exhaustive one. The team should make sure to explore items that do not appear on the checklist. The checklist should be reviewed during project closure to incorporate new lessons learned and improve it for use on future projects.

.4 Assumptions Analysis

Every project and every identified project risk is conceived and developed based on a set of hypotheses, scenarios, or assumptions. Assumptions analysis explores the validity of assumptions as they apply to the project. It identifies risks to the project from inaccuracy, instability, inconsistency, or incompleteness of assumptions.

.5 Diagramming Techniques

Risk diagramming techniques may include:

- **Cause and effect diagrams** (Section 8.3.2.1). These are also known as Ishikawa or fishbone diagrams, and are useful for identifying causes of risks.

- **System or process flow charts.** These show how various elements of a system interrelate, and the mechanism of causation (Section 8.3.2.3).

- **Influence diagrams.** These are graphical representations of situations showing causal influences, time ordering of events, and other relationships among variables and outcomes.

.6 SWOT Analysis

This technique examines the project from each of the SWOT (strengths, weaknesses, opportunities, and threats) perspectives to increase the breadth of identified risks by including internally generated risks. The technique starts with identification of strengths and weaknesses of the organization, focusing on either the project organization or the wider business. These factors are often identified using brainstorming. SWOT analysis then identifies any opportunities for the project that arise from organizational strengths, and any threats arising from organizational weaknesses. SWOT analysis also examines the degree to which organizational strengths offset threats and opportunities that may serve to overcome weaknesses.

.7 Expert Judgment

Risks can be identified directly by experts with relevant experience of similar projects or business areas. Such experts should be identified by the project manager and invited to consider all aspects of the project and suggest possible risks based on their previous experience and areas of expertise. The experts' bias should be taken into account in this process.

11.2.3 Identify Risks: Outputs

The main outputs from Identify Risks are typically contained in the risk register.

.1 Risk Register

The primary outputs from Identify Risks are the initial entries into the risk register. The risk register ultimately contains the outcomes of the other risk management processes as they are conducted, resulting in an increase in the level and type of information contained in the risk register over time. The preparation of the risk register begins in the Identify Risks process with the following information, and then becomes available to other project management and Project Risk Management processes.

- **List of identified risks.** The identified risks are described in as much detail as is reasonable. A simple structure for risks in the list may be applied, such as EVENT may occur, causing IMPACT, or If CAUSE, EVENT may occur, leading to EFFECT. In addition to the list of identified risks, the root causes of those risks may become more evident. These are the fundamental conditions or events that may give rise to one or more identified risks. They should be recorded and used to support future risk identification for this and other projects.

- **List of potential responses.** Potential responses to a risk may sometimes be identified during the Identify Risks process. These responses, if identified in this process, may be useful as inputs to the Plan Risk Responses process (Section 11.5).

11.3 Perform Qualitative Risk Analysis

Perform Qualitative Risk Analysis is the process of prioritizing risks for further analysis or action by assessing and combining their probability of occurrence and impact (see Figures 11-8 and 11-9). Organizations can improve the project's performance by focusing on high-priority risks. Perform Qualitative Risk Analysis assesses the priority of identified risks using their relative probability or likelihood of occurrence, the corresponding impact on project objectives if the risks occur, as well as other factors such as the time frame for response and the organization's risk tolerance associated with the project constraints of cost, schedule, scope, and quality. Such assessments reflect the attitude of the project team and other stakeholders to risk. Effective assessment therefore requires explicit identification and management of the risk attitudes of key participants in the Perform Qualitative Risk Analysis process. Where these risk attitudes introduce bias into the assessment of identified risks, attention should be paid to evaluating bias and correcting for it.

Establishing definitions of the levels of probability and impact can reduce the influence of bias. The time criticality of risk-related actions may magnify the importance of a risk. An evaluation of the quality of the available information on project risks also helps clarify the assessment of the risk's importance to the project.

Perform Qualitative Risk Analysis is usually a rapid and cost-effective means of establishing priorities for Plan Risk Responses and lays the foundation for Perform Quantitative Risk Analysis, if required. The Perform Qualitative Risk Analysis process should be revisited during the project's life cycle to stay current with changes in the project risks. This process can lead into Perform Quantitative Risk Analysis (Section 11.4) or directly into Plan Risk Responses (Section 11.5).

Figure 11-8. Perform Qualitative Risk Analysis: Inputs, Tools & Techniques, and Outputs

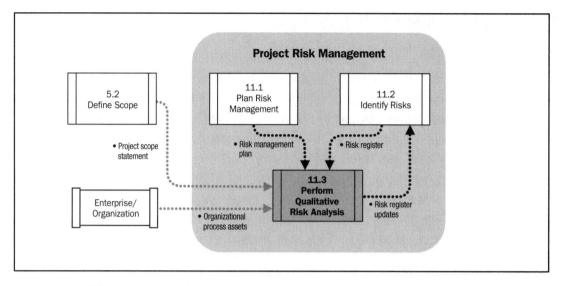

Figure 11-9. Perform Qualitative Risk Analysis Data Flow Diagram

11.3.1 Perform Qualitative Risk Analysis: Inputs

.1 Risk Register

See Section 11.2.3.1.

.2 Risk Management Plan

Key elements of the risk management plan for Perform Qualitative Risk Analysis include roles and responsibilities for conducting risk management, budgets, schedule activities for risk management, risk categories, definitions of probability and impact, the probability and impact matrix, and revised stakeholders' risk tolerances. These inputs are usually tailored to the project during the Plan Risk Management process (Section 11.1). If they are not available they can be developed during the Perform Qualitative Risk Analysis process (Section 11.3).

.3 Project Scope Statement

Projects of a common or recurrent type tend to have more well-understood risks. Projects using state-of-the-art or first-of-its-kind technology, and highly complex projects, tend to have more uncertainty. This can be evaluated by examining the project scope statement (Section 5.2.3.1).

.4 Organizational Process Assets

The organizational process assets that can influence the Perform Qualitative Risk Analysis process include, but are not limited to:

- Information on prior, similar completed projects,
- Studies of similar projects by risk specialists, and
- Risk databases that may be available from industry or proprietary sources.

11.3.2 Perform Qualitative Risk Analysis: Tools and Techniques

.1 Risk Probability and Impact Assessment

Risk probability assessment investigates the likelihood that each specific risk will occur. Risk impact assessment investigates the potential effect on a project objective such as schedule, cost, quality, or performance, including both negative effects for threats and positive effects for opportunities.

Probability and impact are assessed for each identified risk. Risks can be assessed in interviews or meetings with participants selected for their familiarity with the risk categories on the agenda. Project team members and, perhaps, knowledgeable persons from outside the project, are included.

The level of probability for each risk and its impact on each objective is evaluated during the interview or meeting. Explanatory detail, including assumptions justifying the levels assigned, is also recorded. Risk probabilities and impacts are rated according to the definitions given in the risk management plan (Section 11.1.3.1). Risks with low ratings of probability and impact will be included on a watchlist for future monitoring.

.2 Probability and Impact Matrix

Risks can be prioritized for further quantitative analysis and response based on their risk rating. Usually, these risk-rating rules are specified by the organization in advance of the project and included in organizational process assets. Risk-rating rules can be tailored to the specific project in the Plan Risk Management process (Section 11.1). Evaluation of each risk's importance and, hence, priority for attention, is typically conducted using a look-up table or a probability and impact matrix (Figure 11-10). Such a matrix specifies combinations of probability and impact that lead to rating the risks as low, moderate, or high priority. The dark gray area (with the largest numbers) represents high risk, the medium gray area (with the smallest numbers) represents low risk, and the light gray area (with in-between numbers) represents moderate risk.

Probability and Impact Matrix

Probability	Threats					Opportunities				
0.90	0.05	0.09	0.18	0.36	0.72	0.72	0.36	0.18	0.09	0.05
0.70	0.04	0.07	0.14	0.28	0.56	0.56	0.28	0.14	0.07	0.04
0.50	0.03	0.05	0.10	0.20	0.40	0.40	0.20	0.10	0.05	0.03
0.30	0.02	0.03	0.06	0.12	0.24	0.24	0.12	0.06	0.03	0.02
0.10	0.01	0.01	0.02	0.04	0.08	0.08	0.04	0.02	0.01	0.01
	0.05	0.10	0.20	0.40	0.80	0.80	0.40	0.20	0.10	0.05

Impact (numerical scale) on an objective (e.g., cost, time, scope or quality)

Each risk is rated on its probability of occurring and impact on an objective if it does occur. The organization's thresholds for low, moderate or high risks are shown in the matrix and determine whether the risk is scored as high, moderate or low for that objective.

Figure 11-10. Probability and Impact Matrix

As illustrated in Figure 11-5, an organization can rate a risk separately for each objective (e.g., cost, time, and scope). In addition, it can develop ways to determine one overall rating for each risk. An overall project rating scheme can be developed to reflect the organization's preference for one objective over another and using those preferences to develop a weighting of the risks that are assessed by objective. Finally, opportunities and threats can be handled in the same matrix using definitions of the different levels of impact that are appropriate for each.

The risk rating helps guide risk responses. For example, risks that have a negative impact on objectives if they occur (threats), and that are in the high-risk (dark gray) zone of the matrix, may require priority action and aggressive response strategies. Threats in the low-risk (medium gray) zone may not require proactive management action beyond being placed on a watchlist or adding a contingency reserve.

Similarly, opportunities in the high-risk (dark gray) zone that can be obtained most easily and offer the greatest benefit should be targeted first. Opportunities in the low-risk (medium gray) zone should be monitored. The values provided in Figure 11-10 are representative. The number of steps in the scale is organizationally determined and organizationally dependent.

.3 Risk Data Quality Assessment

A qualitative risk analysis requires accurate and unbiased data if it is to be credible. Analysis of the quality of risk data is a technique to evaluate the degree to which the data about risks are useful for risk management. It involves examining the degree to which the risk is understood and the accuracy, quality, reliability, and integrity of the data regarding the risk. If data quality is unacceptable, it may be necessary to gather higher-quality data.

.4 Risk Categorization

Risks to the project can be categorized by sources of risk (e.g., using the RBS), the area of the project affected (e.g., using the WBS), or other useful category (e.g., project phase) to determine areas of the project most exposed to the effects of uncertainty. Grouping risks by common root causes can lead to developing effective risk responses.

.5 Risk Urgency Assessment

Risks requiring near-term responses may be considered more urgent to address. Indicators of priority can include time to affect a risk response, symptoms and warning signs, and the risk rating. In some qualitative analyses the assessment of risk urgency can be combined with the risk ranking determined from the probability and impact matrix to give a final risk severity rating.

.6 Expert Judgment

Expert judgment is required to assess the probability and impact of each risk to determine its location in the matrix shown in Figure 11-10. Experts generally are those having experience with similar projects that occurred in the not-too-distant past. In addition, those who are planning and managing the specific project are experts, particularly about the specifics of that project. Securing expert judgment is often accomplished with the use of risk facilitation workshops or interviews. The experts' bias should be taken into account in this process.

11.3.3 Perform Qualitative Risk Analysis: Outputs

.1 Risk Register Updates

The risk register is started during the Identify Risks process. The risk register is updated with information from Perform Qualitative Risk Analysis and the updated risk register is included in the project documents. The risk register updates from Perform Qualitative Risk Analysis include:

- **Relative ranking or priority list of project risks.** The probability and impact matrix can be used to classify risks according to their individual significance. Using combinations of each risk's probability of occurring and the impact on objectives if it were to occur, risks will be prioritized relative to each other by sorting them into groups of "high risk," "moderate risk," and "low risk." Risks may be listed by priority separately for schedule, cost, and performance since organizations may value one objective over another. The project manager can then use the prioritized list of risks to focus attention on those items of high significance (high risk) to the most important objectives, where responses can lead to better project outcomes. A description of the basis for the assessed probability and impact should be included for risks assessed as important to the project.

- **Risks grouped by categories.** Risk categorization can reveal common root causes of risk or project areas requiring particular attention. Discovering concentrations of risk may improve the effectiveness of risk responses.

- **Causes of risk or project areas requiring particular attention.** Discovering concentrations of risk may improve the effectiveness of risk responses.

- **List of risks requiring response in the near-term.** Those risks that require an urgent response and those that can be handled at a later date may be put into different groups.

- **List of risks for additional analysis and response.** Some risks might warrant more analysis, including Quantitative Risk Analysis, as well as response action.

- **Watchlists of low-priority risks.** Risks that are not assessed as important in the Perform Qualitative Risk Analysis process can be placed on a watchlist for continued monitoring.

- **Trends in qualitative risk analysis results.** As the analysis is repeated, a trend for particular risks may become apparent, and can make risk response or further analysis more or less urgent/important.

11.4 Perform Quantitative Risk Analysis

Perform Quantitative Risk Analysis is the process of numerically analyzing the effect of identified risks on overall project objectives (Figures 11-11 and 11-12). Perform Quantitative Risk Analysis is performed on risks that have been prioritized by the Perform Qualitative Risk Analysis process as potentially and substantially impacting the project's competing demands. The Perform Quantitative Risk Analysis process analyzes the effect of those risk events. It may be used to assign a numerical rating to those risks individually or to evaluate the aggregate effect of all risks affecting the project. It also presents a quantitative approach to making decisions in the presence of uncertainty.

Perform Quantitative Risk Analysis generally follows the Perform Qualitative Risk Analysis process. In some cases, Perform Quantitative Risk Analysis may not be required to develop effective risk responses. Availability of time and budget, and the need for qualitative or quantitative statements about risk and impacts, will determine which method(s) to use on any particular project. Perform Quantitative Risk Analysis should be repeated after Plan Risk Responses, as well as part of Monitor and Control Risks, to determine if the overall project risk has been satisfactorily decreased. Trends can indicate the need for more or less risk management action.

Figure 11-11. Perform Quantitative Risk Analysis: Inputs, Tools & Techniques, and Outputs

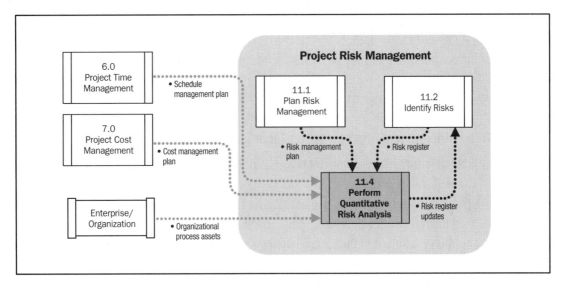

Figure 11-12. Perform Quantitative Risk Analysis Data Flow Diagram

11.4.1 Perform Quantitative Risk Analysis: Inputs

.1 Risk Register

See Section 11.2.3.1.

.2 Risk Management Plan

See Section 11.1.3.1.

.3 Cost Management Plan

The project cost management plan sets the format and establishes criteria for planning, structuring, estimating, budgeting, and controlling project costs (Section 7.0). Those controls may help determine the structure and/or application approach for quantitative analysis of the budget or cost plan.

.4 Schedule Management Plan

The project schedule management plan sets the format and establishes criteria for developing and controlling the project schedule (Section 6.0). Those controls and the nature of the schedule itself may help determine the structure and/or application approach for quantitative analysis of the schedule.

.5 Organizational Process Assets

The organizational process assets that can influence the Perform Quantitative Risk Analysis process include, but are not limited to:

- Information on prior, similar completed projects,

- Studies of similar projects by risk specialists, and

- Risk databases that may be available from industry or proprietary sources.

11.4.2 Perform Quantitative Risk Analysis: Tools and Techniques

.1 Data Gathering and Representation Techniques

- **Interviewing.** Interviewing techniques draw on experience and historical data to quantify the probability and impact of risks on project objectives. The information needed depends upon the type of probability distributions that will be used. For instance, information would be gathered on the optimistic (low), pessimistic (high), and most likely scenarios for some commonly used distributions. Examples of three-point estimates for cost are shown in Figure 11-13. Additional information on three point estimates is in Estimate Activity Durations (Section 6.4.2.4) and Estimate Costs (Section 7.1.2.5). Documenting the rationale of the risk ranges and the assumptions behind them are important components of the risk interview because they can provide insight on the reliability and credibility of the analysis.

Range of Project Cost Estimates

WBS Element	Low	Most Likely	High
Design	$4M	$6M	$10M
Build	$16M	$20M	$35M
Test	$11M	$15M	$23M
Total Project	$31M	$41M	$68M

Interviewing relevant stakeholders helps determine the three-point estimates for each WBS element for triangular, beta or other distributions. In this example, the likelihood of completing the project at or below the most likely estimate of $41 million is relatively small as shown in the simulation results in Figure 11-16 (Cost Risk Simulation Results).

Figure 11-13. Range of Project Cost Estimates Collected During the Risk Interview

- **Probability distributions.** Continuous probability distributions, used extensively in modeling and simulation (Section 11.4.2.2) represent the uncertainty in values such as durations of schedule activities and costs of project components. Discrete distributions can be used to represent uncertain events such as the outcome of a test or a possible scenario in a decision tree. Two examples of widely used continuous distributions are shown in Figure 11-14. These distributions depict shapes that are compatible with the data typically developed during the quantitative risk analysis. Uniform distributions can be used only if there is no obvious value that is more likely than any other between specified high and low bounds, such as in the early concept stage of design.

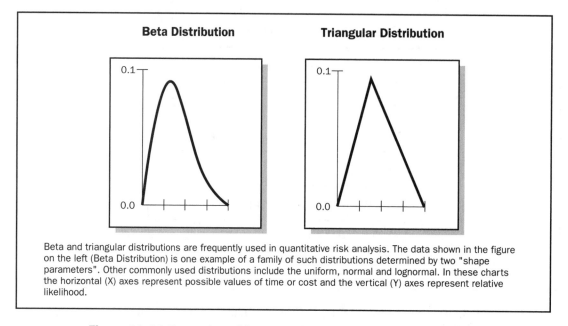

Beta and triangular distributions are frequently used in quantitative risk analysis. The data shown in the figure on the left (Beta Distribution) is one example of a family of such distributions determined by two "shape parameters". Other commonly used distributions include the uniform, normal and lognormal. In these charts the horizontal (X) axes represent possible values of time or cost and the vertical (Y) axes represent relative likelihood.

Figure 11-14. Examples of Commonly Used Probability Distributions

.2 Quantitative Risk Analysis and Modeling Techniques

Commonly used techniques include both event-oriented and project-oriented analysis approaches including:

- **Sensitivity analysis.** Sensitivity analysis helps to determine which risks have the most potential impact on the project. It examines the extent to which the uncertainty of each project element affects the objective being examined when all other uncertain elements are held at their baseline values. One typical display of sensitivity analysis is the tornado diagram, which is useful for comparing relative importance and impact of variables that have a high degree of uncertainty to those that are more stable.

- **Expected monetary value analysis.** Expected monetary value (EMV) analysis is a statistical concept that calculates the average outcome when the future includes scenarios that may or may not happen (i.e., analysis under uncertainty). The EMV of opportunities will generally be expressed as positive values, while those of threats will be negative. EMV requires a risk-neutral assumption, neither risk averse, nor risk seeking. EMV for a project is calculated by multiplying the value of each possible outcome by its probability of occurrence and adding the products together. A common use of this type of analysis is in decision tree analysis (Figure 11-15).

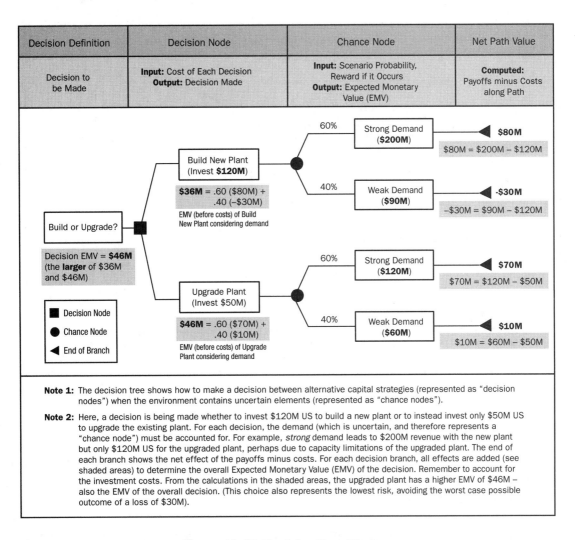

Figure 11-15. Decision Tree Diagram

- **Modeling and simulation.** A project simulation uses a model that translates the specified detailed uncertainties of the project into their potential impact on project objectives. Iterative simulations are typically performed using the Monte Carlo technique. In a simulation, the project model is computed many times (iterated), with the input values (e.g., cost estimates or activity durations) chosen at random for each iteration from the probability distributions of these variables. A probability distribution (e.g., total cost or completion date) is calculated from the iterations. For a cost risk analysis, a simulation uses cost estimates. For a schedule risk analysis, the schedule network diagram and duration estimates are used. The output from a cost risk simulation is shown in Figure 11-16. It illustrates the respective likelihood of achieving specific cost targets. Similar curves can be developed for schedule outcomes.

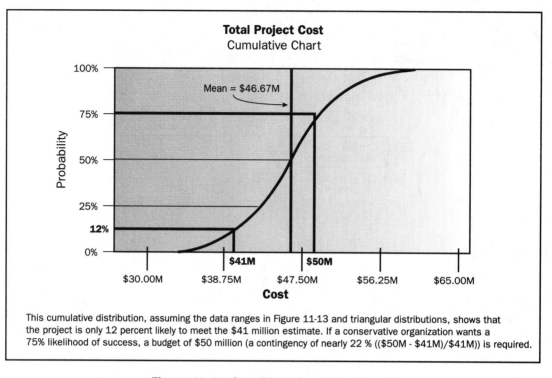

Total Project Cost
Cumulative Chart

This cumulative distribution, assuming the data ranges in Figure 11-13 and triangular distributions, shows that the project is only 12 percent likely to meet the $41 million estimate. If a conservative organization wants a 75% likelihood of success, a budget of $50 million (a contingency of nearly 22 % (($50M - $41M)/$41M)) is required.

Figure 11-16. Cost Risk Simulation Results

.3 Expert Judgment

Expert judgment (ideally using experts with relevant, recent experience) is required to identify potential cost and schedule impacts, to evaluate probability, and to define inputs (such as probability distributions) into the tools.

Expert judgment also comes into play in the interpretation of the data. Experts should be able to identify the weaknesses of the tools as well as their relative strengths. Experts may determine when a specific tool may or may not be more appropriate given the organization's capabilities and culture.

11.4.3 Perform Quantitative Risk Analysis: Outputs

.1 Risk Register Updates

The risk register is further updated to include a quantitative risk report detailing quantitative approaches, outputs, and recommendations. Updates include the following main components:

- **Probabilistic analysis of the project.** Estimates are made of potential project schedule and cost outcomes listing the possible completion dates and costs with their associated confidence levels. This output, often expressed as a cumulative distribution, can be used with stakeholder risk tolerances to permit quantification of the cost and time contingency reserves. Such contingency reserves are needed to bring the risk of overrunning stated project objectives to a level acceptable to the organization. For instance, in Figure 11-16, the cost contingency to the 75th percentile is $9 million US, or about 22% when compared to the $41 million US sum of the most likely estimates shown in Figure 11-13.

- **Probability of achieving cost and time objectives.** With the risks facing the project, the probability of achieving project objectives under the current plan can be estimated using quantitative risk analysis results. For instance, in Figure 11-16, the likelihood of achieving the cost estimate of $41 million US (from Figure 11-13) is about 12%.

- **Prioritized list of quantified risks.** This list of risks includes those that pose the greatest threat or present the greatest opportunity to the project. These include the risks that may have the greatest effect on cost contingency and those that are most likely to influence the critical path. These risks may be identified, in some cases, through a tornado diagram generated as a result of the simulation analyses.

- **Trends in quantitative risk analysis results.** As the analysis is repeated, a trend may become apparent that leads to conclusions affecting risk responses. Organizational historical information on project schedule, cost, quality, and performance should reflect new insights gained through the Perform Quantitative Risk Analysis process. Such history may take the form of a quantitative risk analysis report. This report may be separate from, or linked to, the risk register.

11.5 Plan Risk Responses

Plan Risk Responses is the process of developing options and actions to enhance opportunities and to reduce threats to project objectives (Figures 11-17 and 11-18). It follows the Perform Qualitative Risk Analysis process and the Perform Quantitative Risk Analysis process (if used). It includes the identification and assignment of one person (the "risk response owner") to take responsibility for each agreed-to and funded risk response. Plan Risk Responses addresses the risks by their priority, inserting resources and activities into the budget, schedule and project management plan as needed.

Planned risk responses must be appropriate to the significance of the risk, cost effective in meeting the challenge, realistic within the project context, agreed upon by all parties involved, and owned by a responsible person. They must also be timely. Selecting the best risk response from several options is often required.

The Plan Risk Responses section presents commonly used approaches to planning responses to the risks. Risks include threats and opportunities that can affect project success, and responses are discussed for each.

Inputs	Tools & Techniques	Outputs
.1 Risk register	.1 Strategies for negative risks or threats	.1 Risk register updates
.2 Risk management plan	.2 Strategies for positive risks or opportunities	.2 Risk-related contract decisions
	.3 Contingent response strategies	.3 Project management plan updates
	.4 Expert judgment	.4 Project document updates

Figure 11-17. Plan Risk Responses: Inputs, Tools & Techniques, and Outputs

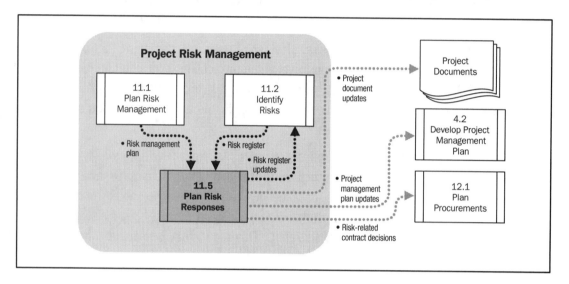

Figure 11-18. Plan Risk Responses Data Flow Diagram

11.5.1 Plan Risk Responses: Inputs

.1 Risk Register

The risk register refers to identified risks, root causes of risks, lists of potential responses, risk owners, symptoms and warning signs, the relative rating or priority list of project risks, a list of risks requiring response in the near term, a list of risks for additional analysis and response, trends in qualitative analysis results, and a watchlist of low-priority risks.

.2 Risk Management Plan

Important components of the risk management plan include roles and responsibilities, risk analysis definitions, timing for reviews (and for eliminating risks from review) and risk thresholds for low, moderate, and high risks. Risk thresholds help identify those risks for which specific responses are needed.

11.5.2 Plan Risk Responses: Tools and Techniques

Several risk response strategies are available. The strategy or mix of strategies most likely to be effective should be selected for each risk. Risk analysis tools, such as decision tree analysis (Section 11.4.2.2), can be used to choose the most appropriate responses. Specific actions are developed to implement that strategy, including primary and backup strategies, as necessary. A fallback plan can be developed for implementation if the selected strategy turns out not to be fully effective or if an accepted risk occurs. Secondary risks (risks driven by the strategies) should also be reviewed. A contingency reserve is often allocated for time or cost. If developed, it may include identification of the conditions that trigger its use.

.1 Strategies for Negative Risks or Threats

Three of the following strategies typically deal with threats or risks that may have negative impacts on project objectives if they occur. The fourth strategy, accept, can be used for negative risks or threats as well as positive risks or opportunities. These strategies, described below, are to avoid, transfer, mitigate, or accept.

- **Avoid.** Risk avoidance involves changing the project management plan to eliminate the threat entirely. The project manager may also isolate the project objectives from the risk's impact or change the objective that is in jeopardy. Examples of this include extending the schedule, changing the strategy, or reducing scope. The most radical avoidance strategy is to shut down the project entirely. Some risks that arise early in the project can be avoided by clarifying requirements, obtaining information, improving communication, or acquiring expertise.

- **Transfer.** Risk transfer requires shifting some or all of the negative impact of a threat, along with ownership of the response, to a third party. Transferring the risk simply gives another party responsibility for its management—it does not eliminate it. Transferring liability for risk is most effective in dealing with financial risk exposure. Risk transference nearly always involves payment of a risk premium to the party taking on the risk. Transference tools can be quite diverse and include, but are not limited to, the use of insurance, performance bonds, warranties, guarantees, etc. Contracts may be used to transfer liability for specified risks to another party. For example, when a buyer has capabilities that the seller does not possess, it may be prudent to transfer some work and its concurrent risk contractually back to the buyer. In many cases, use of a cost-plus contract may transfer the cost risk to the buyer, while a fixed-price contract may transfer risk to the seller.

- **Mitigate.** Risk mitigation implies a reduction in the probability and/or impact of an adverse risk event to be within acceptable threshold limits. Taking early action to reduce the probability and/or impact of a risk occurring on the project is often more effective than trying to repair the damage after the risk has occurred. Adopting less complex processes, conducting more tests, or choosing a more stable supplier are examples of mitigation actions. Mitigation may require prototype development to reduce the risk of scaling up from a bench-scale model of a process or product. Where it is not possible to reduce probability, a mitigation response might address the risk impact by targeting linkages that determine the severity. For example, designing redundancy into a system may reduce the impact from a failure of the original component.

- **Accept.** This strategy is adopted because it is seldom possible to eliminate all threats from a project. This strategy indicates that the project team has decided not to change the project management plan to deal with a risk, or is unable to identify any other suitable response strategy. This strategy can be either passive or active. Passive acceptance requires no action except to document the strategy, leaving the project team to deal with the risks as they occur. The most common active acceptance strategy is to establish a contingency reserve, including amounts of time, money, or resources to handle the risks.

.2 Strategies for Positive Risks or Opportunities

Three of the four responses are suggested to deal with risks with potentially positive impacts on project objectives. The fourth strategy, accept, can be used for negative risks or threats as well as positive risks or opportunities. These strategies, described below, are to exploit, share, enhance, or accept.

- **Exploit.** This strategy may be selected for risks with positive impacts where the organization wishes to ensure that the opportunity is realized. This strategy seeks to eliminate the uncertainty associated with a particular upside risk by ensuring the opportunity definitely happens. Examples of directly exploiting responses include assigning an organization's most talented resources to the project to reduce the time to completion or to provide lower cost than originally planned.

- **Share.** Sharing a positive risk involves allocating some or all of the ownership of the opportunity to a third party who is best able to capture the opportunity for the benefit of the project. Examples of sharing actions include forming risk-sharing partnerships, teams, special-purpose companies, or joint ventures, which can be established with the express purpose of taking advantage of the opportunity so that all parties gain from their actions.

- **Enhance.** This strategy is used to increase the probability and/or the positive impacts of an opportunity. Identifying and maximizing key drivers of these positive-impact risks may increase the probability of their occurrence. Examples of enhancing opportunities include adding more resources to an activity to finish early.

- **Accept.** Accepting an opportunity is being willing to take advantage of it if it comes along, but not actively pursuing it.

.3 Contingent Response Strategies

Some responses are designed for use only if certain events occur. For some risks, it is appropriate for the project team to make a response plan that will only be executed under certain predefined conditions, if it is believed that there will be sufficient warning to implement the plan. Events that trigger the contingency response, such as missing intermediate milestones or gaining higher priority with a supplier, should be defined and tracked.

.4 Expert Judgment

Expert judgment is input from knowledgeable parties pertaining to the actions to be taken on a specific and defined risk. Expertise may be provided by any group or person with specialized education, knowledge, skill, experience, or training in establishing risk responses.

11.5.3 Plan Risk Responses: Outputs

.1 Risk Register Updates

In the Plan Risk Responses process, appropriate responses are chosen, agreed upon, and included in the risk register. The risk register should be written to a level of detail that corresponds with the priority ranking and the planned response. Often, the high and moderate risks are addressed in detail. Risks judged to be of low priority are included in a "watchlist" for periodic monitoring. Components of the risk register at this point can include:

- Identified risks, their descriptions, area(s) of the project (e.g., WBS element) affected, their causes (e.g., RBS element), and how they may affect project objectives;

- Risk owners and assigned responsibilities;

- Outputs from the Perform Qualitative Analysis process (Section 11.3), including prioritized lists of project risks;

- Agreed-upon response strategies;

- Specific actions to implement the chosen response strategy;

- Triggers, symptoms, and warning signs of risks' occurrence;

- Budget and schedule activities required to implement the chosen responses;

- Contingency plans and triggers that call for their execution;

- Fallback plans for use as a reaction to a risk that has occurred and the primary response proves to be inadequate;

- Residual risks that are expected to remain after planned responses have been taken, as well as those that have been deliberately accepted;

- Secondary risks that arise as a direct outcome of implementing a risk response; and

- Contingency reserves that are calculated based on the quantitative risk analysis of the project and the organization's risk thresholds.

.2 Risk-Related Contract Decisions

Decisions to transfer risk, such as agreements for insurance, services, and other items as appropriate are selected in this process. This may happen as a result of mitigating or transferring part or all of the threat or enhancing or sharing part or all of the opportunity. The contract type selected also provides a mechanism for sharing the risks. These decisions are inputs to the Plan Procurements (Section 12.1) process.

.3 Project Management Plan Updates

Elements of the project management plan that may be updated include, but are not limited to:

- **Schedule management plan.** The schedule management plan (Section 6.0) is updated to reflect changes in process and practice driven by the risk responses. This may include changes in tolerance or behavior related to resource loading and leveling, as well as updates to the schedule itself.

- **Cost management plan.** The cost management plan (Section 7.0) is updated to reflect changes in process and practice driven by the risk responses. This may include changes in tolerance or behavior related to cost accounting, tracking, and reports, as well as updates to the budget and the consumption of contingency reserves.

- **Quality management plan.** The quality management plan (Section 8.1.3.1) is updated to reflect changes in process and practice driven by the risk responses. This may include changes in tolerance or behavior related to requirements, quality assurance, or quality control, as well as updates to the requirements documentation.

- **Procurement management plan.** The procurement management plan (Section 12.1.3.1) may be updated to reflect changes in strategy, such as alterations in the make-or-buy decision or contract type(s) driven by the risk responses.

- **Human resource management plan.** The staffing management plan, part of the human resource plan (Section 9.1.3.1), is updated to reflect changes in project organizational structure and resource applications driven by the risk responses. This may include changes in tolerance or behavior related to staff allocation, as well as updates to the resource loading.

- **Work breakdown structure.** Because of new work (or omitted work) generated by the risk responses, the WBS (Section 5.3.3.1) may be updated to reflect those changes.

- **Schedule baseline.** Because of new work (or omitted work) generated by the risk responses, the schedule baseline (Section 6.5.3.2) may be updated to reflect those changes.

- **Cost performance baseline.** Because of new work (or omitted work) generated by the risk responses, the cost performance baseline (Section 7.2.3.1) may be updated to reflect those changes.

.4 Project Document Updates

Project documents that may be updated include, but are not limited to:

- **Assumptions log updates.** As new information becomes available through the application of risk responses, assumptions will inherently change. The assumptions log must be revisited to accommodate this new information. Assumptions may be incorporated in the scope statement or in a separate assumptions log.

- **Technical documentation updates.** As new information becomes available through the application of risk responses, technical approaches and physical deliverables may change. Any supporting documentation must be revisited to accommodate this new information.

11.6 Monitor and Control Risks

Monitor and Control Risks is the process of implementing risk response plans, tracking identified risks, monitoring residual risks, identifying new risks, and evaluating risk process effectiveness throughout the project (see Figures 11-19 and 11-20).

Planned risk responses that are included in the project management plan are executed during the life cycle of the project, but the project work should be continuously monitored for new, changing, and outdated risks.

The Monitor and Control Risks process applies techniques, such as variance and trend analysis, which require the use of performance information generated during project execution. Other purposes of the Monitor and Control Risks process are to determine if:

- Project assumptions are still valid,

- Analysis shows an assessed risk has changed or can be retired,

- Risk management policies and procedures are being followed, and

- Contingency reserves of cost or schedule should be modified in alignment with the current risk assessment.

Monitor and Control Risks can involve choosing alternative strategies, executing a contingency or fallback plan, taking corrective action, and modifying the project management plan. The risk response owner reports periodically to the project manager on the effectiveness of the plan, any unanticipated effects, and any correction needed to handle the risk appropriately. Monitor and Control Risks also includes updating the organizational process assets, including project lessons learned databases and risk management templates, for the benefit of future projects.

Inputs	Tools & Techniques	Outputs
.1 Risk register .2 Project management plan .3 Work performance information .4 Performance reports	.1 Risk reassessment .2 Risk audits .3 Variance and trend analysis .4 Technical performance measurement .5 Reserve analysis .6 Status meetings	.1 Risk register updates .2 Organizational process assets updates .3 Change requests .4 Project management plan updates .5 Project document updates

Figure 11-19. Monitor and Control Risks: Inputs, Tools & Techniques, and Outputs

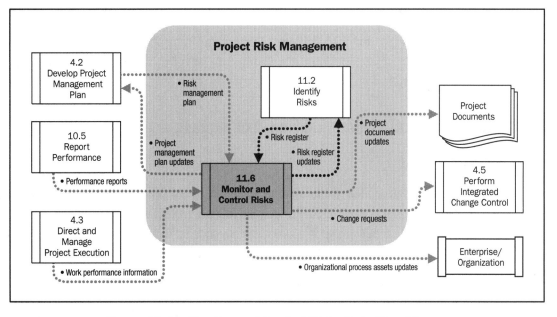

Figure 11-20. Monitor and Control Risks Data Flow Diagram

11.6.1 Monitor and Control Risks: Inputs

.1 Risk Register

The risk register has key inputs that include identified risks and risk owners, agreed-upon risk responses, specific implementation actions, symptoms and warning signs of risk, residual and secondary risks, a watchlist of low-priority risks, and the time and cost contingency reserves.

.2 Project Management Plan

The project management plan described in Section 4.2.3.1 contains the risk management plan, which includes risk tolerances, protocols and the assignment of people (including the risk owners), time, and other resources to project risk management.

.3 Work Performance Information

Work performance information related to various performance results includes, but is not limited to:

- Deliverable status,
- Schedule progress, and
- Costs incurred.

.4 Performance Reports

Performance reports (Section 10.5.3.1) take information from performance measurements and analyze it to provide project work performance information including variance analysis, earned value data, and forecasting data.

11.6.2 Monitor and Control Risks: Tools and Techniques

.1 Risk Reassessment

Monitor and Control Risks often results in identification of new risks, reassessment of current risks, and the closing of risks that are outdated. Project risk reassessments should be regularly scheduled. The amount and detail of repetition that is appropriate depends on how the project progresses relative to its objectives.

.2 Risk Audits

Risk audits examine and document the effectiveness of risk responses in dealing with identified risks and their root causes, as well as the effectiveness of the risk management process. The project manager is responsible for ensuring that risk audits are performed at an appropriate frequency, as defined in the project's risk management plan. Risk audits may be included during routine project review meetings, or separate risk audit meetings may be held. The format for the audit and its objectives should be clearly defined before the audit is conducted.

.3 Variance and Trend Analysis

Many control processes employ variance analysis to compare the planned results to the actual results. For the purposes of monitoring and controlling risk events, trends in the project's execution should be reviewed using performance information. Earned value analysis (Section 7.3.2.1) and other methods of project variance and trend analysis may be used for monitoring overall project performance. Outcomes from these analyses may forecast potential deviation of the project at completion from cost and schedule targets. Deviation from the baseline plan may indicate the potential impact of threats or opportunities.

.4 Technical Performance Measurement

Technical performance measurement compares technical accomplishments during project execution to the project management plan's schedule of technical achievement. It requires definition of objective quantifiable measures of technical performance which can be used to compare actual results against targets. Such technical performance measures might include weight, transaction times, number of delivered defects, storage capacity, etc. Deviation, such as demonstrating more or less functionality than planned at a milestone, can help to forecast the degree of success in achieving the project's scope, and it may expose the degree of technical risk faced by the project.

.5 Reserve Analysis

Throughout execution of the project some risks may occur, with positive or negative impacts on budget or schedule contingency reserves (Sections 6.5.3.3 and 7.1.2.6). Reserve analysis compares the amount of the contingency reserves remaining to the amount of risk remaining at any time in the project in order to determine if the remaining reserve is adequate.

.6 Status Meetings

Project risk management should be an agenda item at periodic status meetings. The amount of time required for that item will vary, depending upon the risks that have been identified, their priority, and difficulty of response. Risk management becomes easier the more often it is practiced. Frequent discussions about risk makes it more likely that people will identify risks and opportunities.

11.6.3 Monitor and Control Risks: Outputs

.1 Risk Register Updates

An updated risk register includes, but is not limited to:

- Outcomes of risk reassessments, risk audits, and periodic risk reviews. These outcomes may include identification of new risk events, updates to probability, impact, priority, response plans, ownership, and other elements of the risk register. Outcomes can also include closing risks that are no longer applicable and releasing their associated reserves.

- Actual outcomes of the project's risks and of the risk responses. This information can help project managers to plan for risk throughout their organizations, as well as on future projects.

.2 Organizational Process Assets Updates

The six Project Risk Management processes produce information that can be used for future projects, and should be captured in the organizational process assets. The organizational process assets that may be updated include, but are not limited to:

- Templates for the risk management plan, including the probability and impact matrix, and risk register;

- Risk breakdown structure; and

- Lessons learned from the project risk management activities.

These documents should be updated as needed and at project closure. Final versions of the risk register and the risk management plan templates, checklists, and risk breakdown structure are included.

.3 Change Requests

Implementing contingency plans or workarounds sometimes results in a change request. Change requests are prepared and submitted to the Perform Integrated Change Control process (Section 4.5). Change requests can include recommended corrective and preventive actions as well.

- **Recommended corrective actions.** Recommended corrective actions include contingency plans and workarounds. The latter are responses that were not initially planned, but are required to deal with emerging risks that were previously unidentified or accepted passively.

- **Recommended preventive actions.** Recommended preventive actions are documented directions to perform on activity that can reduce the probability of negative consequences associated with project risks.

.4 Project Management Plan Updates

If the approved change requests have an effect on the risk management processes, the corresponding component documents of the project management plan are revised and reissued to reflect the approved changes. The elements of the project management plan that may be updated are the same as those in the Plan Risk Responses process (Section 11.5).

.5 Project Document Updates

Project documents that may be updated as a result of the Monitor and Control Risks process are the same as those in the Plan Risk Responses process (Section 11.5).

CHAPTER 12

PROJECT PROCUREMENT MANAGEMENT

Project Procurement Management includes the processes necessary to purchase or acquire products, services, or results needed from outside the project team. The organization can be either the buyer or seller of the products, services, or results of a project.

Project Procurement Management includes the contract management and change control processes required to develop and administer contracts or purchase orders issued by authorized project team members.

Project Procurement Management also includes administering any contract issued by an outside organization (the buyer) that is acquiring the project from the performing organization (the seller), and administering contractual obligations placed on the project team by the contract.

Figure 12-1 provides an overview of the Project Procurement Management processes which include the following:

12.1 Plan Procurements—The process of documenting project purchasing decisions, specifying the approach, and identifying potential sellers.

12.2 Conduct Procurements—The process of obtaining seller responses, selecting a seller, and awarding a contract.

12.3 Administer Procurements—The process of managing procurement relationships, monitoring contract performance, and making changes and corrections as needed.

12.4 Close Procurements—The process of completing each project procurement.

These processes interact with each other and with the processes in the other Knowledge Areas. Each process can involve effort from a group or person, based on the requirements of the project. Each process occurs at least once in every project and occurs in one or more of the project phases, if the project is divided into phases. Although the processes are presented here as discrete components with well-defined interfaces, in practice they overlap and interact in ways not detailed in the *PMBOK® Guide*. Process interactions are discussed in detail in Chapter 3, Project Management Processes.

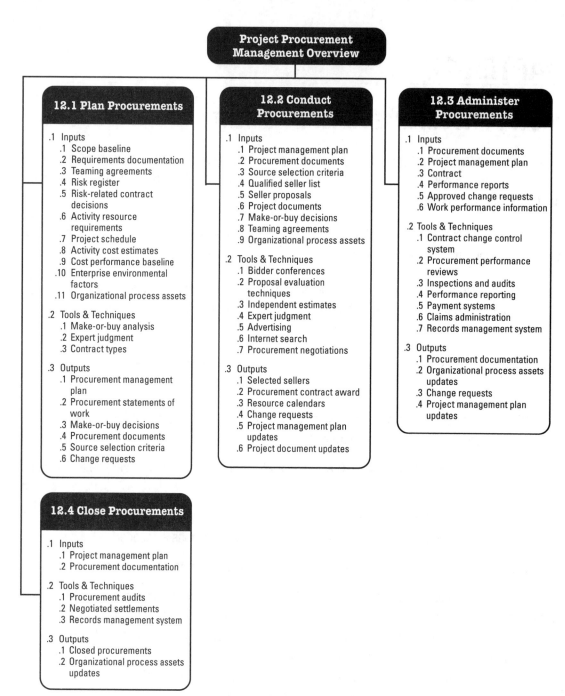

Figure 12-1. Project Procurement Management Overview

The Project Procurement Management processes involve contracts that are legal documents between a buyer and a seller. A contract represents a mutually binding agreement that obligates the seller to provide the specified products, services, or results, and obligates the buyer to provide monetary or other valuable consideration. The agreement can be simple or complex, and can reflect the simplicity or complexity of the deliverables and required effort.

A procurement contract will include terms and conditions, and may incorporate other items that the buyer specifies to establish what the seller is to perform or provide. It is the project management team's responsibility to make certain that all procurements meet the specific needs of the project while adhering to organizational procurement policies. Depending upon the application area, a contract can also be called an agreement, an understanding, a subcontract, or a purchase order. Most organizations will have documented policies and procedures specifically defining the procurement rules and specifying who has authority to sign and administer such agreements on behalf of the organization.

Although all project documents are subject to some form of review and approval, the legally binding nature of a contract usually means that it will be subjected to a more extensive approval process. In all cases, the primary focus of the review and approval process is to ensure that the contract language describes the products, services, or results that will satisfy the identified project need.

The project management team may seek support early from specialists in contracting, purchasing, law, and technical disciplines. Such involvement can be mandated by an organization's policies.

The various activities involved in the Project Procurement Management processes form the life cycle of a contract. By actively managing the contract life cycle and carefully wording the terms and conditions of the procurements, some identifiable project risks can be avoided, mitigated, or transferred to a seller. Entering into a contract for products or services is one method of allocating the responsibility for managing or sharing potential risks.

A complex project can involve managing multiple contracts or subcontracts simultaneously or in sequence. In such cases, each contract life cycle can end during any phase of the project life cycle. Project Procurement Management is discussed within the perspective of the buyer-seller relationship. The buyer-seller relationship can exist at many levels on any one project, and between organizations internal to and external to the acquiring organization.

Depending on the application area, the seller can be called a contractor, subcontractor, vendor, service provider, or supplier. Depending on the buyer's position in the project acquisition cycle, the buyer can be called a client, customer, prime contractor, contractor, acquiring organization, governmental agency, service requestor, or purchaser. The seller can be viewed during the contract life cycle first as a bidder, then as the selected source, and then as the contracted supplier or vendor.

The seller will typically manage the work as a project if the acquisition is not just for shelf material, goods, or common products. In such cases:

- The buyer becomes the customer, and is thus a key project stakeholder for the seller.

- The seller's project management team is concerned with all the processes of project management, not just with those of this Knowledge Area.

- Terms and conditions of the contract become key inputs to many of the seller's management processes. The contract can actually contain the inputs (e.g., major deliverables, key milestones, cost objectives), or it can limit the project team's options (e.g., buyer approval of staffing decisions is often required on design projects).

This chapter assumes that the buyer of items for the project is assigned to the project team and that the sellers are organizationally external to the project team.

It also assumes that a formal contractual relationship will be developed and exist between the buyer and the seller. However, most of the discussion in this chapter is equally applicable to non-contractual intradivisional work, entered into with other units of the project team's organization.

12.1 Plan Procurements

Plan Procurements is the process of documenting project purchasing decisions, specifying the approach, and identifying potential sellers (see Figures 12-2 and 12-3). It identifies those project needs which can best be, or must be, met by acquiring products, services, or results outside of the project organization, versus those project needs which can be accomplished by the project team.

This process involves determining whether to acquire outside support and, if so what to acquire, how to acquire it, how much is needed, and when to acquire it. When the project obtains products, services, and results required for project performance from outside the performing organization, the processes from Plan Procurements through Close Procurements are performed for each item to be acquired.

The Plan Procurements process also includes consideration of potential sellers, particularly if the buyer wishes to exercise some degree of influence or control over acquisition decisions. Consideration should also be given to who is responsible for obtaining or holding any relevant permits and professional licenses that may be required by legislation, regulation, or organizational policy in executing the project.

The requirements of the project schedule can significantly influence the strategy during the Plan Procurements process. Decisions made in developing the procurement management plan can also influence the project schedule and are integrated with Develop Schedule (Section 6.5), Estimate Activity Resources (Section 6.3), and make-or-buy decisions (Section 12.1.3.3).

The Plan Procurements process includes consideration of the risks involved with each make-or-buy decision. It also includes reviewing the type of contract planned to be used with respect to mitigating risks, sometimes transferring risks to the seller.

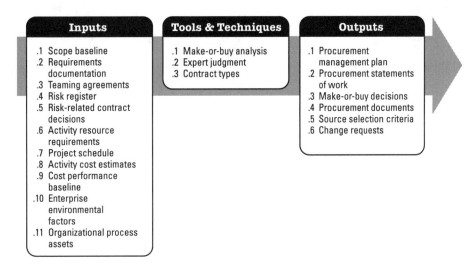

Inputs	Tools & Techniques	Outputs
.1 Scope baseline .2 Requirements documentation .3 Teaming agreements .4 Risk register .5 Risk-related contract decisions .6 Activity resource requirements .7 Project schedule .8 Activity cost estimates .9 Cost performance baseline .10 Enterprise environmental factors .11 Organizational process assets	.1 Make-or-buy analysis .2 Expert judgment .3 Contract types	.1 Procurement management plan .2 Procurement statements of work .3 Make-or-buy decisions .4 Procurement documents .5 Source selection criteria .6 Change requests

Figure 12-2. Plan Procurements: Inputs, Tools and Techniques, and Outputs

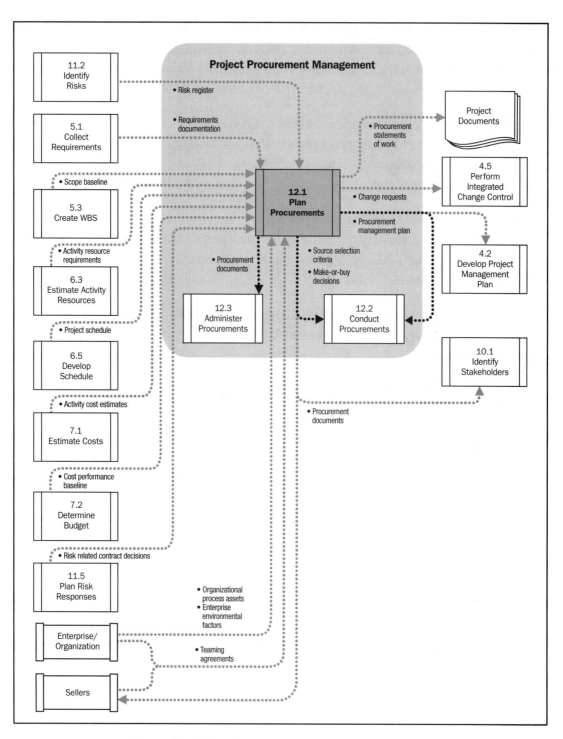

Figure 12-3. Plan Procurements Data Flow Diagram

12.1.1 Plan Procurements: Inputs

.1 Scope Baseline

The scope baseline (Section 5.3.3.3) describes the need, justification, requirements, and current boundaries for the project. It consists of the following components:

- **Scope statement.** The project scope statement contains the product scope description, service description and result description, the list of deliverables, and acceptance criteria, as well as important information regarding technical issues or concerns that could impact cost estimating. Examples of constraints are required delivery dates, available skilled resources, and organizational policies.

- **WBS.** (Section 5.3.3.1).

- **WBS dictionary.** The WBS dictionary (Section 5.3.3.2) and related detailed statements of work provide an identification of the deliverables and a description of the work in each WBS component required to produce each deliverable.

.2 Requirements Documentation

Requirements documentation may include:

- Important information about project requirements that is considered during planning for procurements.

- Requirements with contractual and legal implications that may include health, safety, security, performance, environmental, insurance, intellectual property rights, equal employment opportunity, licenses, and permits—all of which are considered when planning for procurements.

.3 Teaming Agreements

Teaming agreements are legal contractual agreements between two or more entities to form a partnership or joint venture, or some other arrangement as defined by the parties. The agreement defines buyer-seller roles for each party. Whenever the new business opportunity ends, the teaming agreement also ends. Whenever a teaming agreement is in effect, the planning process for the project is significantly impacted. Thus whenever a teaming agreement is in place on a project, the roles of buyer and seller are predetermined, and such issues as scope of work, competition requirements, and other critical issues are generally predefined.

.4 Risk Register

The risk register includes risk-related information such as the identified risks, risk owners, and risk responses (Section 11.2.3.1).

.5 Risk-Related Contract Decisions

Risk-related contract decisions include agreements including insurance, bonding, services, and other items as appropriate, that are prepared to specify each party's responsibility for specific risks (Section 11.5.3.2).

.6 Activity Resource Requirements

Activity resource requirements contain information on specific needs such as people, equipment, or location (Section 6.3.3.1).

.7 Project Schedule

Project schedule contains information on required timelines or mandated deliverable dates (Section 6.5.3.1).

.8 Activity Cost Estimates

Cost estimates developed by the procuring activity are used to evaluate the reasonableness of the bids or proposals received from potential sellers (Section 7.1.3.1).

.9 Cost Performance Baseline

The cost performance baseline provides detail on the planned budget over time (Section 7.2.3.1).

.10 Enterprise Environmental Factors

The enterprise environmental factors that can influence the Plan Procurements process include, but are not limited to:

- Marketplace conditions;
- Products, services, and results that are available in the marketplace;
- Suppliers, including past performance or reputation;
- Typical terms and conditions for products, services, and results or for the specific industry; and
- Unique local requirements.

.11 Organizational Process Assets

The organizational process assets that influence the Plan Procurement process include, but are not limited to:

- Formal procurement policies, procedures, and guidelines. Most organizations have formal procurement policies and buying organizations. When such procurement support is not available, the project team will have to supply both the resources and the expertise to perform such procurement activities.

- Management systems that are considered in developing the procurement management plan and selecting the contract types to be used.

- An established multi-tier supplier system of pre-qualified sellers based on prior experience.

12.1.2 Plan Procurements: Tools and Techniques

.1 Make-or-Buy Analysis

A make-or-buy analysis is a general management technique used to determine whether particular work can best be accomplished by the project team or must be purchased from outside sources. Sometimes a capability may exist within the project organization, but may be committed to working on other projects, in which case the project may need to source such effort from outside the organization in order to meet its schedule commitments.

Budget constraints may influence make-or-buy decisions. If a buy decision is to be made, then a further decision of whether to purchase or lease is also made. A make-or-buy analysis should consider all related costs; both direct costs as well as indirect support costs. For example, the buy-side of the analysis includes both the actual out-of-pocket costs to purchase the product, as well as the indirect costs of supporting the purchasing process and purchased item.

.2 Expert Judgment

Expert technical judgment will often be used to assess the inputs to and outputs from this process. Expert purchasing judgment can also be used to develop or modify the criteria that will be used to evaluate seller proposals. Expert legal judgment may involve the services of legal staff to assist with unique procurement issues, terms, and conditions. Such judgment, including business and technical expertise, can be applied to both the technical details of the acquired products, services, or results and to various aspects of the procurement management processes.

.3 Contract Types

The risk shared between the buyer and seller is determined by the contract type. Although the firm-fixed-price type of contractual arrangement is typically the preferred type which is encouraged and often demanded by most organizations, there are times when another contract form may be in the best interests of the project. If a contract type other than fixed-price is intended, it is incumbent on the project team to justify its use. The type of contract to be used and the specific contract terms and conditions fix the degree of risk being assumed by the buyer and seller.

All legal contractual relationships generally fall into one of two broad families, either fixed-price or cost reimbursable. Also, there is a third hybrid-type commonly in use called the time and materials contract. The more popular of the contract types in use are discussed below as discrete types, but in practice it is not unusual to combine one or more types into a single procurement.

- **Fixed-price contracts.** This category of contracts involves setting a fixed total price for a defined product or service to be provided. Fixed-price contracts may also incorporate financial incentives for achieving or exceeding selected project objectives, such as schedule delivery dates, cost and technical performance, or anything that can be quantified and subsequently measured. Sellers under fixed-price contracts are legally obligated to complete such contracts, with possible financial damages if they do not. Under the fixed-price arrangement, buyers must precisely specify the product or services being procured. Changes in scope can be accommodated, but generally at an increase in contract price.

  ○ **Firm Fixed Price Contracts (FFP).** The most commonly used contract type is the FFP. It is favored by most buying organizations because the price for goods is set at the outset and not subject to change unless the scope of work changes. Any cost increase due to adverse performance is the responsibility of the seller, who is obligated to complete the effort. Under the FFP contract, the buyer must precisely specify the product or services to be procured, and any changes to the procurement specification can increase the costs to the buyer.

  ○ **Fixed Price Incentive Fee Contracts (FPIF).** This fixed-price arrangement gives the buyer and seller some flexibility in that it allows for deviation from performance, with financial incentives tied to achieving agreed to metrics. Typically such financial incentives are related to cost, schedule, or technical performance of the seller. Performance targets are established at the outset, and the final contract price is determined after completion of all work based on the seller's performance. Under FPIF contracts, a price ceiling is set, and all costs above the price ceiling are the responsibility of the seller, who is obligated to complete the work.

○ **Fixed Price with Economic Price Adjustment Contracts (FP-EPA).** This contract type is used whenever the seller's performance period spans a considerable period of years, as is desired with many long-term relationships. It is a fixed-price contract, but with a special provision allowing for pre-defined final adjustments to the contract price due to changed conditions, such as inflation changes, or cost increases (or decreases) for specific commodities. The EPA clause must relate to some reliable financial index which is used to precisely adjust the final price. The FP-EPA contract is intended to protect both buyer and seller from external conditions beyond their control.

- **Cost-reimbursable contracts.** This category of contract involves payments (cost reimbursements) to the seller for all legitimate actual costs incurred for completed work, plus a fee representing seller profit. Cost-reimbursable contracts may also include financial incentive clauses whenever the seller exceeds, or falls below, defined objectives such as costs, schedule, or technical performance targets. Three of the more common types of cost-reimbursable contracts in use are Cost Plus Fixed Fee (CPFF), Cost Plus Incentive Fee (CPIF), and Cost Plus Award Fee (CPAF).

A cost-reimbursable contract gives the project flexibility to redirect a seller whenever the scope of work cannot be precisely defined at the start and needs to be altered, or when high risks may exist in the effort.

○ **Cost Plus Fixed Fee Contracts (CPFF).** The seller is reimbursed for all allowable costs for performing the contract work, and receives a fixed fee payment calculated as a percentage of the initial estimated project costs. Fee is paid only for completed work and does not change due to seller performance. Fee amounts do not change unless the project scope changes.

○ **Cost Plus Incentive Fee Contracts (CPIF).** The seller is reimbursed for all allowable costs for performing the contract work and receives a predetermined incentive fee based upon achieving certain performance objectives as set forth in the contract. In CPIF contracts, if the final costs are less or greater than the original estimated costs, then both the buyer and seller share costs from the departures based upon a prenegotiated cost sharing formula, e.g., an 80/20 split over/under target costs based on the actual performance of the seller.

○ **Cost Plus Award Fee Contracts (CPAF).** The seller is reimbursed for all legitimate costs, but the majority of the fee is only earned based on the satisfaction of certain broad subjective performance criteria defined and incorporated into the contract. The determination of fee is based solely on the subjective determination of seller performance by the buyer, and is generally not subject to appeals.

- **Time and Material Contracts (T&M).** Time and material contracts are a hybrid type of contractual arrangement that contain aspects of both cost-reimbursable and fixed-price contracts. They are often used for staff augmentation, acquisition of experts, and any outside support when a precise statement of work cannot be quickly prescribed.

These types of contracts resemble cost-reimbursable contracts in that they can be left open ended and may be subject to a cost increase for the buyer. The full value of the agreement and the exact quantity of items to be delivered may not be defined by the buyer at the time of the contract award. Thus, T&M contracts can increase in contract value as if they were cost-reimbursable contracts. Many organizations require not-to-exceed values and time limits placed in all T&M contracts to prevent unlimited cost growth. Conversely, T&M contracts can also resemble fixed unit price arrangements when certain parameters are specified in the contract. Unit labor or material rates can be preset by the buyer and seller, including seller profit, when both parties agree on the values for specific resource categories, such as senior engineers at specified rates per hour, or categories of materials at specified rates per unit.

12.1.3 Plan Procurements: Outputs

.1 Procurement Management Plan

The procurement management plan describes how the procurement processes will be managed from developing procurement documents through contract closure. The procurement management plan can include guidance for:

- Types of contracts to be used;

- Risk management issues;

- Whether independent estimates will be used and if they are needed as evaluation criteria;

- Those actions the project management team can take unilaterally, if the performing organization has a prescribed procurement, contracting, or purchasing department;

- Standardized procurement documents, if they are needed;

- Managing multiple suppliers;

- Coordinating procurement with other project aspects, such as scheduling and performance reporting;

- Any constraints and assumptions that could affect planned procurements;

- Handling the required lead times to purchase items from sellers and coordinating them with the project schedule development;

- Handling the make-or-buy decisions and linking them into the Estimate Activity Resource and Develop Schedule processes;

- Setting the scheduled dates in each contract for the contract deliverables and coordinating with the schedule development and control processes;

- Identifying requirements for performance bonds or insurance contracts to mitigate some forms of project risk;

- Establishing the direction to be provided to the sellers on developing and maintaining a work breakdown structure (WBS);

- Establishing the form and format to be used for the procurement/contract statements of work;

- Identifying prequalified sellers, if any, to be used; and

- Procurement metrics to be used to manage contracts and evaluate sellers.

A procurement management plan can be formal or informal, can be highly detailed or broadly framed, and is based upon the needs of each project. The procurement management plan is a subsidiary component of the project management plan (Section 4.2.3.1).

.2 Procurement Statements of Work

The statement of work (SOW) for each procurement is developed from the project scope baseline and defines only that portion of the project scope that is to be included within the related contract. The procurement SOW describes the procurement item in sufficient detail to allow prospective sellers to determine if they are capable of providing the products, services, or results. Sufficient detail can vary based on the nature of the item, the needs of the buyer, or the expected contract form. Information included in a SOW can include specifications, quantity desired, quality levels, performance data, period of performance, work location, and other requirements.

The procurement SOW is written to be clear, complete, and concise. It includes a description of any collateral services required, such as performance reporting or post-project operational support for the procured item. In some application areas, there are specific content and format requirements for a procurement SOW. Each individual procurement item requires a SOW. However, multiple products or services can be grouped as one procurement item within a single SOW.

The procurement SOW can be revised and refined as required as it moves through the procurement process until incorporated into a signed contract award.

.3 Make-or-Buy Decisions

Make-or-buy decisions document the conclusions reached regarding what project products, services, or results will be acquired from outside the project organization, or will be performed internally by the project team. This may also include decisions to require insurance policies or performance bond contracts to address some of the identified risks. The make-or-buy decisions document can be as simple as a listing that includes a short justification for the decisions. These decisions can be altered as subsequent procurement activities indicate a requirement for a different approach.

.4 Procurement Documents

Procurement documents are used to solicit proposals from prospective sellers. Terms such as bid, tender, or quotation are generally used when the seller selection decision will be based on price (as when buying commercial or standard items), while a term such as proposal is generally used when other considerations, such as technical capability or technical approach are paramount. Common terms are in use for different types of procurement documents and may include request for information (RFI), invitation for bid (IFB), request for proposal (RFP), request for quotation (RFQ), tender notice, invitation for negotiation, and invitation for seller's initial response. Specific procurement terminology used may vary by industry and location of the procurement.

The buyer structures procurement documents to facilitate an accurate and complete response from each prospective seller and to facilitate easy evaluation of the responses. These documents include a description of the desired form of the response, the relevant procurement statement of work (SOW) and any required contractual provisions. With government contracting, some or all of the content and structure of procurement documents can be defined by regulation.

The complexity and level of detail of the procurement documents should be consistent with the value of, and risks associated with, the planned procurement. Procurement documents must be sufficient to ensure consistent, appropriate responses, but flexible enough to allow consideration of any seller suggestions for better ways to satisfy the same requirements.

Issuing a procurement request to potential sellers to submit a proposal or bid is normally done in accordance with the policies of the buyer's organization, which can include publication of the request in public newspapers, in trade journals, in public registries, or on the internet.

.5 Source Selection Criteria

Selection criteria are often included as a part of the procurement documents. Such criteria are developed and used to rate or score seller proposals, and can be objective or subjective.

Selection criteria can be limited to purchase price if the procurement item is readily available from a number of acceptable sellers. Purchase price in this context includes both the cost of the item and all ancillary expenses such as delivery.

Other selection criteria can be identified and documented to support an assessment for more complex products, services, or results. Some examples are shown below.

- **Understanding of need.** How well does the seller's proposal address the procurement statement of work?

- **Overall or life-cycle cost.** Will the selected seller produce the lowest total cost of ownership (purchase cost plus operating cost)?

- **Technical capability.** Does the seller have, or can the seller be reasonably expected to acquire, the technical skills and knowledge needed?

- **Risk.** How much risk is embedded in the statement of work, how much risk will be assigned to the selected seller and how does the seller mitigate risk?

- **Management approach.** Does the seller have, or can the seller be reasonably expected to develop, management processes and procedures to ensure a successful project?

- **Technical approach.** Do the seller's proposed technical methodologies, techniques, solutions, and services meet the procurement documents requirements or are they likely to provide more or less than the expected results?

- **Warranty.** What does the seller propose to warrant for the final product, and through what time period?

- **Financial capacity.** Does the seller have, or can the seller reasonably be expected to obtain, the necessary financial resources?

- **Production capacity and interest.** Does the seller have the capacity and interest to meet potential future requirements?

- **Business size and type.** Does the seller's enterprise meet a specific category of business such as small, women-owned, or disadvantaged small business, as defined by the buyer or established by governmental agency and set forth as a condition of the contract award?

- **Past performance of sellers.** What has been the past experience with selected sellers?

- **References.** Can the seller provide references from prior customers verifying the seller's work experience and compliance with contractual requirements?

- **Intellectual property rights.** Does the seller assert intellectual property rights in the work processes or services they will use or in the products they will produce for the project?

- **Proprietary rights.** Does the seller assert proprietary rights in the work processes or services they will use or in the products they will produce for the project?

.6 Change Requests

Change requests (Section 4.3.3.3) to the project management plan, its subsidiary plans and other components may result from the Plan Procurements process. Change requests are processed for review and disposition through the Perform Integrated Change Control process (Section 4.5).

12.2 Conduct Procurements

Conduct Procurements is the process of obtaining seller responses, selecting a seller, and awarding a contract (see Figures 12-4 and 12-5). In this process, the team will receive bids or proposals and will apply previously defined selection criteria to select one or more sellers who are qualified to perform the work and acceptable as a seller.

On major procurement items, the overall process of requesting responses from sellers and evaluating those responses can be repeated. A short list of qualified sellers can be established based on a preliminary proposal. A more detailed evaluation can then be conducted based on a more specific and comprehensive requirements document requested from the sellers on the short list. In addition, tools and techniques described here can be used alone or in combination to select sellers. For example, a weighting system can be used to:

- Select a single seller that will be asked to sign a standard contract, and

- Establish a negotiating sequence by ranking all proposals by the weighed evaluation scores assigned to each proposal.

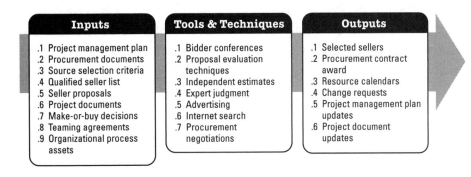

Inputs	Tools & Techniques	Outputs
.1 Project management plan	.1 Bidder conferences	.1 Selected sellers
.2 Procurement documents	.2 Proposal evaluation techniques	.2 Procurement contract award
.3 Source selection criteria	.3 Independent estimates	.3 Resource calendars
.4 Qualified seller list	.4 Expert judgment	.4 Change requests
.5 Seller proposals	.5 Advertising	.5 Project management plan updates
.6 Project documents	.6 Internet search	.6 Project document updates
.7 Make-or-buy decisions	.7 Procurement negotiations	
.8 Teaming agreements		
.9 Organizational process assets		

Figure 12-4. Conduct Procurements: Inputs, Tools & Techniques, and Outputs

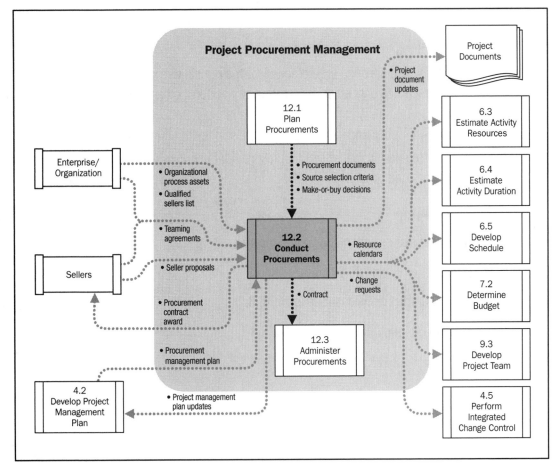

Figure 12-5. Conduct Procurements Data Flow Diagram

12.2.1 Conduct Procurements: Inputs

.1 Project Management Plan

The procurement management plan, part of the project management plan described in Section 4.2.3.1, is an input to Conduct Procurements and describes how the procurement processes will be managed from developing procurement documentation through contract closure (Section 12.1.3.1).

.2 Procurement Documents

Described in Section 12.1.3.4.

.3 Source Selection Criteria

Source selection criteria can include information on the supplier's required capabilities, capacity, delivery dates, product cost, life-cycle cost, technical expertise, and the approach to the contract as described in Section 12.1.3.5.

.4 Qualified Seller List

A listing of sellers who have been pre-screened for their qualifications and past experience, so that procurements are directed to only those sellers who can perform on any resulting contracts.

.5 Seller Proposals

Seller proposals prepared in response to a procurement document package form the basic set of information that will be used by an evaluation body to select one or more successful bidders (sellers).

.6 Project Documents

Project documents that are often considered include:

- Risk register (Section 11.5.1.1), and
- Risk-related contract decisions (Section 11.5.3.2).

.7 Make-or-Buy Decisions

Described in Section 12.1.3.3.

.8 Teaming Agreements

Whenever a teaming agreement is in place, the buyer and seller roles will have already been decided by executive management. In some cases the seller may already be working under some form of interim contract funded by the buyer or jointly by both parties. The effort of the buyer and seller in this process is to collectively prepare a procurement statement of work that will satisfy the requirements of the project. The parties will then negotiate a final contract for award.

.9 Organizational Process Assets

Elements of the organizational process assets that can influence the Conduct Procurements process include, but are not limited to:

- Listings of prospective and previously qualified sellers, and

- Information on relevant past experience with sellers, both good and bad.

12.2.2 Conduct Procurements: Tools and Techniques

.1 Bidder Conferences

Bidder conferences (sometimes called contractor conferences, vendor conferences, and pre-bid conferences) are meetings between the buyer and all prospective sellers prior to submittal of a bid or proposal. They are used to ensure that all prospective sellers have a clear and common understanding of the procurement (both technical and contractual requirements), and that no bidders receive preferential treatment. Responses to questions can be incorporated into the procurement documents as amendments. To be fair, buyers must take great care to ensure that all prospective sellers hear every question from any individual prospective seller and every answer from the buyer.

.2 Proposal Evaluation Techniques

On complex procurements, where source selection will be made based on seller responses to previously defined weighted criteria, a formal evaluation review process will be defined by the buyer's procurement policies. The evaluation committee will make their selection for approval by management prior to the award.

.3 Independent Estimates

For many procurement items, the procuring organization may elect to either prepare its own independent estimate, or have an estimate of costs prepared by an outside professional estimator, to serve as a benchmark on proposed responses. Significant differences in cost estimates can be an indication that the procurement statement of work was deficient, ambiguous, and/ or that the prospective sellers either misunderstood or failed to respond fully to the procurement statement of work.

.4 Expert Judgment

Expert judgment may be used in evaluating seller proposals. The evaluation of proposals may be accomplished by a multi-discipline review team with expertise in each of the areas covered by the procurement documents and proposed contract. This can include expertise from functional disciplines such as contracting, legal, finance, accounting, engineering, design, research, development, sales, and manufacturing.

.5 Advertising

Existing lists of potential sellers can often be expanded by placing advertisements in general circulation publications such as selected newspapers or in specialty trade publications. Some government jurisdictions require public advertising of certain types of procurement items, and most government jurisdictions require public advertising of pending government contracts.

.6 Internet Search

The internet has a major influence on most project procurements and supply chain acquisitions in organizations. While many commodities, components, and off-the-shelf-items can be quickly located and secured at a fixed-price on the internet, the high-risk, highly complex, procurement effort that must be closely monitored cannot be obtained by this means.

.7 Procurement Negotiations

Negotiations clarify the structure, requirements and other terms of the purchases so that mutual agreement can be reached prior to signing the contract. Final contract language reflects all agreements reached. Subjects covered should include responsibilities, authority to make changes, applicable terms and governing law, technical, and business management approaches, proprietary rights, contract financing, technical solutions, overall schedule, payments, and price. Negotiations conclude with a contract document that can be executed by both buyer and seller.

For complex procurement items, contract negotiation can be an independent process with inputs (e.g., issues or an open items listing) and outputs (e.g., documented decisions) of its own. For simple procurement items, the terms and conditions of the contract can be previously set and non-negotiable, and only need to be accepted by the seller.

The project manager may not be the lead negotiator on procurements. The project manager and other members of the project management team may be present during negotiations to provide assistance, and if needed to add clarification of the project's technical, quality, and management requirements.

12.2.3 Conduct Procurements: Outputs

.1 Selected Sellers

The sellers selected are those sellers who have been judged to be in a competitive range based upon the outcome of the proposal or bid evaluation, and who have negotiated a draft contract that will become the actual contract when an award is made. Final approval of all complex, high-value, high-risk procurements will generally require organizational senior management approval prior to award.

.2 Procurement Contract Award

A procurement contract is awarded to each selected seller. The contract can be in the form of simple purchase order or a complex document. Regardless of the document's complexity, a contract is a mutually binding legal agreement that obligates the seller to provide the specified products, services, or results, and obligates the buyer to compensate the seller. A contract is a legal relationship subject to remedy in the courts. The major components in a contract document will vary, but will sometimes include the following:

- Statement of work or deliverables,
- Schedule baseline,
- Performance reporting,
- Period of performance,
- Roles and responsibilities,
- Seller's place of performance,
- Pricing,

- Payment terms,

- Place of delivery,

- Inspection and acceptance criteria,

- Warranty,

- Product support,

- Limitation of liability,

- Fees and retainage,

- Penalties,

- Incentives,

- Insurance and performance bonds,

- Subordinate subcontractor approvals,

- Change request handling, and

- Termination and alternative dispute resolution (ADR) mechanisms. The ADR method can be decided in advance as a part of the procurement award.

.3 Resource Calendars

The quantity and availability of contracted resources and those dates on which each specific resource can be active or idle are documented.

.4 Change Requests

Change requests to the project management plan, its subsidiary plans, and other components are processed for review and disposition through the Perform Integrated Change Control process (Section 4.5).

.5 Project Management Plan Updates

Elements of the Project Management Plan that may be updated include, but are not limited to:

- Cost baseline,

- Scope baseline,

- Schedule baseline, and

- Procurement management plan.

.6 Project Document Updates

Project documents that may be updated include, but are not limited to:

- Requirements documentation,

- Requirements traceability documentation, and

- Risk register.

12.3 Administer Procurements

Administer Procurements is the process of managing procurement relationships, monitoring contract performance, and making changes and corrections as needed (see Figures 12-6 and 12-7). Both the buyer and the seller will administer the procurement contract for similar purposes. Each must ensure that both parties meet their contractual obligations and that their own legal rights are protected. The Administer Procurements process ensures that the seller's performance meets procurement requirements and that the buyer performs according to the terms of the legal contract. The legal nature of the contractual relationship makes it imperative that the project management team is aware of the legal implications of actions taken when administering any procurement. On larger projects with multiple providers, a key aspect of contract administration is managing interfaces among the various providers.

Due to varying organizational structures, many organizations treat contract administration as an administrative function separate from the project organization. While a procurement administrator may be on the project team, this individual typically reports to a supervisor from a different department. This is usually true if the performing organization is also the seller of the project to an external customer.

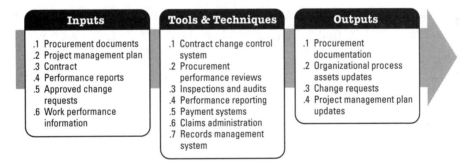

Inputs	Tools & Techniques	Outputs
.1 Procurement documents .2 Project management plan .3 Contract .4 Performance reports .5 Approved change requests .6 Work performance information	.1 Contract change control system .2 Procurement performance reviews .3 Inspections and audits .4 Performance reporting .5 Payment systems .6 Claims administration .7 Records management system	.1 Procurement documentation .2 Organizational process assets updates .3 Change requests .4 Project management plan updates

Figure 12-6. Administer Procurements: Inputs, Tools & Techniques, and Outputs

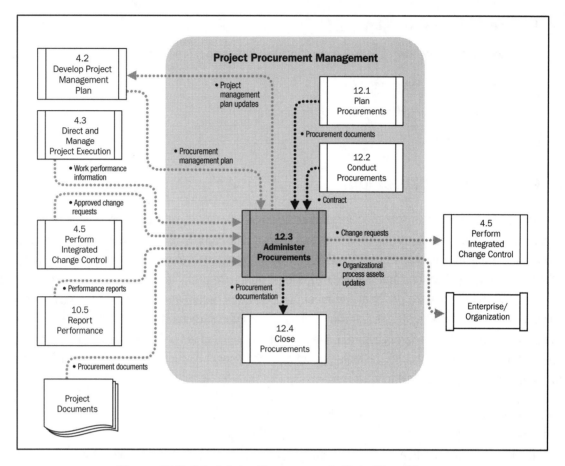

Figure 12-7. Administer Procurements Data Flow Diagram

Administer Procurements includes application of the appropriate project management processes to the contractual relationship(s) and integration of the outputs from these processes into the overall management of the project. This integration will often occur at multiple levels when there are multiple sellers and multiple products, services, or results involved. The project management processes that are applied may include, but are not limited to:

- **Direct and Manage Project Execution** (Section 4.3) to authorize the seller's work at the appropriate time;

- **Report Performance** (Section 10.5) to monitor contract scope, cost, schedule, and technical performance;

- **Perform Quality Control** (Section 8.3) to inspect and verify the adequacy of the seller's product;

- **Perform Integrated Change Control** (Section 4.5) to assure that changes are properly approved and that all those with a need to know are aware of such changes; and

- **Monitor and Control Risks** (Section 11.6) to ensure that risks are mitigated.

Administer Procurements also has a financial management component that involves monitoring payments to the seller. This ensures that payment terms defined within the contract are met and that seller compensation is linked to seller progress, as defined in the contract. One of the principal concerns when making payments to suppliers is that there is a close relationship of payments made to the work accomplished.

The Administer Procurements process reviews and documents how well a seller is performing or has performed based on the contract and establishes corrective actions when needed. This performance review may be used as a measure of the seller's competency for performing similar work on future projects. Similar evaluations are also carried out when it is necessary to confirm that a seller is not meeting the seller's contractual obligations and when the buyer contemplates corrective actions. Administer Procurements includes managing any early terminations of the contracted work (for cause, convenience, or default) in accordance with the termination clause of the contract.

Contracts can be amended at any time prior to contract closure by mutual consent, in accordance with the change control terms of the contract. Such amendments may not always be equally beneficial to both the seller and the buyer.

12.3.1 Administer Procurements: Inputs

.1 Procurement Documents

Procurement documents contain complete supporting records for administration of the procurement processes. This includes procurement contract awards and the statement of work.

.2 Project Management Plan

The procurement management plan (Section 12.1.3.1), part of the project management plan, is an input to Administer Procurements and describes how the procurement processes will be managed from developing procurement documentation through contract closure.

.3 Contract

Described in Section 12.2.3.2.

.4 Performance Reports

Seller performance-related documentation includes:

- Seller-developed technical documentation and other deliverable information provided in accordance with the terms of the contract, and

- Seller performance reports (Section 10.5.3.1). The seller's performance reports indicate which deliverables have been completed and which have not.

.5 Approved Change Requests

Approved change requests can include modifications to the terms and conditions of the contract including the procurement statement of work, pricing, and description of the products, services, or results to be provided. All changes are formally documented in writing and approved before being implemented.

.6 Work Performance Information

Work performance information (Section 4.3.3.2) including the extent to which quality standards are being satisfied, what costs have been incurred or committed, and which seller invoices have been paid, are all collected as part of project execution.

12.3.2 Administer Procurements: Tools and Techniques

.1 Contract Change Control System

A contract change control system defines the process by which the procurement can be modified. It includes the paperwork, tracking systems, dispute resolution procedures, and approval levels necessary for authorizing changes. The contract change control system is integrated with the integrated change control system.

.2 Procurement Performance Reviews

A procurement performance review is a structured review of the seller's progress to deliver project scope and quality, within cost and on schedule, as compared to the contract. It can include a review of seller-prepared documentation and buyer inspections, as well as quality audits conducted during seller's execution of the work. The objective of a performance review is to identify performance successes or failures, progress with respect to the procurement statement of work, and contract non-compliance, which allow the buyer to quantify the seller's demonstrated ability or inability to perform work. Such reviews may take place as a part of project status reviews which would include key suppliers.

.3 Inspections and Audits

Inspections and audits required by the buyer and supported by the seller as specified in the procurement contract can be conducted during execution of the project to verify compliance in the seller's work processes or deliverables. If authorized by contract, some inspection and audit teams can include buyer procurement personnel.

.4 Performance Reporting

Performance reporting provides management with information about how effectively the seller is achieving the contractual objectives.

.5 Payment Systems

Payments to the seller are typically processed by the accounts payable system of the buyer after certification of satisfactory work by an authorized person on the project team. All payments should be made and documented in strict accordance with the terms of the contract.

.6 Claims Administration

Contested changes and potential constructive changes are those requested changes where the buyer and seller cannot reach an agreement on compensation for the change, or cannot agree that a change has occurred. These contested changes are variously called claims, disputes, or appeals. Claims are documented, processed, monitored, and managed throughout the contract life cycle, usually in accordance with the terms of the contract. If the parties themselves do not resolve a claim, it may have to be handled in accordance with alternative dispute resolution (ADR) typically following procedures established in the contract. Settlement of all claims and disputes through negotiation is the preferred method.

.7 Records Management System

A records management system is used by the project manager to manage contract and procurement documentation and records. It consists of a specific set of processes, related control functions, and automation tools that are consolidated and combined as part of the project management information system (Section 4.3.2.2). The system contains a retrievable archive of contract documents and correspondence.

12.3.3 Administer Procurements: Outputs

.1 Procurement Documentation

Procurement documentation includes, but is not limited to, the procurement contract with all supporting schedules, requested unapproved contract changes, and approved change requests. Procurement documentation also includes any seller-developed technical documentation and other work performance information such as deliverables, seller performance reports, warranties, financial documents including invoices and payment records, and the results of contract-related inspections.

.2 Organizational Process Assets Updates

Elements of the organizational process assets that may be updated include, but are not limited to:

- **Correspondence.** Contract terms and conditions often require written documentation of certain aspects of buyer/seller communications, such as the need for warnings of unsatisfactory performance and requests for contract changes or clarification. This can include the reported results of buyer audits and inspections that indicate weaknesses the seller needs to correct. In addition to specific contract requirements for documentation, a complete and accurate written record of all written and oral contract communications, as well as actions taken and decisions made, are maintained by both parties.

- **Payment schedules and requests.** All payments should be made in accordance with the procurement contract terms and conditions.

- **Seller performance evaluation documentation.** Seller performance evaluation documentation is prepared by the buyer. Such performance evaluations document the seller's ability to continue to perform work on the current contract, indicate if the seller can be allowed to perform work on future projects, or rate how well the seller is performing the project work. These documents can form the basis for early termination of the seller's contract or determine how contract penalties, fees, or incentives are administered. The results of these performance evaluations can also be included in the appropriate qualified seller lists (Section 12.2.1.4).

.3 Change Requests

Change requests to the project management plan, its subsidiary plans and other components, such as the cost baseline, project schedule (Section 6.5.3.1) and procurement management plan (Section 12.1.3.1), may result from the Administer Procurements process. Change requests are processed for review and approval through the Perform Integrated Change Control process (Section 4.5).

Requested but unresolved changes can include direction provided by the buyer, or actions taken by the seller, that the other party considers a constructive change to the contract. Since any of these constructive changes may be disputed by one party and can lead to a claim against the other party, such changes are uniquely identified and documented by project correspondence.

.4 Project Management Plan Updates

Elements of the project management plan that may be updated include, but are not limited to:

- **Procurement management plan.** The procurement management plan (Section 12.1.3.1) is updated to reflect any approved change requests that affect procurement management, including impacts to costs or schedules.

- **Baseline schedule.** If there are slippages that impact overall project performance, the baseline schedule may need to be updated to reflect the current expectations.

12.4 Close Procurements

Close Procurements is the process of completing each project procurement (see Figures 12-8 and 12-9). It supports the Close Project or Phase process (Section 4.6), since it involves verification that all work and deliverables were acceptable.

The Close Procurements process also involves administrative activities such as finalizing open claims, updating records to reflect final results and archiving such information for future use. Close Procurements addresses each contract applicable to the project or a project phase. In multi-phase projects, the term of a contract may only be applicable to a given phase of the project. In these cases, the Close Procurements process closes the procurement(s) applicable to that phase of the project. Unresolved claims may be subject to litigation after closure. The contract terms and conditions can prescribe specific procedures for contract closure.

Early termination of a contract is a special case of procurement closure that can result from a mutual agreement of both parties, from the default of one party, or for convenience of the buyer if provided for in the contract. The rights and responsibilities of the parties in the event of an early termination are contained in a terminations clause of the contract. Based upon those procurement terms and conditions, the buyer may have the right to terminate the whole contract or a portion of the contract, at any time for cause or convenience. However, based upon those contract terms and conditions, the buyer may have to compensate the seller for seller's preparations and for any completed and accepted work related to the terminated part of the contract.

Inputs	Tools & Techniques	Outputs
.1 Project management plan	.1 Procurement audits	.1 Closed procurements
.2 Procurement documentation	.2 Negotiated settlements	.2 Organizational process assets updates
	.3 Records management system	

Figure 12-8. Close Procurements: Inputs, Tools & Techniques, and Outputs

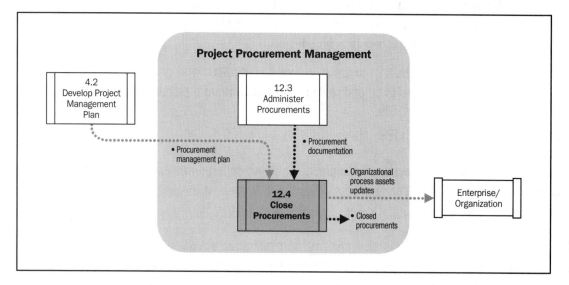

Figure 12-9. Close Procurements Data Flow Diagram

12.4.1 Close Procurements: Inputs

.1 Project Management Plan

Described in Section 4.2.3.1.

.2 Procurement Documentation

To close the contract, all procurement documentation is collected, indexed, and filed. Information on contract schedule, scope, quality, and cost performance along with all contract change documentation, payment records, and inspection results are cataloged. This information can be used for lessons learned information and as a basis for evaluating contractors for future contracts.

12.4.2 Close Procurements: Tools and Techniques

.1 Procurement Audits

A procurement audit is a structured review of the procurement process originating from the Plan Procurements process (Section 12.1) through Administer Procurements (Section 12.3). The objective of a procurement audit is to identify successes and failures that warrant recognition in the preparation or administration of other procurement contracts on the project, or on other projects within the performing organization.

.2 Negotiated Settlements

In all procurement relationships the final equitable settlement of all outstanding issues, claims, and disputes by negotiation is a primary goal. Whenever settlement cannot be achieved through direct negotiation, some form of alternative dispute resolution (ADR) including mediation or arbitration may be explored. When all else fails, litigation in the courts is the least desirable option.

.3 Records Management System

Described in Section 12.3.2.7.

12.4.3 Close Procurements: Outputs

.1 Closed Procurements

The buyer, usually through its authorized procurement administrator, provides the seller with formal written notice that the contract has been completed. Requirements for formal procurement closure are usually defined in the terms and conditions of the contract and are included in the procurement management plan.

.2 Organizational Process Assets Updates

Elements of the organizational process assets that may be updated include, but are not limited to:

- **Procurement file.** A complete set of indexed contract documentation, including the closed contract, is prepared for inclusion with the final project files.

- **Deliverable acceptance.** The buyer, usually through its authorized procurement administrator, provides the seller with formal written notice that the deliverables have been accepted or rejected. Requirements for formal deliverable acceptance, and how to address non-conforming deliverables, are usually defined in the contract.

- **Lessons learned documentation.** Lessons learned, what has been experienced, and process improvement recommendations should be developed for the project file to improve future procurements.

REFERENCES

[1] Project Management Institute. 2006. *Practice Standard for Work Breakdown Structures*—Second Edition. Newtown Square, PA: PMI.

[2] Project Management Institute. 2007. *Practice Standard for Scheduling.* Newtown Square, PA: PMI.

[3] Project Management Institute. 2005. *Practice Standard for Earned Value Management.* Newtown Square, PA: PMI.

[4] International Organization for Standardization. 2005. ISO 9000. *Quality Management Systems—Fundamentals and Vocabulary.* Geneva: ISO Press,

[5] International Organization for Standardization. 1994. ISO 8402. *Quality Management and Quality Assurance.* Geneva: ISO Press (Withdrawn 2000).

[6] Tuckman, Bruce, 1965. *Developmental Sequence in Small Groups. Psychological Bulletin No. 63.* Bethesda, MD: Naval Medical Research Institute.
http://www.businessballs.com/tuckmanformingstormingnormingperforming.htm.

SECTION IV

APPENDICES

APPENDIX A

FOURTH EDITION CHANGES

The purpose of this appendix is to give a detailed explanation of the changes made to *A Guide to the Project Management Body of Knowledge (PMBOK® Guide)*—Third Edition to create the *PMBOK® Guide*—Fourth Edition.

A.1 Consistency and Clarification

The approved scope statement for the *PMBOK® Guide* – Fourth Edition explicitly states that the team should undertake "Any necessary work to make the standard more accurate, up to date, relevant, clear, concise, and easy to understand and implement. This may include the re-organization of content, additional content, refinement of content, or deletion of content."

With that directive in mind, the update team adopted an approach aimed at achieving a greater degree of consistency and clarity by refining the processes, standardizing inputs and outputs where possible, and implementing a global approach for documenting the inputs and outputs.

A.1.1 Consistency

The Fourth Edition, in keeping with the consistency requirement, completed the change to verb noun format for all processes. Standard verbiage was incorporated throughout the document when describing recurring concepts to aid the reader's understanding.

In addition, since process descriptions are located in four places throughout the document, these descriptions were rewritten in a more consistent manner. These areas include:

- In Chapter 3,
- At the beginning of each knowledge area chapter,
- In the first sentence of the applicable process description, and
- In the Glossary.

A.1.2 Clarification

In an effort to provide clarification regarding process interactions, data flow diagrams have been added in order to clarify the input source and the output destination for each process. The project management plan and the project documents have been more clearly differentiated. This was done to highlight subsidiary plans and baselines as the main components of the project management plan. While project documents are used to assist the project manager in managing the project, they are not part of the project management plan. The following is a representative list of project management plan components and project documents.

Table A1. Differentiation between the Project Management Plan and the Project Documents

Project Management Plan	Project Documents	
Change management plan	Activity attributes	Quality metrics
Communications management plan	Activity cost estimates	Responsibility assignment matrix
Configuration management plan	Activity list	Requirements traceability matrix
Cost management plan	Assumption log	Resource breakdown structure
Cost performance baseline	Basis of estimates	Resource calendars
Human resources plan	Change log	Resource requirements
Process improvement plan	Charter	Risk register
Procurement management plan	Contracts	Roles and responsibilities
Quality management plan	Duration estimates	Sellers list
Requirements management plan	Forecasts	Source selection criteria
Risk management plan	Issue log	Stakeholder analysis
Schedule baseline	Milestone list	Stakeholder management strategy
Schedule management plan	Performance reports	Stakeholder register
Scope baseline:	Project funding requirements	Stakeholder requirements
• Scope statement	Proposals	Statement of work
• WBS	Procurement documents	Teaming agreements
• WBS dictionary	Project organizational structure	Team performance assessments
Scope management plan	Quality control measurements	Work performance information
	Quality checklists	Work performance measurements

Another area requiring clarification involved change requests. Corrective action, preventive action, defect repair, and requested changes are now under the general term "change request." This revision helped to streamline the inputs and outputs of many processes while still providing the visibility of the various types of change requests.

The third edition contained a degree of redundancy regarding the components for the project charter and the scope statement. While maintaining some of the spirit of progressive elaboration that takes place between the project charter and the scope statement, we have attempted to distinguish the elements that occur in each document to reduce repetition. The following table lists the elements of each:

Table A2. Elements of the Charter and Scope Statement

Charter	Scope Statement
Project purpose or justification	Product scope description (progressively elaborated)
Measurable project objectives and related success criteria	Project deliverables
High-level requirements	Product user acceptance criteria
High-level project description, product characteristics	Project boundaries
Summary milestone schedule	Project constraints
Summary budget	Project assumptions
Project approval requirements (what constitutes success, who decides it, who signs off)	
Assigned project manager, responsibility and authority level	
Name and responsibility of the person(s) authorizing project charter	

A.2 Process Changes

- *4.2 Develop Preliminary Scope Statement*—Deleted

- *4.7 Close Project*—Changed to 4.6 Close Project or Phase

- *5.1 Plan Scope*—Deleted

- *5.1 Collect Requirements*—Added

- *9.4 Manage Project Team*—Changed from a controlling process to an executing process

- *10.1 Identify Stakeholders*—Added

- *10.4 Manage Stakeholders*—Changed to Manage Stakeholder Expectations; changed from a controlling process to an executing process

- *12.1 Plan Purchases and Acquisitions and 12.2 Plan Contracting*—Changed to 12.1 Plan Procurements

- *12.3 Request Seller Responses and 12.4 Select Sellers*—Changed to 12.2 Conduct Procurements

A.3 Chapter 4—Project Integration Management Changes

Since the project charter contains many of the preliminary goals for the project, and since these goals are elaborated in the Scope Statement, the information relative to Develop Preliminary Project Scope Statement (4.2) was eliminated.

The following table summarizes the Chapter 4 processes:

Table A3. Chapter 4 Changes

Third Edition Sections	Fourth Edition Sections
4.1 Develop Project Charter	4.1 Develop Project Charter
4.2 Develop Preliminary Project Scope Statement	
4.3 Develop Project Management Plan	4.2 Develop Project Management Plan
4.4 Direct and Manage Project Execution	4.3 Direct and Manage Project Execution
4.5 Monitor and Control Project Work	4.4 Monitor and Control Project Work
4.6 Integrated Change Control	4.5 Perform Integrated Change Control
4.7 Close Project	4.6 Close Project or Phase

A.4 Chapter 5—Project Scope Management Changes

In Section 5.1, Scope Planning has been replaced with Collect Requirements. The stakeholder register is used to identify those with interest in the project and involves applying techniques to create the stakeholder requirements document.

The following table summarizes the Chapter 5 processes:

Table A4. Chapter 5 Changes

Third Edition Sections	Fourth Edition Sections
5.1 Scope Planning	5.1 Collect Requirements
5.2 Scope Definition	5.2 Define Scope
5.3 Create WBS	5.3 Create WBS
5.4 Scope Verification	5.4 Verify Scope
5.5 Scope Control	5.5 Control Scope

A.5 Chapter 6—Project Time Management Changes

Chapter 6 reflects changes coming from within the industry and detailed in the *Practice Standard for Scheduling*.

With the use of computer-supported scheduling, the Arrow Diagramming Method (ADM) and its Activity on Arrow (AOA) is rarely used. Therefore it is no longer considered to be used on "most projects, most of the time" and was not included in this chapter.

The following table summarizes the Chapter 6 processes:

Table A5. Chapter 6 Changes

Third Edition Sections	Fourth Edition Sections
6.1 Activity Definition	6.1 Define Activities
6.2 Activity Sequencing	6.2 Sequence Activities
6.3 Activity Resource Estimating	6.3 Estimate Activity Resources
6.4 Activity Duration Estimating	6.4 Estimate Activity Durations
6.5 Schedule Development	6.5 Develop Schedule
6.6 Schedule Control	6.6 Control Schedule

A.6 Chapter 7—Project Cost Management Changes

The Cost Management chapter was updated to more clearly explain the use of the earned value tool and the technique's use, including equations. The "To-Complete Performance Index" calculation was added.

The following table summarizes the Chapter 7 processes:

Table A6. Chapter 7 Changes

Third Edition Sections	Fourth Edition Sections
7.1 Cost Estimating	7.1 Estimate Costs
7.2 Cost Budgeting	7.2 Determine Budget
7.3 Cost Control	7.3 Control Costs

A.7 Chapter 8—Project Quality Management Changes

The following table summarizes the Chapter 8 processes:

Table A7. Chapter 8 Changes

Third Edition Sections	Fourth Edition Sections
8.1 Quality Planning	8.1 Plan Quality
8.2 Perform Quality Assurance	8.2 Perform Quality Assurance
8.3 Perform Quality Control	8.3 Perform Quality Control

A.8 Chapter 9—Project Human Resource Management Changes

The Manage Project Team process was moved into the Executing Process Group as the activities are now more proactive to ensure project performance is optimized. Both Develop Project Team and Manage Project Team have been expanded to recognize and discuss the people skills needed within a successful project team.

The following table summarizes the Chapter 9 processes:

Table A8. Chapter 9 Changes

Third Edition Sections	Fourth Edition Sections
9.1 Human Resource Planning	9.1 Develop Human Resource Plan
9.2 Acquire Project Team	9.2 Acquire Project Team
9.3 Develop Project Team	9.3 Develop Project Team
9.4 Manage Project Team	9.4 Manage Project Team

A.9 Chapter 10—Project Communications Management Changes

Chapter 10 has expanded the recognition and importance of stakeholders within projects. As most project teams cannot necessarily manage their stakeholders but can expect to influence them and their decisions, it was felt that Manage Stakeholder Expectations would better reflect the actual process. This also led to the change from a controlling process to an executing one as the activities are now more about doing than recording/reporting.

The following table summarizes the Chapter 10 processes:

Table A9. Chapter 10 Changes

Third Edition Sections	Fourth Edition Sections
10.1 Communications Planning	10.1 Identify Stakeholders
10.2 Information Distribution	10.2 Plan Communications
10.3 Performance Reporting	10.3 Distribute Information
10.4 Manage Stakeholders	10.4 Manage Stakeholder Expectations
	10.5 Report Performance

A.10 Chapter 11—Project Risk Management Changes

The following table summarizes the Chapter 11 processes:

Table A10. Chapter 11 Changes

Third Edition Sections	Fourth Edition Sections
11.1 Risk Management Planning	11.1 Plan Risk Management
11.2 Risk Identification	11.2 Identify Risks
11.3 Qualitative Risk Analysis	11.3 Perform Qualitative Risk Analysis
11.4 Quantitative Risk Analysis	11.4 Perform Quantitative Risk Analysis
11.5 Risk Response Planning	11.5 Plan Risk Responses
11.6 Risk Monitoring and Control	11.6 Monitor and Control Risks

A.11 Chapter 12—Project Procurement Management Changes

Chapter 12 has consolidated six processes into four processes. Sections 12.1 Plan Purchases and Acquisitions and 12.2 Plan Contracting were combined to create 12.1 Plan Procurements. Sections 12.3 Request Seller Responses and 12.4 Select Sellers were combined to create 12.2 Conduct Procurements. Teaming Agreements were introduced.

The following table summarizes the Chapter 12 processes:

Table A10. Chapter 12 Changes

Third Edition Sections	Fourth Edition Sections
12.1 Plan Purchases and Acquisitions	12.1 Plan Procurements
12.2 Plan Contracting	12.2 Conduct Procurements
12.3 Request Seller Responses	12.3 Administer Procurements
12.4 Select Sellers	12.4 Close Procurements
12.5 Contract Administration	
12.6 Contract Closure	

A.12 Appendices

A new appendix on project management people skills has been added.

A.13 Glossary

The glossary has been expanded and updated to:

- Include those terms within the *PMBOK® Guide* that need to be defined to support an understanding of the document's contents;

- Clarify meaning and improve the quality and accuracy of any translations; and

- Eliminate terms not used within the *PMBOK® Guide* – Fourth Edition.

APPENDIX B

EVOLUTION OF PMI'S *A GUIDE TO THE PROJECT MANAGEMENT BODY OF KNOWLEDGE*

B.1 Initial Development

The Project Management Institute (PMI) was founded in 1969 on the premise that there were many management practices that were common to projects in application areas as diverse as construction and pharmaceuticals. By the time of the PMI Montreal Seminars/Symposium in 1976, the idea that such common practices might be documented as standards began to be widely discussed. This led, in turn, to consideration of project management as a distinct profession.

It was not until 1981, however, that the PMI Board of Directors approved a project to develop the procedures and concepts necessary to support the profession of project management. The project proposal suggested three areas of focus:

- Distinguishing characteristics of a practicing professional (ethics),
- Content and structure of the profession's body of knowledge (standards), and
- Recognition of professional attainment (accreditation).

The project team thus came to be known as the Ethics, Standards, and Accreditation (ESA) Management Group. The ESA Management Group consisted of the following individuals:

Matthew H. Parry, Chair	David C. Aird	Frederick R. Fisher
David Haeney	Harvey Kolodney	Charles E. Oliver
William H. Robinson	Douglas J. Ronson	Paul Sims
Eric W. Smythe		

More than twenty-five volunteers in several local chapters assisted this group. The Ethics statement was developed and submitted by a committee in Washington, DC, chaired by Lew Ireland. The Time Management statement was developed through extensive meetings of a group in Southern Ontario, including Dave MacDonald, Dave Norman, Bob Spence, Bob Hall, and Matt Parry. The Cost Management statement was developed through extensive meetings within the cost department of Stelco, under the direction of Dave Haeney and Larry Harrison. Other statements were developed by the ESA Management Group. Accreditation was taken up by John Adams and his group at Western Carolina University, which resulted in the development of accreditation guidelines. It also resulted in a program of Project Management Professional (PMP®) certification, under the guidance of Dean Martin.

The results of the ESA Project were published in a Special Report in the Project Management Journal in August 1983. The report included the following:

- Code of Ethics, plus a procedure for code enforcement;

- Standards baseline consisting of six major Knowledge Areas: Scope Management, Cost Management, Time Management, Quality Management, Human Resources Management, and Communications Management; and

- Guidelines for both accreditation (recognition of the quality of programs provided by educational institutions) and certification (recognition of the professional qualifications of individuals).

This report subsequently served as the basis for PMI's initial Accreditation and Certification programs. Western Carolina University's Master's Degree in Project Management was accredited in 1983, and the first PMP certifications were awarded in 1984.

B.2 1986–87 Update

Publication of the ESA Baseline Report gave rise to much discussion within PMI about the adequacy of the standards. In 1984, the PMI Board of Directors approved a second standards-related project "to capture the knowledge applied to project management ... within the existing ESA framework." Six committees were then recruited to address each of the six identified Knowledge Areas. In addition, a workshop was scheduled as part of the PMI 1985 Annual Seminars/Symposium.

As a result of these efforts, a revised document was approved in principle by the PMI Board of Directors and published for comment in the *Project Management Journal* in August 1986. The primary contributors to this version of the document were:

R. Max Wideman, Chair *(during development)*	John R. Adams, Chair *(when issued)*	
Joseph R. Beck	Peter Bibbes	Jim Blethen
Richard Cockfield	Peggy Day	William Dixon
Peter C. Georgas	Shirl Holingsworth	William Kane
Colin Morris	Joe Muhlberger	Philip Nunn
Pat Patrick	David Pym	Linn C. Stuckenbruck
George Vallance	Larry C. Woolslager	Shakir Zuberi

In addition to expanding and restructuring the original material, the revised document included three new sections:

- Project Management Framework was added to cover the relationships between the project and its external environment, and between project management and general management;

- Risk Management was added as a separate Knowledge Area in order to provide better coverage of this subject; and

- Contract/Procurement Management was added as a separate Knowledge Area in order to provide better coverage of this subject.

Subsequently, a variety of editorial changes and corrections were incorporated into the material, and the PMI Board of Directors approved it in March 1987. The final manuscript was published in August 1987 as a stand-alone document titled "The Project Management Body of Knowledge."

B.3 1996 Update

Discussion about the proper form, content, and structure of PMI's key standards document continued after publication of the 1987 version. In August 1991, PMI's Director of Standards Alan Stretton initiated a project to update the document based on comments received from the membership. The revised document was developed over several years through a series of widely circulated working drafts and through workshops at the PMI Seminars/Symposia in Dallas, Pittsburgh, and San Diego.

In August 1994, the PMI Standards Committee issued an exposure draft of the document that was distributed for comment to all 10,000 PMI members and to more than twenty other professional and technical associations.

The publication of *A Guide to the Project Management Body of Knowledge (PMBOK® Guide)* in 1996 represented the completion of the project initiated in 1991. Contributors and reviewers are listed later in this section. A summary of the differences between the 1987 document and the 1996 document, which was included in the Preface of the 1996 edition, also is listed later in this section.

The document superseded PMI's *The Project Management Body of Knowledge (PMBOK®)* document that was published in 1987. To assist users of the 1996 document, who may have been familiar with its predecessor, we have summarized the major differences here:

1. Title was changed to emphasize that this document is not the project management body of knowledge. The 1987 document defined the project management body of knowledge as "all those topics, subject areas, and intellectual processes which are involved in the application of sound management principles to ... projects." Clearly, one document will never contain the entire project management body of knowledge.

2. The Framework section was completely rewritten. The new section consisted of three chapters:

    *   Introduction, which set out the purpose of the document and defined at length the terms project and project management

    *   Project Management Context, which covered the context in which projects operate—the project life cycle, stakeholder perspectives, external influences, and key general management skills

    *   Project Management Processes, which described how the various elements of project management interrelate.

3. A revised definition of project was developed, which was both inclusive ("It should not be possible to identify any undertaking generally thought of as a project that does not fit the definition.") and exclusive ("It should not be possible to describe any undertaking that satisfies the definition and is not generally thought of as a project."). Many of the definitions of project in the existing literature were reviewed and all were found to be unsatisfactory in some way. The new definition was driven by the unique characteristics of a project: a project is a temporary endeavor undertaken to create a unique product or service.

4. Revised view of the project life cycle was developed. The 1987 document defined project phases as subdivisions of the project life cycle. This relationship was reordered and project life cycle was defined as a collection of phases whose number and names are determined by the control needs of the performing organization.

5. Names of the major sections were changed from Function to Knowledge Areas. The term "function" had been frequently misunderstood to mean an element of a functional organization. The name change was completed to eliminate this misunderstanding.

6. The existence of a ninth Knowledge Area was formally recognized. There had been widespread consensus for some time that project management is an integrative process. Chapter 4, Project Integration Management, recognized the importance of this subject.

7. The word "Project" was added to the title of each Knowledge Area. Although this may seem redundant, was intended to clarify the scope of the document. For example, Project Human Resource Management covers only those aspects of managing human resources that are unique or nearly unique to the project context.

8. The Knowledge Areas were described in terms of their component processes. The search for a consistent method of presentation led the team to completely restructure the 1987 document into thirty-seven project management processes. Each process was described in terms of its inputs, outputs, and tools and techniques. Inputs and outputs are documents (e.g., a scope statement) or documentable items (e.g., activity dependencies). Tools and techniques are the mechanisms applied to the inputs to create the outputs. In addition to its fundamental simplicity, this approach offered several other benefits:

    - It emphasized the interactions among the Knowledge Areas. Outputs from one process became inputs to another.

    - The structure was flexible and robust. Changes in knowledge and practice were accommodated by adding a new process, by resequencing processes, by subdividing processes, or by adding descriptive material within a process.

    - Processes became the core of other standards. For example, the International Organization for Standardization's quality standards (the ISO 9000 series) are based on identification of business processes.

9. Some illustrations were added to better depict work breakdown structures, network diagrams, and S-curves.

10. The document was reorganized significantly. The following table provides a comparison of the major headings of the 1987 document and the corresponding headings and/or content sources of the 1996 version:

1987 Number and Name	1996 Number and Name
0. PMBOK® Standards	B. Evolution of PMI's *A Guide to the Project Management Body of Knowledge*
1. Framework: The Rationale	1. Introduction (basic definitions) 2. The Project Context (life cycles)
2. Framework: An Overview	1. Various portions 2. Various portions 3. Various portions
3. Framework: An Integrative Model	3. Project Management Processes 4. Project Integration Management
4. Glossary of General Terms	IV. Glossary
A. Scope Management	5. Project Scope Management
B. Quality Management	8. Project Quality Management
C. Time Management	6. Project Time Management
D. Cost Management	7. Project Cost Management
E. Risk Management	11. Project Risk Management
F. Human Resource Management	9. Project Human Resource Management
G. Contract/Procurement Management	12. Project Procurement Management
H. Communications Management	10. Project Communications Management

11. "To classify" was removed from the list of purposes. Both the 1996 document and the 1987 version provided a structure for organizing project management knowledge, but neither was particularly effective as a classification tool. First, the topics included were not comprehensive—they did not include innovative or unusual practices. Second, many elements have relevance in more than one Knowledge Area or process, such that the categories were not unique.

The following individuals, as listed in Appendix C of the 1996 document, contributed in many different ways to various drafts of the 1996 document. PMI is indebted to them for their support.

Standards Committee

The following individuals served as members of the PMI Standards Committee during development of the 1996 update of the PMBOK® document:

William R. Duncan	Frederick Ayer	Cynthia Berg
Mark Burgess	Helen Cooke	Judy Doll
Drew Fetters	Brian Fletcher	Earl Glenwright
Eric Jenett	Deborah O'Bray	Diane Quinn
Anthony Rizzotto	Alan Stretton	Douglas E. Tryloff

Contributors

In addition to the members of the Standards Committee, the following individuals provided original text or key concepts for one or more sections in the chapters indicated:

John Adams (Chapter 3)	Keely Brunner (Chapter 7)
Louis J. Cabano (Chapter 5)	David Curling (Chapter 12)
Douglas Gordon (Chapter 7)	David T. Hulett (Chapter 11)
Edward Ionata (Chapter 10)	John M. Nevison (Chapter 9)
Hadley Reynolds (Chapter 2)	Agnes Salvo (Chapter 11)
W. Stephen Sawle (Chapter 5)	Leonard Stolba (Chapter 8)
Ahmet Taspinar (Chapter 6)	Francis M. Webster Jr. (Chapter 1)

Reviewers

In addition to the Standards Committee and the contributors, the following individuals and organizations provided comments on various drafts of the 1996 document:

Edward L. Averill	C. "Fred" Baker	F. J. "Bud" Baker
Tom Belanger	John A. Bing	Brian Bock
Paul Bosakowski	Dorothy J. Burton	Kim Colenso
Samuel K. Collier	Karen Condos-Alfonsi	E. J. Coyle
Darlene Crane	Russ Darnall	Maureen Dougherty
John J. Downing	Daniel D. Dudek	Lawrence East
Quentin W. Fleming	Rick Fletcher	Greg Githens
Leo Giulianeti	Martha D. Hammonds	Abdulrazak Hajibrahim
G. Alan Hellawell	Paul Hinkley	Wayne L. Hinthorn
Mark E. Hodson	Lew Ireland	Elvin Isgrig
Murray Janzen	Frank Jenes	Walter Karpowski
William F. Kerrigan	Harold Kerzner	Robert L. Kimmons
Richard King	J. D. "Kaay" Koch	Lauri Koskela
Richard E. Little	Lyle W. Lockwood	Lawrence Mack
Christopher Madigan	Michael L. McCauley	Hugh McLaughlin
Frank McNeely	Pierre Menard	Rick Michaels
Raymond Miller	Alan Minson	Colin Morris
R. Bruce Morris	David J. Mueller	Gary Nelson
John P. Nolan	Louise C. Novakowski	James O'Brien
JoAnn C. Osmer	Jon V. Palmquist	Matthew Parry
John G. Phippen	Hans E. Picard	Serge Y. Piotte
PMI Houston Chapter	PMI Manitoba Chapter	PMI New Zealand Chapter
Charles J. Pospisil	Janice Y. Preston	Mark T. Price
Christopher Quaife	Peter E. Quinn	Steven F. Ritter
William S. Ruggles	Ralph B. Sackman	Alice Sapienza
Darryl M. Selleck	Melvin Silverman	Roy Smith
Craig T. Stone	Hiroshi Tanaka	Robert Templeton
Dick Thiel	Saul Thomashow	J. Tidhar
Janet Toepfer	Vijay K. Verma	Alex Walton
Jack Way	R. Max Wideman	Rebecca Winston
Hugh M. Woodward	Robert Youker	Shakir H. Zuberi
Dirk Zwart		

Production Staff

Special mention is due to the following employees of PMI Communications:

Jeannette M. Cabanis, Editor, Book Division

Linda V. Gillman, Office Administrator

Jonathan Hicks, Systems Administrator

Dewey L. Messer, Managing Editor

Mark S. Parker, Production Coordinator

Melissa Pendergast, Information Services Coordinator

Michelle Triggs, Graphic Designer

Misty N. Dillard, Administrative Assistant

Bobby R. Hensley, Publications Coordinator

Sandy Jenkins, Associate Editor

Danell Moses, Marketing Promotion Coordinator

Shirley B. Parker, Business/Marketing Manager

James S. Pennypacker, Publisher/Editor-In-Chief

Lisa Woodring, Administrative Assistant

B.4 2000 Update

The 2000 Edition superseded the Project Management Institute's (PMI®) *A Guide to the Project Management Body of Knowledge (PMBOK® Guide),* published in 1996.

The scope of the project using the 1996 publication as its starting point, was to:

- Add new material, reflecting the growth of the knowledge and practices in the field of project management by capturing those practices, tools, techniques, and other relevant items that have become generally accepted. (Generally accepted means being applicable to most projects most of the time, and having widespread consensus about their value and usefulness.)

- Add clarification to text and figures to make the *PMBOK® Guide* more beneficial to users.

- Correct existing errors in the predecessor document.

Major changes to the 2000 Edition were as follows:

1. Throughout the document, clarified that projects manage to requirements, which emerge from needs, wants, and expectations.

2. Strengthened linkages to organizational strategy throughout the document.

3. Provided more emphasis on progressive elaboration in Section 1.2.3.

4. Acknowledged the role of the Project Office in Section 2.3.4.

5. Added references to project management involving developing economies, as well as social, economic, and environmental impacts, in Section 2.5.4.

6. Added expanded treatment of Earned Value Management in Chapter 4 (Project Integration Management), Chapter 7 (Project Cost Management), and Chapter 10 (Project Communications Management).

7. Rewrote Chapter 11 (Project Risk Management). The chapter now contains six processes instead of the previous four processes. The six processes are Risk Management Planning, Risk Identification, Qualitative Risk Analysis, Quantitative Risk Analysis, Risk Response Planning, and Risk Monitoring and Control.

8. Moved scope verification from an Executing process to a Controlling process.

9. Changed the name of Process 4.3 from Overall Change Control to Integrated Change Control to emphasize the importance of change control throughout the entirety of the project.

10. Added a chart that maps the thirty-nine Project Management processes against the five Project Management Process Groups and the nine Project Management Knowledge Areas in Figure 3-9.

11. Standardized terminology throughout the document from "supplier" to "seller."

12. Added several tools and techniques:

Chapter 4 - Project Integration Management	*Earned Value Management (EVM) Preventive Action*
Chapter 5 - Project Scope Management	*Scope Statement Updates* *Project Plan* *Adjusted Baseline*
Chapter 6 - Project Time Management	*Quantitatively Based Durations* *Reserve Time (Contingency)* *Coding Structure* *Variance Analysis* *Milestones* *Activity Attributes* *Computerized Tools*
Chapter 7 - Project Cost Management	*Estimating Publications* *Earned Value Measurement*
Chapter 8 - Project Quality Management	*Cost of Quality*
Chapter 10 - Project Communications Management	*Project Reports* *Project Presentations* *Project Closure*

PMI Project Management Standards Program Member Advisory Group

The following individuals served as members of the PMI Standards Member Advisory Group (MAG) during development of the 2000 Edition of *A Guide to the Project Management Body of Knowledge (PMBOK® Guide)* standard:

George Belev	Cynthia A. Berg, PMP	Sergio Coronado Arrechedera
Judith A. Doll, PMP	J. Brian Hobbs, PMP	David Hotchkiss, PMP

PMBOK® Guide Update Project Team

The following individuals served as members of the project team for this 2000 Edition of the *PMBOK® Guide*, under the leadership of Cynthia A. Berg, PMP, as Project Manager:

Cynthia A. Berg, PMP	Judith A. Doll, PMP	Daniel Dudek, PMP
Quentin Fleming	Greg Githens, PMP	Earl Glenwright
David T. Hulett, PhD	Gregory J. Skulmoski	

Contributors

In addition to the members of the PMI Standards Member Advisory Group and the *PMBOK® Guide* Project Team, the following individuals provided original text or key concepts for one or more sections in the chapters indicated. Also, the PMI Risk Management Specific Interest Group provided leadership for the rewrite of Chapter 11, Project Risk Management.

Alfredo del Caño (Chapter 11)	Quentin Fleming (Chapters 4 and 12)
Roger Graves (Chapter 11)	David Hillson (Chapter 11)
David Hulett (Chapter 11)	Sam Lane (Chapter 11)
Janice Preston (Chapter 11)	Stephen Reed (Chapter 11)
David Shuster (Chapter 8)	Ed Smith (Chapter 11)
Mike Wakshull (Chapter 11)	Robert Youker (several chapters)

Reviewers

In addition to the PMI Standards Member Advisory Group (MAG), the *PMBOK® Guide* Project Team, and the Contributors, the following individuals provided comments on the Exposure Draft of the 2000 Edition:

Muhamed Abdomerovic, PMP, D. Eng.

Frank Allen, PMP

MaryGrace Allenchey, PMP

Ichizo Aoki

Ronald Auffrédou, PMP

Frederick L. Ayer, PMP

A. C. "Fred" Baker, PMP

Berndt Bellman

Nigel Blampied, PE, PMP

Patrick Brown, PMP

Bruce C. Chadbourne, PMP

Raymond C. Clark, PE

David Coates, PMP

Edmund H. Conrow, PMP

John Cornman, PMP

Kevin Daly, PMP

Thomas Diethelm, PMP

Frank D. Einhorn, PMP

Christian Frankenberg, PMP

Jean-Luc Frere, PMP

Chikako Futamura, PMP

Brian L. Garrison, PMP

Peter Bryan Goldsbury

Jean Gouix, PMP

Franz X. Hake

Chris Herbert, PMP

J. Brian Hobbs, PMP

Robin Hornby

Charles L. Hunt

George Jackelen

Elden F. Jones II, PMP, CMII

Yassir Afaneh

Jon D. Allen, PMP

Robert A. Andrejko, PMP

Paul C. Aspinwall

Edward Averill, PMP

William W. Bahnmaier, PMP

Carole J. Bass, PMP

Sally Bernstein, PMP

John Blatta

Chris Cartwright, PMP

Michael T. Clark, PMP

Elizabeth Clarke

Kim Colenso, PMP

Kenneth G. Cooper

Richard F. Cowan, PMP

Mario Damiani, PMP

David M. Drevinsky, PMP

Edward Fern, PMP

Scott D. Freauf, PMP

Ichiro Fujita, PMP

Serge Garon, PEng, PMP

Eric Glover

Michael Goodman, PMP

Alexander Grassi Sr., PMP

Peter Heffron

Dr. David Hillson, PMP, FAPM

Marion Diane Holbrook

Bill Hubbard

Thomas P. Hurley, PMP

Angyan P. Jagathnarayanan

Sada Joshi, PMP

Lewis Kana, PMP	Subramaniam Kandaswamy, PhD, PMP
Ronald L. Kempf, PMP	Robert Dohn Kissinger, PhD, PMP
Kurt V. Kloecker	Jan Kristrom
Blase Kwok, PMP	Lawrence P. Leach
Philip A. Lindeman	Gábor Lipi
Lyle W. Lockwood, PMP	J. W. Lowthian, PMP
Arif Mahmood, PMP	James Martin (on behalf of INCOSE)
Stephen S. Mattingly	Glen Maxfield
Peter McCarthy	Rob McCormack, PMP
Krik D. McManus	David Michaud
Mary F. Miekoski, PMP	Oscar A. Mignone
Gordon R. Miller, PMP	Roy E. Morgan, PMP
Jim Morris, PMP	Bert Mosterd, PMP
William A. Moylan, PMP	John D. Nelson, PMP
Wolfgang Obermeier	Cathy Oest, PMP
Masato Ohori, PMP	Kazuhiko Okubo, PE, PMP
Edward Oliver	Jerry Partridge, PMP
Francisco Perez-Polo, PMP	James M. Phillips, PMP
Crispin (Kik) Piney, PMP	George Pitagorsky, PMP
David L. Prater, PMP	Bradford S. Price, PMP
Samuel L. Raisch, PMP	Naga Rajan
G. Ramachandran, PMP	Bill Righter, PMP
Bernice L. Rocque, PMP	Wolfgang Theodore Roesch
Fernando Romero Peñailillo	Jon Rude
Linda Rust, PMP	Fabian Sagristani, PMP
James N. Salapatas, PMP	Seymour Samuels
Bradford N. Scales	H. Peter Schiller
John R. Schuyler, PMP	Maria Scott, PMP
Shoukat Sheikh, MBA, PMP	Kazuo Shimizu, PMP
Larry Sieck	(on behalf of the PMI Tokyo, Japan Chapter)
Melvin Silverman, PhD, PE	Loren J. Simer Jr.
Keith Skilling, PE, PMP	Greg Skulmoski
Kenneth F. Smith, PMP	Barry Smythe, PMP
Paul J. Solomon	Joe Soto Sr., PMP
Christopher Wessley Sours, PMP	Charlene Spoede, PMP

Joyce Statz, PMP
Thangavel Subbu
Ahmet N. Taspinar, PMP
Alan D. Uren, PMP
S. Rao Vallabhaneni
Ana Isabel Vazquez Urbina
Stephen E. Wall, PMP
Tammo T. Wilkens, PE, PMP

Emmett Stine, PMP
Jim Szpakowski
John A. Thoren Jr., PMP
Juan Luis Valero, PMP
William Simon Vaughan Robinson
Ricardo Viana Vargas, PMP
William W. Wassel, PMP
Robert Williford, PMP

Contributions to Predecessor Documents

Portions of the 1996 edition and other predecessor documents are included in the 2000 edition. PMI wishes to acknowledge the following volunteers as substantial contributors to the 2000 Edition:

John R. Adams
Alan Stretton

William R. Duncan
R. Max Wideman

Matthew H. Parry

Production Staff

Special mention is due to the following employees of PMI:

Steven L. Fahrenkrog, Standards Manager
Lisa Fisher, Assistant Editor
Lewis M. Gedansky, Research Manager
Linda V. Gillman, Advertising Coordinator/ PMBOK® Guide Copyright Permissions Coordinator
Eva T. Goldman, Technical Research & Standards Associate
Paul Grace, Certification Manager
Sandy Jenkins, Managing Editor
Toni D. Knott, Book Editor
John McHugh, Interim Publisher
Dewey L. Messer, Design and Production Manager
Mark S. Parker, Production Coordinator
Shirley B. Parker, Business/Book Publishing Manager
Michelle Triggs Owen, Graphic Designer
Iesha D. Turner-Brown, Standards Administrator

B.5 Third Edition Update

The Third Edition, published in 2004, superseded the Project Management Institute's (PMI®) *A Guide to the Project Management Body of Knowledge (PMBOK® Guide)*, published in 2000.

Structural Changes

One of the most pronounced changes to the Third Edition of the *PMBOK® Guide* was the structure. The Third Edition was structured to emphasize the importance of the Process Groups as described in Table B1, which displays a side-by-side comparison of the changes. Chapter 3 was renamed "Project Management Processes for a Project" and was moved from Section I to a new Section II entitled "The Standard for Project Management of a Project." As part of this change, Chapter 3 was extensively revised to clearly indicate that the processes, inputs, and outputs called out in the chapter are the basis of the standard for project management of a single project.

Table B1. Structural Changes

2000 Edition Sections	Third Edition Sections
Section I - The Project Management Framework Chapters 1, 2, and 3	Section I - The Project Management Framework Chapters 1 and 2
	Section II - The Standard for Project Management of a Project Chapter 3 - Project Management Processes for a Project
Section II - The Project Management Knowledge Areas Chapters 4 through 12	Section III - The Project Management Knowledge Areas Chapters 4 through 12
Section III - Appendices Appendix D - Notes Appendix E - Application Area Extensions	Section IV - Appendices Appendix D - Application Area Extensions
Section IV - Glossary and Index	Section V – References, Glossary, and Index

Process Name Changes

In the Third Edition, seven processes have been added, thirteen renamed, and two deleted for a net gain of five processes.

The names of processes in the various chapters of the *PMBOK® Guide* – 2000 Edition were in different formats and styles. Inconsistent naming styles can cause confusion for project management students and experienced individuals as well. For example, the processes in the Scope Knowledge Area were Initiation, Scope Planning, Scope Definition, Scope Verification, and Scope Change Control. Some of these are active voice; some are present participles. The effect of these different styles was that readers were unable, at a glance, to determine whether a term is an activity (a process) or a deliverable (a work-product or artifact). The project team proposed a wholesale change of all process names to the verb-object format in the *PMBOK® Guide* – Third Edition. However, PMI was concerned that changing all of the names would be too large a change; therefore, PMI authorized only an incremental change in the *PMBOK® Guide* – Third Edition to include only those approved new processes and a small number of other processes for specific reasons explained later in this appendix.

Elimination of Facilitating and Core Process Designations

The terms "Facilitating Processes" and "Core Processes" were eliminated to ensure that all project management processes in the Project Management Process Groups have the same level of importance. The project management processes are still grouped within the Project Management Process Groups, as indicated in Figure 3-5 Initiating Process Group; Figure 3-6 Planning Process Group; Figure 3-7 Executing Process Group; Figure 3-8 Monitoring and Controlling Process Group; and Figure 3-9 Closing Process Group. The 44 project management processes are mapped into both the Project Management Process Groups and the Knowledge Areas, as shown in Table 3-45.

Writing Styles

A Style Guide was developed and used by the project team to create and finalize the input. Attention was focused on using active voice language and content consistency throughout the document to prevent an occurrence of different writing styles.

Chapter 1 – Introduction Changes

Chapter 1 changes were intended to clarify and improve organization within the chapter. Chapter 1 clarified the differences between a project and operations. Standard definitions were provided for program and program management, portfolio and portfolio management, and included a more detailed discussion of project management office (PMO) variations. Additional revisions included the following:

- General management skills were moved to Chapter 1.

- A section identifying the many areas of expertise needed by the project team was added.

Chapter 2 – Project Life Cycle and Organization Changes

Chapter 2 changes clarified the distinctions between project life cycles and product life cycles, and explained project phases. Stakeholders were defined in relation to the project team. A PMO's role and responsibility in the organization were defined, and the concept of a project management system was introduced.

Chapter 3 – Project Management Processes for a Project Changes

Chapter 3 was completely rewritten and expanded to focus on the Project Management Process Groups and processes within the Knowledge Areas. For emphasis, Chapter 3 was renamed "Project Management Processes for a Project" and moved into a new Section II, "The Standard for Project Management of a Project." Chapter 3 was extensively revised to serve as a standard for managing a single project and clearly indicates the five required Project Management Process Groups and their constituent processes. The Initiating Process Group and the Closing Process Group were given more emphasis than in previous editions. The Controlling Process Group was expanded to include Monitoring and is retitled the "Monitoring and Controlling Process Group." Material was added to clarify the distinction between the Project Management Process Groups and project phases, which have sometimes mistakenly been viewed as one and the same.

Chapter 4 – Project Integration Management Changes

Chapter 4 was completely rewritten to enhance the discussion of integrating project management processes and activities. The chapter describes integration from the aspect of the Project Management Process Groups, and provides a clear description of integration across all Project Management Process Groups and among all project management processes. Four new processes were included in the chapter and two processes were renamed:

- Develop Project Charter process formally authorizes a project.

- Develop Preliminary Project Scope Statement process provides a high-level scope narrative.

- Develop Project Management Plan process documents the actions necessary to define, prepare, integrate, and coordinate all subsidiary plans into the project management plan.

- Direct and Manage Project Execution process executes the work defined in the project management plan to achieve the project's objectives.

- Monitor and Control Project Work process defines the processes to monitor and control the project activities needed to initiate, plan, execute, and close a project.

- Close Project process finalizes all activities across all of the Process Groups to formally close the project.

Table B2 summarizes the Chapter 4 changes:

Table B2. Chapter 4 Changes

2000 Edition Sections	Third Edition Sections
	4.1 Develop Project Charter
	4.2 Develop Preliminary Project Scope Statement
4.1 Project Plan Development	4.3 Develop Project Management Plan
4.2 Project Plan Execution	4.4 Direct and Manage Project Execution
	4.5 Monitor and Control Project Work
4.3 Integrated Change Control	4.6 Integrated Change Control
	4.7 Close Project

Chapter 5 – Project Scope Management Changes

Chapter 5 was modified to clarify the role of the project scope management plan in developing the project scope statement. The chapter provided an extensive discussion and clarified the importance of a work breakdown structure (WBS), with the addition of a new section on creating the WBS. The Initiation section was rewritten and moved to Chapter 4. The following table summarizes the Chapter 5 changes:

Table B3. Chapter 5 Changes

2000 Edition Sections	Third Edition Sections
5.1 Initiation	Rewritten and moved to Chapter 4
5.2 Scope Planning	5.1 Scope Planning
5.3 Scope Definition	5.2 Scope Definition
	5.3 Create WBS
5.4 Scope Verification	5.4 Scope Verification
5.5 Scope Change Control	5.5 Scope Control

Chapter 6 – Project Time Management Changes

Chapter 6 changes included moving the Resource Planning section into the chapter and renaming it Activity Resource Estimating. Several figures were deleted (e.g., PERT) and other figures were reworked to clarify the use and meaning (e.g., bar or Gantt chart, milestone chart). Another figure was added to show the difference between a milestone schedule, summary schedule, and detailed schedule. The chapter introduction described the need for a schedule management plan, a subsidiary component of the project management plan. Subsections were also added to provide information on project cost estimates, resource leveling, and progress reporting to reflect how these processes influence the project's schedule. The following table summarizes the Chapter 6 changes:

Table B4. Chapter 6 Changes

2000 Edition Sections	Third Edition Sections
6.1 Activity Definition	6.1 Activity Definition
6.2 Activity Sequencing	6.2 Activity Sequencing
	6.3 Activity Resource Estimating
6.3 Activity Duration Estimating	6.4 Activity Duration Estimating
6.4 Schedule Development	6.5 Schedule Development
6.5 Schedule Control	6.6 Schedule Control

Chapter 7 – Project Cost Management Changes

Chapter 7 processes were expanded to integrate project budget directly with the WBS and to cover controlling costs. There were significant structural changes to the inputs, tools and techniques, as well. The chapter introduction was modified to describe the need for a cost management plan, a subsidiary component of the project management plan. The Resource Planning process was moved to Chapter 6 and renamed Activity Resource Estimating. This chapter contains the majority of the information on Earned Value Management. The following table summarizes the Chapter 7 changes:

Table B5. Chapter 7 Changes

2000 Edition Sections	Third Edition Sections
7.1 Resource Planning	Moved to Project Time Management (Chapter 6)
7.2 Cost Estimating	7.1 Cost Estimating
7.3 Cost Budgeting	7.2 Cost Budgeting
7.4 Cost Control	7.3 Cost Control

Chapter 8 - Project Quality Management Changes

Chapter 8 was changed to include two revised project management process names to better reflect the activities of those processes. An emphasis was made to integrate quality activities with the overall Monitoring and Controlling process, as defined in Chapter 4. The following table summarizes the Chapter 8 changes:

Table B6. Chapter 8 Changes

2000 Edition Sections	Third Edition Sections
8.1 Quality Planning	8.1 Quality Planning
8.2 Quality Assurance	8.2 Perform Quality Assurance
8.3 Quality Control	8.3 Perform Quality Control

Chapter 9 – Project Human Resource Management Changes

Chapter 9 identifies several aspects of human resource planning, as well as the staffing management plan. Manage Project Team was added as a Monitoring and Controlling process. Several key explanations were also added, including organizational charts and position descriptions. The figures in this chapter were changed to reflect current project management techniques, such as virtual teams, ground rules, and issues log. The following table summarizes the Chapter 9 changes:

Table B7. Chapter 9 Changes

2000 Edition Sections	Third Edition Sections
9.1 Organizational Planning	9.1 Human Resource Planning
9.2 Staff Acquisition	9.2 Acquire Project Team
9.3 Team Development	9.3 Develop Project Team
	9.4 Manage Project Team

Chapter 10 – Project Communications Management Changes

Chapter 10 was updated with the addition of a Manage Stakeholders process. The Manage Stakeholders process manages communications to satisfy the needs of, and resolve issues with, project stakeholders. The following table summarizes the Chapter 10 changes:

Table B8. Chapter 10 Changes

2000 Edition Sections	Third Edition Sections
10.1 Communications Planning	10.1 Communications Planning
10.2 Information Distribution	10.2 Information Distribution
10.3 Performance Reporting	10.3 Performance Reporting
10.4 Administrative Closure	10.4 Manage Stakeholders

Chapter 11 – Project Risk Management Changes

Chapter 11 was updated to increase focus on opportunities (versus threats). It now includes options based on project complexity, enhances Risk Management Planning activities, adds the risk register, and provides closer integration with other processes. The following table summarizes the Chapter 11 changes:

Table B9. Chapter 11 Changes (no process name changes were made)

2000 Edition Sections	Third Edition Sections
11.1 Risk Management Planning	11.1 Risk Management Planning
11.2 Risk Identification	11.2 Risk Identification
11.3 Qualitative Risk Analysis	11.3 Qualitative Risk Analysis
11.4 Quantitative Risk Analysis	11.4 Quantitative Risk Analysis
11.5 Risk Response Planning	11.5 Risk Response Planning
11.6 Risk Monitoring and Control	11.6 Risk Monitoring and Control

Chapter 12 – Project Procurement Management Changes

Chapter 12 was updated to provide a consistent use of the terms "buyer" and "seller." The changes clarified the difference between the project team as a buyer of products and services, and as the seller of products and services. The chapter was updated to include a process on seller performance evaluation to contract administration, and the words "procure," "solicit," and "solicitation" were removed to recognize the negative connotation of these words in various areas around the world. The following table summarizes the Chapter 12 changes:

Table B10. Chapter 12 Changes

2000 Edition Sections	Third Edition Sections
12.1 Procurement Planning	12.1 Plan Purchases and Acquisitions
12.2 Solicitation Planning	12.2 Plan Contracting
12.3 Solicitation	12.3 Request Seller Responses
12.4 Source Selection	12.4 Select Sellers
12.5 Contract Administration	12.5 Contract Administration
12.6 Contract Closeout	12.6 Contract Closure

Glossary

The glossary was expanded and updated to:

- Include those terms within the *PMBOK® Guide* that need to be defined to support an understanding of the document's contents

- Clarify meaning and improve the quality and accuracy of any translations

- Eliminate terms not used within the *PMBOK® Guide* – Third Edition.

PMBOK® Guide – Third Edition Project Leadership Team

The following individuals were contributors of text or concepts and served as leaders within the Project Leadership Team (PLT):

Dennis Bolles, PMP, Project Manager

Darrel G. Hubbard, PE, Deputy Project Manager

J. David Blaine, PMP (Quality Control Coordinator)

Theodore R. Boccuzzi, PMP (Document Research Team Leader)

Elden Jones, PMP (Configuration Management Coordinator)

Dorothy Kangas, PMP (Product Overview Team Leader)

Carol Steuer, PMP (Framework Team Leader)

Geree Streun, PMP (Process Groups Team Leader)

Lee Towe, PMP (Special Appointment)

PMBOK® Guide – Third Edition Project Core Team

In addition to the Project Leadership Team, the following individuals served as contributors of text or concepts and as co-leaders within the Project Core Team (PCT):

Nigel Blampied, PE, PMP (Framework Team Co-Leader)

J. David Blaine, PMP (Product Overview Team Co-Leader)

Andrea Giulio Demaria, PMP (Document Research Team Co-Leader)

Greg Githens, PMP (Framework Team Co-Leader)

Dana J. Goulston, PMP (Framework Team Co-Leader)

David T. Hulett, PhD (Knowledge Areas Team Co-Leader)

Elden Jones, MSPM, PMP (Process Groups Team Co-Leader)

Carol Rauh, PhD, PMP (Knowledge Areas Team Co-Leader)

Michael J. Schollmeyer, PMP (Product Overview Team Co-Leader)

PMBOK® Guide – Third Edition Project Sub-Teams

The following individuals served as contributors of text or concepts and as leaders of the Project Sub-Teams (PST):

W. Clifton Baldwin, PMP (Index and Input Guidance Leader)

Barbara Borgmann, PMP (Knowledge Areas Chapter 8 Leader)

Kim D. Colenso, PMP, CSQE (Glossary Leader)

Earl Glenwright, PE, VEA (Knowledge Areas Chapter 7 Leader)

Darrel G. Hubbard, PE (Knowledge Areas Chapter 12 Leader)

David T. Hulett, PhD, PMP (Knowledge Areas Chapter 11 Leader)

Jim O'Brien, PMP (Knowledge Areas Chapter 6 Leader)

Brian Salk, MA Ed, PMP (Knowledge Areas Chapter 5 Leader)

Geree Streun, PMP (Knowledge Areas Chapters 3 and 4 Leader)

John A. Thoren, Jr., PMP, PhD (Knowledge Areas Chapter 10 Leader)

Lee Towe, PMP, MBA (Knowledge Areas Chapter 9 Leader)

Significant Contributors

In addition to the members of the Project Leadership Team, the Project Core Team, and the Sub-Team Leaders, the following individuals provided significant input or concepts:

Sumner Alpert, PMP, CMC

Cynthia A. Berg, PMP

Edmund H. Conrow, PhD, PMP

Bradford Eichhorn, PMP

Steve Grey, PhD, PMP

David Hillson, PhD, PMP

Yan Bello Mendez, PMP

Crispin "Kik" Piney, BSc, PMP

Massimo Torre, PhD, PMP

Cornelis (Kees) Vonk, PMP

Linda Westfall, PE, CSQE

PMBOK® Guide – Third Edition Project Team Members

In addition to those listed above, the following PMBOK® Guide – Third Edition Project Team Members provided input to and recommendations on drafts of the PMBOK® Guide – Third Edition, or submitted Enterprise Change Requests (ECRs):

Abdallah Abi-Aad, PMP, PEng

Adrian Abramovici, PMP

Mark Allyn, PMP

Lionel Andrew, MBA, ISP

Prabu V. Ayyagari, PhD, PMP

Pamela M. Baker, PMP

James S. Bennett, PMP

Howland Blackiston

Charles W. Bosler, Jr.

Carolyn Boyles, MBA, PMP

Alex S. Brown, PMP

Stephen C. Burgan, PMP

Muhamed Abdomerovic, PMP

Jamie K. Allen, PMP

Scott C. Anderson, PMP

Russell Archibald, PMP

Ernest Baker, PMP

Kevin E. Bast, PMP

Ionut C. Bibac

Ray Blake, PMP

Rollin O. Bowen, Jr.

Wayne R. Brantley, PMP, MS Ed

Timothy S. Brown

Anne Cagle, PMP

Dean J. Calabrese, PMP

Giuseppe A. Caruso, PMP

Clare Chan

Gene Chiappetta, PMP

Mark T. Chism, PMP

Robert L. Cutler, PMP

Mario Damiani, PMP

Robert de Jong, PMP

John M. Dery, PMP

Jerry Dimos, PMP

Capt. Nick Doralp, PMP

Peter Duignan, PMP

Suhas Dutta, PMP

Gary S. Elliott, MS, MD

Morten Fangel, PhD

Eve Featherman

Flynn M. Fernandes, PMP, MSPM

David Foley, MBA

Gary W. Fortune, PMP

Scott D. Freauf, PMP

Ichiro Fujita, PMP

Donald G. Gardner, PMP

Jose A. George, B Tech, PGDM

Leo A. Giulianetti, PMP

Donna Golden

Margarida Goncalves, PhD

Neal S. Gray, PMP

Patrick D. Guest, PMP

Navneet Gupta, PMP

J. Ray Harwood, PMP

Ralph Hernandez

Bobby Tsan Fai Ho, PMP, CISM

Keith D. Hornbacher, MBA

Clinton in't Veld

Don R. James, PMP

Wei Jing

Granville H. Jones, Sr., MBA, PMP

Neil R. Caldwell

Bill Chadick, PMP

Porfirio Chen Chang, MBA, PMP

Tomio Chiba, PMP

Andy Crowe, PMP

Darren Dalcher, PhD, MAPM

Pranab Das, PMP

Connie Delisle

Barbara De Vries, PMP

James A. Doanes

Magnus Karl Drengwitz, PMP

Lloyd R. Duke, Jr., PMP

Bradford R. Eichhorn, PMP

Gregory William Fabian, PMP

Martin Christopher Fears, PMP

AnnaMaria Felici

John C. "Buck" Field, MBA, PMP

Kirby Fortenberry, PMP

John M. Foster, PMP, MBA

Denis Freeland

John S. Galliano

Stainslaw Gasik

Dan Georgopulos

Christopher A. Goetz, PMP

Neil P. Goldman, PMP

John C. Goodpasture, PMP

Robert J. Gries, PE, PMP

Jinendra Gunathilaka, PE

Aaron S. Hall, PMP

Ali Hassan, PMP

Pat Hillcoat, PMP

Gopi V. Hombal

Kenneth Alan Hudacsko, PMP

Adesh Jain, PMP, MPD

Noel C. Jensen, PMP

Bruce Johnson, PMP

Kevin B. Jones, BMath, PMP

Tom Kerr, PMP

Asadullah Khan, PMP

Mihail Kitanovski

Takahiko Kuki, PMP, PE

Avis Kunz

John S. Layman, PMP

Elizabeth Ann Long, PMP

Pier Paolo Lo Valvo, PMP

Sajith K. Madapatu, PMP

Enrique Martinez

David L. McPeters, PMP

Godfrey I. Meertens, PMP

Gordon R. Miller, PMP, CCP

Andrew H. Moore, MBA, PMP

Mhlabaniseni Moses Mitmunye

K.S. Keshava Murthy

AnathaKrishnan S. Nallepally, PMP

Vijayalakshimi Neela, MCA, PMP

Brian D. Nelson, PMP

Kazuhiko Okubo, PE, PMP

Jeffery L. Ottesen, PE

Laura Dorival Paglione

Jerry L. Partridge, PMP

Eric Patel

Manohar Powar, PMP

Ge Qun

Prem Ranganath, PMP

Ulka Rathi

Vijay Sai Reddy, PMP, CSQA

Steven Ricks, PMP

Dee Rizor

Michael C. Roach

Cheryl N. Rogers, PMP

Ed Rosenstein, PMP

Joseph A. Roushdi

Paul S. Royer, PMP

Frank Ryle, PMP

Ajmal Afzal Khan

Lucy Kim, PMP, PE

Jennifer Eileen Kraft

Polisetty V.S. Kumar, M Tech, PMP

Antonio Carlos Laranjo da Silva

Erik D. Lindquist, PMP, PE

Raul S. Lopez, PE, PMP

Karen Griffin MacNeil, PMP

Vijaya Kumar Mani, PMP

Victor J. Matheron, PMP

Ed Mechler, PMP

Richard Meertens, MBA, PMP

Liu Min

Colin Morris, PE, PMP

Charles L. Munch, PMP

Jo Musto, PMP

NB Narayanan

Beatrice Nelson, PMP

Isabella Nizza, PMP

David M. Olson, MBA (ITM)

Michael T. Ozeranic

Glen R. Palmer

George Pasieka, PMP

Sreenivasa Rao Potti, MCA, PMP

Patrick J. Quairoli

Vara Prasad Raju Kunada

Raju Rao, PMP

Tony Raymond

J. Logan C. Rice

Thad B. Ring, PMP

Susan Rizzi

Alexandre G. Rodrigues, PhD

Scott A. Rose, PMP

Samuel S. Roth, PMP

Gurdev Roy, PMP

James J. Rutushni, PMP

Anjali Sabharwal, PMP

Srinivasa R. Sajja, PMP

Markus Scheibel, PMP, Dipl-Ing

Amy Schneider, PMP

Andrea R. Scott

Tufan Sevim, PMP

Mundaje S. Shetty, PMP

Rali Shital

Larry Sieck

Richard L. Sinatra, PMP, PhD

Edward Smith

Richard Spector, PMP

Donglin Su

Karen Z. Sullivan, PMP

David E. Taylor, PMP

Sai K. Thallam, MBA, PMP

Massimo Torre, PhD, PMP

Rufis A. Turpin, CQA, CSQE

M. Raj Ullagaraj, PhD

JR Vanden Eynde, PMP

Thomas G. Van Scoyoc, PMP

Ricardo Viana Vargas, MSc, PMP

Craig Veteto, PMP, CPIM

Eduardo Newton Vieira, PMP

Cornelius (Kees) Vonk, PMP

Thomas M. Walsh, PMP

Kevin R. Wegryn, PMP, CPM

Gwen Whitman, PMP

Alan K. Williams, Sr., PMP

Stephen D. Wise

Thomas Wuttke, PMP, CPM

Angela F. Young, PMP

Eire E. Zimmermann, PMP

Nashaat A. Salman, PMP

John Schmitt, PMP

Randa Schollmeyer, PMP

Benjamin R. Sellers, PMP, CPCM

Sanjay Shah, PMP

Kazuo Shimizu, PMP

Ganga Siebertz

Melvin Silverman, PhD, PE

Raghavendra Singh

Patricia Smith

Allison St. Jean

Sambasivam S., PMP, CSQA

Karen Tate, PMP, MBA

James E. Teer, Jr.

Surendra Tipparaju, ME

Rogerio Carlos Traballi

Marion J. Tyler, PMP

Eric Uyttewaal, PMP

Gerrit van Otterdijk, BSc Mgt Science

Paula X. Varas, PMP

Mark M. Vertin, PE, PMP

Roberto Viale, PMP

Desmond Joseph Vize, PMP

J. Wendell Wagner, PMP

Patrick Weaver, PMP, FAICD

Timothy E. Welker, PMP

Tammo T. Wilkens, PE, PMP

Charles M. Williamson, MBA, PMP

Robert Wood

Uma S. Yalamanchili, PMP

Kathy Zandbergen

Final Exposure Draft Reviewers and Contributors

In addition to team members, the following individuals provided recommendations for improving the Exposure Draft of the PMBOK® Guide – Third Edition:

Fred Abrams, PMP, CPL	Yassir Afaneh
Mohammed Abdulla Al-Kuwari, Eur Ing, Ceng	Hussain Ali Al-Ansari, Eur Ing, CEng
Frank Anbari	William W. Bahnmaier, PMP
Alfred Baker	B. D. Barnes
Jefferson Bastreghi	Mohammed Safi Batley, MIM
Cynthia A. Berg, PMP	Sally Bernstein, PMP
Mamoun A. Besaiso, CE	J. David Blaine, PMP, CSQE
Nigel Blampied, PE, PMP	Dennis Bolles, PMP
Stephen Bonk	Gregory M. Bowen, CSDP
David Bradford, PMP	James (Jim) P. Branden, MBA, PMP
Gary D. Brawley, P.Eng., PMP	Edgard P. Cerqueira Neto, PhD, PMP
Bruce Chadbourne	Tomio Chiba, PMP
Aaron Coffman, PMP, CQM	Kim D. Colenso, PMP, CSQE
Edmund H. Conrow, PhD, PMP	Helen S. Cooke, PMP
Michael Corish	John E. Cormier, PMP
John Cornman, PMP, MBA	Aloysio da Silva
Mario Damiani	Arindam Das
Allan E. Dean	Alfredo del Cano, PE, PhD
Juan De La Cruz	M. Pilar De La Cruz
Ravi Kumar Dikshit, PMP	John Downing
Daniel Dudek	Judith Edwards, PhD, PMP
Robert L. Emerson, PMP	Alison Evanish
Keith Farndale, PEng, PMP	Linda Fitzgerald
Quentin W. Fleming	Scott D. Freauf, PMP
Ichiro Fujita, PMP	Paul H. Gil, MCP, PMP
Jackelen George	Mike Griffiths, PMP
David R. Haas, PMP, FLMI	Robert W. Harding, RA
Delbert K. Hardy, PMP	Rick Hiett
Bob Hillier, PMP	Guy N. Hindley, MAPM, MILT
Danny N. Hinton, PMP	Ho Lee Cheong, PhD, MIMechE
J. Brian Hobbs, PhD, PMP	Piet Holbrouck, MSc
Martin Hopkinson, BSc, APMP	Darrel G. Hubbard, PE
Grant Jefferson	Howard J. Kalinsky, PMP, MPM

Constance Katsanis

Takahiko Kuki, PMP, PE

Craig Letavec

Pier Paolo Lo Valvo, PMP

Enrique Lopez-Mingueza, PMP

Stephen S. Mattingly

Giuseppe Mauri

Santosh Kumar Mishra, PMP, CSQA

Saradhi Motamarri, M Tech, PMP

Jeffrey S. Nielsen, PMP

Peter Ostrom, PhD, PMP

Ravindranath Palahalli

Nick Palumbo, PMP

Francisco Perez-Polo

Crispin (Kik) Piney, BSc, PMP

Gurdev Randhawa

Steven F. Ritter, PMP

David W. Ross, PMP

Kyoichi Sato

Benjamin R. Sellers, PMP, CPCM

Kazuo Shimizu, PMP

Fernando Demattio de O. Simoes, PMP

Cynthia Snyder, PMP, MBA

Paul Solomon, PMP

Juergen Sturany

Luis Eduardo Torres Calzada, PMP, MBA

Gary Van Eck

J.R. Vanden Eynde, PMP

Aloysio Vianna, Jr.

Thomas M. Walsh, PMP

Patrick Weaver, PMP, FAICD

Linda Westfall, PE, CSQE

Clement C.L. Yeung, PMP

Cristine Zerpa

Roger Kent

Lawrence (Larry) P. Leach, PMP

Ben Linders

Mary K. Lofsness

Mark Marlin, PMP

Christopher J. Maughan, CEng, PMP

Yves Mboda, PMP

Colin Morris, PEng, PMP

Rita Mulcahy, PMP

Kazuhiko Okubo, PE, PMP

Ravindranath P S

Jon Palmquist

Anil Peer, PEng, PMP

Paul W. Phister, Jr., PhD, PE

Polisetty V.S. Kumar, M Tech, PMP

Raju Rao, PMP

Hans (Ron) Ronhovde, PMP

Robbi Ryan

Suzanne Lee Schmidt, PMP

Tufan Sevim, PMP

Melvin Silverman

John E. Singley, PhD, PMP

Antonio Soares

Michael Stefanovic, PEng, PMP

George Sukumar, MSChe, OE

Dalton L. Valeriano-Alves, M.E.

Judy Van Meter

Ricardo Vargas

Dave Violette, MPM, PMP

William W. Wassel, PE, PMP

Kevin R. Wegryn, PMP, CPM

Allan Wong

John Zachar, BSc, APMP

Paul Zilmer

PMI Standards Member Advisory Group (MAG)

The following individuals served as members of the PMI Standards Member Advisory Group during development of *A Guide to the Project Management Body of Knowledge (PMBOK® Guide)* – Third Edition:

Julia M. Bednar, PMP

Sergio R. Coronado

J. Brian Hobbs, PMP

Carol Holliday, PMP

Thomas Kurihara

Asbjorn Rolstadas, PhD

Bobbye Underwood, PMP

Dave Violette, MPM, PMP

Production Staff

Special mention is due to the following employees of PMI:

Steven L. Fahrenkrog, PMP, Manager, Standards

Kristin L. Wright, Standards Program Administrator

Shari M. Daniel, PMP, Project Manager—Translations

Dan Goldfischer, Editor-in-Chief

Patti Harter, Project Manager

David Parker, Manager, Publications

Natasha Pollard, Translation Verification Committee Coordinator

Richard E. Schwartz, Product Editor

Barbara Walsh, Publications Planner

APPENDIX C

CONTRIBUTORS AND REVIEWERS OF
PMBOK® GUIDE – FOURTH EDITION

PMI volunteers first attempted to codify the Project Management Body of Knowledge in the *Special Report on Ethics, Standards, and Accreditation,* published in 1983. Since that time, other volunteers have come forward to update and improve that original document and contribute to this globally recognized standard for project management, PMI's *A Guide to the Project Management Body of Knowledge (PMBOK® Guide).* This appendix lists, alphabetically within groupings, those individuals who have contributed to the development and production of the *PMBOK® Guide* – Fourth Edition. No simple list or even multiple lists can adequately portray all the contributions of those who have volunteered to develop the *PMBOK® Guide* – Fourth Edition.

The Project Management Institute is grateful to all of these individuals for their support and acknowledges their contributions to the project management profession.

C.1 *PMBOK® Guide*—Fourth Edition Project Core Team

The following individuals served as members were contributors of text or concepts and served as leaders within the Project Core Team (PCT):

Cynthia Stackpole, MBA, PMP, Project Manager

Karen Rasmussen Noll, Deputy Project Manager

Murray Grooms, BA, PMP (Communications)

Sandra Hyman, PMP, (Chapter Coordinator)

Joseph W. Kestel, PMP, MSIS (Chapter 3 & 5 Lead)

Tom Malicki (Volunteer Lead, Front & Back Lead)

Clifford W. Sprague, PMP (Volunteer Coordinator)

Geree V. Streun, CSQE, PMP (Chief Architect)

Kristin L. Vitello, Standards Project Specialist

C.2 *PMBOK® Guide* 2004 Update Project Sub-Teams

The following individuals served as contributors of text or concepts and as leaders of the Project Sub-Teams (PST):

Quentin W. Fleming (Chapters 7 & 12 Leader)

Xue Gang (Gabriel), PMP, QSLA (Chapter 1 Leader)

Marie Gunnerson (Chapter 6 Leader)

Marylinda Jones, PMP, Six Sigma Greenbelt (Chapter 8 Leader)

George Jucan, PMP (Chapter 10 Leader)

Joseph W. Kestel, PMP, MSIS (Chapters 3 & 5 Leader)

Carl L. Pritchard, PMP, EVP (Chapter 11 Leader)

Geree V. Streun, CSQE, PMP (Chapter 4 Leader)

Vijay K. Verma, PMP, MBA (Chapter 9 Leader)

Mark Wilfer, PMP (Chapter 2 Leader)

C.3 Significant Contributors

In addition to the members of the Project Core Team and the Sub-Team Leaders, the following individuals provided significant input or concepts:

Michael C. Broadway, PMP

John A. Dullnig, PMP

Merleen Cowie Hilley

Beth Ouellette, MBA, PMP

Dave Violette, MPM, PMP

Linda Westfall, CSQE, PE

C.4 *PMBOK® Guide*—Fourth Edition Operation Team Members

In addition to those listed above, the following *PMBOK® Guide*—Fourth Edition project team members assisted in project operations for *PMBOK® Guide*—Fourth Edition.

Operation Team Members:

Janet P. Burns, PMP   Betty Corbin, PMP

Judith A. Edwards, PhD, PMP   Suhail Iqbal, PE, PMP

Tony Jacob, PMP   Merna M. Johnson, PMP

Mark Krahn, PhD, PMP   Rich Maltzman, PMP

Colleen A. McGraw, PMP

Daniel Picard, PMP

Randy Tangco, PMP, CSM

Audrey R. Wojcik

Saradhi Motamarri, MTech, PMP

Carolina Gabriela Spindola, SSBB, PMP

John Wilson, PhD, PMP

C.5 *PMBOK® Guide*—Fourth Edition Project Content Contributors

In addition to those listed above, the following *PMBOK® Guide*—Fourth Edition project team members were contributors of text or concepts, or provided recommendations on drafts of the *PMBOK® Guide*—Fourth Edition.

Content Contributors:

Wayne F. Abba

Upinder Aggarwal, PMP

Graeme A. Allan, BSc(Hons), PMP

Nazir M. Bashir, PMP

Wayne R. Brantley, MS.Ed, PMP

Camper Bull, PMP

Noman Zafar Chaudry, PE, PMP

Anthony R. Corridore, PMP

Phillip Dyer, PMP

Waleed M. ElToukhy, PMP

Bruce E. Falk, PMP

Marcelo B. Ferreira

Scott D. Freauf, PMP

Kel Henderson

David T. Hulett, PhD

David S. Jacob, MS, PE

Puja Kasariya, PMP

Sasi Kumar, PMP

Vijaya Kurada, MBA, PMP

Richard G. Larson, PMP, CBAP

Adrian Lovel-Hall

Lou Marks, PMP

Muhammad Nasir

Mohit Agarwal

Neil F. Albert

Muhammad Waqar Asghar, PMP

Al Bornmann, PMP, PE

Jeannine Allison Bryan

Ka-Keung Chan, PMP, MBA

David Christensen

Claudio D'Arcangelo, PMP

Nigel O. D'Souza, PMP, ITIL

Patricia A. David-Gentsch

AnnaMaria Felici PMP, CMC

Cheryl Fitzgarrald, PMP

Vivek Goel, PMP

David A. Hillson, PhD, PMP

George Jackelen

Dhanojkumar D. Jadhav

Tom Kendrick, PMP

Karthikeyan Kumaraguru, MS, PMP

Mary-Elizabeth Larson, PMP, CBAP

Arden Lockwood, MBA, PMP

Robin Maher

John L. Murphy, PE, PMP

Kazuhiko Okubo, PMP, PE

Crispin (Kik) Piney, BSc, PMP

Roberto Henrique Nogueira Pons

Janice Preston, PMP

Satheesh Santhangopalan, PMP

John Singley, PhD, PMP

Jaimini Thakore

Paul E. Waits, Jr, PMP, CPM

Mark A. Wright, PMP

Morris A. Pondfield, MBA, MS

Steven R. Potter, PMP

V. Raja, PMP

Anna Self

Amin Tabatabayi, BEng, MBA

Ricardo Triana, PMP

Dale K. Williams, PMP, CSM

K. Kimi Hirotsu Ziemski, PMP

C.6 *PMBOK® Guide*—Fourth Edition Project Content Reviewers

In addition to those listed above, the following *PMBOK® Guide*—Fourth Edition Project Team Members performed reviews of drafts of the *PMBOK® Guide*—Fourth Edition.

Content Reviewers:

Yasser Thiab Ali Afaneh

Syed Asghar, PMP

Mamoun A. Besaiso, CE

Craig Nicholas Blackford

Charles Cain, PMP

Alejandro M. Polanco Carrasco

Tomio Chiba, PMP

William T. Craddock

Peter Ewart-Brookes, PMP

Joseph Sanju George

Paul A. Green, BSc (Hons)

George H. Hopman, PhD , PE

Raj Kumar Jhajharia, PMP

Ramakrishna Kavirayani, PMP

Milan Kumar, MCM, ITIL

Chuanqing James Lu, PMP

Brian J. Mangravite

Nael Mattar

Alberto Moreno, PMP

Carlo Muzzarelli

Charis Ogbonna

Eva D. Aimable

Rozinah Bachik, PMP, MSc (PM)

Shantanu Bhamare, PMP

Roberto Alejandro Cadena

Franco Caron, PhD

William A Cather, PhD, PMP

Manuel Cisneros, PMP, MBA

Alexandre Coelho, PMP

Ann Marie Ficarra, PMP

Jonathan Glaser, PhD, PMP

Torben Grut, PMP

Ganesh Jambunathan, PMP

Edwin J. Kapinus, PMP, PE

Konstantinos Kirytopoulos, PhD, PMP

Juanita Jane Lightfoot

Catryana C. Malcolm, PMP

Rebecca P. Masucci

Sumith Alvet Miranda, PMP

Mridul Paul, PMP, MBA

Jeffrey S. Nielsen, PMP

Tara Pangakis, PMP

Almir dos Santos Pereira, PMP

Dave Randell, PMP

Curt Schlonies, PMP

Eng. S.M. Saliha Sheriff, MBA, PMP

Bernd Spiehl

Chinta V.N. Subrahmanyam, PMP

Masanori Takahashi, PMP, MA

Gangesh Thakur, CPIM, CSCP

Ali Vahedi Diz, MSc, PMP

John A. Weber, PMP

Carl W. Pro, PMP

Nani Sadowski-Alvarez, PMP

Salvatore J. Sciascia, PMP

Manas Singh

Jolene R. Staruch, PMP

Shoji Tajima

Nilesh Adrian Pieris Tavarayan, AMBCS, MACS (Prov)

Lulu V. Tobin, PMP

Pepijn Visser

Tan EE Yuen Yvonne

C.7 *PMBOK® Guide*—Fourth Edition Project Team Members

In addition to those listed previously, the following individuals participated on the *PMBOK® Guide*—Fourth Edition Project Team.

Team Members:

Shigeru Akiba, PMP

Mohammad M. Ali

Fayez Mosaed Al-Talhi, PMP

Abel Andrew Anderson, CBM, PMP

Jagathnarayanan P. Angyan, FIE, CE

Mahadhir Aziz, PMP

Alok Bhaskar, MBA, PMP

Edward Bogak, MBA

Jean-Luc Boulanger, PMP

Kenny E. Burrow, PhD, PMP

Roberto Castro

Zhen Cheng

Hsing-Tung Chou, PhD

Darren D. Criglar, MLA, MA

Venkatesh Dakshinamurthy

Rahul P. Deshpande

Nick Doralp, PMP, ECM

Teresa Duvall, PMP, CDR

Giovanni Fanduiz, MSc, PMP

Luis Cláudio Tavares Fernandes, PMP

Ir Hj Ahmad Khairiri Abdul Ghani, Int PE, ASEAN Eng

Marcia de Almeida

Ketal Amin, BB, PMP

Andrew Lam Tug Wye, PMP, CITPM (Associate)

Usman Asif, PMP

Ricardo do Rêgo Barros, PMP

Artur Bialy, PMP

Lyn Bos, MHA, MBA

Joan Browne

Bernardo O. Bustamante, PE, PMP

Ashish Chawla, MS

David Kwok Keung Chenung

Richard J. Coffelt, PMP

Jacqueline M. Cruit, PMP

Madhavi Desai, MS, PMP

David Dominguez

Nicolas Douliez

G. Ebynayagam

Sabeeh U. Faruqui, BE Elect, PMP

Gloria Elena Folle Estrada

Dean J. Fragos

Jay D. Gassaway

Subir Ghosh, PMP

Priyesh Gopalakrishnan

Matthew W. Handi, PMP

Gary Higgs

Nilesh D. Jaltare, PMP

Nancy A. Joseph, PMP

Sanjay Kapoor

Genny Kelly

Takahiko Kuki, PMP, PEJ

Jerry D. Lainhart, PMP

David K. Larson

Michelle Z. Lim-Watson

John D. Lissaman, BEng, PMP

Carmelene Mangahis

Robert A. Marshall, PhD, PMP

Jamie Mata

David McKenna, MSc, PMP

Gregg Mohrmann

Gerald Mulenburg, DBA, PMP

Prakash Nagaraju, PMP

Mohammed Taher Netarwala, BE Mech, PMP

Priya Padmanabhan, PMP

Peter B. Paulauskas, PMP

Bruce T. Petro, PMP

Regina Rahmilov

Shrish Rangaramanujam, PMP

Krupakara Reddy, PMP, PRINCE2 Practitioner

Ana I. Rodríguez García, PMP

Laurie M. Rudnitsky, PMP

Gladstone Leslie Samuel

Ramanathan Sathianaraynan, PMP, CSQA

Dhilan N. Shah, CPA, PMP

Shervin Shariatpanahi Mojtabanejad

Anand Swaroop Garg

Mitchlyn Gentry, MISM

Sulema de Oliveira Barcelos Gobato, PMP, MSc

Joy Gumz, PMP, CPA

Mohamed Hassan, PMP, CSWP

Lecia L. Hogan, MPM

Marco Antonio Jimenez, PMP, MBA

Marijana Jurgec

Kenichi Kawamata, PMP

Hamed Keyvanfar

S Lakshminarasimhan, MBA(Fin), PMP

Tim K.Y. Lam, PMP, MBA

Charlene Lattier, PMP

Michael Linegar, PMP, MBA

Vasantha R. Manda, MS, PMP

Joachim Manz, PhD, PMP

Cristinel Damian Martalogu

Laura McDonough, PMP

Purvi Sheth Mishra

Bhagchand S. Motwani

Pradeep Murti

John T. Napier

Dmitry Ostroushko, PhD

Kent D. Paris, PMP

Sitarama Chakravarthy Peruvel, PMP

Rama P. Pokala, PMP

Aditya Rajguru, PMP

Banshidhar Rayaguru, PMP, M Tech

Caroline Robison, PMP

Jaideep Roy

Lee Ryan

Paul Sanghera, PhD, PMP

Kathakali Seth

Manar Shami, PhD, PMP

Pawan Sharma

Rachna Sharma

Jinmei Shen, PMP

Evandro L.P. Silva

Nicklaus B. Sims, PMP

Kathy J. Slater, PMP

Nguyen Hoanh Son

Rob Spurgeon

Varadarajan Sriram

Rashid M. Syed, MBA, PMP

Pham Minh Thang

Rocky Thurston, PMP

Victoria Todas-Lozada, PMP

Shi-Ja Tseng

Malay Verma, PMP, PGCBM

John White

Kazuo Yamamoto, PMP

Xuyan Zhang

John Sheers, PMP

Toshihiro Shoji, PMP

Michael D. Simants

Siddharth Singh

Juliette A. Soczka

Mauro Sotille, PMP

Delores Stimpson, PMP

Raghavan Sundararajan, PMP

Paraminder Talwar, PMP

Claire-Jodane Thermidor

Surendra Tipparaju, ME

Nagla Toma, MA

William Stephen Turner

Cornelis (Kees) Vonk

Vicki Wrona, PMP

Masakazu Yonezaki

Rob Zilay, MBA, PMP

C.8 Final Exposure Draft Reviewers and Contributors

In addition to team members, the following individuals provided recommendations for improving the Exposure Draft of the *PMBOK® Guide* – Fourth Edition:

Ahmed Taha Abd El Hameed

Biju B. Abraham, PMP

Phill C. Akinwale, PMP

Hussain Ali Al-Ansari, Eur Ing, Ceng

Wasel A. Al-Muhammad, MBA, PMP

Alonso Loaiza A., PMP

Alok N. Anadkat, PMP, BS

Chet R. Anderson, PMP

Ondiappan Arivazhagan "Ari", PMP, CSSBB

Naing Moe Aung, PMP

Mike Awuah, PMP, MBA

Jacklyn Ayoung-Chee, MBA, PMP

Ernest Baker, PMP

Klaus Abert

Ed Adelman, PMP

James E. Aksel, MS, PMP

Mohammed Abdulla Al-Kuwari, Eur Ing, PMP

Noor Hamad Alnisif, PMP

Barnabas Seth Amarteifio, PMP

P. Lingesh Ananth, PMP

Niels Erik Andersen, MSc CS

Syed S. Asghar, MSA, PMP

Shigeo Awamura

Tanin I. Ayabakan, MD, PMP

Karthegesan B, MBA, PMP

Ramanan Balakrishna, PMP

Sunil Bansal, PMP

Herminia Bastos, PMP, CMC

Fred Beckmann, PMP

Eric Berry, PMP

Dale L. Beyer, MBA, PMP

Kurmarao V. Bhavanasi, PMP

Dennis L. Bolles, PMP, LLC

Adolfo Borja, PMP, MBA

Didier Brackx, PMP, EMS Prof

Carlos Eduardo M. F. Braga, PMP

Ralf Braune, PhD, PMP

Ian A. Brown, MBA, PMP

Pat Buckna, PMP

John Buxton, PE, PMP

Teresa W. Calhoon, PMP

Luis Eduardo Torres Calzada, PMP, MPM

Brian L. Cassita

Bruce C. Chadbourne, PMP, PgMP

Krishna Datta Nallani Chakravartula, MBA, PMP

Supriyo Chatterji, MCA, PMP

Ramesh Chepur, CSQA, PMP

Chiba, Tomio, PMP

Lung-Hung Roger Chou, PMP, MCT

Brenda Connor, PMP

John E. Cormier, PMP

Larry E. Criger, PE, PMP

Michael J. Cunningham, PMP

Robert L. Cutler, PMP

Claudio Da Rold, PMP

Venkateswarlu B. Dasigi, PMP, PhD

Jim Delrie, PE, PMP

Laurie Diethelm, CAPM

Bernadine Douglas

Francine J. Duncan, MIEEE, PMP

Susan Holly Edelman, PMP

Patricia J. Bartl, PMP

Mohammed Safi Batley, MIM

Debra C. Bedford

Stephen Berté, PhD, PMP

Shantanu Bhamare, PMP

Rhonda R. Blevins, PMP

Stephen F. Bonk, PMP, PE

Lynda Bourne, DPM, PMP

Robin G. Bradshaw, PMP

Wayne R. Brantley, MS Ed, PMP

Alex S. Brown, PMP IPMA-C

Jerry L. Brown, PMP

Mitchell S. Burke, MS, MBA

Andrea Caccamese, PMP, PRINCE2 Practitioner

Sergio A. Calvo, PMP

Chris Cartwright, MPM, PMP

Roberto Celkevicius, PMP, ITIL

K. K. Chakraborty, PMP, BE

Paul E. Chaney, PMP

Tony Tze Wai Chau, PMP, MAPM

David K. Cheung, MSc, MBA

Ananaba Marcellinus Chikwendu, MBA, PMP

Darrell S. Cleavenger, PMP

Edmund H. Conrow, PhD, PMP

Mauricio E. Cornejo, PMP

Mary Colleen Cullinan, PMP

Craig Curran-Morton, MA, PMP

Barbara Y. DaCosta, MPA, PMP

Anirban Das, PMP

Allan Edward Dean, MBA, PMP

Anita Dhir, PMP

George R. Dorer, PMP MBA

John A. Dullnig, PMP

Azra Duric, PMP

Paul J. Egan

Tarek El-Misalami, PMP, PhD

Brian M. Evans, PMP

Bruce E. Falk, PMP

Kathleen M. Federici, MEd, CAPM

Michael H. Fisher, MSPM, PMP

Edgardo J. Fitzpatrick, PMP

Joel E. Fleiss, PMP

Charles T. Follin, PMP

Mark R. Friedman, CISA, PMP

Andrew H. Furber, PMP, PRINCE2

Ravindra Gajendragadkar, PMP

George F. Garas, MBA

Stanisław Gasik

Carl M. Gilbert, PMP, OPM3A/C

Theofanis Giotis, MSc, PMP

Joelle A. Godfrey, PMP

Roger K. Goodman, PMP

Derek R. Grant, BSc, PMP

Roy Greenia, MPM, PMP

Mireya Grieco, PMP

Jeff Jianfei Gu, PMP, MBA

Joy Gumz, PMP, CPA

Swati Gupta, PMP

Anne N. Gwankobe, PMP, CSSGB

Edward Hall, PMP, CQM

Sharad S. Harale, PMP, MIM

Donna M. Harrison, PMP

Sheriff Hashem, PhD, PMP

Larry J. Hawkins, DSc, PMP

Jim Hayden, PMP

Mohamed S. Hefny, MSc, PMP

Robert Hierholtz

Bob Hillier, PMP

Felicia Hong, PMP, MBA

Gheorghe Hriscu, PMP, OCP

Ramon Espinoza, PMP

Peter Ewart-Brookes, PMP

John L. Fallon, PMP

AnnaMaria Felici, PMP, CMC

Matthew J. Fiske, PE, PMP

Martin Flank, MBA, PMP

Quentin W. Fleming

Scott D. Freauf, PMP

Scott J. Friedman, PMP

W. Anders Fusia, PMP

Sharyn H. Gallagher, Ed.D., PMP

Jose Eduardo Motta Garcia, MBA, PMP

David P. Gent, CEng, PMP

Peter James Gilliland, PMP

Fernando Hurtado Giraldo

Marshall Goldman, PMP

Jean Gouix, Eng, PMP

Thomas J. Gray, PMP, PE

Stephen Grey, PhD

Liz Grinzo, PMP

Pier Luigi Guida, Ing, PMPt

Marie Gunnerson

Raj Guttha

Mustafa Hafizoglu, PMP

John Haneiko, PMP

Kurt J. Harris, PMP

Akkiraju V. Harshavardhan, PMP

Lawrence Hattenburg, PMP

Ernesto Yo Hayashi, MEng

Gary R. Heerkens, PMP, PE

Krzysztof Hejduk, PhD, PMP

Hideyuki Hikida, PMP

Mark Holdrege

Tim Hornett, PMP

Chih-Yang Hsia, PMP, MBA

Jeff M Hughes, BA (Hons), PMP

Theresa L. Hunt, CSQE, CSTE

Jean-Pierre Husereau, PMP, OPM3-CC

Zulfiqar Hussain, PE, PMP

George Jackelen

T.D. Jainendrakumar, PMP

Elden F. Jones II, PMP, MSPM

Michele J. Jones, PMP

Nils Kandelin, PhD, PMP

Kenneth P. Katz, PMP

Lance Kelson, CISSP, PMP

Rameshchandra B. Ketharaju

Tausif Khawaja

Joan Knutson, PMP

Roman S. Kosarzycki, PMP

Edie E. Kubomoto, PMP, CQM

Thomas M. Kurihara

Philippe Landucci, PMP

Richard Larson, PMP, CBAP

Jim Lee Sr., PMP

Donald Likens

Robin Lindenmeier, PMP

Mary K. Lofsness

Alberto Lopez, PMP

Margaret L. Love, PMP

Yves M. Lucas, PMP

Raymond Maczka

Konstantinos Maliakas, PMP

Rick Mandarino, PMP, MBA

Ammar W. Mango, PgMP, PMP

Mark Marlin, PMP, PE

Mohit Raj Mathur, PMP

Yan Bello Méndez, PMP

Su Mei-Shih, PMP

Predrag Fred Mikanovic, MBA, PMP

David T. Hulett, PhD

Marta Hurst, CLSSBB

Huma Hydari, MBA, PMP

Midori Ito

Ashok Jain, PAHM, PMP

Tony Johnson, PMP, PgMP

Marylinda Jones, PMP, Six Sigma Greenbelt

Lenin Babu Kamma, PMP

Carl Karshagen, PMP

Ramakrishna Kavirayani, PMP

Roger Kent, PMP

Thomas C. Keuten, PMP, OPM3-CC

Jim Kinard, PMP

Kimberly A. Kook, PMP, ITIL Foundations

Chetana S. Koulagi, PMP, CSQA

Takahiko Kuki, PMP, JPE

Lisa M. LaCourse, PMP

David J. Lanners, MBA, PMP

Marta M. Laszcz, PMP

Patty Leung

Diana Lilla, MA, PMP

Kristin Linoski, PMP

Anand Lokhande, PMP

Enrique López-Mingueza, PMP

Angela Cheng-Jui Lu, PhD, PMP

Christina Luik

Shankar Mahadevan, PMP, CWA

Rich Maltzman, PMP

Srinivas Mandgi, PMP, SAP HR

Joachim Manz, PhD, PMP

John A. Marzullo, PMP

Rahma Mbarki Eng, MSc, MBA

Louis J. Mercken, PMI Fellow, PMP

Kenneth Merten

Berne C. Miller, PMP, CPL

Walter Warren Miller III, PhD, PMP

Gary Monti, PMP

John Morck

Kaoru Mori, PMP

Stephen E. Mueller, PMP, EVP

Rita Mulcahy, PMP

Takamichi Nagano

Faig Nasibov, PMP

Edgard Pedreira de Cerqueira Neto, PhD, PMP

Thuthuy C. Nguyen, PMP

Jeffrey S. Nielsen, PMP

Michael C. Nollet, MBA, PMP

Jeff Nuding, PMP

Edward A. O'Connor, PMP

James Ostad, PMP

Nariman Panahian, PhD, PMP

Leah Paras, PMP

Hyung Ki Park, PMP

Frank R. Parth, MBA, PMP

George Pasieka, aCPP, PMP

Seenivasan Pavanasam, B Tech, PMP

Robert E. Perrine, PMP

George Pitagorsky, PMP

Steven S. Popovich

Javier Pumar, PMP

S. Ramani, PgMP, PMP

Claudia Elisa Ramírez, PMP

Rafael Fernando Ronces Rosas, PMP

Prakash Roshan, PMP

Osamu Sakamoto, PMP

Otavio Ritter Santos, PMP

Vikas Sarin, ME(SS),MCA

Curt Schlonies, PMP

John Schuyler, PE, PMP

Mark B. Shadowens, PMP

Mark A. Monteleone, PMP, CBAP

Carlos Morais, PMP

Paola Morgese, PE, PMP

Rogan Morrison, PMP

Hazim Muhssin, PMP

Philips Tharakan Mulackal, PMP, CCE

Kalyanraman Narayanswamy, PMP

John T. Nelson, BSc

Michael Newell, PMP

Praveen K. Nidumolu, PMP

James S. Niziurski, PMP

Peter Ntiforo, PMP, BSc (Hons)

Michael O'Brochta, MPM, PMP

Kazuhiko Okubo, PE, PMP

Beth Ouellette, MBA, PMP

Mohan Pandey, MPharm, PGDM(IIMA)

Balaji Parasuraman

William J. Parkes, PMP

Jerry L. Partridge, PMP

Marcello Patrese, PMP, MPM

Nancy Perosio, PMP

Crispin ("Kik") Piney, BSc, PMP

Charles M. Poplos, EdD, PMP

Nathan Pryce, EMTM, PMP

Jan F.M. Raes, PhD, PMP

Ananthakrishnan Ramaswami, PMP

Gurdev S. Randhawa, PMP

Kenneth H. Rose, PMP

Neal L. Rowland, PMP

Brian Salk, MA Ed, PMP

Rick B. Santos, MBA, PMP

Kyoichi Sato, PMP

Eugene Schreiner

Benjamin R. Sellers, PMP, CPCM

Paul E. Shaltry, PMP

Archana Sharma, MS, PMP	Nitin Shende
Kazuo Shimizu, PMP	Toshihiro Shoji, PMP
Hilary Shreter, MBA, PMP	João Carlos A. Silva Neto, Msc, PMP
Michael Simmering, PE, OPM3-CC	Marzena Zych- Skrzypkowska
Martin J. Smit, PMP	Carolyn E. Smith, PMP
Bruce F. Snow	Jorge Garcia Solano, PMP
John P. Soltesz, PE, PMP	Brijesh Sonawane, PMP
Patricia Spadea, PMP	Clifford W. Sprague, PMP
Pranay Srivastava, PMP, CISA	Joyce Statz, PhD, PMP
Doug Stephon	Samuel N. Stevens III, PhD
Kenneth D Strang, PhD, PMP	Michael E. (Mike) Strom, PMP
Juergen Sturany, PMP	Brian T. Sullivan, PMP
Yasuji Suzuki, PMP	Michal Szymaczek, PMP
Shoji Tajima, PMP	John Terdik, PMP, DCB
William M. Thom, PMP	Darin Thomas, PMP
William J. Thompson, PE, PMP	Linus G. Tibayan, FLMI, PMP
Mark Tolbert	Carolyn A. Toomer, PMP
Terry D. Tosh, PMP	Lee Towe, PMP, MBA
Biagio Tramontana, Ing, PMP	R. Trant, BA, C Mar Eng
Daniel J. Troxell, MBA, PMP	Vidyasagar Uddagiri, PMP
Nnanna Charles Ukaegbu, PE, PMP	Krishnakant T. Upadhyaya, PMP
Eric Uyttewaal, MS Business, PMP	Jorge Valdés Garciatorres, PMP, ITIL
Dennis K. Van Gemert, MS, PMP	Paula Ximena Varas, PMP
Ricardo Viana Vargas, MSc, PMP	Jouko Vaskimo, PMP
Thierry Verlynde, PMP	Aloysio Vianna Jr.
Mike Wakshull, PMP, MSc	Ronald P. C. Waller, PMI Fellow, PMP
Thomas M. Walsh, PMP	Steve J. Walter, PhD, CSEP, PMP
Xiaojin Wang, PhD, PMP	Lou Ware, PMP
William W. Wassel, PE, PMP	Ian J. Watson, PMP
Michael D. Watson, PMP	Patrick Weaver, PMP, FAICD
Kevin R. Wegryn, PMP, CPM	Mark Wilfer, PMP
Donald Wilkinson, PMP	Terry Williams, PhD, PMP
Rebecca A. Winston, JD	Michael Witzorky, PMP
Rick Woods, SSBB, PMP	Vicki Wrona, PMP
Shahrzad Yazdani, PMP, LSS GB	Clement C.L. Yeung, PMP

Azam M. Zaqzouq, MCT, PMP

Omran M. Zbeida

Paul W. Zilmer, PMP

William A. Zimmer, PMP

Heinz Zimmermann, MSc, PMP

C.9 PMI Standards Member Advisory Group (MAG)

The following individuals served as members of the PMI Standards Member Advisory Group (MAG) during development of *A Guide to the Project Management Body of Knowledge (PMBOK® Guide)* – Fourth Edition:

Julia M. Bednar, PMP

Chris Cartwright, MPM, PMP

Douglas Clark

Terry Cooke-Davies, PhD, FCMI

Carol Holliday, MA, PMP

Deborah O'Bray, CIM (Hons)

Asbjørn Rolstadås, PhD, Ing

David W. Ross, PMP, PgMP

Paul E. Shaltry, PMP

David Violette, MPM, PMP

John Zlockie, MBA, PMP

C.10 Staff Contributors

Special mention is due to the following employees of PMI:

Christie Biehl, EdD, PMP, Former Project Manager

Steven L. Fahrenkrog, PMP, VP Regional Development

Amanda Freitick, Standards Program Administrator

Donn Greenberg, Manager, Publications

Ruth Anne Guerrero, MBA, PMP, Former Standards Manager

Roberta Storer, Product Editor

Barbara Walsh, CAPM, Publications Planner

Nan Wolfslayer, AStd, Standards Compliance Specialist

Nancy Wilkinson, MBA, PMP, OPM3® Project Specialist

APPENDIX D

APPLICATION AREA EXTENSIONS

D.1 Need for Application Area Extensions

Application area extensions are necessary when there are generally accepted knowledge and practices for a category of projects in one application area that are not generally accepted across the full range of project types in most application areas. Application area extensions reflect:

- Unique or unusual aspects of the project environment of which the project management team must be aware, in order to manage the project efficiently and effectively, and

- Common knowledge and practices that, if followed, will improve the efficiency and effectiveness of the project (e.g., standard work breakdown structures).

Application area-specific knowledge and practices can arise as a result of many factors, including, but not limited to, differences in cultural norms, technical terminology, societal impact, or project life cycles. For example:

- In construction, where virtually all work is accomplished under contract, there are common knowledge and practices related to procurement that do not apply to all categories of projects;

- In bioscience, there are common knowledge and practices driven by the regulatory environment that do not apply to all categories of projects;

- In government contracting, there are common knowledge and practices driven by government acquisition regulations that do not apply to all categories of projects; and

- In consulting, there are common knowledge and practices created by the project manager's sales and marketing responsibilities that do not apply to all categories of projects.

Application area extensions are:

- Additions to the core material of *PMBOK® Guide* Chapters 1 through 12—not substitutes for it;

- Organized in a fashion similar to the *PMBOK® Guide*—that is, by identifying and describing the project management processes unique to that application area; and

- Unique additions to the core material. Such content may:

    o Identify new or modified processes,

    o Subdivide existing processes,

    o Describe different sequences or interactions of processes,

    o Increase elements or modifying the common process definitions, and

    o Define special inputs, tools and techniques, and/or outputs for the existing processes.

Application area extensions are not:

- "How-to" documents or "practice guidelines"—such documents may be issued as PMI standards, but they are not what are intended as extensions; or

- A lower level of detail than is addressed in the *PMBOK® Guide*—such details may be addressed in handbooks or guidebooks that may be issued as PMI standards, but they are not what is intended as extensions.

D.2 Criteria for Development of Application Area Extensions

Extensions will be developed under the following criteria:

- There is a substantial body of knowledge that is both project-oriented and unique or nearly unique to that application area;

- There is an identifiable PMI component (e.g., a PMI Specific Interest Group, College, or Chapter); or an identifiable external organization is willing and able to commit the necessary resources to subscribe to and support the PMI standards program with the development and maintenance of a specific PMI standard; or, the extension may be developed by PMI itself; and

- The proposed extension is able to pass the same level of rigorous PMI project management standard-setting process as any other PMI standard.

D.3 Publishing and Format of Application Area Extensions

Application area extensions are developed and/or published by PMI, or they are developed and/or published by either a PMI component or an external organization under a formal agreement with PMI.

- Extensions match the *PMBOK® Guide* in style and content. They use the same paragraph and subparagraph numbers for the material that has been extended.

- Sections and paragraphs of the *PMBOK® Guide* that are not extended are not repeated in extensions.

- Extensions contain a rationale/justification about the need for an extension and its material.

- Extensions are delimited in terms of what they are not intended to do.

D.4 Process for Development and Maintenance of Application Area Extensions

When approved in accordance with the PMI standards-setting process, application area extensions become PMI standards. They will be developed and maintained in accordance with the process described below.

- An extension must be sponsored by PMI, a formally chartered PMI component (e.g., a Specific Interest Group, College, or Chapter), or another organization external to PMI, which has been approved by the PMI Standards Program Member Advisory Group and the PMI Standards Manager. Co-sponsorship with PMI is the preferred arrangement. All approvals will be by formal written agreement between PMI and the sponsoring entity; such agreement will include, among other things, the parties' agreement as to intellectual property ownership rights and publications rights to the extension.

- A project to develop, publish, and/or maintain an extension must be approved by the PMI standards program. Permission to initiate, develop, and maintain an extension must be received from PMI and will be the subject of an agreement between or among the organizations. If there is no other sponsoring organization, the PMI standards program may elect to proceed alone.

- The sponsoring group will notify and solicit advice and support from the PMI Standards Member Advisory Group (MAG) and the PMI Standards Manager throughout the development and maintenance process. They will concur with the appropriateness of the sponsoring organization for the proposed extension and will review the extension during its development to identify any conflicts or overlaps with other similar projects that may be under way.

- The sponsoring group will prepare a proposal to develop the extension. The proposal will include a justification for the project with a matrix of application-area-specific processes and the affected sections of this document (i.e., the *PMBOK® Guide*). It will also contain the commitment of sufficient qualified drafters and reviewers; identification of funding requirements, including reproduction, postage, telephone costs, desktop publishing, etc.; commitment to the PMI procedures for PMI standards extension development and maintenance; and a plan and schedule for extension development and maintenance.

- Following acceptance of the proposal, the project team will prepare a project charter for approval by the sponsoring group and the PMI standards program team. The charter will include sources of funding and any funding proposed to be provided by PMI. It will include a requirement for periodic review of the extension with reports to the PMI standards program team and will specify when, and under what conditions, the extension will be removed from active status as a PMI standard.

- The proposal will be submitted to the PMI Standards Manager in accordance with the PMI standards-setting process. The PMI Standards Manager will determine if the proposal can be expected to result in a document that will meet the requirements for a PMI standard and whether adequate resources and sources of support have been identified. To help with this determination, the PMI Standards Manager will seek review and comment by the PMI Standards Member Advisory Group (MAG) and, if appropriate, a panel of knowledgeable persons not involved with the extension.

- The PMI Standards Manager, with the support of the PMI Standards Member Advisory Group (MAG), will monitor and support the development of the approved project.

- The sponsoring organization will develop the extension according to the approved project charter, including coordinating with the PMI standards program team for support, review, and comment.

- When the extension has been completed to the satisfaction of the sponsoring organization, it will be submitted to the PMI Standards Manager, who will manage the final approval and publication processes in accordance with the PMI standards-setting process. This final submittal will include a listing of and commitment by the sponsoring organization to the PMI extension maintenance processes and efforts.

- Following approval of the extension as a PMI standard, the sponsoring organization will implement the extension maintenance process in accordance with the approved plan.

APPENDIX E

ADDITIONAL SOURCES OF INFORMATION ON PROJECT MANAGEMENT

Project management is a growing, dynamic field; books and articles on the subject are published regularly. The entities listed below provide a variety of products and services that may be of use to those interested in project management.

E.1 Professional and Technical Organizations

This document was developed and published by the Project Management Institute (PMI). PMI can be contacted at:

Project Management Institute
14 Campus Boulevard
Newtown Square, PA 19073-3299 USA
Phone: +1-610-356-4600
Fax: +1-610-356-4647
E-mail: pmihq@pmi.org
Internet: http://www.pmi.org

EMEA Service Center
300 Avenue Tervueren
B-1150 Brussels, Belgium
Tel: +32-2-743-15-73
Fax: +32-2-743-15-50
Email: customercare.emea@pmi.org

Asia Pacific Service Center
73 Bukit Timah Road
#04-01 Rex House
Singapore 229832
Tel: +65-6496-5501
Fax: -65-6336-2263
E-mail: customercare.asiapac@pmi.og
R.E.P. Related E-mail: repsupport-pac@pmi

©2008 Project Management Institute. *A Guide to the Project Management Body of Knowledge (PMBOK® Guide) — Fourth Edition*

PMI India

PMI Organization Centre Private Limited

#1031 Regus

Level Ground & 1, Trade Centre

Bandra Kurla Complex, Bandra (E)

Mumbai, India-400 051

Tel: +91-22-4070-0325

Fax: +91-22-4070-0800

E-mail: pmi.india@pmi.org

PMI (Beijing) Project Management Technology Co. Ltd.

Room 05A

16th Floor

Ideal International Plaza

No. 58

Northwest Ring Road

Haidian District

Beijing 100080

P.R. China

Tel: +86-10-8260-7906

Fax: +86-10-8260-7909

E-mail: yongtao.chen@pmi.org

India Regional Service Centre

New Delhi, IndiaTel: +91-124-4517140

E-mail: customercare.india@pmi.org

There are numerous organizations that may be able to provide additional information about project management. For example:

Academy of Management

American Management Association International

American Society for Quality

Construction Industry Institute

Construction Management Association of America (CMAA)

Institute of Electrical and Electronics Engineers (IEEE)

Institute of Industrial Engineers (IIE)

International Council on Systems Engineering (INCOSE)

National Association for Purchasing Management

National Contract Management Association

Society for Human Resource Management

American Society of Civil Engineers

Current contact information for these and other professional and technical organizations worldwide can generally be found on the Internet.

E.2 Commercial Publishers

PMI is the premier publisher of books on project management. Many commercial publishers produce books on project management and related fields. Commercial publishers that regularly produce such materials include:

Addison-Wesley

AMACOM

Gower Press

John Wiley & Sons

Marcel Dekker

McGraw-Hill

Prentice-Hall

Probus

Van Nostrand Reinhold

Most project management books from these publishers are available from PMI. Many of the books available from these sources include extensive bibliographies or lists of suggested readings.

E.3 Product and Service Vendors

Companies that provide software, training, consulting, and other products and services to the project management profession often provide monographs or reprints.

The PMI Registered Education Provider (R.E.P.) program facilitates the ongoing professional development of PMI members, Project Management Professional (PMP®) certificants, and other project management stakeholders by linking stakeholders and training coordinators with qualified educational providers and products. A listing of R.E.P.s and their associated educational offerings is found at http://www.pmi.org/education/rep.

E.4 Educational Institutions

Many universities, colleges, and junior colleges offer continuing education programs in project management and related disciplines. Many of these institutions also offer graduate or undergraduate degree programs.

APPENDIX F

SUMMARY OF PROJECT MANAGEMENT KNOWLEDGE AREAS

F.1 Project Integration Management

Project Integration Management includes the processes and activities needed to identify, define, combine, unify, and coordinate the various processes and project management activities within the Project Management Process Groups. In the project management context, integration includes characteristics of unification, consolidation, articulation, and integrative actions that are crucial to project completion, successfully managing stakeholder expectations, and meeting requirements.

The Project Integration Management processes include:

- **Develop Project Charter**—The process of developing a document that formally authorizes a project or a phase and documenting initial requirements that satisfy the stakeholder's needs and expectations.

- **Develop Project Management Plan**—The process of documenting the actions necessary to define, prepare, integrate, and coordinate all subsidiary plans.

- **Direct and Manage Project Execution**—The process of performing the work defined in the project management plan to achieve the project's objectives.

- **Monitor and Control Project Work**—The process of tracking, reviewing, and regulating the progress to meet the performance objectives defined in the project management plan.

- **Perform Integrated Change Control**—The process of reviewing all change requests, approving changes, and managing changes to the deliverables, organizational process assets, project documents, and project management plan.

- **Close Project or Phase**—The process of finalizing all activities across all of the Project Management Process Groups to formally complete the project or phase.

F.2 Project Scope Management

Project Scope Management includes the processes required to ensure that the project includes all the work required, and only the work required, to complete the project successfully. Managing the project scope is primarily concerned with defining and controlling what is and is not included in the project. Project Scope Management processes include:

- **Collect Requirements**—The process of defining and documenting stakeholders' needs to meet the project objectives.

- **Define Scope**—The process of developing a detailed description of the project and product.

- **Create WBS**—The process of subdividing project deliverables and project work into smaller, more manageable components.

- **Verify Scope**—The process of formalizing acceptance of the completed project deliverables.

- **Control Scope**—The process of monitoring the status of the project and product scope and managing changes to the scope baseline.

F.3 Project Time Management

Project Time Management includes the processes required to accomplish timely completion of the project. Project Time Management processes include:

- **Define Activities**—The process of identifying the specific actions to be performed to produce the project deliverables.

- **Sequence Activities**—The process of identifying and documenting relationships among the project activities.

- **Estimate Activity Resources**—The process of estimating the type and quantities of material, people, equipment, or supplies required to perform each activity.

- **Estimate Activity Durations**—The process of approximating the number of work periods needed to complete individual activities with estimated resources.

- **Develop Schedule**—The process of analyzing activity sequences, durations, resource requirements, and schedule constraints to create the project schedule.

- **Control Schedule**—The process of monitoring the status of the project to update project progress and managing changes to the schedule baseline.

F.4 Project Cost Management

Project Cost Management includes the processes involved in estimating, budgeting, and controlling costs so that the project can be completed within the approved budget. Project Cost Management processes include the following:

- **Estimate Costs**—The process of developing an approximation of the monetary resources needed to complete project activities.

- **Determine Budget**—The process of aggregating the estimated costs of individual activities or work packages to establish an authorized cost baseline.

- **Control Costs**—The process of monitoring the status of the project to update the project budget and managing changes to the cost baseline.

F.5 Project Quality Management

Project Quality Management includes the processes and activities of the performing organization that determine quality policies, objectives, and responsibilities so that the project will satisfy the needs for which it was undertaken. It implements the quality management system through policy and procedures with continuous process improvement activities conducted throughout, as appropriate. Project Quality Management processes include:

- **Plan Quality**—The process of identifying quality requirements and/or standards for the project and product, and documenting how the project will demonstrate compliance.

- **Perform Quality Assurance**—The process of auditing the quality requirements and the results from quality control measurements to ensure appropriate quality standards and operational definitions are used.

- **Perform Quality Control**—The process of monitoring and recording results of executing the quality activities to assess performance and recommend necessary changes.

F.6 Project Human Resource Management

Project Human Resource Management includes the processes that organize, manage, and lead the project team. The project team is comprised of the people with assigned roles and responsibilities for completing the project. The Project Human Resource Management processes include:

- **Develop Human Resource Plan**—The process of identifying and documenting project roles, responsibilities, required skills, reporting relationships, and creating the staffing management plan.

- **Acquire Project Team**—The process of confirming human resource availability and obtaining the team necessary to complete project assignments.

- **Develop Project Team**—The process of improving the competencies, team interaction, and the overall team environment to enhance project performance.

- **Manage Project Team**—The process of tracking team member performance, providing feedback, resolving issues, and managing changes to optimize project performance.

F.7 Project Communications Management

Project Communications Management includes the processes required to ensure timely and appropriate generation, collection, distribution, storage, retrieval, and ultimate disposition of project information. The Project Communications Management processes include:

- **Identify Stakeholders**—The process of identifying all people or organizations impacted by the project, and documenting relevant information regarding their interests, involvement and impact on project success.

- **Plan Communications**—The process of determining the project stakeholder information needs and defining a communication approach.

- **Distribute Information**—The process of making relevant information available to project stakeholders as planned.

- **Manage Stakeholder Expectations**—The process of communicating and working with stakeholders to meet their needs and addressing issues as they occur.

- **Report Performance**—The process of collecting and distributing performance information, including status reports, progress measurements, and forecasts.

F.8 Project Risk Management

Project Risk Management includes the processes of conducting risk management planning, identification, analysis, response planning, and monitoring and control on a project. The objectives of Project Risk Management are to increase the probability and impact of positive events, and decrease the probability and impact of negative events in the project. The Project Risk Management processes include:

- **Plan Risk Management**—The process of defining how to conduct risk management activities for a project.

- **Identify Risks**—The process of determining which risks may affect the project and documenting their characteristics.

- **Perform Qualitative Analysis**—The process of prioritizing risks for further analysis or action by assessing and combining their probability of occurrence and impact.

- **Perform Quantitative Analysis**—The process of numerically analyzing the effect of identified risks on overall project objectives.

- **Plan Risk Responses**—The process of developing options and actions to enhance opportunities and to reduce threats to project objectives.

- **Monitor and Control Risks**—The process of implementing risk response plans, tracking identified risks, monitoring residual risks, identifying new risks, and evaluating the risk process throughout the project.

F.9 Project Procurement Management

Project Procurement Management includes the processes necessary to purchase or acquire products, services, or results needed from outside the project team to perform the work. Project Procurement Management includes the contract management and change control processes required to develop and administer contracts or purchase orders issued by authorized project team members.

The Project Procurement Management processes include:

- **Plan Procurements**—The process of documenting project purchasing decisions, specifying the approach, and identifying potential sellers.

- **Conduct Procurements**—The process of obtaining seller responses, selecting a seller, and awarding a contract.

- **Administer Procurements**—The process of managing procurement relationships, monitoring contract performance, and making changes and corrections as needed.

- **Close Procurements**—The process of completing each project procurement.

©2008 Project Management Institute, *A Guide to the Project Management Body of Knowledge (PMBOK® Guide)* — Fourth Edition

APPENDIX G

INTERPERSONAL SKILLS

Project managers accomplish work through the project team and other stakeholders. Effective project managers acquire a balance of technical, interpersonal, and conceptual skills that help them analyze situations and interact appropriately. This appendix describes important interpersonal skills, such as:

- Leadership
- Team building
- Motivation
- Communication
- Influencing
- Decision making
- Political and cultural awareness
- Negotiation

While there are additional interpersonal skills that project managers use, the appropriate use of these skills assists the project manager in effectively managing the project.

G.1 Leadership

Leadership involves focusing the efforts of a group of people toward a common goal and enabling them to work as a team. In general terms, leadership is the ability to get things done through others. Respect and trust, rather than fear and submission, are the key elements of effective leadership. Although important throughout all project phases, effective leadership is critical during the beginning phases of a project when the emphasis is on communicating the vision and motivating and inspiring project participants to achieve high performance.

Throughout the project, the project team leaders are responsible for establishing and maintaining the vision, strategy, and communications; fostering trust and team building; influencing, mentoring, and monitoring; and evaluating the performance of the team and the project.

G.2 Team Building

Team building is the process of helping a group of individuals, bound by a common sense of purpose, to work interdependently with each other, the leader, external stakeholders, and the organization. The result of good leadership and good team building is teamwork.

Team building activities consist of tasks (establish goals, define, and negotiate roles and procedures) and processes (interpersonal behavior with emphasis on communication, conflict management, motivation, and leadership). Developing a team environment involves handling project team problems and discussing these as team issues without placing blame on individuals. Team building can be further enhanced by obtaining top management support, encouraging team member commitment, introducing appropriate rewards, recognition and ethics, creating a team identity, managing conflicts effectively, promoting trust and open communication among team members, and providing leadership.

While team building is essential during the front end of a project, it is an ongoing process. Changes in a project environment are inevitable. To manage these changes effectively, a continued or renewed teambuilding effort is required. Outcomes of team building include mutual trust, high quality of information exchange, better decision making, and effective project control.

G.3 Motivation

Project teams are comprised of team members with diverse backgrounds, expectations, and individual objectives. The overall success of the project depends upon the project team's commitment, which is directly related to their level of motivation.

Motivating in a project environment involves creating an environment to meet project objectives while offering maximum self-satisfaction related to what people value most. These values may include job satisfaction, challenging work, a sense of accomplishment, achievement and growth, sufficient financial compensation, and other rewards and recognition the individual considers necessary and important.

G.4 Communication

Communication has been identified as one of the single biggest reasons for project success or failure. Effective communication within the project team and between the project manager, team members, and all external stakeholders is essential. Openness in communication is a gateway to teamwork and high performance. It improves relationships among project team members and creates mutual trust.

To communicate effectively, the project manager should be aware of the communication styles of other parties, cultural issues, relationships, personalities, and overall context of the situation. Awareness of these factors leads to mutual understanding and thus to effective communication. Project managers should identify various communication channels, understand what information they need to provide, what information they need to receive, and which interpersonal skills will help them communicate effectively with various project stakeholders. Carrying out team-building activities to determine team member communications styles (e.g. directive, collaborative, logical, explorer, etc), allows managers to plan their communications with appropriate sensitivity to relationships and cultural differences.

Listening is an important part of communication. Listening techniques, both active and effective give the user insight to problem areas, negotiation and conflict management strategies, decision making, and problem resolution.

G.5 Influencing

Influencing is a strategy of sharing power and relying on interpersonal skills to get others to cooperate towards common goals. Using the following guidelines can influence team members:

- Lead by example, and follow through with commitments
- Clarify how a decision will be made
- Use a flexible interpersonal style, adjust the style to the audience
- Apply your power skillfully and cautiously. Think of long-term collaboration.

G.6 Decision Making

There are four basic decision styles normally used by project managers: command, consultation, consensus, and coin flip (random). There are four major factors that affect the decision style: time constraints, trust, quality, and acceptance. Project managers may make decisions individually, or they may involve the project team in the decision-making process.

Project managers and project teams sometimes use a decision-making model or process such as the six-phase model shown below.

1. **Problem Definition**—Fully explore, clarify, and define the problem.

2. **Problem Solution Generation**—Prolong the new idea generating process by brainstorming multiple solutions and discouraging premature decisions.

3. **Ideas to Action**—Define evaluation criteria, rate pros and cons of alternatives, select best solution.

4. **Solution Action Planning**—Involve key participants to gain acceptance and commitment to making the solution work.

5. **Solution Evaluation Planning**—Post-implementation analysis, evaluation, and lessons learned.

6. **Evaluation of the Outcome and Process**—Evaluate how well the problem was solved or project goals were achieved (extension of previous phase).

G.7 Political and Cultural Awareness

Organizational politics are inevitable in project environments due to the diversity in norms, backgrounds and expectations of the people involved with a project. The skillful use of politics and power helps the project manager to be successful. Conversely, ignoring or avoiding project politics and inappropriate use of power can lead to difficulty in managing projects.

Today project managers operate in a global environment, and many projects exist in an environment of cultural diversity. By understanding and capitalizing on cultural differences, the project management team is more likely to create an environment of mutual trust and a win/win atmosphere. Cultural differences can be both individual and corporate in nature and may involve both internal and external stakeholders. An effective way to manage this cultural diversity is through getting to know the various team members and the use of good communication planning as part of the overall project plan.

Culture at a behavioral level includes those behaviors and expectations that occur independently of geography, ethnic heritage, or common and disparate languages. Culture can impact the speed of working, the decision-making process, and the impulse to act without appropriate planning. This may lead to conflict and stress in some organizations, thereby affecting the performance of project managers and project teams.

G.8 Negotiation

Negotiation is a strategy of conferring with parties of shared or opposed interests with a view to compromise or reach an agreement. Negotiation is an integral part of project management and done well, increases the probability of project success.

The following skills and behaviors are useful in negotiating successfully:

- Analyze the situation.

- Differentiate between wants and needs—both theirs and yours.

- Focus on interests and issues rather than on positions.

- Ask high and offer low, but be realistic.

- When you make a concession, act as if you are yielding something of value, don't just give in.

- Always make sure both parties feel as if they have won. This is win-win negotiating. Never let the other party leave feeling as if he or she has had advantage taken of them.

- Do a good job in listening and articulating.

G.9 References

Covey, S. R. *Seven Habits of Highly Effective People*, A Fireside Book. New York, NY: Simon and Schuster, 1990.

Dinsmore, P.C. *Human Factors in Project Management* (Revised Edition). New York, NY: American Management Association, 1990.

Levin, G. and Flannes. S. *Essential People Skills for Project Managers*. Vienna, VA: Management Concepts Inc., 2005.

Verma, V. K. *Organizing Projects for Success*. Newtown Square, PA: PMI, 1995.

Verma, V. K. *Human Resource Skills for the Project Manager*. Newtown Square, PA: PMI, 1995.

Verma, V. K. *Managing the Project Team*. Newtown Square, PA: PMI, 1997.

GLOSSARY

1. Inclusions and Exclusions

This glossary includes terms that are:

- Unique or nearly unique to project management (e.g., project scope statement, work package, work breakdown structure, critical path method).

- Not unique to project management, but used differently or with a narrower meaning in project management than in general everyday usage (e.g., early start date, schedule activity).

This glossary generally does not include:

- Application area-specific terms (e.g., project prospectus as a legal document—unique to real estate development).

- Terms used in project management which do not differ in any material way from everyday use (e.g., calendar day, delay).

- Compound terms whose meaning is clear from the combined meanings of the component parts.

- Variants when the meaning of the variant is clear from the base term (e.g., exception report is included, exception reporting is not).

As a result of the above inclusions and exclusions, this glossary includes:

- A preponderance of terms related to Project Scope Management, Project Time Management, and Project Risk Management, since many of the terms used in these Knowledge Areas are unique or nearly unique to project management.

- Many terms from Project Quality Management, since these terms are used more narrowly than in their everyday usage.

- Relatively few terms related to Project Human Resource Management and Project Communications Management, since most of the terms used in these Knowledge Areas do not differ significantly from everyday usage

- Relatively few terms related to Project Cost Management, Project Integration Management, and Project Procurement Management, since many of the terms used in these Knowledge Areas have narrow meanings that are unique to a particular application area.

2.   Common Acronyms

AC	actual cost
ACWP	actual cost of work performed
BAC	budget at completion
BCWP	budgeted cost of work performed
BCWS	budgeted cost of work scheduled
CCB	change control board
COQ	cost of quality
CPAF	cost plus award fee
CPF	cost plus fee
CPFF	cost plus fixed fee
CPI	cost performance index
CPIF	cost plus incentive fee
CPM	critical path methodology
CV	cost variance
EAC	estimate at completion
EF	early finish date
EMV	expected monetary value
ES	early start date
ETC	estimate to complete
EV	earned value
EVM	earned value management
FF	finish-to-finish
FFP	firm fixed price
FMEA	failure mode and effect analysis
FP-EPA	fixed price with economic price adjustment
FPIF	fixed price incentive fee

FS	finish to start
IFB	invitation for bid
LF	late finish date
LOE	level of effort
LS	late start date
OBS	organizational breakdown structure
PDM	precedence diagramming method
PMBOK	Project Management Body of Knowledge
PMIS	project management information system
PMP®	Project Management Professional
PV	planned value
QA	quality assurance
QC	quality control
RACI	responsible, accountable, consult, and inform
RAM	responsibility assignment matrix
RBS	risk breakdown structure
RFI	request for information
RFP	request for proposal
RFQ	request for quotation
SF	start-to-finish
SOW	statement of work
SPI	schedule performance index
SS	start-to-start
SV	schedule variance
SWOT	strengths, weaknesses, opportunities, and threats
T&M	time and material
TQM	Total Quality Management
WBS	work breakdown structure

3. Definitions

Many of the words defined here have broader, and in some cases different, dictionary definitions.

The definitions use the following conventions:

- In some cases, a single glossary term consists of multiple words (e.g., risk response planning).
- When synonyms are included, no definition is given and the reader is directed to the preferred term (i.e., see preferred term).
- Related terms that are not synonyms are cross-referenced at the end of the definition (i.e., see also related term).

Acceptance Criteria. Those criteria, including performance requirements and essential conditions, which must be met before project deliverables are accepted.

Acquire Project Team [Process]. The process of confirming human resource availability and obtaining the team necessary to complete project assignments.

Activity. A component of work performed during the course of a project.

Activity Attributes [Output/Input]. Multiple attributes associated with each schedule activity that can be included within the activity list. Activity attributes include activity codes, predecessor activities, successor activities, logical relationships, leads and lags, resource requirements, imposed dates, constraints, and assumptions.

Activity Code. One or more numerical or text values that identify characteristics of the work or in some way categorize the schedule activity that allows filtering and ordering of activities within reports.

Activity Duration. The time in calendar units between the start and finish of a schedule activity. See also *duration*.

Activity Identifier. A short unique numeric or text identification assigned to each schedule activity to differentiate that project activity from other activities. Typically unique within any one project schedule network diagram.

Activity List [Output/Input]. A documented tabulation of schedule activities that shows the activity description, activity identifier, and a sufficiently detailed scope of work description so project team members understand what work is to be performed.

Actual Cost (AC). Total costs actually incurred and recorded in accomplishing work performed during a given time period for a schedule activity or work breakdown structure component. Actual cost can sometimes be direct labor hours alone, direct costs alone, or all costs including indirect costs. Also referred to as the actual cost of work performed (ACWP). See also *earned value management and earned value technique*.

Actual Cost of Work Performed (ACWP). See *actual cost* (AC).

©2008 Project Management Institute. *A Guide to the Project Management Body of Knowledge (PMBOK® Guide) — Fourth Edition*

Actual Duration. The time in calendar units between the actual start date of the schedule activity and either the data date of the project schedule if the schedule activity is in progress or the actual finish date if the schedule activity is complete.

Administer Procurements [Process]. The process of managing procurement relationships, monitoring contract performance, and making changes and corrections as needed.

Analogous Estimating [Technique]. An estimating technique that uses the values of parameters, such as scope, cost, budget, and duration or measures of scale such as size, weight, and complexity from a previous, similar activity as the basis for estimating the same parameter or measure for a future activity.

Application Area. A category of projects that have common components significant in such projects, but are not needed or present in all projects. Application areas are usually defined in terms of either the product (i.e., by similar technologies or production methods) or the type of customer (i.e., internal versus external, government versus commercial) or industry sector (i.e., utilities, automotive, aerospace, information technologies, etc.). Application areas can overlap.

Approved Change Request [Output/Input]. A change request that has been processed through the integrated change control process and approved.

Assumptions. Assumptions are factors that, for planning purposes, are considered to be true, real, or certain without proof or demonstration.

Assumptions Analysis [Technique]. A technique that explores the accuracy of assumptions and identifies risks to the project from inaccuracy, inconsistency, or incompleteness of assumptions.

Authority. The right to apply project resources, expend funds, make decisions, or give approvals.

Backward Pass. The calculation of late finish dates and late start dates for the uncompleted portions of all schedule activities. Determined by working backwards through the schedule network logic from the project's end date. See also *schedule network analysis*.

Baseline. An approved plan for a project, plus or minus approved changes. It is compared to actual performance to determine if performance is within acceptable variance thresholds. Generally refers to the current baseline, but may refer to the original or some other baseline. Usually used with a modifier (e.g., cost performance baseline, schedule baseline, performance measurement baseline, technical baseline).

Bottom-up Estimating [Technique]. A method of estimating a component of work. The work is decomposed into more detail. An estimate is prepared of what is needed to meet the requirements of each of the lower, more detailed pieces of work, and these estimates are then aggregated into a total quantity for the component of work. The accuracy of bottom-up estimating is driven by the size and complexity of the work identified at the lower levels.

Brainstorming [Technique]. A general data gathering and creativity technique that can be used to identify risks, ideas, or solutions to issues by using a group of team members or subject-matter experts.

Budget. The approved estimate for the project or any work breakdown structure component or any schedule activity. See also *estimate*.

Budget at Completion (BAC). The sum of all the budgets established for the work to be performed on a project or a work breakdown structure component or a schedule activity. The total planned value for the project.

Budgeted Cost of Work Performed (BCWP). See *earned value* (EV).

Budgeted Cost of Work Scheduled (BCWS). See *planned value* (PV).

Buffer. See *reserve*.

Buyer. The acquirer of products, services, or results for an organization.

Calendar Unit. The smallest unit of time used in scheduling a project. Calendar units are generally in hours, days, or weeks, but can also be in quarter years, months, shifts, or even in minutes.

Change Control. Identifying, documenting, approving or rejecting, and controlling changes to the project baselines.

Change Control Board (CCB). A formally constituted group of stakeholders responsible for reviewing, evaluating, approving, delaying, or rejecting changes to a project, with all decisions and recommendations being recorded.

Change Control System [Tool]. A collection of formal documented procedures that define how project deliverables and documentation will be controlled, changed, and approved. In most application areas, the change control system is a subset of the configuration management system.

Change Request. Requests to expand or reduce the project scope, modify policies, processes, plans, or procedures, modify costs or budgets, or revise schedules.

Charter. See *project charter*.

Claim. A request, demand, or assertion of rights by a seller against a buyer, or vice versa, for consideration, compensation, or payment under the terms of a legally binding contract, such as for a disputed change.

Close Procurements [Process]. The process of completing each project procurement.

Close Project or Phase [Process]. The process of finalizing all activities across all of the Project Management Process Groups to formally complete the project or phase.

Closing Processes [Process Group]. Those processes performed to finalize all activities across all Project Management Process Groups to formally close the project or phase.

Code of Accounts [Tool]. Any numbering system used to uniquely identify each component of the work breakdown structure.

Collect Requirements [Process]. Collect Requirements is the process of defining and documenting stakeholders' needs to meet the project objectives.

Co-location [Technique]. An organizational placement strategy where the project team members are physically located close to one another in order to improve communication, working relationships, and productivity.

Common Cause. A source of variation that is inherent in the system and predictable. On a control chart, it appears as part of the random process variation (i.e., variation from a process that would be considered normal or not unusual), and is indicated by a random pattern of points within the control limits. Also referred to as random cause. Contrast with *special cause.*

Communication Management Plan [Output/Input]. The document that describes: the communications needs and expectations for the project; how and in what format information will be communicated; when and where each communication will be made; and who is responsible for providing each type of communication. The communication management plan is contained in, or is a subsidiary plan of, the project management plan.

Conduct Procurements [Process]. The process of obtaining seller responses, selecting a seller, and awarding a contract.

Configuration Management System [Tool]. A subsystem of the overall project management system. It is a collection of formal documented procedures used to apply technical and administrative direction and surveillance to: identify and document the functional and physical characteristics of a product, result, service, or component; control any changes to such characteristics; record and report each change and its implementation status; and support the audit of the products, results, or components to verify conformance to requirements. It includes the documentation, tracking systems, and defined approval levels necessary for authorizing and controlling changes.

Constraint [Input]. The state, quality, or sense of being restricted to a given course of action or inaction. An applicable restriction or limitation, either internal or external to a project, which will affect the performance of the project or a process. For example, a schedule constraint is any limitation or restraint placed on the project schedule that affects when a schedule activity can be scheduled and is usually in the form of fixed imposed dates.

Contingency. See *reserve.*

Contingency Allowance. See *reserve.*

Contingency Reserve [Output/Input]. The amount of funds, budget, or time needed above the estimate to reduce the risk of overruns of project objectives to a level acceptable to the organization.

Contract [Output/Input]. A contract is a mutually binding agreement that obligates the seller to provide the specified product or service or result and obligates the buyer to pay for it.

Control. Comparing actual performance with planned performance, analyzing variances, assessing trends to effect process improvements, evaluating possible alternatives, and recommending appropriate corrective action as needed.

Control Account [Tool]. A management control point where scope, budget (resource plans), actual cost, and schedule are integrated and compared to earned value for performance measurement. See also *work package*.

Control Chart [Tool]. A graphic display of process data over time and against established control limits, and that has a centerline that assists in detecting a trend of plotted values toward either control limit.

Control Costs [Process]. The process of monitoring the status of the project to update the project budget and managing changes to the cost baseline.

Control Limits. The area composed of three standard deviations on either side of the centerline, or mean, of a normal distribution of data plotted on a control chart that reflects the expected variation in the data. See also *specification limits*.

Control Schedule [Process]. The process of monitoring the status of the project to update project progress and managing changes to the schedule baseline.

Control Scope [Process]. The process of monitoring the status of the project and product scope and managing changes to the scope baseline.

Controlling. See *control*.

Corrective Action. Documented direction for executing the project work to bring expected future performance of the project work in line with the project management plan.

Cost Management Plan [Output/Input]. The document that sets out the format and establishes the activities and criteria for planning, structuring, and controlling the project costs. The cost management plan is contained in, or is a subsidiary plan of, the project management plan.

Cost of Quality (COQ) [Technique]. A method of determining the costs incurred to ensure quality. Prevention and appraisal costs (cost of conformance) include costs for quality planning, quality control (QC), and quality assurance to ensure compliance to requirements (i.e., training, QC systems, etc.). Failure costs (cost of non-conformance) include costs to rework products, components, or processes that are non-compliant, costs of warranty work and waste, and loss of reputation.

Cost Performance Baseline. A specific version of the time-phased budget used to compare actual expenditures to planned expenditures to determine if preventive or corrective action is needed to meet the project objectives.

Cost Performance Index (CPI). A measure of cost efficiency on a project. It is the ratio of earned value (EV) to actual costs (AC). CPI = EV divided by AC.

Cost-Plus-Fixed-Fee (CPFF) Contract. A type of cost-reimbursable contract where the buyer reimburses the seller for the seller's allowable costs (allowable costs are defined by the contract) plus a fixed amount of profit (fee).

Cost-Plus-Incentive-Fee (CPIF) Contract. A type of cost-reimbursable contract where the buyer reimburses the seller for the seller's allowable costs (allowable costs are defined by the contract), and the seller earns its profit if it meets defined performance criteria.

Cost-Reimbursable Contract. A type of contract involving payment to the seller for the seller's actual costs, plus a fee typically representing seller's profit. Cost-reimbursable contracts often include incentive clauses where, if the seller meets or exceeds selected project objectives, such as schedule targets or total cost, then the seller receives from the buyer an incentive or bonus payment.

Cost Variance (CV). A measure of cost performance on a project. It is the difference between earned value (EV) and actual cost (AC). CV = EV minus AC.

Crashing [Technique]. A specific type of project schedule compression technique performed by taking action to decrease the total project schedule duration after analyzing a number of alternatives to determine how to get the maximum schedule duration compression for the least additional cost. Typical approaches for crashing a schedule include reducing schedule activity durations and increasing the assignment of resources on schedule activities. See also *fast tracking* and *schedule compression*.

Create WBS (Work Breakdown Structure) [Process]. The process of subdividing project deliverables and project work into smaller, more manageable components.

Criteria. Standards, rules, or tests on which a judgment or decision can be based, or by which a product, service, result, or process can be evaluated.

Critical Activity. Any schedule activity on a critical path in a project schedule. Most commonly determined by using the critical path method. Although some activities are "critical," in the dictionary sense, without being on the critical path, this meaning is seldom used in the project context.

Critical Chain Method [Technique]. A schedule network analysis technique that modifies the project schedule to account for limited resources.

Critical Path. Generally, but not always, the sequence of schedule activities that determines the duration of the project. It is the longest path through the project. See also *critical path methodology*.

Critical Path Methodology (CPM) [Technique]. A schedule network analysis technique used to determine the amount of scheduling flexibility (the amount of float) on various logical network paths in the project schedule network, and to determine the minimum total project duration. Early start and finish dates are calculated by means of a forward pass, using a specified start date. Late start and finish dates are calculated by means of a backward pass, starting from a specified completion date, which sometimes is the project early finish date determined during the forward pass calculation. See also *critical path*.

Data Date. The date up to or through which the project's reporting system has provided actual status and accomplishments. Also called as-of date and time-now date.

Decision Tree Analysis [Technique]. The decision tree is a diagram that describes a decision under consideration and the implications of choosing one or another of the available alternatives. It is used when some future scenarios or outcomes of actions are uncertain. It incorporates probabilities and the costs or rewards of each logical path of events and future decisions, and uses expected monetary value analysis to help the organization identify the relative values of alternate actions. See also *expected monetary value analysis.*

Decomposition [Technique]. A planning technique that subdivides the project scope and project deliverables into smaller, more manageable components, until the project work associated with accomplishing the project scope and providing the deliverables is defined in sufficient detail to support executing, monitoring, and controlling the work.

Defect. An imperfection or deficiency in a project component where that component does not meet its requirements or specifications and needs to be either repaired or replaced.

Defect Repair. The formally documented identification of a defect in a project component with a recommendation to either repair the defect or completely replace the component.

Define Activities [Process]. The process of identifying the specific actions to be performed to produce the project deliverables.

Define Scope [Process]. The process of developing a detailed description of the project and product.

Deliverable [Output/Input]. Any unique and verifiable product, result, or capability to perform a service that must be produced to complete a process, phase, or project. Often used more narrowly in reference to an external deliverable, which is a deliverable that is subject to approval by the project sponsor or customer. See also *product and result.*

Delphi Technique [Technique]. An information gathering technique used as a way to reach a consensus of experts on a subject. Experts on the subject participate in this technique anonymously. A facilitator uses a questionnaire to solicit ideas about the important project points related to the subject. The responses are summarized and are then recirculated to the experts for further comment. Consensus may be reached in a few rounds of this process. The Delphi technique helps reduce bias in the data and keeps any one person from having undue influence on the outcome.

Dependency. See *logical relationship.*

Determine Budget [Process]. The process of aggregating the estimated costs of individual activities or work packages to establish an authorized cost baseline.

Develop Human Resource Plan [Process]. The process of identifying and documenting project roles, responsibilities, and required skills, reporting relationships, and creating a staffing management plan.

Develop Project Charter [Process]. The process of developing a document that formally authorizes a project or a phase and documenting initial requirements that satisfy the stakeholder's needs and expectations.

Develop Project Management Plan [Process]. The process of documenting the actions necessary to define, prepare, integrate, and coordinate all subsidiary plans.

Develop Project Team [Process]. The process of improving the competencies, team interaction, and the overall team environment to enhance project performance.

Develop Schedule [Process]. The process of analyzing activity sequences, durations, resource requirements, and schedule constraints to create the project schedule.

Direct and Manage Project Execution [Process]. The process of performing the work defined in the project management plan to achieve the project's objectives.

Distribute Information [Process]. The process of making relevant information available to project stakeholders as planned.

Duration (DU or DUR). The total number of work periods (not including holidays or other nonworking periods) required to complete a schedule activity or work breakdown structure component. Usually expressed as workdays or workweeks. Sometimes incorrectly equated with elapsed time. Contrast with *effort.*

Early Finish Date (EF). In the critical path method, the earliest possible point in time on which the uncompleted portions of a schedule activity (or the project) can finish, based on the schedule network logic, the data date, and any schedule constraints. Early finish dates can change as the project progresses and as changes are made to the project management plan.

Early Start Date (ES). In the critical path method, the earliest possible point in time on which the uncompleted portions of a schedule activity (or the project) can start, based on the schedule network logic, the data date, and any schedule constraints. Early start dates can change as the project progresses and as changes are made to the project management plan.

Earned Value (EV). The value of work performed expressed in terms of the approved budget assigned to that work for a schedule activity or work breakdown structure component. Also referred to as the budgeted cost of work performed (BCWP).

Earned Value Management (EVM). A management methodology for integrating scope, schedule, and resources, and for objectively measuring project performance and progress. Performance is measured by determining the budgeted cost of work performed (i.e., earned value) and comparing it to the actual cost of work performed (i.e., actual cost).

Earned Value Technique (EVT) [Technique]. A specific technique for measuring the performance of work and used to establish the performance measurement baseline (PMB).

Effort. The number of labor units required to complete a schedule activity or work breakdown structure component. Usually expressed as staff hours, staff days, or staff weeks. Contrast with *duration*.

Enterprise Environmental Factors [Output/Input]. Any or all external environmental factors and internal organizational environmental factors that surround or influence the project's success. These factors are from any or all of the enterprises involved in the project, and include organizational culture and structure, infrastructure, existing resources, commercial databases, market conditions, and project management software.

Estimate [Output/Input]. A quantitative assessment of the likely amount or outcome. Usually applied to project costs, resources, effort, and durations and is usually preceded by a modifier (i.e., preliminary, conceptual, feasibility, order-of-magnitude, definitive). It should always include some indication of accuracy (e.g., ± x percent). See also *budget* and *cost*.

Estimate Activity Durations [Process]. The process of approximating the number of work periods needed to complete individual activities with estimated resources.

Estimate Activity Resources [Process]. The process of estimating the type and quantities of material, people, equipment or supplies required to perform each activity.

Estimate at Completion (EAC) [Output/Input]. The expected total cost of a schedule activity, a work breakdown structure component, or the project when the defined scope of work will be completed. The EAC may be calculated based on performance to date or estimated by the project team based on other factors, in which case it is often referred to as the latest revised estimate. See also *earned value technique* and *estimate to complete*.

Estimate Costs [Process]. The process of developing an approximation of the monetary resources needed to complete project activities.

Estimate to Complete (ETC) [Output/Input]. The expected cost needed to complete all the remaining work for a schedule activity, work breakdown structure component, or the project. See also *earned value technique* and *estimate at completion*.

Execute. Directing, managing, performing, and accomplishing the project work, providing the deliverables, and providing work performance information.

Executing Processes [Process Group]. Those processes performed to complete the work defined in the project management plan to satisfy the project objectives.

Expected Monetary Value (EMV) Analysis. A statistical technique that calculates the average outcome when the future includes scenarios that may or may not happen. A common use of this technique is within decision tree analysis.

Expert Judgment [Technique]. Judgment provided based upon expertise in an application area, knowledge area, discipline, industry, etc. as appropriate for the activity being performed. Such expertise may be provided by any group or person with specialized education, knowledge, skill, experience, or training.

Failure Mode and Effect Analysis (FMEA) [Technique]. An analytical procedure in which each potential failure mode in every component of a product is analyzed to determine its effect on the reliability of that component and, by itself or in combination with other possible failure modes, on the reliability of the product or system and on the required function of the component; or the examination of a product (at the system and/or lower levels) for all ways that a failure may occur. For each potential failure, an estimate is made of its effect on the total system and of its impact. In addition, a review is undertaken of the action planned to minimize the probability of failure and to minimize its effects.

Fast Tracking [Technique]. A specific project schedule compression technique that changes network logic to overlap phases that would normally be done in sequence, such as the design phase and construction phase, or to perform schedule activities in parallel. See also *crashing* and *schedule compression.*

Finish Date. A point in time associated with a schedule activity's completion. Usually qualified by one of the following: actual, planned, estimated, scheduled, early, late, baseline, target, or current.

Finish-to-Finish (FF). The logical relationship where completion of work of the successor activity cannot finish until the completion of work of the predecessor activity. See also *logical relationship.*

Finish-to-Start (FS). The logical relationship where initiation of work of the successor activity depends upon the completion of work of the predecessor activity. See also *logical relationship.*

Firm-Fixed-Price (FFP) Contract. A type of fixed price contract where the buyer pays the seller a set amount (as defined by the contract), regardless of the seller's costs.

Fixed-Price-Incentive-Fee (FPIF) Contract. A type of contract where the buyer pays the seller a set amount (as defined by the contract), and the seller can earn an additional amount if the seller meets defined performance criteria.

Float. Also called slack. See *total float* and *free float.*

Flowcharting [Technique]. The depiction in a diagram format of the inputs, process actions, and outputs of one or more processes within a system.

Forecast. An estimate or prediction of conditions and events in the project's future based on information and knowledge available at the time of the forecast. The information is based on the project's past performance and expected future performance, and includes information that could impact the project in the future, such as estimate at completion and estimate to complete.

Forward Pass. The calculation of the early start and early finish dates for the uncompleted portions of all network activities. See also *schedule network analysis* and *backward pass.*

Free Float. The amount of time that a schedule activity can be delayed without delaying the early start date of any immediately following schedule activities. See also *total float.*

Functional Manager. Someone with management authority over an organizational unit within a functional organization. The manager of any group that actually makes a product or performs a service. Sometimes called a line manager.

Functional Organization. A hierarchical organization where each employee has one clear superior, and staff are grouped by areas of specialization and managed by a person with expertise in that area.

Gantt Chart. [Tool] A graphic display of schedule-related information. In the typical bar chart, schedule activities or work breakdown structure components are listed down the left side of the chart, dates are shown across the top, and activity durations are shown as date-placed horizontal bars.

Grade. A category or rank used to distinguish items that have the same functional use (e.g., "hammer"), but do not share the same requirements for quality (e.g., different hammers may need to withstand different amounts of force).

Hammock Activity. See *summary activity.*

Historical Information. Documents and data on prior projects including project files, records, correspondence, closed contracts, and closed projects.

Human Resource Plan. A document describing how roles and responsibilities, reporting relationships, and staffing management will be addressed and structured for the project. It is contained in or is a subsidiary plan of the project management plan.

Identify Risks [Process]. The process of determining which risks may affect the project and documenting their characteristics.

Identify Stakeholders [Process]. The process of identifying all people or organizations impacted by the project, and documenting relevant information regarding their interests, involvement, and impact on project success.

Imposed Date. A fixed date imposed on a schedule activity or schedule milestone, usually in the form of a "start no earlier than" and "finish no later than" date.

Influence Diagram [Tool]. A graphical representation of situations showing causal influences, time ordering of events, and other relationships among variables and outcomes.

Initiating Processes [Process Group]. Those processes performed to define a new project or a new phase of an existing project by obtaining authorization to start the project or phase.

Input [Process Input]. Any item, whether internal or external to the project that is required by a process before that process proceeds. May be an output from a predecessor process.

Inspection [Technique]. Examining or measuring to verify whether an activity, component, product, result, or service conforms to specified requirements.

Invitation for Bid (IFB). Generally, this term is equivalent to request for proposal. However, in some application areas, it may have a narrower or more specific meaning.

Issue. A point or matter in question or in dispute, or a point or matter that is not settled and is under discussion or over which there are opposing views or disagreements.

Lag [Technique]. A modification of a logical relationship that directs a delay in the successor activity. For example, in a finish-to-start dependency with a ten-day lag, the successor activity cannot start until ten days after the predecessor activity has finished. See also *lead*.

Late Finish Date (LF). In the critical path method, the latest possible point in time that a schedule activity may be completed based upon the schedule network logic, the project completion date, and any constraints assigned to the schedule activities without violating a schedule constraint or delaying the project completion date. The late finish dates are determined during the backward pass calculation of the project schedule network.

Late Start Date (LS). In the critical path method, the latest possible point in time that a schedule activity may begin based upon the schedule network logic, the project completion date, and any constraints assigned to the schedule activities without violating a schedule constraint or delaying the project completion date. The late start dates are determined during the backward pass calculation of the project schedule network.

Lead [Technique]. A modification of a logical relationship that allows an acceleration of the successor activity. For example, in a finish-to-start dependency with a ten-day lead, the successor activity can start ten days before the predecessor activity has finished. A negative lead is equivalent to a positive lag. See also *lag*.

Lessons Learned [Output/Input]. The learning gained from the process of performing the project. Lessons learned may be identified at any point. Also considered a project record, to be included in the lessons learned knowledge base.

Lessons Learned Knowledge Base. A store of historical information and lessons learned about both the outcomes of previous project selection decisions and previous project performance.

Leveling. See *resource leveling*.

Life Cycle. See *project life cycle*.

Log. A document used to record and describe or denote selected items identified during execution of a process or activity. Usually used with a modifier, such as issue, quality control, action, or defect.

Logical Relationship. A dependency between two project schedule activities, or between a project schedule activity and a schedule milestone. The four possible types of logical relationships are: Finish-to-Start; Finish-to-Finish; Start-to-Start; and Start-to-Finish. See also *precedence relationship*.

Manage Project Team [Process]. The process of tracking team member performance, providing feedback, resolving issues, and managing changes to optimize project performance.

Manage Stakeholder Expectations [Process]. The process of communicating and working with stakeholders to meet their needs and addressing issues as they occur.

Master Schedule [Tool]. A summary-level project schedule that identifies the major deliverables and work breakdown structure components and key schedule milestones. See also *milestone schedule.*

Material. The aggregate of things used by an organization in any undertaking, such as equipment, apparatus, tools, machinery, gear, material, and supplies.

Matrix Organization. Any organizational structure in which the project manager shares responsibility with the functional managers for assigning priorities and for directing the work of persons assigned to the project.

Methodology. A system of practices, techniques, procedures, and rules used by those who work in a discipline.

Milestone. A significant point or event in the project.

Milestone Schedule [Tool]. A summary-level schedule that identifies the major schedule milestones. See also *master schedule.*

Monitor. Collect project performance data with respect to a plan, produce performance measures, and report and disseminate performance information.

Monitor and Control Project Work [Process]. The process of tracking, reviewing, and regulating the progress to meet the performance objectives defined in the project management plan.

Monitor and Control Risks [Process]. The process of implementing risk response plans, tracking identified risks, monitoring residual risks, identifying new risks, and evaluating risk process throughout the project.

Monitoring and Controlling Processes [Process Group]. Those processes required to track, review, and regulate the progress and performance of the project, identify any areas in which changes to the plan are required, and initiate the corresponding changes.

Monte Carlo Analysis. A technique that computes or iterates, the project cost or project schedule many times using input values selected at random from probability distributions of possible costs or durations, to calculate a distribution of possible total project cost or completion dates.

Monte Carlo Simulation. A process which generates hundreds or thousands of probable performance outcomes based on probability distributions for cost and schedule on individual tasks. The outcomes are then used to generate a probability distribution for the project as a whole.

Near-Critical Activity. A schedule activity that has low total float. The concept of near-critical is equally applicable to a schedule activity or schedule network path. The limit below which total float is considered near critical is subject to expert judgment and varies from project to project.

Network. See *project schedule network diagram.*

Network Analysis. See *schedule network analysis.*

Network Logic. The collection of schedule activity dependencies that makes up a project schedule network diagram.

Network Path. Any continuous series of schedule activities connected with logical relationships in a project schedule network diagram.

Node. One of the defining points of a schedule network; a junction point joined to some or all of the other dependency lines.

Objective. Something toward which work is to be directed, a strategic position to be attained, or a purpose to be achieved, a result to be obtained, a product to be produced, or a service to be performed.

Opportunity. A condition or situation favorable to the project, a positive set of circumstances, a positive set of events, a risk that will have a positive impact on project objectives, or a possibility for positive changes. Contrast with *threat.*

Organizational Breakdown Structure (OBS) [Tool]. A hierarchically organized depiction of the project organization arranged so as to relate the work packages to the performing organizational units.

Organizational Process Assets [Output/Input]. Any or all process related assets, from any or all of the organizations involved in the project that are or can be used to influence the project's success. These process assets include formal and informal plans, policies, procedures, and guidelines. The process assets also include the organizations' knowledge bases such as lessons learned and historical information.

Output [Process Output]. A product, result, or service generated by a process. May be an input to a successor process.

Parametric Estimating [Technique]. An estimating technique that uses a statistical relationship between historical data and other variables (e.g., square footage in construction, lines of code in software development) to calculate an estimate for activity parameters, such as scope, cost, budget, and duration. An example for the cost parameter is multiplying the planned quantity of work to be performed by the historical cost per unit to obtain the estimated cost.

Pareto Chart [Tool]. A histogram, ordered by frequency of occurrence, that shows how many results were generated by each identified cause.

Path Convergence. The merging or joining of parallel schedule network paths into the same node in a project schedule network diagram. Path convergence is characterized by a schedule activity with more than one predecessor activity.

Path Divergence. Extending or generating parallel schedule network paths from the same node in a project schedule network diagram. Path divergence is characterized by a schedule activity with more than one successor activity.

Percent Complete. An estimate, expressed as a percent, of the amount of work that has been completed on an activity or a work breakdown structure component.

Perform Integrated Change Control [Process]. The process of reviewing all change requests, approving changes, and managing changes to the deliverables, organizational process assets, project documents, and project management plan.

Performance Measurement Baseline. An approved integrated scope-schedule-cost plan for the project work against which project execution is compared to measure and manage performance. Technical and quality parameters may also be included.

Performance Reports [Output/Input]. Documents and presentations that provide organized and summarized work performance information, earned value management parameters and calculations, and analyses of project work progress and status.

Performing Organization. The enterprise whose personnel are most directly involved in doing the work of the project.

Perform Qualitative Risk Analysis [Process]. The process of prioritizing risks for further analysis or action by assessing and combining their probability of occurrence and impact.

Perform Quality Assurance [Process]. The process of auditing the quality requirements and the results from quality control measurements to ensure appropriate quality standards and operational definitions are used.

Perform Quality Control [Process]. The process of monitoring and recording results of executing the quality activities to assess performance and recommend necessary changes.

Perform Quantitative Risk Analysis [Process]. The process of numerically analyzing the effect of identified risks on overall project objectives.

Phase. See *project phase*.

Plan Communications [Process]. The process of determining project stakeholder information needs and defining a communication approach.

Plan Procurements [Process]. The process of documenting project purchasing decisions, specifying the approach, and identifying potential sellers.

Plan Quality [Process]. The process of identifying quality requirements and/or standards for the project and product, and documenting how the project will demonstrate compliance.

Plan Risk Management [Process]. The process of defining how to conduct risk management activities for a project.

Plan Risk Responses [Process]. The process of developing options and actions to enhance opportunities and to reduce threats to project objectives.

Planned Value (PV). The authorized budget assigned to the scheduled work to be accomplished for a schedule activity or work breakdown structure component. Also referred to as the budgeted cost of work scheduled (BCWS).

Planning Package. A work breakdown structure component below the control account with known work content but without detailed schedule activities. See also *control account.*

Planning Processes [Process Group]. Those processes performed to establish the total scope of the effort, define and refine the objectives, and develop the course of action required to attain those objectives.

Portfolio. A collection of projects or programs and other work that are grouped together to facilitate effective management of that work to meet strategic business objectives. The projects or programs of the portfolio may not necessarily be interdependent or directly related.

Portfolio Management [Technique]. The centralized management of one or more portfolios, which includes identifying, prioritizing, authorizing, managing, and controlling projects, programs, and other related work, to achieve specific strategic business objectives.

Practice. A specific type of professional or management activity that contributes to the execution of a process and that may employ one or more techniques and tools.

Precedence Diagramming Method (PDM) [Technique]. A schedule network diagramming technique in which schedule activities are represented by boxes (or nodes). Schedule activities are graphically linked by one or more logical relationships to show the sequence in which the activities are to be performed.

Precedence Relationship. The term used in the precedence diagramming method for a logical relationship. In current usage, however, precedence relationship, logical relationship, and dependency are widely used interchangeably, regardless of the diagramming method used. See also *logical relationship.*

Predecessor Activity. The schedule activity that determines when the logical successor activity can begin or end.

Preventive Action. A documented direction to perform an activity that can reduce the probability of negative consequences associated with project risks.

Probability and Impact Matrix [Tool]. A common way to determine whether a risk is considered low, moderate, or high by combining the two dimensions of a risk: its probability of occurrence and its impact on objectives if it occurs.

Procurement Documents [Output/Input]. The documents utilized in bid and proposal activities, which include the buyer's Invitation for Bid, Invitation for Negotiations, Request for Information, Request for Quotation, Request for Proposal and seller's responses.

Procurement Management Plan [Output/Input]. The document that describes how procurement processes from developing procurement documentation through contract closure will be managed.

Product. An artifact that is produced, is quantifiable, and can be either an end item in itself or a component item. Additional words for products are material and goods. Contrast with *result*. See also *deliverable*.

Product Life Cycle. A collection of generally sequential, non-overlapping product phases whose name and number are determined by the manufacturing and control needs of the organization. The last product life cycle phase for a product is generally the product's retirement. Generally, a project life cycle is contained within one or more product life cycles.

Product Scope. The features and functions that characterize a product, service, or result.

Product Scope Description. The documented narrative description of the product scope.

Program. A group of related projects managed in a coordinated way to obtain benefits and control not available from managing them individually. Programs may include elements of related work outside of the scope of the discrete projects in the program.

Program Evaluation and Review Technique (PERT). A technique for estimating that applies a weighted average of optimistic, pessimistic, and most likely estimates when there is uncertainty with the individual activity estimates.

Program Management. The centralized coordinated management of a program to achieve the program's strategic objectives and benefits.

Progressive Elaboration [Technique]. Continuously improving and detailing a plan as more detailed and specific information and more accurate estimates become available as the project progresses, and thereby producing more accurate and complete plans that result from the successive iterations of the planning process.

Project. A temporary endeavor undertaken to create a unique product, service, or result.

Project Calendar. A calendar of working days or shifts that establishes those dates on which schedule activities are worked and nonworking days that determine those dates on which schedule activities are idle. Typically defines holidays, weekends, and shift hours. See also *resource calendar*.

Project Charter [Output/Input]. A document issued by the project initiator or sponsor that formally authorizes the existence of a project, and provides the project manager with the authority to apply organizational resources to project activities.

Project Communications Management [Knowledge Area]. Project Communications Management includes the processes required to ensure timely and appropriate generation, collection, distribution, storage, retrieval, and ultimate disposition of project information.

Project Cost Management [Knowledge Area]. Project Cost Management includes the processes involved in estimating, budgeting, and controlling costs so that the project can be completed within the approved budget.

Project Human Resource Management [Knowledge Area]. Project Human Resource Management includes the processes that organize and manage the project team.

Project Initiation. Launching a process that can result in the authorization of a new project.

Project Integration Management [Knowledge Area]. Project Integration Management includes the processes and activities needed to identify, define, combine, unify, and coordinate the various processes and project management activities within the Project Management Process Groups.

Project Life Cycle. A collection of generally sequential project phases whose name and number are determined by the control needs of the organization or organizations involved in the project. A life cycle can be documented with a methodology.

Project Management. The application of knowledge, skills, tools, and techniques to project activities to meet the project requirements.

Project Management Body of Knowledge. An inclusive term that describes the sum of knowledge within the profession of project management. As with other professions, such as law, medicine, and accounting, the body of knowledge rests with the practitioners and academics that apply and advance it. The complete project management body of knowledge includes proven traditional practices that are widely applied and innovative practices that are emerging in the profession. The body of knowledge includes both published and unpublished materials. This body of knowledge is constantly evolving. PMI's *PMBOK® Guide* identifies that subset of the project management body of knowledge that is generally recognized as good practice.

Project Management Information System (PMIS) [Tool]. An information system consisting of the tools and techniques used to gather, integrate, and disseminate the outputs of project management processes. It is used to support all aspects of the project from initiating through closing, and can include both manual and automated systems.

Project Management Knowledge Area. An identified area of project management defined by its knowledge requirements and described in terms of its component processes, practices, inputs, outputs, tools, and techniques.

Project Management Office (PMO). An organizational body or entity assigned various responsibilities related to the centralized and coordinated management of those projects under its domain. The responsibilities of a PMO can range from providing project management support functions to actually being responsible for the direct management of a project.

Project Management Plan [Output/Input]. A formal, approved document that defines how the project is executed, monitored, and controlled. It may be a summary or detailed and may be composed of one or more subsidiary management plans and other planning documents.

Project Management Process Group. A logical grouping of project management inputs, tools and techniques, and outputs. The Project Management Process Groups include initiating processes, planning processes, executing processes, monitoring and controlling processes, and closing processes. Project Management Process Groups are not project phases.

Project Management System [Tool]. The aggregation of the processes, tools, techniques, methodologies, resources, and procedures to manage a project.

Project Management Team. The members of the project team who are directly involved in project management activities. On some smaller projects, the project management team may include virtually all of the project team members.

Project Manager (PM). The person assigned by the performing organization to achieve the project objectives.

Project Organization Chart [Output/Input]. A document that graphically depicts the project team members and their interrelationships for a specific project.

Project Phase. A collection of logically related project activities, usually culminating in the completion of a major deliverable. Project phases are mainly completed sequentially, but can overlap in some project situations. A project phase is a component of a project life cycle. A project phase is not a Project Management Process Group.

Project Procurement Management [Knowledge Area]. Project Procurement Management includes the processes to purchase or acquire the products, services, or results needed from outside the project team to perform the work.

Project Quality Management [Knowledge Area]. Project Quality Management includes the processes and activities of the performing organization that determine quality policies, objectives, and responsibilities so that the project will satisfy the needs for which it was undertaken.

Project Risk Management [Knowledge Area]. Project Risk Management includes the processes concerned with conducting risk management planning, identification, analysis, responses, and monitoring and control on a project.

Project Schedule [Output/Input]. The planned dates for performing schedule activities and the planned dates for meeting schedule milestones.

Project Schedule Network Diagram [Output/Input]. Any schematic display of the logical relationships among the project schedule activities. Always drawn from left to right to reflect project work chronology.

Project Scope. The work that must be performed to deliver a product, service, or result with the specified features and functions.

Project Scope Management [Knowledge Area]. Project Scope Management includes the processes required to ensure that the project includes all the work required, and only the work required, to complete the project successfully.

Project Scope Statement [Output/Input]. The narrative description of the project scope, including major deliverables, project assumptions, project constraints, and a description of work, that provides a documented basis for making future project decisions and for confirming or developing a common understanding of project scope among the stakeholders.

Project Team Directory. A documented list of project team members, their project roles, and communication information.

Project Time Management [Knowledge Area]. Project Time Management includes the processes required to manage the timely completion of a project.

Projectized Organization. Any organizational structure in which the project manager has full authority to assign priorities, apply resources, and direct the work of persons assigned to the project.

Quality. The degree to which a set of inherent characteristics fulfills requirements.

Quality Management Plan [Output/Input]. The quality management plan describes how the project management team will implement the performing organization's quality policy. The quality management plan is a component or a subsidiary plan of the project management plan.

Regulation. Requirements imposed by a governmental body. These requirements can establish product, process, or service characteristics, including applicable administrative provisions that have government-mandated compliance.

Report Performance [Process]. The process of collecting and distributing performance information, including status reports, progress measurements, and forecasts.

Request for Information (RFI). A type of procurement document whereby the buyer requests a potential seller to provide various pieces of information related to a product or service or seller capability.

Request for Proposal (RFP). A type of procurement document used to request proposals from prospective sellers of products or services. In some application areas, it may have a narrower or more specific meaning.

Request for Quotation (RFQ). A type of procurement document used to request price quotations from prospective sellers of common or standard products or services. Sometimes used in place of request for proposal and in some application areas, it may have a narrower or more specific meaning.

Requested Change [Output/Input]. A formally documented change request that is submitted for approval to the integrated change control process.

Requirement. A condition or capability that must be met or possessed by a system, product, service, result, or component to satisfy a contract, standard, specification, or other formally imposed document. Requirements include the quantified and documented needs, wants, and expectations of the sponsor, customer, and other stakeholders.

Requirements Traceability Matrix. A table that links requirements to their origin and traces them throughout the project life cycle.

Reserve. A provision in the project management plan to mitigate cost and/or schedule risk. Often used with a modifier (e.g., management reserve, contingency reserve) to provide further detail on what types of risk are meant to be mitigated.

Reserve Analysis [Technique]. An analytical technique to determine the essential features and relationships of components in the project management plan to establish a reserve for the schedule duration, budget, estimated cost, or funds for a project.

Residual Risk. A risk that remains after risk responses have been implemented.

Resource. Skilled human resources (specific disciplines either individually or in crews or teams), equipment, services, supplies, commodities, material, budgets, or funds.

Resource Breakdown Structure. A hierarchical structure of resources by resource category and resource type used in resource leveling schedules and to develop resource-limited schedules, and which may be used to identify and analyze project human resource assignments.

Resource Calendar. A calendar of working days and nonworking days that determines those dates on which each specific resource is idle or can be active. Typically defines resource specific holidays and resource availability periods. See also *project calendar.*

Resource Histogram. A bar chart showing the amount of time that a resource is scheduled to work over a series of time periods. Resource availability may be depicted as a line for comparison purposes. Contrasting bars may show actual amounts of resources used as the project progresses.

Resource Leveling [Technique]. Any form of schedule network analysis in which scheduling decisions (start and finish dates) are driven by resource constraints (e.g., limited resource availability or difficult-to-manage changes in resource availability levels).

Responsibility Assignment Matrix (RAM) [Tool]. A structure that relates the project organizational breakdown structure to the work breakdown structure to help ensure that each component of the project's scope of work is assigned to a person or team.

Result. An output from performing project management processes and activities. Results include outcomes (e.g., integrated systems, revised process, restructured organization, tests, trained personnel, etc.) and documents (e.g., policies, plans, studies, procedures, specifications, reports, etc.). Contrast with *product.* See also *deliverable.*

Rework. Action taken to bring a defective or nonconforming component into compliance with requirements or specifications.

Risk. An uncertain event or condition that, if it occurs, has a positive or negative effect on a project's objectives.

Risk Acceptance [Technique]. A risk response planning technique that indicates that the project team has decided not to change the project management plan to deal with a risk, or is unable to identify any other suitable response strategy.

Risk Avoidance [Technique]. A risk response planning technique for a threat that creates changes to the project management plan that are meant to either eliminate the risk or to protect the project objectives from its impact.

Risk Breakdown Structure (RBS) [Tool]. A hierarchically organized depiction of the identified project risks arranged by risk category and subcategory that identifies the various areas and causes of potential risks. The risk breakdown structure is often tailored to specific project types.

Risk Category. A group of potential causes of risk. Risk causes may be grouped into categories such as technical, external, organizational, environmental, or project management. A category may include subcategories such as technical maturity, weather, or aggressive estimating.

Risk Management Plan [Output/Input]. The document describing how project risk management will be structured and performed on the project. It is contained in or is a subsidiary plan of the project management plan. Information in the risk management plan varies by application area and project size. The risk management plan is different from the risk register that contains the list of project risks, the results of risk analysis, and the risk responses.

Risk Mitigation [Technique]. A risk response planning technique associated with threats that seeks to reduce the probability of occurrence or impact of a risk to below an acceptable threshold.

Risk Register [Output/Input]. The document containing the results of the qualitative risk analysis, quantitative risk analysis, and risk response planning. The risk register details all identified risks, including description, category, cause, probability of occurring, impact(s) on objectives, proposed responses, owners, and current status.

Risk Tolerance. The degree, amount, or volume of risk that an organization or individual will withstand.

Risk Transference [Technique]. A risk response planning technique that shifts the impact of a threat to a third party, together with ownership of the response.

Role. A defined function to be performed by a project team member, such as testing, filing, inspecting, coding.

Rolling Wave Planning [Technique]. A form of progressive elaboration planning where the work to be accomplished in the near term is planned in detail at a low level of the work breakdown structure, while the work far in the future is planned at a relatively high level of the work breakdown structure, but the detailed planning of the work to be performed within another one or two periods in the near future is done as work is being completed during the current period.

Root Cause Analysis [Technique]. An analytical technique used to determine the basic underlying reason that causes a variance or a defect or a risk. A root cause may underlie more than one variance or defect or risk.

Schedule. See *project schedule* and see also *schedule model.*

Schedule Baseline. A specific version of the schedule model used to compare actual results to the plan to determine if preventive or corrective action is needed to meet the project objectives.

Schedule Compression [Technique]. Shortening the project schedule duration without reducing the project scope. See also *crashing* and *fast tracking.*

Schedule Management Plan [Output/Input]. The document that establishes criteria and the activities for developing and controlling the project schedule. It is contained in, or is a subsidiary plan of, the project management plan.

Schedule Model [Tool]. A model used in conjunction with manual methods or project management software to perform schedule network analysis to generate the project schedule for use in managing the execution of a project. See also *project schedule.*

Schedule Network Analysis [Technique]. The technique of identifying early and late start dates, as well as early and late finish dates, for the uncompleted portions of project schedule activities. See also *critical path method, critical chain method,* and *resource leveling.*

Schedule Performance Index (SPI). A measure of schedule efficiency on a project. It is the ratio of earned value (EV) to planned value (PV). The SPI = EV divided by PV.

Schedule Variance (SV). A measure of schedule performance on a project. It is the difference between the earned value (EV) and the planned value (PV). SV = EV minus PV.

Scheduled Finish Date (SF). The point in time that work was scheduled to finish on a schedule activity. The scheduled finish date is normally within the range of dates delimited by the early finish date and the late finish date. It may reflect resource leveling of scarce resources. Sometimes called planned finish date.

Scheduled Start Date (SS). The point in time that work was scheduled to start on a schedule activity. The scheduled start date is normally within the range of dates delimited by the early start date and the late start date. It may reflect resource leveling of scarce resources. Sometimes called planned start date.

Scope. The sum of the products, services, and results to be provided as a project. See also *project scope* and *product scope.*

Scope Baseline. An approved specific version of the detailed scope statement, work breakdown structure (WBS), and its associated WBS dictionary.

Scope Change. Any change to the project scope. A scope change almost always requires an adjustment to the project cost or schedule.

Scope Creep. Adding features and functionality (project scope) without addressing the effects on time, costs, and resources, or without customer approval.

Scope Management Plan [Output/Input]. The document that describes how the project scope will be defined, developed, and verified and how the work breakdown structure will be created and defined, and that provides guidance on how the project scope will be managed and controlled by the project management team. It is contained in or is a subsidiary plan of the project management plan.

S-Curve. Graphic display of cumulative costs, labor hours, percentage of work, or other quantities, plotted against time. Used to depict planned value, earned value, and actual cost of project work. The name derives from the S-like shape of the curve (flatter at the beginning and end, steeper in the middle) produced on a project that starts slowly, accelerates, and then tails off. Also a term used to express the cumulative likelihood distribution that is a result of a simulation, a tool of quantitative risk analysis.

Secondary Risk. A risk that arises as a direct result of implementing a risk response.

Seller. A provider or supplier of products, services, or results to an organization.

Sensitivity Analysis. A quantitative risk analysis and modeling technique used to help determine which risks have the most potential impact on the project. It examines the extent to which the uncertainty of each project element affects the objective being examined when all other uncertain elements are held at their baseline values. The typical display of results is in the form of a tornado diagram.

Sequence Activities [Process]. The process of identifying and documenting relationships among the project activities.

Simulation. A simulation uses a project model that translates the uncertainties specified at a detailed level into their potential impact on objectives that are expressed at the level of the total project. Project simulations use computer models and estimates of risk, usually expressed as a probability distribution of possible costs or durations at a detailed work level, and are typically performed using Monte Carlo analysis.

Slack. Also called float. See *total float* and *free float.*

Special Cause. A source of variation that is not inherent in the system, is not predictable, and is intermittent. It can be assigned to a defect in the system. On a control chart, points beyond the control limits, or non-random patterns within the control limits, indicate it. Also referred to as assignable cause. Contrast with *common cause.*

Specification. A document that specifies, in a complete, precise, verifiable manner, the requirements, design, behavior, or other characteristics of a system, component, product, result, or service and, often, the procedures for determining whether these provisions have been satisfied. Examples are: requirement specification, design specification, product specification, and test specification.

Specification Limits. The area, on either side of the centerline, or mean, of data plotted on a control chart that meets the customer's requirements for a product or service. This area may be greater than or less than the area defined by the control limits. See also *control limits.*

Sponsor. The person or group that provides the financial resources, in cash or in kind, for the project.

Staffing Management Plan. The document that describes when and how human resource requirements will be met. It is contained in, or is a subsidiary plan of, the human resource plan.

Stakeholder. Person or organization (e.g., customer, sponsor, performing organization, or the public) that is actively involved in the project, or whose interests may be positively or negatively affected by execution or completion of the project. A stakeholder may also exert influence over the project and its deliverables.

Standard. A document that provides, for common and repeated use, rules, guidelines, or characteristics for activities or their results, aimed at the achievement of the optimum degree of order in a given context.

Start Date. A point in time associated with a schedule activity's start, usually qualified by one of the following: actual, planned, estimated, scheduled, early, late, target, baseline, or current.

Start-to-Finish (SF). The logical relationship where completion of the successor schedule activity is dependent upon the initiation of the predecessor schedule activity. See also *logical relationship*.

Start-to-Start (SS). The logical relationship where initiation of the work of the successor schedule activity depends upon the initiation of the work of the predecessor schedule activity. See also *logical relationship*.

Statement of Work (SOW). A narrative description of products, services, or results to be supplied.

Strengths, Weaknesses, Opportunities, and Threats (SWOT) Analysis. This information gathering technique examines the project from the perspective of each project's strengths, weaknesses, opportunities, and threats to increase the breadth of the risks considered by risk management.

Subnetwork. A subdivision (fragment) of a project schedule network diagram, usually representing a subproject or a work package. Often used to illustrate or study some potential or proposed schedule condition, such as changes in preferential schedule logic or project scope.

Subphase. A subdivision of a phase.

Subproject. A smaller portion of the overall project created when a project is subdivided into more manageable components or pieces.

Successor Activity. The schedule activity that follows a predecessor activity, as determined by their logical relationship.

Summary Activity. A group of related schedule activities aggregated at some summary level, and displayed/reported as a single activity at that summary level. See also *subproject* and *subnetwork*.

Team Members. See *project team members*.

Technical Performance Measurement [Technique]. A performance measurement technique that compares technical accomplishments during project execution to the project management plan's schedule of planned technical achievements. It may use key technical parameters of the product produced by the project as a quality metric. The achieved metric values are part of the work performance information.

Technique. A defined systematic procedure employed by a human resource to perform an activity to produce a product or result or deliver a service, and that may employ one or more tools.

Template. A partially complete document in a predefined format that provides a defined structure for collecting, organizing, and presenting information and data.

Threat. A condition or situation unfavorable to the project, a negative set of circumstances, a negative set of events, a risk that will have a negative impact on a project objective if it occurs, or a possibility for negative changes. Contrast with *opportunity*.

Three-Point Estimate [Technique]. An analytical technique that uses three cost or duration estimates to represent the optimistic, most likely, and pessimistic scenarios. This technique is applied to improve the accuracy of the estimates of cost or duration when the underlying activity or cost component is uncertain.

Threshold. A cost, time, quality, technical, or resource value used as a parameter, and which may be included in product specifications. Crossing the threshold should trigger some action, such as generating an exception report.

Time and Material (T&M) Contract. A type of contract that is a hybrid contractual arrangement containing aspects of both cost-reimbursable and fixed-price contracts. Time and material contracts resemble cost-reimbursable type arrangements in that they have no definitive end, because the full value of the arrangement is not defined at the time of the award. Thus, time and material contracts can grow in contract value as if they were cost-reimbursable-type arrangements. Conversely, time and material arrangements can also resemble fixed-price arrangements. For example, the unit rates are preset by the buyer and seller, when both parties agree on the rates for the category of senior engineers.

Time-Scaled Schedule Network Diagram [Tool]. Any project schedule network diagram drawn in such a way that the positioning and length of the schedule activity represents its duration. Essentially, it is a bar chart that includes schedule network logic.

To-Complete-Performance-Index (TCPI). The calculated projection of cost performance that must be achieved on the remaining work to meet a specified management goal, such as the budget at completion (BAC) or the estimate at completion (EAC). It is the ratio of "remaining work" to the "funds remaining."

Tool. Something tangible, such as a template or software program, used in performing an activity to produce a product or result.

Total Float. The total amount of time that a schedule activity may be delayed from its early start date without delaying the project finish date, or violating a schedule constraint. Calculated using the critical path method technique and determining the difference between the early finish dates and late finish dates. See also *free float*.

Trend Analysis [Technique]. An analytical technique that uses mathematical models to forecast future outcomes based on historical results. It is a method of determining the variance from a baseline of a budget, cost, schedule, or scope parameter by using prior progress reporting periods' data and projecting how much that parameter's variance from baseline might be at some future point in the project if no changes are made in executing the project.

Triggers. Indications that a risk has occurred or is about to occur. Triggers may be discovered in the risk identification process and watched in the risk monitoring and control process. Triggers are sometimes called risk symptoms or warning signs.

Validation. The assurance that a product, service, or system meets the needs of the customer and other identified stakeholders. It often involves acceptance and suitability with external customers. Contrast with *verification*.

Value Engineering. An approach used to optimize project life cycle costs, save time, increase profits, improve quality, expand market share, solve problems, and/or use resources more effectively.

Variance. A quantifiable deviation, departure, or divergence away from a known baseline or expected value.

Variance Analysis [Technique]. A method for resolving the total variance in the set of scope, cost, and schedule variables into specific component variances that are associated with defined factors affecting the scope, cost, and schedule variables.

Verification. The evaluation of whether or not a product, service, or system complies with a regulation, requirement, specification, or imposed condition. It is often an internal process. Contrast with validation.

Verify Scope [Process]. The process of formalizing acceptance of the completed project deliverables.

Virtual Team. A group of persons with a shared objective who fulfill their roles with little or no time spent meeting face to face. Various forms of technology are often used to facilitate communication among team members. Virtual teams can be comprised of persons separated by great distances.

Voice of the Customer. A planning technique used to provide products, services, and results that truly reflect customer requirements by translating those customer requirements into the appropriate technical requirements for each phase of project product development.

Work Authorization. A permission and direction, typically written, to begin work on a specific schedule activity or work package or control account. It is a method for sanctioning project work to ensure that the work is done by the identified organization, at the right time, and in the proper sequence.

Work Authorization System [Tool]. A subsystem of the overall project management system. It is a collection of formal documented procedures that defines how project work will be authorized (committed) to ensure that the work is done by the identified organization, at the right time, and in the proper sequence. It includes the steps, documents, tracking system, and defined approval levels needed to issue work authorizations.

Work Breakdown Structure (WBS) [Output/Input]. A deliverable-oriented hierarchical decomposition of the work to be executed by the project team to accomplish the project objectives and create the required deliverables. It organizes and defines the total scope of the project.

Work Breakdown Structure Component. An entry in the work breakdown structure that can be at any level.

Work Breakdown Structure Dictionary [Output/Input]. A document that describes each component in the work breakdown structure (WBS). For each WBS component, the WBS dictionary includes a brief definition of the scope or statement of work, defined deliverable(s), a list of associated activities, and a list of milestones. Other information may include: responsible organization, start and end dates, resources required, an estimate of cost, charge number, contract information, quality requirements, and technical references to facilitate performance of the work.

Work Package. A deliverable or project work component at the lowest level of each branch of the work breakdown structure. See also *control account.*

Work Performance Information [Output/Input]. Information and data, on the status of the project schedule activities being performed to accomplish the project work, collected as part of the direct and manage project execution processes. Information includes: status of deliverables; implementation status for change requests, corrective actions, preventive actions, and defect repairs; forecasted estimates to complete; reported percent of work physically completed; achieved value of technical performance measures; start and finish dates of schedule activities.

Workaround [Technique]. A response to a negative risk that has occurred. Distinguished from contingency plan in that a workaround is not planned in advance of the occurrence of the risk event.

INDEX